LATIN AMERICAN DEMOCRACIES IN THE NEW GLOBAL ECONOMY

edited by

Ana Margheritis

North·South Center Press
UNIVERSITY OF MIAMI

The publisher of this book is the North-South Center Press at the University of Miami.

The mission of the North-South Center is to promote better relations and serve as a catalyst for change among the United States, Canada, and the nations of Latin America and the Caribbean by advancing knowledge and understanding of the major political, social, economic, and cultural issues affecting the nations and peoples of the Western Hemisphere.

© 2003 North-South Center Press at the University of Miami.

 Published by the North-South Center Press at the University of Miami and distributed by Lynne Rienner Publishers, Inc., 1800 30th Street, Suite 314, Boulder, CO 80301-1026. All rights reserved under International and Pan-American Conventions. No portion of the contents may be reproduced or transmitted in any form, or by any means, including photocopying, recording, or any information storage retrieval system, without prior permission in writing from the North-South Center Press.

All copyright inquiries should be addressed to the publisher: North-South Center Press, 1500 Monza Avenue, Coral Gables, Florida 33146-3027, U.S.A., phone 305-284-8912, fax 305-284-6370, or e-mail mmapes@miami.edu.

To order or to return books, contact Lynne Rienner Publishers, Inc., 1800 30th Street, Suite 314, Boulder, CO 80301-1026, 303-444-6684, fax 303-444-0824.

Library of Congress Cataloging-in-Publication Data

Latin American democracies in the new global economy /edited by Ana Margheritis

   p. cm.

Includes bibliographical references and index.

ISBN 1-57454-124-2 (hard cover: alk. paper) ISBN 1-57454-129-3 (pbk: alk.paper)

1. Latin America—Economic conditions—1982- 2. Globalization—Economic aspects—Latin America. 3. Democratization—Latin America. 4. Latin America—Politics and government—1980- I. Margheritis, Ana.

HC125.L347955 2003

330.98—dc22   2003061423

Printed in the United States of America/TS

08 07 06 05 04 03   6 5 4 3 2 1

TABLE OF CONTENTS

ACKNOWLEDGMENTS

I am particularly grateful to Neil A. Allen for his support in this endeavor.

The Fletcher School of Law and Diplomacy provided an excellent environment in which to carry out this project. Thanks to my colleagues there who actively participated: Michael Klein, Carsten Kowalczyk, Lisa Lynch, and John Coatsworth, Director of the David Rockefeller Center for Latin American Studies at Harvard University.

The chapters greatly benefited from comments and suggestions made by Merilee Grindle, Michael Klein, Lisa Lynch, John Sheahan, William C. Smith, and Andrés Velasco, as well as from the editorial and design assistance of the staff at the North-South Center Press. Many thanks to all of them.

Ana Margheritis

FOREWORD

L atin American politicians, policymakers, and ordinary citizens not only must cope with the uncertainties generated by the vertiginous globalization of their economies and societies, they also must contend with unilateralist projects emanating from official circles in Washington who pay scant heed to the sensitivities, needs, and priorities of Latin American democracies. Latin America's experiment with democratic governance and market capitalism remains problematic. The advent of democracy and the inauguration of a new, market-driven regime of economic growth have been highly traumatic for the elites as well as the masses. Elections and representative government remain the only acceptable formulas for the legitimate exercise of political power, but public opinion polls reveal that popular expectations for the rule of law, broadened political participation, and the extension of citizenship rights to excluded sectors of society have been frustrated. Likewise, the orthodoxies of the market have yielded disappointing results. Growth rates remain significantly lower than in the previous era of state-led industrialization. Very little has been done to ameliorate the region's stubborn poverty or to combat egregious social inequalities.

That these recent transformations in politics and economics remain problematic stems not only from disappointing economic performance or elite intransigence and unwillingness to compensate losers — from neoliberal reforms, including the millions of middle-class and working-class people in the public and private sectors thrown into precarious informal employment, as well as the owners of firms driven out of business by cheap imports — but also from the poor quality of the policy debates and the sad truth that no one has come up with original ideas on what to do next. For political, economic, and other reasons, this discussion has been always postponed. Even today, facing widespread discontent, the multilateral funding agencies and other advocates of the free market continue to insist on "deepening the reforms" without due attention to their political viability or consideration of other, more daring alternatives — if someone could ever articulate a coherent alternative proposal. Even those who suggest to "reform the reforms" generally limit their proposals to marginal tinkering within the parameters of the same package, on the assumption that the Latin American economies are in better shape now than before the reforms. Such opinions still elicit considerable consensus among elites. Dissident views have been discussed with increasing intensity in the last few years, but they have not crystallized in a project that could appeal to electoral majorities.

Fortunately, the contributors to *Latin American Democracies in the New Global Economy* eschew the pessimism that these painful realities could trigger in many observers. Instead, while duly recognizing the constraints that powerfully condition reformist options, Ana Margheritis and her collaborators conscientiously seek to explore the possible opportunities for innovative policy alternatives and to expand the range of choices open to Latin American societies. Their volume originated at a conference organized in late 2001 by Margheritis while she was Neil Allen Visiting Chair of Latin American Studies at The Fletcher School of Law and

Diplomacy, Tufts University. As one of the *comentaristas*, I recall wondering whether papers written by such a heterogeneous group of economists and political scientists could coalesce into a coherent intellectual product. My concerns obviously were misplaced. Margheritis' skill, tact, and intellectual vision are in no small measure to be credited for this collection's readily accessible, clearly argued, and sophisticated chapters, which make analytical and empirical contributions to fuel this long-awaited debate by examining four broad policy domains — economic integration, financial instability, human capital, and democratic governance.

The future course of regional economic integration is a vital core concern of governmental policymakers and businesspeople, as well as union and civil society activists, anxious to safeguard national interests and sovereignty from the negative effects of the unregulated globalization of production, commerce, and finance. Multilateral negotiations involving the expansion of the North American Free Trade Agreement (NAFTA); the revival of the Southern Common Market (Mercado Común del Sur — MERCOSUR); and the implementation of the Free Trade Area of the Americas (FTAA) are complex undertakings, fraught with risks but also offering promising opportunities. If pursued with skill and determination, strengthened subregional and regional cooperation may partially compensate for the region's massive power asymmetries vis-à-vis the United States. Simultaneous negotiations with the European Union, Japan, and new players, such as India and China, along with constant attention to global negotiations conducted in the venue of the World Trade Organization's Doha Round, may well contribute to Latin America's more competitive international insertion in global markets.

Finding innovative ways to cope with the vagaries of global capital markets is a similar imperative. Some Latin American governments have not exercised sufficient control over flows of short-term, sometimes volatile, speculative capital; thus, they have failed to reap the potential benefits of foreign direct investment (FDI). Far from promoting optimal efficiency in allocating capital, when global financial markets are largely free from public governance (the status quo as of mid-2003), capital flows into Latin American economies all too frequently simply serve to compensate for current account deficits. Even more perverse, in times of political and economic uncertainty, the flows often fuel conspicuous consumption by globalized elites and finance capital flight to safe havens outside Latin America. These are not merely technical issues. Reducing the volatility of speculative capital and promoting greater domestic savings and investment are eminently political tasks. However, they require effective national and multilateral regulatory mechanisms that operate transparently under the supervision of competent technocrats, who are, in turn, monitored closely by democratically elected officials.

The pursuit of equity and improvements in popular welfare are intimately linked to the accumulation of human capital. But to promote meaningful human capital accumulation demands comprehensive steps to achieve rapid reductions in poverty and significant changes in prevailing patterns of inequality. Such shifts in strategy and policy are particularly urgent in Latin America because it has the highest level of inequality in income distribution of any region in the world-economy. In this regard, more rapid economic growth together with a more competitive insertion in global markets are important but clearly insufficient.

Similarly, improvements in the quality of and access to education, better public health coverage, and more adequate training of the labor force are crucial; however, by themselves policies in these areas will not necessarily achieve improved standards of living. In fact, mounting evidence suggests that increased investments in education, public health, and training to upgrade job skills may generate only modest wage returns. Transformations in underlying institutional arrangements to assure better coordination among governments, schools, industry, and civil society actors are also necessary. Moreover, the positive effects of policies to foment human capital accumulation can be easily swamped by the orthodox precepts central to the conventional market reform packages demanded by global markets and multilateral financial institutions. In sum, effective human capital accumulation requires significant innovations in institutional design to make macro and microeconomic policy management compatible with the goals of social inclusion and distributive justice.

Sophisticated quantitative analyses with large data sets find a strong connection between social and economic performance and the quality of political institutions. Less well understood is how the reform of specific institutional configurations, represented by federalism, can impact the quality of democracy. In general, there is ample reason to hope that stronger, more representative, accountable, and transparent political institutions and regulatory mechanisms will be conducive to combating corruption and enforcing voluntary compliance with legal norms. Better, more encompassing institutional arrangements can also help resolve principal-agent dilemmas, reduce information asymmetries, and improve coordination among governmental and between state agencies and civil society actors. Similarly, contentious institutional reforms in conflictive areas, such as social security and the decentralization of fiscal authority and the delivery of services, proceed more rapidly, with more democratic and efficient outcomes, when the political process provides for a measure of deliberation, inclusiveness, and concern with equity.

There is a final angle to the issue of governance and institutions worth highlighting. Despite the exigencies of the new era of globalization, there is a growing consensus that international competitiveness does not have to impose an inexorable "race to the bottom" under the aegis of repressive, authoritarian regimes. In fact, there are persuasive theoretical arguments, backed by considerable empirical data from both Europe and East Asia, that countries with stable, legitimate democratic governments; high-quality institutions; coherent, effective regulatory agencies; and pro-equity public policies are likely to offer long-term predictability and sustainable, market-friendly growth.

These brief reflections touch on just some of issues treated clearly and provocatively by the contributors to this volume. The readers of these chapters will be in their debt, as I am.

William C. Smith
University of Miami
Editor, *Latin American Politics and Society*
Rio de Janeiro
July 2003

Introduction

FOREIGN POLICY AND DOMESTIC RESTRUCTURING IN LATIN AMERICA: RECENT ACHIEVEMENTS AND FUTURE CHALLENGES

Ana Margheritis

In Latin America, as elsewhere, the beginning of a new century seems to be a particularly auspicious moment to evaluate and speculate on past choices, ongoing developments, and future options. The complexity of current political and economic problems in many Latin American countries, including some dramatic ongoing crises, adds impetus to the exercise.

Many countries in the region have recently opened their economies as part of a broader search for a more competitive position in the international economic system. Trade liberalization, regional economic integration, and capital flows deregulation have translated into greater exchanges, but also greater external vulnerability. Although outcomes varied across countries (and economic sectors within countries), most of these economies still face structural problems and recurrent crises, such as poor export performance, low savings rate, increasing indebtedness, and permanent fiscal imbalance, while improvement in living conditions has been only very modest and not shared by the majority. Deteriorating educational and health standards, high unemployment and poverty rates, concentration of wealth, and social polarization are indicators of that trend.

In addition, the process of democratization in Latin America has also led to a diversity of political developments. Together with strong commitments to the maintenance and consolidation of democratic institutions, authoritarian legacies and violations of the rule of law still remain as parts of usual political practices in several countries. The region still has a long way to go in building stable, transparent, and accountable democratic institutions and practices that may efficiently complement the working of market economies.

Thus, from the perspective of countries still seeking social and economic growth in a highly competitive international context, there are some remaining puzzles to be solved, such as what to do next, how to improve what has been done, whether more and/or different reforms are needed, and, if so, how to make them viable. The search for integration into the world economy still requires Latin American elites to be more innovative and flexible when redefining policy priorities. Social disenchantment throughout the region due to recent transformations demonstrates an urgent need to elaborate a socio-political-economic approach to reforms, one that goes beyond simple technical fixes and narrow attempts to "get economics right." Open market policies will not translate into sustained growth and widely shared development if they are not accompanied by a whole set of complementary social and political measures.

For these reasons, this volume argues that the analysis of such an outward-oriented development strategy must necessarily include the economic, political, and social dimensions of the processes already underway. These considerations led to this study's emphasis on four policy areas. The first two areas of study, economic integration and finance, have traditionally been considered to be part of foreign economic relations. The remaining two policy areas examined — human capital development and democratic institution building — are nontraditional but increasingly relevant issues within the economic foreign policy agenda today.

In addition, given the intermestic, or international and domestic, character of all governments' agendas and the high politicization of international economic relations today, the analysis of foreign economic policy must pay due attention to both domestic and international variables. Hence, the chapters amply and effectively illustrate the interplay of actors, the overlap of issues, and the intertwining of processes at both levels of analysis. They show how the forces of globalization are constraining policy options, while profound transformations already underway in the domestic arena, such as democratization and decentralization, can have an impact on many policy areas and are redefining actors' perceptions and relations in a complex, multiple-level game. This explains our interest in integrating the intermestic and politico-economic perspectives of Latin America's current place in the international context that is different from what has been traditionally included in the study of foreign economic relations.

In this way, this book aims to contribute not only a fresh and more comprehensive understanding of current foreign economic policy in Latin America, but also seeks to expand the debate about what the policy priorities and options are — and ought to be — in the region.

These are the concerns that guide this volume. The essays that follow place these concerns in four different policy domains and explore each from the perspective of specific issues that are claiming the attention of various governments. Some chapters cover those issues at a regional level, while others focus on case studies. The rest of this introductory chapter sets the context for discussion and summarizes the main findings of contributors to this book.

ON POLICY DILEMMAS AND OPPORTUNITIES

Within policy science literature, policy dilemmas are conceptualized in a particular way. It is assumed that societies face problems when there is a gap between reality and desires, when the ongoing situation does not fulfill people's expectations. If the general public or a particular interest group or groups are able to organize and exert considerable pressure on governmental structures, or if a political entrepreneur takes over such demands and works to promote a solution, the problem will likely become part of a government's agenda (Kingdon 1995).

Should this happen, decisionmakers will be faced with the difficult task of choosing a course of action. Their decisions will always be the result of a selection process among competing alternatives. The adoption of a decision often creates a dilemma because the number of alternatives are frequently reduced and making a choice among those alternatives can involve costly trade-offs. Thus, decisionmakers usually have to balance different kinds of social, political, and economic costs and gains with the impact their policy decisions may have in external contexts and on their own chances of staying in power. The fact is that decisionmaking is always embedded in politics — an element usually neglected by rational policy analyses — and decisions are the ultimate expression of a struggle over different alternatives. As Deborah Stone reminds us, the decision-making process follows a political reasoning that is not completely rational; instead, it is "reasoning by metaphor and analogy [that tries] to get others to see a situation as one thing rather than another" (Stone 1997, 9).

In other words, problems can be regarded as pressures on policymakers to act and, at the same time, as opportunities to implement new resolution alternatives that would be inconceivable in normal times. The politics of launching and implementing recent structural reforms in Latin America, for example, is very much the story of a dramatic crisis portrayed by policymakers as an extremely constraining context; during this time, no other policy alternatives were feasible.

Nonetheless, besides the messy context created by politics, policymakers are usually expected to find the least costly and most efficient policy option. This is basically the dilemma of making a choice that is both right and timely in an unpredictably changing context. Indeed, it is worth underlining that the challenge includes the spicy and elusive ingredient of timing. To a considerable extent, cost and efficiency are related to the ability to solve problems within a reasonable time framework. Although the term "reasonable" may have different meanings across political systems, such as the Brazilian muddling-through decisionmaking style versus more expeditious methods, a reasonable time framework may be assumed to be one defined as appropriate by social expectations. A proper time horizon is determined by how long key actors involved are willing to wait for a resolution to a certain problem.

In addition, policy innovations tend to generate specific dilemmas. For instance, by definition, structural reforms involve major transformations that trigger political and economic effects and reactions not usually associated with noninnovative policies. Their content implies changes in wealth distribution within a society, so policymakers need to watch closely the reactions of winners and losers in order to achieve their goals, while obtaining support and neutralizing opposition. The results of these efforts are crucial to building up and maintaining electoral and governing coalitions.

Hence, within the restricted scenario that decisionmakers act, the following two factors make their task more complex:

1. Governments can pay serious attention to only a few issues at a time, making the selection of priorities a risky political calculus.

2. Policy windows[1] present themselves occasionally and stay open only for short periods of time.

As for the latter, there is an unsettled discussion about the role of crises in broadening the maneuvering room of policymakers. Crises are seen as opening a window of opportunity for policy innovation or, in other words, authorizing governments to use extraordinary policy-making mechanisms to launch radical and ambitious programs of reforms. However, crises are also understood as an intervening variable that, although important in generating a propitious context, cannot explain per se — much less predict — outcomes.[2] Beyond the plausibility of such arguments, it is worth noting that in Latin America, crises have been more the norm rather than the exception, thus rendering policymaking in the region to the management of emergencies by governments in trouble.

On top of that, although windows of opportunity may open due to objective factors, such as a change of administration, a dramatic economic crisis, or other pressing problems, a question of perception is also involved. Actors have to perceive the window or estimate the likelihood of its future emergence in order to act appropriately, but they may well misperceive or misestimate its occurrence, or simply be unable to seize the opportunity when it arises. In other words, the short list of issues that get on a governmental agenda and urge it to make decisions is not only defined by sociopolitical and economic developments, but also by the subjective perceptions and estimations of policymakers. Thus, it is possible that those in charge of making decisions may well let windows of opportunity slip away or set policy priorities that do not necessarily reflect the most urgent problems facing their societies.

How have these factors played in recent Latin American history? What was the role of crises in launching structural reforms? What use did policy elites make of the windows of opportunity presented? What kinds of policy dilemmas and opportunities did governments confront at the beginning of the reformist process? Almost two decades later, what are the main challenges facing these governments in the management of their foreign economic relations, and what are feasible options for coping with them?

FOREIGN POLICY AND STRUCTURAL REFORMS

The last two decades of the twentieth century were a period of deep transformation for the international system in general and for Latin America in particular. Actually, since the mid-1970s, the main elements and institutions of political and economic postwar order started to transform and were progressively abandoned or reformed. Economies and societies became increasingly integrated, and policymakers had to learn to deal with global problems for which they lacked — and still lack — adequate tools.

During these decades, Latin America passed from the last hopeful phase of industrialization through indebtedness to external debt crisis, and from the latter to the painful period of adjustment and structural reforms that reversed decades of state interventionism and fostered in its place the development of private initiative within the framework of free market economies. This last process was painful, not only because it required a deep restructuring of old, well-entrenched institutions and actors' attitudes and strategies, but also because it involved considerable social costs for a large part of the population in terms of deterioration of living standards, such as employment conditions and rate, poverty levels, access and quality of education, and health coverage (Korzeniewicz and Smith 1996, 1-31).

This aspect of the process was probably not part of the calculus of Latin American policymakers in the 1980s. Faced with the enormous challenge of managing two complex transitions (to democracy and to the market) in an adverse international context, they seized the opportunity presented by the crisis and tried to take advantage of the window of opportunity that suddenly appeared to open. The executives,[3] in particular, led the economic transformation with the help of new technocratic cadres fully committed to the new policy paradigm. They interpreted the dilemma in terms of extreme crisis, stagnation, and marginalization versus liberalization, growth, and increasing integration in a globalized world economy. Policy priorities were selected almost inevitably by a combination of urgency and necessity; political and institutional reforms were left for a later moment in time when the waters would calm on the economic side and growth could resume. Thus, while issues such as drug trafficking and international crime, human rights defense, democracy promotion, migration flows across borders, and environmental degradation were still crucial for specific countries, from the mid-1980s on, the economic dimension of external relations played a key role in the foreign policy agenda of the whole region (Domínguez 2000).

Consequently, at different times and applying distinct implementation styles, most Latin American countries experienced a shift in economic policy. Following neoliberal ideas that were dominant worldwide and the exigencies of financial conditionality, Latin American governments set clear policy goals to attain monetary stabilization, ending the recurrent problem of high inflation; to open their economies fully; and to withdraw the state from past economic and social welfare commitments.

The new foreign policy orientation aimed to make these economies competitive in international markets. The means chosen to make this happen were a combined set of structural reforms that included trade liberalization; export promotion; deregulation of capital markets and stimulus to foreign capital investment; privatization of state-owned enterprises, in the framework of broader reforms of state structures and public administration functioning; and the formation of regional blocs, through deeper and faster economic integration with neighboring countries. Hope was focused on the beneficial effects that would be obtained from both economic stabilization and structural market-oriented reforms. Political and institutional reforms, although absolutely necessary for the correct functioning of markets, were indefinitely postponed or implemented only partially (Haggard and Kaufman 1992; Smith et al. 1994a, 1994b; Diamond and Plattner 1995; Nelson 1994b; Oxhorn and Ducatenzeiler 1998).

The impact of the economic measures taken has been mixed. As described in the following paragraphs, progress lagged behind the initial expectations of policy elites in several areas, while in others some new problems arose. So, what went wrong? Did governments lack commitment, persistence, or the capacities to carry out the necessary transformations? Is it plausible, perhaps, that they overestimated the size of the policy window?

In general terms, evidence across the region shows that the following important goals were achieved:

- Hyperinflation was eliminated, and the inflation rate was considerably reduced.
- Budget balances, though not completely attained, were improved, and significant amounts of international reserves were accumulated.
- Exports were expanded and, in some cases, diversified.
- Large-scale deregulation and privatization of economic activities were carried out in most countries.

However, these achievements were accompanied by significant economic imbalances and unfortunate records, such as the persistence of huge fiscal deficits and low domestic savings rates; a moderate growth rate of the regional gross domestic product (GDP); increasing foreign indebtedness; and poor export performance in some countries, not to mention a generalized social setback in terms of labor conditions and social equity (Lora and Panizza 2002; Inter-American Development Bank 1997).

Many of the remaining structural problems and some of the new issues generated by reforms are closely related to the way the changes were implemented. The debate is not yet settled regarding the benefits and disadvantages of gradualism versus speed, pragmatism versus dogmatism, radical "bitter pill" approaches versus incremental ones, decree-driven imposed initiatives versus those supported by negotiated consensus building, and the impact of these issues on the success of reform implementation (Sturzenegger and Tommasi 1998). Yet, there is a generalized consensus within institutionalist political science approaches that, to a large extent, the characteristics of the transition have shaped the kinds of relations and institutions of the new reformed economy (Smith and Korzeniewicz 1997, 21-36). This is so because any structural adjustment process is essentially a process of change. Its dynamic goes beyond the passage from one type of socioeconomic organization to another, for example, from a state- to a market-centered model. The transition itself is very relevant, as future conditions are molded while the transition is taking place. In other words, the mechanisms used to implement reforms, the sequence and speed of the measures, as well as the conditions agreed upon during the transition between public and private actors all have clear impacts on the relations and institutions that will define the new model. Latin American policymakers, in general, pressured by time and political and economic constraints, neglected this aspect of the process. Hence, significant institutional deficits are now acting as obstacles to further and deeper transformations.

Indeed, the post-reform scenario in Latin America reflects the relative ability governments have had to make use of opportunities for policy innovation. Some of them managed to reform more effectively than others; that had to do, to a certain extent, with the fact that each starting point was different, and not all governments had the same institutional capacities to launch and sustain necessary changes. The new landscape combines old and new elements that are a hybrid mix of market-oriented practices, sectoral protectionist policies, and some degree of state intervention that is different from that of the past. Underlying these trends have been simultaneous processes of deep destructuring and restructuring of states' powers and functions, economic agents' organization and relations, and social actors' conditions and political representation (Smith and Korzeniewicz 1997, 37-53). The picture is not static and varies considerably across countries, acquiring many nuances and making it very difficult to assess accurately achievements and shortcomings at the regional level.

Yet, in general terms and from a long-term historical perspective, the current situation can be read as one more opportunity for Latin American countries to redefine their foreign policies. Previous attempts at redefinition also involved an active position, especially since the 1970s, when most major countries in the region were engaged in individual and cooperative endeavors to defend their interests and produce a change in the international economic order. Like today, that effort had a very high economic policy content. The 1980s not only reflected the failure of that attempt, but also the harsh difficulties of getting out of an extremely serious crisis. The fragile Latin American democracies of this transition period then focused more on their domestic problems, while negotiations to solve the external debt crisis dominated their foreign economic policy agenda. There was a turning away from global issues toward more internal and regional ones (Huntington and Nye 1985, 161-198).

Now, at the beginning of the twenty-first century, Latin American countries again face the challenge of strategically rethinking their options for active participation in world affairs. In an international context where power is more diffuse, societies and economies are highly interdependent, nontraditional issues and actors have considerable leverage, and ideological models of all sorts are under question, so there may be more room for innovative proposals (Tulchin and Espach 2001).

However, the region still has to work against the scant attention it gets from the United States (with the exceptions, to some extent, of Mexico and Colombia) and the ineffectiveness of its regional institutions to solve collective and individual problems. In addition, policy innovation seems to have reached some limits, and more comprehensive approaches that integrate and properly address economic, political, and social problems have yet to be designed.

Latin American governments currently face the new policy choice of having to decide whether and how to deepen the path taken in the last few decades. The international context has pressed them to persist in free-market-oriented experiments, even if these policies proved to be the source of many frustrations. Domestic constituencies demand better wealth distribution and a way out of harsh situations affecting a large part of the population. How are these conflicting demands to be reconciled? It is beyond the aim and scope of this volume to answer this general political question. The main purpose here is to identify the areas in which governmental action is urgently required and to suggest some alternatives.

Four policy areas seem particularly relevant to Latin America's current foreign economic policy agenda because they pose specific and pressing dilemmas. They involve the issues of trade, economic integration, capital flows, and financial relations, which have been traditionally included in the realm of foreign economic policy and some others that are relatively new, but just as important in light of ongoing developments in the world economy. These include social policies for human capital development, institution building, and democratic governance. It is our aim to underline the importance of raising these newer issues to the top of governments' agendas.

First, how can domestic, regional, and international markets be enlarged, and is economic integration a good and feasible option for doing so? In order to promote growth, governments have to find a way to enlarge and diversify markets. The path taken so far has been to liberalize trade and engage in economic integration processes with other nations. This strategy has shown some limits and unforeseen consequences that cast doubt on whether this should be the main bet, that is, the engine of a restructuring process that will place these economies competitively in regional and world markets.

Second, how can recurrent external crises be coped with, and to what extent is it possible to prevent financial instability? Policymakers urgently need to design mechanisms to attain long-term monetary stabilization, strengthen their nation's finances, and find a positive balance between a generalized context of capital markets deregulation and the need to reduce their economies' vulnerability to external shocks.

Third, how can human capital be created and accumulated to promote economic competitiveness and more broadly shared standards of living? Both educational reforms and job training programs are an important component of any economic and social development strategy, especially in a global economy driven by knowledge- and technology- based industries. Latin American governments still have to incorporate human capital development as a top priority in their policy agendas.

Fourth, how can democratic institutions be built and consolidated to make governmental action efficient, accountable, and credible? Markets do not function in a vacuum. They require an appropriate legal and institutional framework that, among other things, guarantees respect for property rights, enforces contracts, and provides certainty and an extended time horizon for business. Although important progress has been achieved in the last two decades, the process of democratic consolidation is far from complete in Latin America. Not only is the efficiency and transparency of governmental action seriously questioned across the region, but in some cases, so is governmental legitimacy in terms of representativeness and delivery capacity.

The next sections turn to a brief analysis of these four general concerns and some specific policy alternatives.

BETTING ON ECONOMIC INTEGRATION

E conomic integration has been the cornerstone of Latin American trade policy since the mid-1980s and a crucial component of the new development strategy of both large and small countries. Unilateral trade liberalization and the formation of subregional trade blocs served as the main instruments to promote countries' economic interests in the international sphere, to gain and maintain access to foreign markets, and to foster domestic productivity. Trade blocs have also been viewed as having some potential political side benefits, such as helping to build up governmental credibility by showing the strength of their commitments to free market policies, supporting democratic consolidation by including respect for democratic practices as a requirement for membership, and increasing the bargaining power of member states vis-à-vis world powers and other blocs in order to reduce discrimination.

This recent trend of regionalism differs considerably from previous experiments. It has more ambitious political and economic goals than earlier cooperation agreements. It not only includes the political dimension previously mentioned, but also greater tariff reductions in a larger number of economic sectors than in the past. It reflects a more pragmatic and flexible approach than before. It is also closely linked to the economic structural reforms carried out at the domestic level. It is primarily outward-oriented; that is, it is based on an open borders policy and export-oriented insertion in international markets that is in opposition to the inward-oriented integration schemes pursued within the import-substitution strategy. Thus, it is aimed at adjusting Latin American economies to a highly dynamic and competitive globalized economic environment (Mace and Thérien 1996; Mace and Bélanger 1999).

José Salazar-Xirinachs' chapter in this volume provides a thoughtful account of the last two decades, which witnessed a proliferation of bilateral and multilateral trade agreements. These agreements differed considerably in terms of the areas they covered and the institutional arrangements on which they were based. Their impact has been multiple, too. In general terms, both trade reforms and the revitalization of integration initiatives had a great impact on the acceleration of growth, especially during the first half of the 1990s. Regional export performance improved notably in comparison with the previous decade and was remarkable for countries such as Mexico. The region also modified its traditional basket of goods, incorporating an important proportion of goods of medium- and high-technology content. Intraregional trade grew more rapidly than trade with nonregional partners. This trend was particularly pronounced in the case of exports, while a large part of the region's imports are still supplied by extrahemispheric countries. And it is mainly through trade relations within the region that these economies have increased their exchange of technology-intensive products, this being a potential way to move toward more value-added exports to other markets (Inter-American Development Bank 1997, Parts I and II, and IDB 2001, chapter 4; Stallings and Peres 2000, chapter 2).

The way that trade liberalization was pursued also had an impact on the outcome and contrasts sharply with the experiences of other regions, especially Southeast Asia. Most Latin American countries carried out liberalization rapidly and set a passive role for the state, while Asian economies went through a long process of state-led liberalization that oriented the production structure toward international markets (Ffrench-Davis 2000). More concretely, structural transformations and the development of manufactured exports preceded import liberalization in Asia, and the latter took place in a context of macroeconomic equilibrium and a high investment rate. In contrast, import liberalization in Latin America was drastic and took place in the midst of recessive stabilization programs, low rates of capital accumulation, and incipient internalization strategies. In such an environment, private economic agents lacked time and incentives to adjust to the changes, and some industrial capacity was lost. No reciprocity model between governments and the business sector was implemented to stimulate export performance, much less a strategy to develop national capacities on knowledge-based activities.[4] In addition, the interrelation of trade liberalization with other reforms hampered the efficient reallocation of resources expected. As explained in the next section, capital markets deregulation in the 1990s led to exchange rate appreciation and high real interest rates, thus discouraging productive investment necessary to produce structural change and pushing resources away from the production of tradable goods toward financial investment.

In contrast, as Salazar-Xirinachs suggests in his chapter, the impact of regional trade agreements goes beyond the trade domain and includes several nontrade issues. For instance, such agreements imply a good commitment mechanism that has helped to increase the credibility of reformist initiatives; created interdependencies that have helped reduce historical rivalries and encourage cooperation; promoted certain discipline and coordinated responses to external shocks; and altered the incentives to compete and, thus, indirectly affected private firms' strategies, forcing them to restructure and adjust to new international standards.

Within that multilayered framework created by different paths taken to trade reform in Latin America, it is possible to identify the following distinct strategies:

- *Integration in world markets through unilateral liberalization and trade diversification (both of products and partners).* This involves the dismantling of tariff and nontariff barriers and an export-led development strategy, as well as the pursuit of further access to foreign markets and preferential agreements with multiple trade partners. It is a relatively easy alternative that avoids the economic and political costs involved in any cooperation effort and in the long-term and strong commitments required by multilateral formal agreements. To some extent, this option was taken in Latin America as part of the policy recommendations of the Washington Consensus. Chile is the best example of a country that adopted it as the main feature of its foreign economic policy.

- *Integration in a subregional bloc through bilateral or multilateral formal agreements with neighboring countries.* This assumes a progressive process of economic integration among member states that is initially driven by trade liberalization and proceeds through stages that may eventually lead to the formation of a common market but often includes many other dimensions. The most relevant case in terms of market size in Latin America is the Southern Common Market (Mercado Común del Sur — MERCOSUR), created in 1991 by Argentina, Brazil, Uruguay, and Paraguay (Chile and Bolivia are associate members). The fact that the other most relevant case in the hemisphere is the North American Free Trade Agreement (NAFTA), in which Mexico participates together with the United States and Canada, has opened up at least two alternative scenarios for the rest of the Latin American countries (Roett 1999; Wise 1998). One is to achieve preferential trade agreements with Mexico or the United States. The second is to concentrate efforts in the consolidation of subregional blocs. This second option may be seen either as an instrument to increase individual member states' bargaining power and improve their chances of attracting foreign investment and obtaining unilateral accession to NAFTA (Argentina played with this possibility for a while), or it can be viewed as a way of building a counterbalancing economic bloc that might allow implementation of a more assertive foreign policy and competition with other blocs for a share of world markets (Brazil's position may well reflect such an attempt) (Mace and Thérien 1996, 199-218; Smith 2000).

- *Trade partnership with extrahemispheric actors through broad bilateral cooperation agreements.* This implies seeking establishment of close economic and political ties with outside powers. It aims at diversifying economic and financial partnership, thus gaining access to nontraditional export markets and sources of foreign investment and financial aid. This course has been pursued by major Latin American governments in the last decade as a complement to previously mentioned strategies. The European Union and some countries in the Asia-Pacific Rim (especially Japan) have been the main targets of this strategy.

Undoubtedly, selecting one of these strategies depends on varying combinations of each country's interests and capacities. It is obvious that not all options are available to all countries. Mexico, for instance, is a peculiar case. As this volume's chapter by Gustavo Vega Cánovas shows, trade policy in Mexico has been a crucial component of its development strategy. The successful promotion of an export manufacture sector has made important contributions to financial recovery and economic growth in the 1980s and 1990s. Participation in NAFTA has been the top priority of trade policy and largely explains the outcomes. However, the persistence of significant asymmetries among NAFTA members, the vicissitudes of U.S. foreign policy, and the marginalization of a large part of the Mexican population from the benefits of modernization and growth cast doubt on the desirability of making economic integration with the United States the main focus. Moreover, the events of September 11, 2001, have made evident that the prospects of NAFTA largely depend on the capacity of the United States and Mexican governments to redefine their relationship and find cooperative solutions to very sensitive issues, such as security and migration.

Still, the future feasibility of each alternative will be determined not only by the evolution of the subregional integration processes already in place, but also by the progress attained by the initiative to create a Free Trade Area of the Americas (FTAA). According to Roberto Bouzas, in his chapter in this volume, MERCOSUR has reached a critical point. It is currently undergoing a slow and difficult phase that puts into question the viability and desirability of the custom union. Indeed, the initial progress made toward the liberalization of intraregional trade flows has, since 1999, been slowed by the serious obstacles created by disagreement over issues such as lowering nontariff barriers, enforcing a common external trade policy, and dealing with the impact of the divergent monetary policies of its lead members. These problems reflect underlying differences in perceptions and goals, a lack of willingness and ability to lead by both Argentina and Brazil, and the absence of an agreed-upon cooperative agenda. Hence, the challenge ahead for bloc members still involves the hard work of defining common interests and strategies, harmonizing policy in several realms, and developing institutional structures and enforcing mechanisms. Although a reversal of the integration process seems unlikely, its progress depends on the capacity of member countries to renew their political commitment and reassess costs and benefits from a broad and long-term perspective. It goes without saying that Argentina's default in December 2001 has seriously affected MERCOSUR's prospects.

As for the FTAA project, potential economic and political gains abound. Salazar-Xirinachs' chapter provides a full account of them. However, there is still much work to do to attain the expected outcome by 2005, and prospects are highly dependent on the shifting priorities of U.S. foreign policy and domestic agendas. The project itself remains slightly vague, and no agreement has been reached on contentious issues, such as labor and environmental considerations (Stark 2001, 161-184). Although President George W. Bush has said, since his term began, that he is seriously committed to the FTAA initiative, it is not yet clear how he will use the recently obtained trade promotion authority (TPA, formerly called the "fast track mechanism") (*New York Times* 2002, 5). Since then, other priorities have been shifting the executive's attention away from Latin America.

COPING WITH FINANCIAL INSTABILITY

Financial crises have been recurring phenomena in Latin America since the early 1980s. Every few years, financial collapses originating in Latin American countries or elsewhere have battered the region. The immediate negative impact of individual debacles and their longer-term recessionary effects spread to neighboring economies. Some spillover effects have also shaken developed countries and required further aid from them. Even more, in the context of the considerable effort undertaken by Latin American countries to reform their economies according to the policy prescriptions designed and enforced by Washington and international financial bodies, these frequent crises have seriously brought into question those prescriptions and the ability of international financial institutions to cope with the undesired results.

The diagnosis from which those recommendations were based indicated that governments' control over capital in the past not only encouraged the formation of black markets in foreign currency and rent-seeking behavior, but also put limits on local firms' access to foreign capital and other resources, such as technology. Thus, reforms to eliminate exchange controls and restrictions on foreign direct investment (FDI) and capital flows in general were carried out. As a complement, domestic financial reforms were also encouraged. In this case, the argument was made that Latin American governments' control of the domestic financial system was responsible for a series of negative effects, such as low savings rates, low access to credit, and credit allocation on the basis of political nonefficient considerations. Thus, changes were required to let markets determine the interest rates, lower reserve requirements, limit or end subsidized credit, and privatize or close state-owned banks. These changes were generally complemented by a policy trend toward strengthening the autonomy of central banks.

The new norms, as well as a more stable macroeconomic and political scenario, had an impact on the behavior of capital flows during the 1990s. This domestic stimulus, together with some international factors, such as recession in industrialized countries and a decrease in the U.S. interest rate, served to redirect flows of capital toward emerging countries in the first half of the nineties. Inflows of capital to Latin America were characterized by high volatility. Fluctuations took place at a more frequent rate. Portfolio flows grew more than FDI. The higher proportion of short-term inflows contributed to high volatility. Only in a few cases was this increase in capital inflow accompanied by a higher investment rate; typically, most of the capital went to consumption or to compensate for worsening terms of trade (Stallings 2000; Ffrench-Davis 2000). Economic recovery and increasing capital inflows went hand in hand with exchange rate appreciation, decreasing trade surpluses, and increasing current account deficits, which eventually ended up in financial and banking meltdowns (Krueger 2000, 511-547).

In light of the successive crises in emerging and transitional economies, much of the debate has concentrated on whom to blame for the disasters. Positions divide between those who blame Latin American governments for their lack of willingness and/or commitment to go further with the proper structural reforms and those who point a finger at the role played by lending institutions (specifically, their neglect toward heterodox programs or their incapacity to enforce conditionality) or structural characteristics of international financial markets. Sidney Weintraub's chapter in this volume is conceptualized in those terms. He takes a comparative look at the Mexican (1994-1995), Brazilian (1998-1999), and Argentine (from late 1998 on) crises, asking whether the sources of trouble originated with the international financial system or lie at the domestic level where wrong choices were made. Weintraub identifies the following systemic factors working in all three crises: increases in the interest rate by the U.S. government, contagion effects from financial debacles in other regions, and the capacity of international capital to flow in easily and rapidly during good times and flow out when conditions worsened. As for the policy failures attributable to Latin American governments, he points to insufficient efforts to resolve fiscal deficits, which led to increasing public debts, and real exchange rate appreciation and overvaluation, which, in turn, translated into current account imbalances and eventual crises. Some specific characteristics of each political system are also mentioned as intertwining factors that made the carrying out of fiscal adjustment more difficult. He concludes that, although systemic forces played a role in all three cases, the policies chosen by governments at the domestic level were the overwhelming cause of financial collapse.

Weintraub's account has captured a very important angle of the problem. However, it is worth looking at how international variables interplay with domestic ones. For instance, a combination of factors, such as the inherent vulnerability of developing countries to sudden stops in capital flows and the absence of a lender of last resort at the global level, also seem to play important roles. In addition, there are some peculiarities of Latin American financial systems that do not all derive from a government's policy choices, for example, a lower ratio of financial intermediation in relation to GDP, lower investor willingness to commit long-term funds, and higher volatility in deposit markets. These characteristics, in turn, derive from institutional deficits, such as an underdeveloped legal framework regulating financial markets and accounting standards that are relatively weak (Hausmann and Rojas-Suárez 1996, 3-21). Although Latin American countries, such as Mexico,

Argentina, and Venezuela, have recently carried out important reforms of their banking sectors and financial liberalization, these deficits persist and add to the fragility of their economies.

Once again, the modality of implementing the changes is an important variable in explaining the outcomes. These reforms were carried out under the assumption that deregulation of capital accounts was needed in order to raise national savings, deepen domestic financial markets, reduce the costs of financial intermediation, satisfy the demand for risk diversification, and optimize resource allocation. However, successive crises suggest not only the failure of international financial markets and some lending practices, but also some flaws in the sequencing and speed of the liberalization reforms. As for the latter, the main lesson has been that capital account liberalization was premature and should have been postponed until other major reforms, for example, in trade and the domestic financial sector, had been consolidated (Ffrench-Davis 2000).

For the reasons specific to Latin America cited above, the lessons derived from crisis resolution in industrialized countries do not always apply to the regional context. In addition, there is widespread consensus that financial crises will persist in the region in the near future and will probably continue to be more severe than the crises experienced in the industrialized world. To diminish external vulnerability and contagion effects is a long-term and complex process that would require not only sound policies at home but also serious cooperation between developed and developing countries on harmonizing regulatory and supervisory standards. Meanwhile, policy recommendations for economies in constant trouble have refocused on the design of efficient bank regulations and safety nets, strengthening legal rules and enforcement mechanisms that protect investors' rights, and improving the general governance context by asserting the rule of law and increasing the judicial system's efficiency (Burki and Perry 1998).

No alternatives have been designed at the international level to prevent these episodes from occurring. The ball is again in each individual government's court, creating pressure to pursue further domestic reforms. There are several things that governments can do to cope with financial instability. In her chapter for this volume, Sylvia Maxfield suggests the following four interrelated policy recommendations:

- To manage national capital structures through either capital account regulations or innovative incentive structures;
- To promote the deepening of local financial markets;
- To build up institutional capacities to supervise and regulate the bank sector and creditor rights; and
- To conduct countercyclical macroeconomic practices, especially through flexible fiscal policies.

These four measures aim at improving market functioning and do not necessarily involve increasing government intervention. But they all fall in the realm of economic policymaking and will require some governmental action. The crises have taught us that inactivity and procrastination can produce significant costs. Nonetheless, only governments with strong capacities and institutions in place will be capable of implementing all of these policy recommendations. Thus, the challenge for policymakers will be to sort out in each national context the degree of necessity, urgency, and feasibility of each policy option open on this front.

ACCUMULATING HUMAN CAPITAL

To position national economies more effectively in world markets today implies a series of changes within the whole productive process, including those that directly affect the labor force. Some examples required by new international standards include the incorporation of technological advances, a new distribution of workers among economic sectors, new and more qualifications, the restructuring of firms' organization and processes, different management techniques, and more flexible labor relations. Global trends have also hit Latin America in this realm and have forced firms to adapt to the new dominant production paradigm. Within that restructuring process, the main consequences for the labor force have been three-fold. First, changes have occurred in its composition, such as fewer industrial workers, and working conditions, for example, flexibilization. Second, technological changes have given rise to greater demand for more educated workers who can perform various tasks and upgrade their skills. Qualifications become, as a result, less structured, hierarchical, and specialized. Third, the need to manage human resources beyond hiring — through constant training, participatory schemes, and compliance and motivation techniques — has increased (Tokman and O'Donnell 1998, 91-118).

In short, knowledge, in the form of qualifications and broad abilities, has become a crucial element in increasing productivity. Thus, education and on-the-job training policies are a key component of any development strategy. As Nancy Birdsall has pointed out, "The earliest postwar models of development emphasized accumulation of physical capital, and saw spending on health and education as a drain on the accumulation of 'productive' assets. . . . Sustainable growth in these models [the more recent endogenous growth models] is the result in part of positive externalities generated by education, an important form of capital. In these models, new ideas and new technologies that are critical to high sustained growth rely fundamentally on high levels of human capital" (Birdsall 2001, 14).

Moreover, education is extremely relevant in increasing productivity because the ability to incorporate and even create new technologies is mediated by the knowledge and capacity of workers to learn. Higher productivity is not related only to financial markets, infrastructure development, and technology; it is also associated with the following three human capital-related issues: education through formal schooling, on-the-job training, and cooperative labor relations.

Nonetheless, the questions of human capital, as well as poverty and inequality, have only recently become topics of considerable discussion in Latin America. Educational reforms have received much less and much later attention than first-generation reforms on the agendas of scholars and practitioners. This is surprising in a region where many countries have attained only relatively low education levels and training systems have largely failed.

Indeed, progress in education in the last few decades has been slower than in other regions and plagued with obstacles. A large majority of children have access to primary school, but high repetition and dropout rates push them away from secondary school. Training programs at the workplace suffer from many deficiencies and are usually reserved for the most educated workers, thus deepening initial inequalities. Labor relations have been far from cooperative; rather, conflict and distrust have prevailed, working against the creation of conditions that might have raised workers' motivation (IDB 2001).

Moreover, according to the same source, recent problems of competitiveness in Latin American economies have also been related to human development issues. Modest regional economic growth has been attributed to the low rate of accumulation of productive factors and very poor performance in productivity. Indicators include low investment rates over the last two decades that determined a relatively low growth rate of capital stocks (2.6 percent annually in the 1980s and 3.7 percent in the 1990s, much less than in other developing countries) and educational levels that have been growing at a much slower pace than regions with even lower standards, such as the Middle East or some parts of Asia. Consequently, it has been estimated that Latin America could sustain a growth rate of no more than 4 percent annually on the basis of the accumulation of factors of production only. However, during the 1990s, the rate of growth was even lower (3.3 percent) because declines in productivity subtracted 0.6 percent. The decline in productivity in most countries has been attributed to an incapacity to assimilate technological changes. This type of incapacity results mainly from a labor force insufficiently educated to take advantage of these changes (IDB 2001).

The challenge ahead is even more compelling if the interrelationship of educational standards with other dimensions of human development,[5] such as life expectancy, GDP per capita, employment rate, and salary levels are taken into account. There is a vicious cycle of poverty, low level of education, low level of training, and un- or underemployment in the region. Each life experience shows a distinct combination of basic formal education largely determined by socioeconomic background and family situations. The quality of education, as well as access to specialized training and even job opportunities, are less the result of individual decisions than of the constraining and/or enabling conditions generated within the family and social context. In this respect, governmental action is required in Latin America to break this cycle.

Demographic changes already underway are expected to produce an important impact on Latin American labor markets, such as an expanded labor force and shift from larger proportions of younger workers to greater proportions of older ones (IDB 2000). These changes will require further adjustments in labor regulations and income policies, two areas where scant progress has been made.

Although market-oriented reforms accelerated regional economic growth, they also slowed the pace of job creation and have been one of the reasons for increasing unemployment rates. At the same time, poverty increased during the 1990s, and income distribution did not improve and in some cases even worsened. Concrete evaluations differ in important ways across countries and according to the source. While some analysts hold the more benign view that stresses positive achievements and de-emphasizes the negative effects of reforms (IDB 1997), others have pointed out some striking negative facts. For instance, about one out of three individuals lives on an income below US$2 per day. Acknowledged urban unemployment consistently increased from 5.7 to 8.6 percent from 1991 to 2000. The same trend is evident in the rate of underemployment, while wage differentials between skilled and unskilled workers increased considerably (Stark 2001, 5-7).

Policy alternatives need to take into account these realities. So far, the first phase of education reforms in Latin America focused on broad dimensions of the whole institutional system. This phase included decentralization, legal changes, development of pilot innovations, and creation of testing and evaluation mechanisms. The stage was set for further and deeper changes that would focus on issues such as pedagogical practices, learning mechanisms, access and use of information, definition of new roles and empowerment of some actors, and accountability problems. The goal during the second phase would be to make sure that structural changes in the legal framework translate into changes in actors' values and behaviors. This would require movement from a top-down to a bottom-up approach to policy innovation (Burki and Perry 1998).

The chapters in this section of the book provide important insights about the relative contribution and feasibility of various policy alternatives. Wendy Hunter, for example, points out that policymakers are working in this field without a master plan, with less urgency than in other areas, and are facing stronger resistance to innovation from domestic interest groups and weaker pressure from external actors to reform. She also argues that the lack of technical consensus for reforming education leads to controversies over paths taken. In particular, investment strategies are questioned because they have apparently been guided by inappropriate priorities, such as too much concentration on higher education, as well as the excessive administrative and financial centralization that characterizes Latin American educational systems. The chapter gathers some evidence that efforts to decentralize have been relatively more successful than attempts to shift the allocation of investments. Political and economic changes have contributed to open a window of opportunity for policy elites to carry out decentralization initiatives, while reforms such as instituting tuition charges at public universities still face serious obstacles.

From another perspective, the chapter by Suzanne Duryea and Carmen Pagés links education policy with productivity and poverty levels. Duryea and Pagés argue that low educational standards in Latin America (lower than in other developing regions) have been one of the most important obstacles to achieving sustained productivity growth and poverty reduction. They examine the ability of education to lift labor incomes above poverty levels and find that in many countries, education by itself has a positive, although limited, potential to increase wages above minimum level. In general, they have found that prospects are dim because progress in raising average schooling levels has been slow even under the best historical scenarios. Duryea and Pagés also explore whether the apparent failure of education can be explained by low wage returns to schooling and poor underlying conditions. Their findings suggest that investment in education continues to yield important payoffs, but poor underlying conditions result in modest prospects for the role of education in the short run. This conclusion leads the authors to consider additional policies that could be pursued in order to ensure higher productivity for workers in the region, such as improving the institutions and government regulations that would prevent diversion of resources away from productive uses, motivating workers with schemes that increase their stake and participation in their firms' successes, developing mechanisms that improve the diffusion of information, and expanding the provision of basic infrastructure.

It is possible and desirable, of course, to go beyond education to identify policy opportunities. It is necessary to develop more integrated approaches that help to complement investments in human capital with other conditions and policies, such as physical and social infrastructure, the rule of law, regulatory frameworks, and governance quality. Moreover, education is not the only source of human capital development. Thus, it is necessary to pay more attention to the role of skills acquired outside school. Like education, training institutions and programs show some important deficits in the region and can hardly meet the skill needs of the workforce today. For instance, most recent innovations in training systems in Latin America have been implemented as temporary devices to cope with unemployment and poverty (IDB 2001).

Therefore, it is necessary for governments to expand their understanding of the problem and place this issue at the top of their agendas. As the performance of training institutions is closely linked to education policy, tax policies, and labor market regulations, the coordination of measures among these areas is crucial to promote investments in human capital development. Demographic changes, technological progress, and globalization trends are demanding that Latin American countries work on reforming and making more complementary their education and training systems.

IMPROVING DEMOCRATIC GOVERNANCE

S cholarly speculation at the beginning of the 1990s pointed to uncertainty about the type of social and institutional formations that would emerge from economic and political liberalization in Latin America. Taking into account the increasing differences that existed in various countries, alternative scenarios were postulated to accommodate the relative achievements of Latin American countries in terms of both democratic consolidation and economic restructuring (Smith et al. 1994, 1-28). Scholars, in general, were concerned with the relatively fragmented and weak character of societies in Latin America, a structural feature accentuated by the neoliberal reforms and the most recent generalized dismantling of already poor state capacities. Some analyses centered the problem on the reconstruction of those capacities in the difficult context of a transition to democracy that was not yet completely finished (Grindle 1996). No doubt, simultaneous management of two very complex processes (the political and economic transitions) put still fragile democratic governments under serious stress. The literature on reforms also accounted for those difficulties (Nelson 1994a, 1-36).

Intellectual exercises, as well as cross-regional evidence, contributed to produce a certain redefinition of the Washington Consensus' policy prescriptions for developing countries. From the early 1990s, international financial agencies started to include questions about the quality of government in their packages of conditional lending (Gore 2000; Burki and Perry 1997, 1998). A growing demand for institutional reforms, from both domestic and foreign actors concerned with the consolidation of democracy and the improvement of political practices, accompanied this move.

The underlying reasons for this evolution can be found in the prerequisites of free-market-oriented socioeconomic organizations; specifically, the recognition that markets need an appropriate legal and institutional framework that guarantees the development of private initiative. Markets, in fact, are embodied in institutions, which may be defined in broad terms as the formal and informal rules that shape the behavior of individuals. Some of the most important functions that institutions play in relation to markets have to do with access to information and enforcing mechanisms. By affecting these two elements, institutions shape agents' perceptions of the costs and risks involved in transactions and, consequently, the likelihood and level of investment. It is plausible, then, to expect that institutions have an influence on economic growth in the long run (North 1990).

Indeed, empirical evidence from a large number of countries in various regions and policy areas confirms these assumptions (Burki and Perry 1998). In the case of Latin America, certain characteristics of institutional frameworks seem particularly relevant today in relation to national economies' competitiveness. The decline in productivity in the 1990s has been attributed not only to the educational factors mentioned above, but also to the fragility of public institutions. Examples include the absence or weakness of a stable and respected system of laws, governments' inefficiency, high levels of corruption, and a lack of institutions for social protection and for the resolution of distributive conflicts. It is noteworthy that productivity rose substantially faster during the same decade in countries with better institutions (IDB 2001).

These problems, shared by a large number of developing countries and transitional democracies, have recently led to the development of a set of indicators and cross-country indexes of institutional performance. Using these indices, a positive association between governance indicators and development outcomes has been demonstrated (Kaufmann et al. 1999a, 1999b).[6] These tools have also allowed measuring the evolution in time of three key aspects of governance — the process by which authorities are selected and made accountable, the capacity of the state to implement policies, and the respect for the rule of law — in a sample of 178 countries (Kaufmann et al. 2002). These studies aim not only at measuring important aspects of governance, but also at using systematized knowledge to help governments and civil societies approach institutional change (Kaufmann et al. 2000).

As for Latin America, the region presents some problems in the following four critical and interrelated areas: the rule of law, the control of corruption, the effectiveness of public administration, and the quality of regulatory frameworks (IDB 2000). The first refers to the degree of respect of citizens and the state toward the formal institutions that govern their relations; it represents a crucial principle without which democratic consolidation is virtually impossible. Corruption adopts many forms within Latin American political systems and spreads across policy areas largely because of the near absence of accountability mechanisms and deficits in the administration of justice. Public administration problems are long-standing and translate into a lack of capacity to deliver public services, incompetence of the bureaucracy, political interference, and lack of credibility of governmental actions. The regulatory frameworks governing markets have developed considerably in the last few years but still show some shortcomings.

Those same factors, together with policy instability, have been mentioned by the business sector as obstacles to the development of economic activities in Latin America. This is the case not only for domestic entrepreneurs but also for foreign investors. Good quality institutions not only facilitate and reduce the costs of doing business, but also increase the predictability of the environment in which long-term strategies then make more sense.

Indeed, this volume's chapter by Richard Youngs provides evidence of the increasing importance placed by foreign investors on democratic quality. Contrary to the common view that argues that multinationals prioritize firm, stable, and expeditious governments over pluralism, this study shows their growing concern with different aspects of the political process and structures. In particular, foreign investors appear to be sensitive to issues such as the maintenance of social stability, forms of resolution of conflict, and sustainability and predictability of public policies such as market reforms. Nonetheless, their opinions are quite heterogeneous, thus rendering the relationship between FDI trends and the quality of democracy more complex than what most analysts have often assumed. Nevertheless, the issue is a clear indicator of the opportunity open to governments eager to attract foreign direct investment. Besides their value per se, institutional reforms have become an important tool for achieving that goal.

The set of policy areas targeted by institutional reforms is very broad and involves sensitive issues. Two — finance and education — have already been mentioned in the previous sections. Another crucial transformation has been tried in the realm of social security systems. Several Latin American countries have recently redesigned the principles, norms, and mechanisms regulating the provision of social security benefits. The process has often encountered opposition and resistance. Laws have been difficult to pass and executive branches' initiatives delayed. The chapter by Peter Kingstone in this volume clearly illustrates these difficulties in the Brazilian case. It provides detailed explanations of the political and economic struggles involved in the attempt to reform the system. Kingstone's account evaluates the relative achievements in terms of democratic governance according to the criteria of deliberation, inclusiveness, and equity. The evidence that Brazil has met a certain, albeit minimalist, criteria related to these democratic concerns is a significant finding that challenges often simplistic arguments about low-intensity democracy. In contrast, Kingstone shows that the combination of sharp deficits in the social security system and uncertainty about continuous federal government transfers has made the reform particularly urgent. International pressure has also contributed to the promotion of policy innovation, as fiscal imbalances and poor economic performance tended to increase country risk, discourage private investment, and give incentives to international financial agencies to exert pressure for reform. Thus, in economies dependent on foreign capital, the performance of social security systems may have critical consequences for foreign economic relations. Nonetheless, Kingstone's account warns us against purely systemic explanations and highlights the impact of domestic politics on the outcomes. The incremental Brazilian path to reform in this policy area reflects the government's attempt to cope with the dilemma of balancing necessary and politically possible changes.

Decentralization is another crucial institutional reform that has advanced considerably during the 1990s and cuts across several policy areas. It is an excellent example of the intermestic politico-economic character of policy issues emphasized in this volume. Decentralization involves very sensitive changes in norms regarding, for instance, the assignment of expenditure responsibilities among different levels of government, the increasing political autonomy suddenly acquired by local governments, and the design of mechanisms of intergovernmental transfers of resources and management of new functions. This trend has not advanced uniformly across the region. As Kent Eaton shows in his chapter, progress has been faster and deeper in Brazil, Colombia, Argentina, and Bolivia, while other countries, such as Chile, Uruguay, Venezuela, and Peru, have implemented only partial decentralization measures. This pattern of aggressive versus tentative decentralizers sheds light on the obstacles to an institutional reform of such magnitude and, at the same time, on the risks and costs of extreme alternatives and insufficient policy coordination between central and local governments.

Moreover, the payoff outcomes are being decisively shaped by strategic interactions of national elites with supranational actors, such as international financial institutions, governmental agencies from developed states, and transnational advocacy networks, as well as by subnational actors, such as oligarchic elites, local leaders, and local social movements. Thus, decentralization becomes a good laboratory to test how globalization is reshaping national power configurations from above and below the nation-state. In addition, the issue relates not only to the quality of democratic institutions but also to the new orientation of Latin American countries' foreign economic policy because it can potentially have an impact on the sustainability of structural economic reforms. Particularly, it makes it more difficult for national governments to maintain fiscal discipline and to implement countercyclical policies. It also affects the dynamics of integration processes not only because their prospects are highly dependent on fiscal balance and macroeconomic stability, but also because the devolution of authority to subnational actors makes it harder for national policymakers to delegate policy authority to supranational bodies at the same time.

Thus, it is obvious that institutional reforms involve very difficult, though possible, changes. Part of the difficulty has to do with prior inexperience with institutional innovation and the vagueness of policy tools. The previously mentioned approaches were based on large surveys in hundreds of developed and developing countries and a broad array of indicators; they reflect the growing activity developed in this field by governmental and non-governmental organizations. These studies have contributed to our understanding of the relationship between the quality of governance and economic development. However, these instruments have the following limits: they fall short of providing good guidance on some specific reforms; they measure some aspects of government performance but cannot account for some processes and political dynamics that lead to certain institutional arrangements; they check governance performance at much too broad an aggregate level; they have a substantial margin of error; and they do not allow precise comparisons across countries (Knack and Manning 2000). Also, the studies tend to ignore some social and political dimensions of the process, thus neglecting the study of how weak and inefficient institutions have varying impacts on different sectors of the population and may exclude some of them from the benefits of economic growth. This is not a minor issue for societies highly dissatisfied with democracy and governments whose delivery and representation capacities are under serious criticism.

The World Bank has only very recently addressed these aspects of the problem. Although its last report on development suffers from the same vagueness when it comes to recommendations for policymakers,[7] it correctly points to the impact of institutions on the poor and to another key aspect of the challenge involving how structural and contextual conditions, such as other supporting institutions, available technology and skills, level of corruption, and the costs of accessing and maintaining the institution can determine whether a particular institution is appropriate for a country (World Bank 2002). In sum, it seems that all agree that institutions matter. However, what institutions are needed? Little is known about the interrelation between those contextual conditions and new policy recommendations that are largely untested.

Indeed, after two decades or so of initiated changes, major institutional reforms are still pending or are advancing very slowly. This is not surprising, as the institutional reforms involve a tremendous effort for which political and economic elites do not perceive clear incentives. Borrowing Merilee S. Grindle's term, the previously mentioned institutional reforms may well be characterized as audacious in the sense that they imply the creation of new rules about the distribution of power, a process in which the key actors involved lack motivation to engage (Grindle 2000). With a degree of truth, the reform of the state was labeled some years ago as the "politicians' dilemma" (Geddes 1994).

CONCLUSION

The list of foreign economic policy dilemmas in Latin America offered in this work is not exhaustive. To be complete, it should also include environmental degradation and international migration flows, issues that are both closely related to trade policies. However, this volume aims to cover in depth only four basic areas that currently demand urgent government attention and to make the case for a broader understanding of what is at stake in terms of policy options and priorities. The order in which the four issues are presented does not reflect any ranking of importance. Their relative position can only emerge from political considerations in a country-specific foreign policy agenda. However, it is evident that improving the quality of institutions is an absolutely pressing demand that cuts across all other policy areas.

Scenarios for the future do not include the reversal of an open-market foreign policy orientation. Although new approaches and substantial modifications of the paths taken are being discussed, alternatives are framed within the same paradigm.

This is not surprising, given that ideational consensus takes time to emerge, let alone be embodied in actors, institutions, and policies. The last wave of liberal ideas in Latin America is clearly embedded in a new regime of accumulation, one that reflects the strong political and economic interests of some domestic and international groups. The long silence around alternatives to neoliberalism helped to postpone crucial institutional changes indefinitely. This is a clear example of how some issues have been kept out of public debate and governments' agendas for almost a decade.

When it comes to what to do next in each policy area, as usual, the feasibility of different alternatives will be determined by a contingent combination of international and domestic conditions. Regarding the former, a new technological paradigm will continue shaping production, trade, and investment patterns at a global level. U.S. foreign economic policy, including its traditional (albeit assertive) neglect of Latin America, will keep setting the parameters for the rest of the continent. With regard to the latter, policy elites are expected to demonstrate a great deal of innovative capacity. The opening of new windows of opportunity in the near future is uncertain, and some bridges have been burned. Social disenchantment with the inability of democratic governments to address the needs of majorities may make constituencies less prone to acquiesce to delegative practices, thus making more complex the advancement of pending reforms. The question remains open as to whether policymakers will be able to live up to the challenge of managing this two-level game involved in foreign policy.

NOTES

1.   Policy windows are opportunities for advocates of certain projects to get attention paid to specific problems and to promote their preferred solutions.

2.   See an illustration of the first point of view in Keeler 1993, and of the second in Corrales 1997; Haggard and Kaufman 1995, chapters 5 and 6. For a formalization of the benefits expected from crises, see Drazen, Allan, and Vittorio Grilli, "The Benefits of Crises for Economic Reforms," in Sturzeneger and Tommasi 1998, 127-142.

3.   I refer here to the executive branch of government.

4.   On the reciprocity mechanism and its results, see Amsden 2001.

5.   The United Nations Human Development Index, for instance, combines the following four elements: life expectancy at birth; literacy rate of people over 15; combined rate of school enrollment in primary, secondary, and postsecondary education; and GDP per capita.

6.   See Kaufmann et al., 1999, *Governance Matters*, World Bank Policy Research Department Working Paper # 2196 (Washington, D.C.: The World Bank). On the methodology used to design indicators and indexes, see Kaufmann et al., 1999, *Aggregating Governance Indicators*, World Bank Policy Research Department Working Paper # 2195 (Washington, D.C.: The World Bank).

7.   These four broad principles are suggested as guidelines: to complement what exists, to innovate, to connect, and to promote competition.

REFERENCES

Amsden, Alice. 2001. *The Rise of "the Rest": Challenges to the West from Late Industrializing Economies*. Oxford: Oxford University Press.

Birdsall, Nancy. 2001. "Human Capital and the Quality of Growth." *Development Outreach* (Winter): 14-17.

Burki, Shahid Javed, and Guillermo E. Perry. 1997. *The Long March: A Reform Agenda for Latin America and the Caribbean in the Next Decade*. Washington, D.C.: The World Bank.

Burki, Shahid Javed, and Guillermo E. Perry. 1998. *Beyond the Washington Consensus: Institutions Matter*. Washington, D.C.: The World Bank.

Corrales, Javier. 1997. "Do Economic Crises Contribute to Economic Reform? Argentina and Venezuela in the 1990s." *Political Science Quarterly* 112 (4): 617-644.

Diamond, Larry, and Marc F. Plattner, eds. 1995. *Economic Reform and Democracy*. Baltimore: The Johns Hopkins University Press.

Domínguez, Jorge I., ed. 2000. *The Future of Inter-American Relations*. New York: Routledge.

Ffrench-Davis, Ricardo. 2000. *Reforming the Reforms in Latin America: Macroeconomics, Trade, Finance*. London: Macmillan/ Palgrave

Geddes, Barbara. 1994. *Politicians' Dilemma: Building State Capacity in Latin America*. Berkeley, Calif.: University of California Press.

Gore, Charles. 2000. "The Rise and Fall of the Washington Consensus as a Paradigm for Developing Countries." *World Development* 28 (5): 789-804.

Grindle, Merilee S. 1996. *Challenging the State: Crisis and Innovation in Latin America and Africa*. Cambridge, UK: Cambridge University Press.

Grindle, Merilee, S. 2000. *Audacious Reforms: Institutional Invention and Democracy in Latin America*. Baltimore: The Johns Hopkins University Press.

Haggard, Stephan, and Robert R. Kaufman. 1995. *The Political Economy of Democratic Transitions*. Princeton, N.J.: Princeton University Press.

Haggard, Stephan, and Robert R. Kaufman, eds. 1992. *The Politics of Economic Adjustment*, Princeton, N.J.: Princeton University Press.

Hausmann, Ricardo, and Liliana Rojas-Suárez, eds. 1996. *Banking Crises in Latin America*. Washington, D.C.: Inter-American Development Bank.

Huntington, Samuel P., and Joseph S. Nye, Jr., eds. 1985. *Global Dilemmas*. Cambridge, Mass.: The Center for International Affairs, Harvard University; and Lanham, Md.: University Press of America.

Inter-American Development Bank (IDB). 1997. *Latin America After a Decade of Reforms: Economic and Social Progress in Latin America*. Washington, D.C.: IDB.

IDB. 2000. *Development Beyond Economics: Economic and Social Progress in Latin America*. Washington, D.C.: IDB.

IDB. 2001. *Competitiveness: The Business of Growth. Economic and Social Progress in Latin America*. Washington, D.C.: IDB.

Kaufmann, Daniel, Aart Kraay, and Pablo Zoido-Lobatón. 1999a. *Aggregating Governance Indicators*. Working Paper 2195 from the World Bank Policy Research Department. Washington, D.C.: The World Bank.

Kaufmann, Daniel, Aart Kraay, and Pablo Zoido-Lobatón. 1999b. *Governance Matters*. Working Paper 2196 from the World Bank Policy Research Department. Washington, D.C.: The World Bank.

Kaufmann, Daniel, Aart Kraay, and Pablo Zoido-Lobatón. 2000. "Governance Matters: From Measurement to Action." *Finance and Development* 37 (2).

Kaufmann, Daniel, Aart Kraay, and Pablo Zoido-Lobatón. 2002. *Governance Matters, II: Updated Indicators for 2000-01*. Washington, D.C.: The World Bank. Preliminary Draft. January 17.

Keeler, John T.S. 1993. "Opening the Window for Reform: Mandates, Crises, and Extraordinary Policy-Making." *Comparative Political Studies* 25 (4): 433-486.

Kingdon, John W. 1995. *Agendas, Alternatives, and Public Policies*. New York: Longman.

Knack, Stephen, and Nick Manning. 2000. "Toward More Operationally Relevant Indicators of Governance." *PREM Notes* 49 (December).

Korzeniewicz, Roberto P., and William C. Smith, eds. 1996. *Latin America in the World-Economy*. Westport, Conn.: Greenwood Press.

Krueger, Anne O., ed. 2000. *Economic Policy Reform: The Second Stage*. Chicago: The University of Chicago Press.

Lora, Eduardo, and Ugo Panizza, 2002. *Structural Reforms in Latin America under Scrutiny*. Working Paper Series 470. Washington, D.C.: Inter-American Development Bank. Research Department. March.

Mace, Gordon, and Jean-Philippe Thérien, eds. 1996. *Foreign Policy and Regionalism in the Americas*. Boulder, Colo.: Lynne Rienner Publishers.

Mace, Gordon, and Louis Bélanger. 1999. *The Americas in Transition: The Contours of Regionalism*. Boulder, Colo.: Lynne Rienner Publishers.

Muñoz, Heraldo, and Joseph S. Tulchin, eds. 1996. *Latin American Nations in World Politics*. Boulder, Colo.: Westview Press.

Nelson, Joan M. 1994a. *Intricate Links: Democratization and Market Reforms in Latin America and Eastern Europe*. New Brunswick, N.J.: Transaction Publishers.

Nelson, Joan M., ed. 1994b. *A Precarious Balance: Democracy and Economic Reforms in Latin America*. San Francisco: International Center for Economic Growth, Overseas Development Council, and ICS Press.

North, Douglas. 1990. *Institutions, Institutional Change, and Economic Performance*. New York: Cambridge University Press.

Oxhorn, Philip D., and Graciela Ducatenzeiler, eds. 1998. *What Kind of Democracy? What Kind of Market? Latin America in the Age of Neoliberalism*. University Park, Pa.: The Pennsylvania State University Press.

Roett, Riordan, ed. 1999. *Mercosur: Regional Integration, World Markets*. Boulder, Colo.: Lynne Rienner Publishers.

Smith, Peter H. 2000. *Talons of the Eagle: Dynamics of U.S.-Latin American Relations*. 2nd. ed. New York: Oxford University Press.

Smith, William C., Carlos H. Acuña, and Eduardo A. Gamarra, eds. 1994a. *Democracy, Markets, and Structural Reform in Latin America: Argentina, Bolivia, Brazil, Chile, and Mexico*. Coral Gables, Fla.: North-South Center Press at the University of Miami.

Smith, William C., Carlos H. Acuña, and Eduardo A. Gamarra, eds. 1994b. *Latin American Political Economy in the Age of Neoliberal Reform: Theoretical and Comparative Perspectives for the 1990s*. Coral Gables, Fla.: North-South Center Press at the University of Miami.

Smith, William C., and Roberto P. Korzeniewicz, eds. 1997. *Politics, Social Change, and Economic Restructuring in Latin America*. Coral Gables, Fla.: North-South Center Press at the University of Miami.

Stallings, Barbara, and Wilson Peres. 2000. *Growth, Employment, and Equity: The Impact of the Economic Reforms in Latin America and the Caribbean*. Washington, D.C.: The Brookings Institution Press.

Stark, Jeffrey, ed. 2001. *The Challenge of Change in Latin America and the Caribbean*. Coral Gables, Fla.: North-South Center Press at the University of Miami.

Stone, Deborah. 1997. *Policy Paradox: The Art of Political Decision Making*. New York: W.W. Norton & Company.

Sturzeneger, Federico, and Mariano Tommasi, eds. 1998. *The Political Economy of Reform*. Cambridge, Mass.: The MIT Press.

The New York Times. 2002. "Bush Signs Trade Bill, Restoring Broad Presidential Authority," August 7.

The World Bank. 2002. *World Development Report: Building Institutions for Markets*. New York: Oxford University Press.

Tokman, Víctor E., and Guillermo O'Donnell, eds. 1998. *Poverty and Inequality in Latin America: Issues and New Challenges*. Notre Dame, Ind.: University of Notre Dame Press.

Tulchin, Joseph S., and Ralph H. Espach, eds. 2001. *Latin America in the New International System*. Boulder, Colo.: Lynne Rienner Publishers.

Wise, Carol, ed. 1998. *The Post-NAFTA Political Economy: Mexico and the Western Hemisphere*. University Park, Pa.: The Pennsylvania State University Press.

PART I

BETTING ON ECONOMIC INTEGRATION

Chapter One

ECONOMIC INTEGRATION AND TRADE NEGOTIATIONS IN LATIN AMERICA AND THE CARIBBEAN AT THE TURN OF THE CENTURY

José M. Salazar-Xirinachs[1]

For the last 10 to 15 years, most, if not all, Latin American and Caribbean (LAC) countries have pursued integration of their national economies into the world economy as the key strategic objective of their growth and development policies. They have sought multiple paths to market expansion and global integration by way of unilateral liberalization, multilateral engagement in the General Agreement on Tariffs and Trade (GATT)/World Trade Organization (WTO), regional integration via the Free Trade Area of the Americas (FTAA), as well as subregional and bilateral trade agreements. Indeed, regional trade agreements (RTAs) are proliferating throughout the region and have become a central component of these countries' development strategies.

This chapter analyzes the LAC experience with international economic integration and discusses the main challenges that will have to be faced in the next stage of trade policy reform. The following five interrelated arguments are made:

- Despite criticism of the "Washington Consensus" and the risk of populist backlash, economic integration into world markets will most likely continue to be a key element in the economic reform programs of most LAC countries.

- In the next stage of trade policy reform, countries will be better served by a multiple-path strategy of trade negotiations that will maximize benefits by moving simultaneously on several negotiating fronts.

- The creation of the FTAA should and most likely will continue to be a priority despite the launching of a new multilateral round of trade negotiations.

- The next stage of trade policy will be the most negotiation- and implementation-intensive ever that Latin American countries have had to face, placing the issue of trade-related capacity building at the center of policy concerns not only for LAC countries, but also for aid-providing governments and for inter-American and global development agencies.

- Although economic integration and trade openness are the right ways to go, reaping their long-term benefits in terms of growth, development, and poverty reduction requires consistent work within a much broader national development agenda in each country, supported by international cooperation.

The chapter is organized as follows: The first section provides a brief diagnosis of the economic and trade policy reform experience in Latin America and the Caribbean in the last decade, including an overview of the proliferation of RTAs in this period. The second section analyzes some of the main options for economic integration and market enlargement. The third section reviews the case for the creation of the FTAA as well as its prospects. The fourth section discusses some of the links and dilemmas posed by simultaneous multilateral and regional negotiations. The final section presents a five-part policy framework to summarize the main challenges Latin American and Caribbean countries face in the next stage of their trade and development policies.

ECONOMIC REFORMS, TRADE, GROWTH, AND INTERDEPENDENCE DURING THE 1990S

What general assessment can be made of economic reforms implemented by Latin American and Caribbean countries during the last 10 to 15 years? Has increased trade openness contributed to higher growth and poverty reduction? How has economic interdependence changed among economies in the Americas?

The Economic Reforms Balance Sheet

The economic reforms' scorecard can be summarized by recognizing the important achievements of controlling inflation, reducing fiscal deficits and foreign debt, increasing the flows of foreign direct investment (FDI), and expanding exports in some countries. However, there were also disappointing results in other areas, including economic growth, employment, poverty reduction, income distribution, and social conditions.

The Washington Consensus, which oversaw many of these economic reforms, is often blamed for the region's slow growth and disappointing social results. While there is plenty of room for valid criticism, those who question the strategic direction of integrating LAC countries into the world economy must answer the question: What is the alternative?

Nancy Birdsall and Augusto de la Torre (2001) reached the following important general conclusions about the intense debate over the deficiencies of the Washington policy consensus: without the reforms, the LAC situation would have been worse because per capita income and output would have been lower, volatility higher, and poverty and income inequality deeper. However, the original Washington policy consensus was too narrow and somewhat simplistic. The current disappointment with the reforms is closely associated with their inability to restore growth, increase employment, reduce inequality, as well as address the institutional failures and increased corruption observed in a number of countries. Combating institutional decay in public-sector institutions, from executive to judicial systems; strengthening the rule of law; and enabling the functioning of markets and their regulatory frameworks have emerged as new priorities. Strong, efficient state institutions and strong, well-functioning markets — not one to the detriment of the other — are what is needed for good economic performance. *The Economist* summarized the situation in a recent survey, "The problem is not that . . . the wrong course [was adopted] a decade ago but that the road is longer and more complicated than many hoped" (2002, 11).[2]

Changing Paradigms in Trade and Aid for Development

Based on the experiences of Latin America and elsewhere, the 1990s saw a dramatic change in the international community's and organizations' approaches toward policy reform and development. Poverty reduction and equity and institutional strengthening came to occupy center stage in the lending operations and programs of international financial institutions (IFIs). Unfortunately, this refocusing of effort was associated with a reduction in the priority some donors and IFIs assigned to trade and productive sector development versus social policies, humanitarian concerns, and other priorities. This has been unfortunate because, as will be explained in the next section of this chapter, recent economic research has made it clear that growth is important for poverty reduction, and insertion into larger markets and open trade policies are essential for growth. In this context, the Doha Development Agenda marks a turning point, partly because a new trade round has been launched, but also because it reflects a new international consensus that reasserts the role of trade in development (trade "mainstreaming") that at the same time places broader development issues and institutional capacity building at the center of the international cooperation agenda. This is partly a reflection of the new WTO developing country membership and partly an expression of developing countries' frustration with a world trading system that is perceived to be unbalanced and in need of opening more opportunities available to them.[3] One of the most profound implications of the Doha Development Agenda is that it has created incentives to bridge the (often abysmal) differences between the trade and development communities that have plagued national and international policy discussions for years.[4] This salutary effect is complemented by the realization that there is no single big idea, miracle cure, or magic formula in the quest for growth and development (Easterly 2001).

Trade, Growth, and Development: Some Lessons Learned

There is a growing consensus in the economics of development that growth is important for poverty reduction and trade is important for growth. On the growth-poverty relationship, it has been shown that fast growth is associated with fast poverty reduction, and economic contraction is associated with increased poverty. This result has put to rest the widely held view that economic growth leaves the poor behind (Dollar and Kraay 2001). For poverty to increase with economic growth, there would have to be a drastic worsening of income distribution, and this is not generally the case in most countries. It is also clear that growth by itself does not necessarily improve income distribution; such an improvement requires a complex array of accompanying social policies (Cooper 2002).

With regard to the trade-growth relationship, a number of researchers using different approaches have found positive correlations between growth and trade, or economic openness or trade liberalization.[5] However, there is an ongoing scholarly debate about the methodology and interpretation of this cross-country empirical research.[6] Some economists are skeptical of both the results and the progress that can be made from further cross-country empirical research without a better theoretical understanding of how trade and trade policy affect total factor productivity, income levels, and growth.[7] This skepticism does not stem so much from disagreement over the basic proposition that economic openness enhances growth, but rather from the limitations presented by cross-country research methods that lack a better understanding and specification of causalities and mechanisms. At a general level, it is widely agreed that the main channels by which trade and economic openness promote growth are increased specialization, according to comparative advantage; greater exploitation of increasing returns; importing of ideas, knowledge and technological capacities, including benefits from the acceleration of learning and larger variety of technological inputs; positive effects of increased competition on productivity; and improving economic performance through positive impacts on institutions and the political process.

The following three policy conclusions, relevant for the next stage of trade and integration policies in Latin America, can be drawn from this debate:

1. Although applied economic research needs to provide improved calibration of empirical models, the available theory and evidence create a strong presumption in favor of the proposition that international trade and open trade policies to the rest of the world are major contributing factors for growth.

2. However, as Cooper points out, "The key policy issue is whether for each country, starting where it is, some liberalization of trade (or foreign investment) would improve its economic performance. The answer lies not in cross-section country regressions, however carefully specified, but in detailed analysis of each country under study" (Cooper 2002, 126).

3. This issue is important because different visions about the nature of the links among trade, growth, poverty reduction, and income distribution will generate different answers regarding the priority of trade policies and trade-related capacity building in the development programs of countries and the cooperation programs of donors and financial institutions.

Here again, the Doha Development Agenda's emphasis on the need to mainstream trade in national development strategies in least-developed countries is a step in the right direction.[8] And so would be similar parallel efforts for LAC countries in the context of the FTAA. The adoption of a Hemispheric Cooperation Program by FTAA Ministers at their Meeting in Quito, Ecuador, on November 1, 2002, provides a unique opportunity to integrate further a development dimension into the FTAA negotiations.

Interdependence

The fundamental empirical fact about economic interdependence in the Americas is that today, all the LAC economies are much more open and interdependent within their region, with the United States, and with the world economy than they were a decade ago. It is useful to think of interdependence in the following three mutually reinforcing dimensions: 1) in terms of the business dynamism that has transformed trade and investment structures; 2) in terms of the legally binding commitments associated with the proliferation of regional and bilateral trade agreements in the hemisphere; and 3) in terms of a convergence in political, strategic, and collective security interests.

The indicators of increased economic interdependence include the following:

- Average tariffs have been drastically reduced since 1985, which is one of the main factors that explains why the share of trade in gross domestic product (GDP) increased in all countries of the Americas during the last decade.

- For Latin America as a whole, the two engines for export expansion were the U.S. market and the rest of the LAC markets. The rates of growth of exports to these destinations were around 14 percent per year from 1988 to 1998, much higher than the business activity and the dynamism of exports to Asia, Europe, and Japan. From 1990 to the present, the share of intraregional trade in total trade increased consistently for the Southern Common Market (Mercado Común del Sur — MERCOSUR), the Andean Community, the Caribbean Community and Common Market (CARICOM), and the North American Free Trade Agreement (NAFTA).

- FDI flows into LAC countries, as a whole, increased from levels between US$10 to $15 billion in the early 1990s and between US$80 to $90 billion at the end of the decade.

A second dimension of interdependence is associated with the dramatic proliferation of trade agreements. LAC countries are now bound by a new generation of trade agreements unlike any other time in their history, and there is sufficient liberalizing momentum in the agreements already negotiated to increase interdependence even more from now until 2010. Table 1 classifies agreements into Customs Unions and Free Trade Agreements.[9] The Central American Common Market (CACM), created in 1961; the Andean Community, created in 1969; CARICOM, created in 1973; and MERCOSUR, created in 1991; are the four Customs Unions in the Americas. The former three, originally created under the old inward-looking strategy of industrialization, were significantly restructured and relaunched in the 1990s with a much lower common external tariff and new, deeper disciplines, while MERCOSUR was conceived under the principles of "open regionalism" since its inception.[10]

With regard to free trade agreements (FTAs), there was an explosion in the negotiation of FTAs by LAC countries, starting with Mexico's participation in NAFTA in 1994. These so-called "new generation" agreements more or less closely followed the NAFTA model and included, besides liberalization of trade in goods, new sectors such as services and agriculture and new areas of discipline such as investment, competition policy, intellectual property rights, and dispute settlement mechanisms. LAC countries have negotiated 14 FTAs among themselves and with the United States and Canada since 1990 and are in the process of negotiating nine more. One of the most notable developments in this new picture is that since 1998, the 34 countries of the Western Hemisphere (with the exception of Cuba) have been formally negotiating the FTAA.

Countries in the Western Hemisphere have also been negotiating new generation agreements with other countries outside the hemisphere. Eight of these agreements were completed from 1997 to 2002, and another 10 are under negotia-

Table 1.
Customs Unions and Free Trade Agreements in the Western Hemisphere

Agreement	Signed	Entered into Force
Customs Unions		
1. CACM (Central American Common Market)	1960	1961[c]
2. Andean Community	1969[a]	1969
3. CARICOM (Caribbean Community and Common Market)[b]	1973	1973
4. MERCOSUR (Southern Common Market)[d]	1991	1995
Free Trade Agreements		
1. NAFTA (North American Free Trade Agreement)[e]	1992	1994
2. Costa Rica-Mexico	1994	1995
3. Group of Three (Colombia, Mexico, Venezuela)	1994[f]	1995
4. Bolivia-Mexico	1994	1995
5. Canada-Chile	1996	1997
6. Mexico-Nicaragua	1997	1998
7. Central America-Dominican Republic	1998	2001-2002[g]
8. Chile-Mexico	1998[h]	1999
9. CARICOM-Dominican Republic	1998[i]	Pending
10. Central America-Chile	1999	2002-2003[j]
11. Mexico-Northern Triangle (El Salvador, Guatemala, Honduras)	2000	2001
12. Costa Rica-Canada	2001	2002
13. Central America-Panama	2002	Pending
14. Chile-United States	2003	Pending
15. Andean Community-MERCOSUR	In negotiation	
16. CA-4-Canada	In negotiation	
17. Mexico-Ecuador	In negotiation	
18. Mexico-Panama	In negotiation	
19. Mexico-Peru	In negotiation	
20. Mexico-Trinidad and Tobago	In negotiation	
21. Central America-U.S. (CAFTA)	In negotiation	
22. Chile-Bolivia	In negotiation	
23. Costa Rica-CARICOM	In negotiation	
Agreements with Countries Outside the Hemisphere		
1. United States-Israel	—	1985
2. Canada-Israel	1996	1997
3. Mexico-European Union	2000	2000
4. Mexico-Israel	2000	2000

Agreement	Signed	Entered into Force
5. Mexico-EFTA	2000	2001
6. United States-Vietnam	2000	2001
7. United States-Jordan	2000	2001
8. Chile-South Korea	2003	Pending
9. Chile-European Union	2002	2003
10. Canada-EFTA	In negotiation	
11. Canada-Singapore	In negotiation	
12. Chile-EFTA	In negotiation	
13. MERCOSUR-European Union	In negotiation	
14. MERCOSUR-South Africa	In negotiation	
15. Mexico-Singapore	In negotiation	
16. Mexico-Japan	In negotiation	
17. United States-Singapore	In negotiation	
18. United States-Morocco	In negotiation	
19. United States-Australia	In negotiation	

Source: Updated from *Towards Free Trade In the Americas*, eds. José M. Salazar-Xirinachs and Maryse Robert. 2001. Washington, D.C.: Brookings Institution Press/OAS General Secretariat.

a. With the signing of the Trujillo Protocol in 1996 and the Sucre Protocol in 1997, the five Andean countries — Bolivia, Colombia, Ecuador, Peru, and Venezuela — restructured and revitalized their regional integration efforts under the name Andean Community.

b. The members of the Caribbean Community are Antigua and Barbuda, the Bahamas, Barbados, Belize, Dominica, Grenada, Guyana, Jamaica, St. Kitts and Nevis, St. Lucia, St. Vincent and the Grenadines, Suriname, Trinidad and Tobago, and Montserrat (an overseas territory of the United Kingdom). The Bahamas is an associate but not a full member of the Common Market. Haiti will become the fifteenth member of CARICOM once it deposits its instruments of accession with the group's secretary general. The British Virgin Islands and the Turks and Caicos Islands count as associate members of CARICOM.

c. The agreement entered into force on this date for El Salvador, Guatemala, and Nicaragua; on April 27, 1962, for Honduras; and on September 23, 1963, for Costa Rica. With the signing of the Tegucigalpa Protocol in 1991 and the Guatemala Protocol in 1996, the countries of the Central American Common Market — El Salvador, Costa Rica, Guatemala, Honduras, and Nicaragua — restructured and revitalized their regional integration efforts.

d. The full members are Argentina, Brazil, Paraguay, and Uruguay. Chile and Bolivia are associate members.

e. Before signing NAFTA, Canada and the United States had concluded the Canada-U.S. Free Trade Agreement, which entered into force on January 1, 1989.

f. Chapters III (national treatment and market access for goods), IV (automotive sector), V (Sec. A) (agricultural sector), VI (rules of origin), VIII (safeguards), IX (unfair practices in international trade), XVI (state enterprises), and XVIII (intellectual property) do not apply between Colombia and Venezuela. See Article 103 (1) of the agreement.

g. This agreement applies bilaterally between each Central American country and the Dominican Republic. In 2001, it entered into force between the Dominican Republic and El Salvador, Guatemala and Honduras, and in 2002, between Costa Rica and the Dominican Republic.

h. On September 22, 1991, Chile and Mexico had signed a free trade agreement within the framework of the Latin American Integration Association (ALADI).

i. A protocol to implement the agreement was signed on April 28, 2000.

j. This agreement applies bilaterally between each Central American country and Chile. The Chile-Costa Rica bilateral agreement entered into force on February 15, 2002. The Chile-El Salvador bilateral agreement entered into force in June 2002.

tion.[11] The new agreements embody much more than trade barrier reduction at the border for goods and present important similarities, partly due to the fact that most of them have been modeled on NAFTA in terms of their structure, scope, and coverage. However, there are also important differences in terms of disciplines included as well as in institutional arrangements. For instance, only some of them include significant disciplines in financial services, government procurement, competition policy, and air transportation. While most include the telecommunication sector, this is not the case in the Costa Rica-Mexico agreement and in the Central America-Dominican Republic agreement.

FTAs in Latin America and the Caribbean have also been fertile ground for experimentation both in traditional disciplines and in linking trade and nontrade objectives. For instance, the Canada-Chile agreement eliminates the use of anti-dumping among the parties. Several agreements have moved beyond the GATT/ WTO into areas such as environment and labor standards. NAFTA contains two side agreements on labor and environmental cooperation that envisage the possibility of trade sanctions. The Canada-Chile FTA also includes side agreements in these areas but eliminates the possibility of sanctions and instead introduces a system of monetary fines in case of violations. The recently concluded Canada-Costa Rica FTA also includes side agreements but does not include sanctions or monetary fines, only transparency and a series of institutional instances for cooperative actions.

MERCOSUR incorporates a democratic clause that has quite successfully been used at least once to exercise pressure on Paraguay, when the constitutional order was about to be permanently broken in that country. Ongoing discussions in the context of the Summit of the Americas process are exploring how to strengthen the democratic provisions in the inter-American system, including possible cross references to the FTAA.

The proliferation of bilateral and regional trade agreements (RTAs) in Latin America and their diversity in terms of coverage and institutional arrangements is linked to a complex interaction of economic, political, and security objectives. As a practical matter, a wide range of considerations enter when countries seek to negotiate RTAs. In LAC countries, as in countries around the world, objectives include market access; investment attraction; strengthening domestic policy reform and positive signaling to investors; increased bargaining power vis-à-vis third countries (a particularly strong motivation in the case of MERCOSUR); political, security, or strategic linkage objectives (an important motivation from the U.S. perspective in the negotiation of the FTAA); and the actual or potential use of regional agreements for tactical purposes by countries seeking to achieve multilateral objectives.[12]

Proliferation in Latin America and the Caribbean was grounded first and foremost in the decisive shift in development and trade policy toward outward-looking, market-friendly policies where integration into larger markets and FDI are seen as the keys to higher growth. In terms of sequencing, the typical pattern has been for countries first to engage in unilateral liberalization and in joining the GATT/WTO as part of the process of economic reform. Unilateral liberalization was then taken further in the direction of deeper integration with neighboring countries. From this perspective, as Ethier (1998) has argued, national liberalization, both unilateral and that generated by the multilateral system, has promoted the revitalization of regionalism in Latin America. Bilateral agreements and RTAs have also induced additional liberalization.

In addition, the fact that national competitive strategies are based to an important degree on the attraction of FDI provides a new logic to subregional integration efforts and to the role of trade agreements in the global repositioning of countries. In a number of smaller economies in Latin America and the Caribbean, a strong motivation to engage in bilateral and other RTAs, particularly with larger and relatively more developed countries, has begun to develop a competitive edge in attracting investment.

Finally, the interdependence involved in the new regional integration effort has a political and strategic rationale, not just an economic one. How this applies depends on the precise grouping of countries. For instance, the key original rationale for MERCOSUR was closely related to the objective of diffusing long-standing tensions between Argentina and Brazil and fostering better relations between them. MERCOSUR is also based on much more than a desire to liberalize trade. It is part of a vision to assert the role of this group of countries in the Western Hemisphere and as global players. As explained in a later section, the effort to create an FTAA also has strong political, strategic, and security dimensions.

With these elements of analysis as background, the following sections analyze some of the main challenges facing Latin America and the Caribbean in the area of trade and integration over the next few years.

TRADE STRATEGY OPTIONS AND PATHS FOR MARKET ENLARGEMENT

In the next few years, LAC countries will have at least five avenues — unilateral; multilateral (WTO); regional (FTAA); subregional (MERCOSUR, Andean Community, CACM, CARICOM); and bilateral — for market expansion and trade reform. Should countries pursue these avenues simultaneously? Should they prioritize unilateral liberalization? Should they concentrate their scarce negotiating capital and efforts at the multilateral level, rather than on regional, subregional, or bilateral exercises? What opportunities and dilemmas emerge from the linkage or interdependence between negotiations in different forums? The following section tries to answer some of these important questions.

Unilateral Liberalization

LAC countries have come a long way in terms of unilateral liberalization. A strong economic argument has been made that further unilateral liberalization and improvements in regulation in specific sectors will bring about important additional benefits and is, therefore, in the self-interest of these countries. In theory, unilateral liberalization is the most direct route to free trade, maximizing gains from trade and avoiding the delays, inefficiencies, and arbitrariness of political negotiations. However, there are well-known drawbacks to unilateralism. Also, given the unilateral effort already undertaken and ongoing multilateral and regional negotiations, there remain a number of obstacles to further unilateral liberalization in Latin America and the Caribbean.

The first group of drawbacks can be found in the classical arguments for reciprocity over unilateralism. Reciprocity is important for a liberalizing country because it deters the protectionism of its partners. Reciprocity, or collective coordination and enforcement, solves collective action "free-rider" problems, makes it costly for others to go back on commitments, and, thus, puts the floor on a potential downward spiral of protectionism and economic contraction. This is one of the major advantages of a reciprocity-based multilateral trading system, particularly during periods of economic turbulence and/or downturn. From the point of view of an individual country, a powerful reason to prefer reciprocity-based trade negotiations is to reduce uncertainty by locking in market access with its main trading partners. With unilateral actions, countries renounce the possibility of gaining additional reciprocal benefits in exchange for local economic adjustments. Also lost is the option of bargaining for free trade collectively or as a group, an attractive option for smaller economies with little individual leverage.[13] For these reasons, LAC countries face the practical dilemma of whether to proceed with further unilateral measures or delay them for later use as possible "concessions" in multilateral, regional, or bilateral negotiations. It has been estimated that at around a 10-percent level of tariffs, the benefits of reciprocal negotiations outweigh those of unilateral liberalization. The downside is that if both multilateral and regional negotiations are protracted, they might have the perverse effect of delaying economic openness when countries "wait" to use trade reform measures as "concessions" during a mercantilist exchange in trade negotiations.[14]

In addition to external trade negotiating tactics, the attitude toward unilateral actions is influenced by internal political economy dynamics. If the starting point involves high levels of protection and "anti-export bias," as was the case in Latin America and the Caribbean 10 to 15 years ago, then the benefits of unilateral liberalization override external trade negotiating tactics and increase the domestic political feasibility of trade reform. However, once countries have reached relatively low levels of trade barriers and a minimum of export competitiveness — as is the case in most of Latin America and the Caribbean today — the short-term costs for domestic producers and workers of increased openness become more evident, and the politics of trade would require a clear identification of winners that gain from additional market access, granted by trading partners to offset the resistance of local losers, who could be hurt by increased imports and competition. While consumers benefit via lower prices and more choice, they are normally not sufficiently organized to influence the politics of trade.

Under the present circumstances, characterized by a new WTO round and ongoing regional negotiations, and given the strong unilateral liberalization effort of the decade of the 1990s, it is unlikely that LAC countries will be prepared to continue to engage in ambitious across-the-board unilateral initiatives except in certain specific sectors. Hence, trade policy in Latin America and the Caribbean in the next few years will most likely be dominated by multilateral, regional, and bilateral negotiations.

Multilateral Negotiations:
Opportunities and Dilemmas for Latin America

Despite their proactive regional and bilateral agendas, in the last few years Latin American countries have also been engaged more than ever in multilateral negotiations, reflecting the general change of attitude toward the multilateral system of many developing countries after the Uruguay Round of GATT. As is the case with many other developing countries, LAC countries' priorities in the new round lie principally in traditional market access issues for goods and services, such as tariff peaks on products of interest; tariff escalation; agriculture; labor-intensive manufactures, such as textiles and apparel; disciplining of antidumping measures; and nontariff barriers rather than in the new areas of rules and domestic regulatory policies (investment, competition, trade facilitation, transparency in government procurement, and the environment) on which the European Union (EU), in particular, sought to launch negotiations. Progress in market access in goods and services in the Doha Development Agenda can have a strong, positive, growth impact on developing countries. This potential mainly involves the four areas of agriculture, industrial tariffs, textiles and apparel, and services.[15]

In contrast to market access, some of the new areas of rules and domestic regulatory policies have been regarded with suspicion by many developing countries, including some countries in Latin America and the Caribbean. Among the reasons for this are the lack of trial-and-error experience about the real-world impact of these regulatory areas (Finger 2001); the high cost of implementation of resource intensive agreements; the idea that in some of the new areas, voluntary "good practice" norms are better developed and enforced outside the WTO by technical and specialized bodies; and the reluctance to accept linkage of issues where the developmental impact is either not clear or could distract the negotiations from focusing on market access priorities (Hoekman 2001). There are also strong concerns over the risk that some of the new rules may constrain the use of policy instruments to promote economic growth.

LAC countries, and particularly smaller economies, are also acutely aware of supply-side and competitive constraints they face to benefit from freer trade and insist on the need to expand cooperation to strengthen supply capacity and improve competitiveness and the investment climate.[16] While some would like to raise technical assistance to the level of a binding commitment, others recognize that most of this effort should happen outside of the WTO or trade agreements.[17]

The wide range of issues under discussion and their complexity; the number of countries involved; and the fact that initial offers in agriculture and services are to be submitted by mid- to late 2003, while negotiations on the so-called Singapore issues (investment, competition, trade facilitation, and government procurement) "will take place after the Fifth Session of the Ministerial Conference on the basis of a decision to be taken, by explicit consensus, at that Session on the modalities of negotiations," have led many to consider highly unrealistic the January 1, 2005, target date to conclude multilateral negotiations.

The fact remains that the benefits of a new round are potentially very significant for LAC countries and some market access issues of prime interest to

Latin American countries will only make progress at the multilateral level on issues such as agricultural subsidies. Therefore, these countries face the challenge of allocating a very significant amount of negotiating resources to the WTO process in the years to come.

THE FTAA: BENEFITS AND STATE OF PLAY

The general rationale for the FTAA stems from the following three forces working to increase interdependence in the Americas: business dynamics in response to the new open regionalism; new legal frameworks associated with trade agreement proliferation; and convergence in political, strategic, and collective security interests. With regard to the latter, the FTAA was conceived from the beginning as part of a broader effort of rapprochement and interdependence in the context of the Summit of the Americas process. The new agenda of hemispheric cooperation includes areas that go from the protection of democracy and human rights to the fight against corruption and drug trafficking, and from hemispheric infrastructure to sustainable development and labor issues. In addition, future FTAA members are already parties to the set of principles, rules, and legal and diplomatic instruments of the Inter-American System and the Organization of American States.[18] Within this new hemispheric context, what are the benefits of the FTAA for its prospective members? In the final analysis, this is a question that can only be answered by each individual country. However, it is possible and useful to outline a rationale and make some general considerations for the main countries or groups of countries.

What Latin America and the Caribbean Stand to Gain

From the point of view of Latin America and the Caribbean, the FTAA presents numerous potential economic benefits. Some of them apply to all countries; others require making a distinction between the larger and smaller economies of the hemisphere. Economic benefits from the FTAA include growth and developmental impacts, increased investment, better and more secure access to large markets, increased competitiveness, and improvement in market economy institutions and fundamentals.

Growth and Developmental Benefits

The main reason why the FTAA is beneficial to countries is grounded in basic textbook material about the gains from trade known since the time of Adam Smith (1776). Market size is essential to the division of labor, economies of scale, and increases in productivity. The smaller an economy's market is, the harder it will be to achieve high rates of growth. As explained in a previous section, recent economic research has reinforced these old truths with new evidence and a better understanding of the many channels by which trade and economic openness promote growth. In addition, the general conclusion of various integration and trade liberalization scenarios in Latin America, using multicountry computable general equilibrium (CGE) models, is that RTAs, such as the FTAA or the potential agreement between MERCOSUR and the EU, are good for the participants and have little impact on nonparticipants. Trade creation greatly exceeds trade diversion in most cases. And in general, the gains are found to be more significant for Latin American participants than for their larger or potential partners, the United States and the EU. These results are consistent with earlier studies of NAFTA, which also predicted small positive gains for the United States and large gains for Mexico.[19] Despite these positive results, it should be noted that the gains from agreements such as the FTAA are probably underestimated in these CGE exercises, due to the imperfect treatment in these models of dynamic gains from trade.

The inclusion of dynamic effects would strengthen the argument that by promoting increased investment; accelerating the importation of goods, services, and knowledge through improved technological capacities; and strengthening market institutions the FTAA has the potential to contribute to growth and become a major force for economic transformation and modernization in Latin American economies. While smaller economies stand to lose the most in the short term, due to import competition and the fact that they maintain higher trade barriers than the United States and Canada, they could also gain the most in terms of economic growth and modernization.[20] Let us consider some of the mechanisms in more detail.

Investment

As a result of the economic reforms of the 1980s and 1990s, of which economic openness is a key component, the LAC region increased the inflows of FDI from US$10 to $15 billion per year in the early 1990s and from $70 to $90 billion per year from 1998 to 2000. By expanding markets, reducing uncertainty, improving the investment climate, and providing common rules in areas such as the treatment of investment, intellectual property protection, technical standards, and dispute resolution, the FTAA will contribute to sustaining this increased role of FDI flows in the growth and development of LACs.

FDI has multiple benefits in terms of modernization; job creation; intangible assets (including technology transfer, marketing, best management practices, and skills); and other potential spillovers and externalities that are highly beneficial for host-country economic growth. Properly defined rules in the context of the FTAA will not only help to maximize the benefits from FDI, but will also minimize the dangers and costs of locational incentive competition among countries to attract the externality-rich sourcing patterns of international investors (Moran 1999).

Increased and More Secure Access to Large Markets

The U.S. market represents 78 percent of the aggregate GDP of the Western Hemisphere. This figure alone underlines the importance for LAC countries to achieve increased and more secure access to the U.S. market. Between 40 and 50 percent of total Central American, Caribbean, and Andean countries' exports are destined for the United States and Canada. Those economies enjoy quite extensive access to U.S. and Canadian markets via the Generalized System of Preferences (GSP), the Caribbean Basin Initiative (CBI), and the Andean Trade Preferences Act. However, these are unilateral preferences, and, as such, present the following drawbacks: they are more uncertain than a reciprocal arrangement, they do not have a dispute resolution mechanism, and key products are excluded. Therefore, in terms of market access, these countries still have an important margin of benefit to gain from the FTAA.

In the case of MERCOSUR, 20 percent of its total exports are destined for the United States and Canada, 26 percent for Europe, 31 percent to the rest of Latin America and the Caribbean, and 16 percent to the rest of the world. Although it is often pointed out that the share of exports going to the United States is less important for MERCOSUR than for the other LAC countries, the fact remains that more than 50 percent of total MERCOSUR exports go to other countries in the Americas. This makes the FTAA project potentially very significant for the economic dynamics of MERCOSUR.[21]

It is not only better access to the United States and Canadian markets that makes the FTAA beneficial for all countries, but also the reciprocal access between and among the LAC group of countries themselves. For instance, from 1990 to 1999 the growth rates of exports to other LAC countries as a group were higher for all LAC subregions than the growth rates of exports to other regions in the world.

Security in market access also involves disciplining the application of trade remedy measures, such as countervailing and antidumping duties and safeguards.[22] Further benefits are also associated with appropriate dispute settlement mechanisms, particularly in light of the growth of intrahemispheric trade flows previously mentioned.

Increased Competitiveness and Services

The FTAA will serve to reduce distortions and increase the global competitiveness of LAC economies by allowing learning and knowledge transfers associated with trade and by inducing countries to reduce or eliminate domestic distortions that are incompatible with free trade. For instance, in many countries, the prospect and the reality of increased import competition has led not only the government but also the local business communities to be more interested in reducing domestic distortions in transportation costs, the costs of telephone calls, electricity rates, and interest rates that hinder the ability to compete with firms in countries with which free trade agreements have been entered.

The FTAA would also promote higher competitiveness in key services sectors of the economies, such as banking and financial services, telecommunications and transportation, tourism, and professional services. Besides, there is an increasing recognition that services activities are critical for the economic dynamism of economies in the Americas. Services represent, on average, 60 percent of the hemispheric GDP. In trade terms, services are even more important to the smaller economies of the Caribbean and Central America; for many such economies, services exports are the main source of employment and of foreign exchange earnings. In addition, several studies show that on average, 60 percent of manufacturing value added is represented by services inputs, which means that competitiveness in manufacturing products is strongly dependent on competitiveness in services activities. Highly priced and inefficient services raise costs for all users, imposing a "tax" on the whole economy. This is why a recent report by the World Bank argues that the services sector is one of the most important areas to liberalize for developing countries' competitiveness (World Bank 2001). All this makes the

FTAA services negotiations, along with the liberalization and competitiveness that they might induce, one of the principal benefits of the FTAA for participating countries.[23]

Improvement of Market Economy Fundamentals

The integration of national economies into wider markets, either on a world scale or regionally, will bring about increased trade liberalization, not only in the traditional sense of measures at the border, but also a significant amount of institutional and regulatory "harmonization" of markets with regard to trade policy, treatment of investment, legal codes, tax systems, government procurement, ownership, and competition patterns. In these and other areas, international norms today play a key role in defining the terms of reform policies. Whether this effect of trade and trade agreements is called "deep integration" (Lawrence 1997) or "importing institutions" or "institutional arbitrage" (Rodrik 1999), the point is that as a comprehensive agreement, the FTAA will have a major impact in influencing the economic policies, institutions, regulatory frameworks, and traditional market governance practices of LAC countries. The FTAA will be a major force to promote transparency, predictability, competition, nondiscrimination, and rule-bound behavior in many areas of the economic systems of Latin America, reducing the scope for discretion, corruption, collusion, rent-seeking, and arbitrariness. It is not just that markets will be more open, but that their institutional and legal fundamentals will also be stronger as a result of FTAA rules and commitments.

For instance, the impact of NAFTA in locking in not only a broad range of economic reforms, but democracy as well, has been widely recognized. NAFTA was instrumental in determining the policy response of both the Mexican and the U.S. governments to the 1995 peso crisis. Mexico maintained the reforms and increased its credibility as a location for international investment, and the U.S. response demonstrated that NAFTA meant more than just trade policy.[24]

In fact, even though the major benefits of the FTAA will accrue to countries when this agreement comes into effect in 2005, the FTAA process has already been generating collateral benefits and positive externalities for the countries involved. These benefits include strategic direction and a sense of urgency for economic reforms; positive signaling to investors; improved compliance with WTO obligations; renewed vigor in subregional integration efforts; positive effects on private sector behavior via reduced rent-seeking, improved competitive strategies, and networking; increased mutual knowledge and trust among negotiators; and stepped-up technical assistance in trade-related capacity building.[25]

In conclusion, as it is with most modern RTAs, the FTAA is not limited to trade measures at the border. It will provide a framework for governments to adopt better policies, strengthen trade-related institutions, and promote cooperation among members. How precisely the FTAA would help its members integrate into the world economy and benefit in terms of growth and development will, of course, depend on how the agreement is designed and the availability of additional development assistance induced by the agreement by mechanisms internal or external to the agreement.

What the United States Stands to Gain

The executive branch of the United States government has consistently expressed strong economic and strategic interest in the FTAA. Politically and strategically, it is part of U.S. foreign policy to strengthen peace and democracy in the hemisphere, promote prosperity and better standards of living, and reduce the incidence of problems that are perceived as national security threats to the United States, such as excessive immigration, money laundering, and drug trafficking. As pointed out by Gary Hufbauer, Jeffrey Schott, and Barbara Kotschwar:

> Closer trade relations have important spillover effects on overall U.S. relations with the region. Trade pacts act as a magnet for attracting support among hemispheric neighbors for other important political and foreign policy goals: its antidrug efforts, its immigration concerns, its emphasis on better environmental and labor conditions and its efforts to engender simultaneous gains in market-oriented policies and democratic practices. The most important carrot the U.S. government can hold out for broad cooperation in the social agenda is trade and investment talks (Hufbauer et al. 1999, 64).[26]

An important question on the political front is whether one of the effects of the tragic events of September 11, 2001, will be to strengthen or weaken the link between the geopolitical/security elements and prosperity components of U.S. policy toward Latin America. In terms of the executive branch, the answer seems to be positive. In a speech delivered at the Organization of American States (OAS) on January 16, 2002, President Bush explained that "the future of this hemisphere depends on the strength of three commitments: democracy, security, and market-based development. These commitments are inseparable. . . ." On this occasion, the president also announced his disposition to explore a free trade agreement with Central American countries. Negotiations were officially started in January 2003.

Whether Congress will allow implementation of this integrated trade, political, and security approach toward Latin America is a more difficult question. The approval of trade promotion authority (TPA) legislation by the House of Representatives on July 27, 2002, and by the Senate on August 2, 2002, is a major positive development in this respect, although the price for obtaining TPA was a series of concessions to domestic protectionist interests that have generated serious concerns among trading partners.[27]

With regard to economic benefits, Latin America and the Caribbean are one of the main markets for U.S. exports. From total U.S. exports to the world of US$695 billion in 1999, Europe represented $171 billion; Asia, $190 billion; and the Western Hemisphere, $308 billion, of which Canada and Mexico accounted for $253 billion and the rest of the countries in the Americas accounted for $55 billion.[2828] U.S. exports to its partners in the Americas, excluding Canada and Mexico, almost doubled from $30 billion in 1991 to $55 billion in 1999, making this the most dynamic market after the other NAFTA partners in those years. The Caribbean Basin by itself (Central America and the Caribbean) is a larger market for U.S. exports than the U.S. sales to Russia, India, and Indonesia combined and is not far behind total U.S. exports to Brazil. Central American and Caribbean countries buy from the United States more than double the combined purchases of the African subcontinent, including South Africa, and it is the third market in the world for U.S. services exports. So, economic, political, and strategic reasons make the FTAA an important foreign policy priority for the United States.

To conclude this section, all the countries of the Americas have important economic, political, and strategic reasons to be interested in creating the FTAA. The FTAA can also be seen as a natural step in light of the forces at work inducing increased interdependence in the hemisphere. However, the feasibility of completing the FTAA negotiations by January 2005 will depend critically on the capacity of all participating countries to accommodate each other's interests and generate a balanced package of significant market access and other reciprocal concessions. Some of the areas of conflict and factors at work are analyzed next.

State of Play

The FTAA countries have now entered the fourth and final phase of negotiations. As requested by the ministers before the Quito, Ecuador, Ministerial meeting of November 1, 2002, the vice ministers had agreed on most aspects of the methods and modalities to begin market access negotiations in nonagricultural goods, agriculture, services, investment, and government procurement.[29] The following timetable was established for the presentation of offers and requests:

- Presentation of offers: December 15, 2002, to February 15, 2003.
- Submission of requests for improvements to the offers: February 16, 2003, to June 15, 2003.
- Initiation of process for the presentation of revised offers: July 15, 2003.

During 2002, the negotiating groups and vice ministers continued to work on reducing brackets in the draft text and presented a new version to the ministers at their Quito, Ecuador, meeting, which they decided to make public. In addition, according to the timetable above, in February 2003, countries started to exchange their offers for market access negotiations. The adoption of TPA by the U.S. Congress in July-August 2002 went a long way to ensure that market access talks in the FTAA would be fully engaged and that the political commitment would be there so all participants could show their cards at the negotiating table.

However, if negotiations are to be concluded no later than January 1, 2005, numerous challenges need to be addressed on the negotiating and political fronts. On the negotiating front, the interests of the LAC countries are not uniform, but a broad characterization is possible. As explained, the priority objectives of most LAC countries are related to larger and more secure access to large-country markets and to each other's markets to boost their growth and development prospects. These priorities include elimination of high tariffs and nontariff barriers in sectors where they have comparative advantage (textiles, clothing, footwear, leather, food, and agriculture); elimination of tariff escalation; tougher discipline in the application of trade remedies by large industrial countries; further strengthening of dispute resolution mechanisms; and enhanced access for their skilled labor in services contracts. LAC countries are also very interested in increased access to international investment flows, yet they recognize that this is fundamentally a matter for domestic policies — to improve the investment climate, from macrodisciplines to normative frameworks for investment protection, and to the core factors of competitiveness. Although there is broad consensus that the major developmental impacts of the

FTAA for Latin America and the Caribbean are on the market access side and the associated increased investment dynamics, LAC countries also recognize that there are many positive developmental impacts and benefits in adopting modern domestic regulations in areas such as investment, services, competition policy, intellectual property, environmental standards, and labor rights. However, on the rules side, a number of apprehensions and doubts exist that include issues such as how convenient it is to import developed-country regulations in certain areas, whether it is convenient to lock themselves into rules that may preclude the use of certain development policy instruments, or what the appropriate sequence for a more development-friendly trade liberalization is. There are also concerns about the vulnerability to protectionist abuse by interest groups that some of these new rules might be subject to, in particular in areas such as labor and the environment.

The U.S. principal negotiating objectives include more open and reciprocal market access in Latin America and the Caribbean for U.S. exports. As a major exporter of capital and given its global competitive interests, the United States has a particularly strong interest in opening up Latin America's markets and ensuring national treatment for U.S. investors in both goods and services and government procurement contracts, as well as in the adoption and enforcement of intellectual property rights, investment protection, and upgrading of labor and environmental standards.[30] Significant opening up of key sectors where LAC countries are competitive, such as textiles, clothing, footwear, leather, food and agriculture, and revision of trade remedy laws are particularly sensitive issues in the United States and Canada, and yet those areas are where the largest potential benefits for LAC countries are.

Another make-or-break issue in the FTAA is the treatment of smaller economies. Smaller economies have been insisting on their specificities associated with size, vulnerabilities, difficulties for resource reallocation, and sluggish economic adjustment capacities. What differential treatment and what additional mobilization of resources for trade-related capacity building they might receive are key issues for them.[31] Just as the interests of large countries must be reconciled and their costs and benefits balanced, the FTAA will not succeed unless the interests of the smaller economies are similarly addressed. Additional challenges on the negotiating front related to links between FTAA and WTO negotiations are addressed in the next section.

On the political front, one of the main hurdles to the completion of the FTAA — approval of TPA by the U.S. Congress — was overcome in mid-2002. This means U.S. negotiators now know the parameters defined for trade agreements and can fully engage in negotiations again. In addition to providing a boost to WTO and FTAA negotiations, the negotiations with Chile became unstuck and were finalized in December 2002. These are being followed by bilateral negotiations with Central America and Singapore. However, overoptimism is not warranted because approval of TPA does not mean that the traditionally strong U.S. trade policy consensus, broken since the early 1990s, has been fully rebuilt. The fact remains that trade liberalization no longer commands broad bipartisan backing; TPA passed by a narrow majority, and protectionist constituencies will continue to resist liberalization on issues such as textiles, agriculture, banking and insurance at the subfederal level, coastal shipping, and changes in antidumping laws, among others, and will watch trade negotiators closely.

In Latin America and the Caribbean, economic and political fundamentals experienced a significant deterioration during 2001 and 2002, increasing the risk of populist, antiglobalization backlash, as trade liberalization and market-friendly policies become more unpopular. This trend cuts both ways by exacerbating the constraints (fiscal, social, and political) binding even those reformist governments committed to freer trade and by making progress toward and completion of the FTAA more necessary as a way to anchor economic policies, attract investment, and promote growth. The stability of the Brazilian economy and the attitude of the new Brazilian government toward the FTAA will be another key element in the political and economic scenario for further trade integration in the Americas. Although the United States cannot solve Latin America's problems, renewed U.S. leadership and engagement in the region that build on the shared Summit of the Americas values of peace, security, and prosperity can make an enormous difference.[32] Whether the FTAA will be completed successfully and on time will depend critically on the nature of the overall U.S. response to the predicament of LAC countries in the next few years. It will also depend on the links between different negotiations, particularly multilateral negotiations.

SIMULTANEOUS WTO AND FTAA NEGOTIATIONS: SOME CHALLENGES AND LINKS

A Pragmatic Approach to Multilateralism and Regionalism

A cademic economists in particular have been very concerned with the negotiation of regional and bilateral agreements and have warned and written extensively about the costs and risks of proliferating these agreements to the detriment of unilateral liberalization or multilateral negotiations. The case in favor of multilateral negotiations is based on the following three main types of arguments: the economic costs of regionalism in terms of trade diversion; the practical inefficiencies and costs of overlapping trade agreements in terms of inconsistent rules of origin and dispute settlement mechanisms that can create what Jagdish Bhagwati, professor and trade expert, has likened to a "spaghetti bowl"[33] that could hinder, rather than facilitate, business; and the distraction effect of RTAs in pulling both resources and political attention away from the multilateral system.

While some of these costs can be real, it can be argued that the multilateralism versus regionalism debate is based on a false dilemma for at least three fundamental reasons. First, the evidence from Latin America and the Caribbean does not support the view that the new bilateral and RTAs negotiated in the region have been seriously trade diverting.[34]

Second, there are many plausible trajectories in pursuing a two- or three-track strategy (multilateral, regional, and bilateral) that might get countries to free trade quicker than relying only on one track. Historical experience shows evidence of patterns of mutually reinforcing interdependence, where the pursuit of regionalism triggers or induces the pursuit of multilateralism.[35] In addition, the multilateral system is far from being as quick and efficient as is sometimes portrayed because it is slow to achieve results and weak in a number of fundamental areas. Still, it is a major achievement in the area of global governance and must be protected and strengthened. A positive view of the competition to negotiate is also at the center of the new three-tiered approach to trade negotiations, promoted by the Bush administration and what United States Trade Representative (USTR) Robert Zoellick has called "competitive negotiations." This approach radically changes the structure of incentives for other countries and regions and opens up new scenarios for them that include the possibility for certain countries to be excluded or be the last to enjoy the benefits of a bilateral trade agreement with the United States. Thus, it has served the objective of reinvigorating the FTAA negotiations.

Third, the evidence from Latin America shows that these countries did not adopt the new regionalism instead of or as an alternative to multilateralism. As previously observed, the typical sequence was that countries first engaged in unilateral liberalization as part of the process of economic reform in the 1980s and early 1990s. The new regionalism was a consequence of this process of reform. Countries also actively participated in the Uruguay Round, and it was in the climate of protracted negotiations and uncertainty about the results of the round that they simultaneously engaged in the revitalization of their customs unions and in the negotiation of FTAs.

The most valid criticism of the costs of RTAs is the increased transactions costs involved in a "spaghetti bowl" world of proliferation. The risks here are quite real, and governments should make every effort to design trade agreements to minimize these costs and risks.

However, in practice, governments will most likely continue to pursue a multiple-path strategy of trade negotiations. In Doha, regional exercises gained increased legitimacy. Paragraph four of the Doha Ministerial Declaration recognizes "that RTAs can play an important role in promoting the liberalization and expansion of trade and in fostering development." So, if RTAs are here to stay, the key question becomes how to harness and orient regionalism so that it maximizes its role as a building block for a more open world trading system. Given the disappointing record of the GATT/WTO mechanisms for examining consistency of RTAs with the conditions of Article XXIV of GATT and Article V of GATS, in Doha, the Ministers agreed to "negotiations aimed at clarifying and improving disciplines and procedures under the existing WTO provisions applying to regional agreements. The negotiations shall take into account the developmental aspects of regional trade agreements" (Doha 2001). As Hoekman and Kostecki have noted: "At the end of the day, the more successful the WTO is in reducing external barriers through multilateral trade negotiations, the less problematical RTAs will be from a systemic and non-member perspective" (Hoekman and Kostecki 2001, 367).

Can the FTAA Be Achieved Faster?

Although potentially major gains for LAC countries may result from the new round, there is reason to believe that the benefits of the FTAA can be achieved faster and, in some respects with larger benefits, than would be achieved with multilateral negotiations. This is not an argument to give priority to the FTAA over multilateral negotiations, but an argument for why the priority of the FTAA should not be reduced with the launching of the Doha Development Agenda.

First, with regard to market access issues, the new round of WTO negotiations will not deliver global free trade at the end of the round. The goal is to achieve a significant further step in market access, but it is not to eliminate tariffs and nontariff barriers or subsidies completely. The list of exceptions and unfinished business at the end of the round is likely to be long. Besides, negotiations are complex and will probably take longer than the formally planned date to finish by January 1, 2005.

In contrast, the objective of FTAA negotiations is to create a free trade area, which means complete elimination of tariffs for trade in goods. Although there will probably be exceptions and reservations, the list will probably be smaller than in the WTO. Whether liberalization of services in the FTAA could go beyond the WTO is an open question, but it is also likely that, given the smaller number of countries and the fact that LAC countries have been engaged in substantial liberalization of services in recent years, the FTAA will be able to go deeper into the area of services than would have been possible in the WTO negotiations.

Since the beginning of negotiations, rulemaking in the areas of competition, government procurement, and investment have been on the FTAA agenda with more ambitious objectives than those defined in the Doha Work Program, where they are new issues. Moreover, although many important issues remain to be decided and negotiated, the FTAA negotiations on rules are already well advanced.

Thus, because of the potential benefits of this agreement, the momentum already achieved, and the potential in terms of speed and depth, the FTAA negotiations are not likely to be dropped by countries, even if they have to be continued at the same time as WTO negotiations.

FTAA-WTO Linkages

FTAA-WTO negotiations are linked in complex ways. Links can be identified on the negotiating and political and policymaking fronts. On the negotiating front, the areas where links are more apparent are agriculture, antidumping, trade-related aspects of intellectual property rights (TRIPS), and subsidies. In these four areas, there are some specific issues where progress is likely to be possible only at the multilateral level. In the other areas of the negotiations, in particular in the key market access issues of tariffs and services, there is no reason why the FTAA could not make progress with relative independence from the new round.

On the political and policymaking front, managing two major negotiations simultaneously poses a daunting challenge. The sheer complexity and intensity of both negotiations will demand a tremendous effort and additional resources for the negotiating teams of all countries. This involves practical/managerial issues, such as minimal capacity to be present or being meaningfully represented at meetings, appropriate organization of the negotiating teams, ensuring an adequate flow of information about what goes on in each forum, and the domestic and international coordination of negotiating positions. On the positive side, it can be argued that the FTAA has already had "positive learning externalities" and has contributed to significant capacity building that will allow countries to engage more effectively at the multilateral level.

Concurrent negotiations will require not only strengthened trade technocracies able to engage internationally, but also increased transparency and heightened engagement locally with broad sectors of civil society, in order to arbitrate the distributional conflict inherent in trade policy reform, articulate national positions, and develop a sense of "local ownership" and support for what is being negotiated.

SUMMARY OF CHALLENGES FOR THE NEXT STAGE

B ased on the analysis in this paper, this section presents a five-part policy framework as a way of integrating and summarizing the main challenges Latin American and Caribbean countries face in their next stages of trade and development policy. The first two parts refer to external negotiations, and the others relate to the complementary domestic development policy agenda.

The first part concerns the question of trade strategy options countries should pursue. This paper argues that despite current criticism of neoliberal policies and populist rhetoric to the contrary, economic integration into world markets should be, and most likely will continue to be, a key element in the economic reform programs of all LAC countries. It was also argued that countries will be better served by a multiple-path strategy of trade negotiations that can maximize benefits by moving simultaneously on the following negotiating fronts: multilateral, regional, and bilateral. Reasons were given why the creation of the FTAA should continue to be a priority despite the launching of a new round. With regard to unilateral liberalization efforts, however, given the significant liberalization already undertaken by most countries and ongoing multilateral and regional negotiations, incentives for further unilateral liberalization in the region have been reduced for the next stage.

The second component of the five-part policy agenda also involves external negotiations, but it refers to the need for a concerted effort with other developing countries and with like-minded industrialized countries to promote a more development-friendly global trade and financial architecture. The agenda for reshaping the global trade architecture for development contained in the 2002 Global Economic Prospects report issued by the World Bank provides a real manifesto for strengthening the global trade system in a development-friendly way, and many of its proposals should be embraced by LAC countries.[36]

The third component is upgrading trade-related public- and private-sector institutions. The next stage of trade policy will be the most negotiation intensive ever that Latin American countries have had to face. This is exacerbated by the inevitable fact that all these negotiations are linked in different and complex ways. Thus, despite the intensity of the 1990s on the trade front, the present decade promises to be even more intense. And, of course, down the road and in the not too distant future, LAC countries face the challenge of implementing the new commitments negotiated in the Doha Development Agenda, in the FTAA, and in other agreements. Negotiating on several fronts at the same time and complying with new rules and obligations will require more trade capacity building than ever before. This represents a challenge not only for the countries themselves, but also to aid-providing governments and to inter-American and global development agencies. The Hemispheric Cooperation Program, adopted by FTAA ministers at their meeting in Quito in November 2002, has the potential to address some of these challenges.

The fourth part is adoption of pro-growth and pro-competitive policies to augment supply-side response capacities. Achieving improved market access is a necessary condition to create opportunities for growth; an active trade negotiating agenda can take care of this, but it is not sufficient. To take advantage of such opportunities, countries must develop supply-side capacity and provide an attractive investment climate. There is a whole array of initiatives countries should consider to create this pro-growth policy environment. The right incentives for growth include a stable macroeconomic framework; promotion of efficiency in services sectors that are essential to trade and international competitiveness, such as transport, telecommunications, financial activities, business services, and others; policies to promote technological innovation and maximize knowledge diffusion in society; and investment in human capital and education.[37]

The final part of this policy framework is social development policies. Even if satisfactory rates of growth are achieved, growth alone will be inadequate for facing the social challenges of Latin America.

The point of enumerating this broad spectrum of policies is partly to underline that even though trade policy and economic integration into larger markets are essential, they are but one component of a much broader set of challenges. Trade and integration can deliver broad-based improvements in standards of living only if accompanied by a wider range of policies. A more development-friendly international environment can go a long way toward facilitating the task ahead for developing countries, but, ultimately, it is up to national governments and societies to find the unique combination of economic and social policies to achieve sustained growth and development. The international trade agenda should not be confused with nor be a substitute for a development agenda founded on a clear national vision and a strong national policy consensus.

NOTES

1.   The author is grateful to Karsten Steinfatt, Juan Pablo Villegas, and Laurent Pipitone for research assistance with this paper. The views expressed are those of the author and should not be attributed to the Organization of American States or to its member states.

2.   For detailed discussions of the Washington Consensus and influential views on the way forward for policy reform in Latin America and the Caribbean, see Williamson 1997; Ocampo 1998; Stiglitz 1998; Naim 1999; and Rodrik 2001a and 2001b.

3.   See Martin Wolf 2001; Oxfam 2001; and World Bank 2002.

4.   For instance, how these two communities have traditionally understood the term "cooperation" is very different. Trade negotiators are accustomed to delivering courses and training on trade rules, agreements, and other issues close to negotiations. More recently, their agenda has expanded to include a concern for trade agreement implementation, particularly in behind-the-border issues. The development community is used to a much broader spectrum of policy areas where, in many cases, trade, market institutions, or private sector development might not even appear or have only secondary importance. One of the major challenges is, then, to bridge these differences between the development community and institutions and the trade community and institutions, a difference that is sometimes expressed not only at the international level, but also between different national agencies and institutions. See Salazar-Xirinachs 2002b.

5.   See Levine and Renault 1992; Sachs and Warner 1995; Sala-i-Martin 1997; Frankel and Romer 1999; and Irwin and Tervio 2000.

6.   Rodríguez and Rodrik 2000 and Rodrik 2001 are skeptical about the robustness of some of these results regarding the relationship between trade openness and growth. Jones 2000, however, focusing on trade policy variables, concludes that trade restrictions are almost invariably harmful to long-run growth, although the magnitude of the effect is uncertain. For Rodrik, "The appropriate conclusion to draw . . . is not that trade protection should be preferred to trade liberalization as a rule. The point is simply that the benefits of trade openness should not be oversold" (Rodrik 2001b, 39).

7.   See Cooper 2002; Klenow and Rodríguez-Clare 1997; and Rodríguez-Clare 2002.

8.   Trade mainstreaming can be defined as the process and methods for identifying priority areas for trade-capacity building and integrating them into the overall country development program.

9.   Note that the table does not include nonreciprocal trade agreements, of which there are five in the Americas: the Caribbean Basin Initiative, the Andean Trade Preferences Act, CARIBCAN, and the agreements between CARICOM and Venezuela and between CARICOM and Colombia. It also does not include the "partial scope" agreements negotiated under the Latin American Integration Association (La Asociación Latinoamericana de Integración — ALADI). For an analysis of nonreciprocal agreements in the Western Hemisphere, see Steinfatt 2001.

10. For the history, characteristics and recent evolution of customs unions, see Salazar-Xirinachs, Wetter, Steinfatt and Ivascanu 2001; and for free trade agreements, see Robert 2001.

11. For an assessment of key analytical and policy issues posed by proliferation in the Americas, see Salazar-Xirinachs 2002.

12. Important discussions of country objectives in pursuing RTAs are Ethier 1998; Perroni and Whalley 1994; and Whalley 1996.

13. For a more detailed explanation of the advantages and disadvantages of unilateral actions, see Aggarwal and Espach 2001.

14. One proposal is to grant credit to countries for "autonomous liberalization" to avoid, at least in part, this perverse effect. However, there is not much support for this proposal in the WTO or in the FTAA.

15. See World Bank 2000 and Hoekman 2001 for an overview of scenarios and estimates of gains for developing countries from the new round in these areas.

16. This is the case both in the WTO, where the Doha Declaration itself is the prime evidence of the priority developing countries have assigned to capacity building and technical assistance, and in the FTAA, where smaller economies, including the Caribbean, Central American, and Andean ones have insisted on special treatment of the differences in size and level of development and on the importance of developing a hemispheric cooperation program.

17. Rodrik (1999; 2001a; 2001b) has stressed the need to complement trade openness with a range of policies, including institutional reform, infrastructure, trade-capacity building, and social safety nets in order to "make openness work" for growth and development. Hoekman 2001 argues that in order to strengthen the WTO and the multilateral system from a development perspective, the following four key elements are necessary: a) giving priority in the new WTO round to negotiations to improve market access conditions for both goods and services; b) pro-development rules, that is, ensuring that trade rules are useful or "friendly" for developing countries; c) a major aid effort outside of the WTO to improve trade performance of low-income countries by helping them deal with their supply-side and institutional constraints; and d) unilateral actions by industrialized countries to facilitate market access by the least-developed countries.

18. Presidential Summits of the Americas have been held in Miami in 1994; Santiago, Chile, in April 1998; and Quebec, Canada, in April 2001. For analyses of the political, strategic, and security objectives of countries in the Americas and of the Summit process, see Gaviria 2001; Weintraub 2000; Franco 2000; Feinberg 1997; and The Leadership Council for Inter-American Summitry 2001.

19. For a survey of this literature, see Robinson and Thierfelder 1999. For recent regional scenarios, see also Diao, Diaz-Bonilla, and Robinson 2001; Roland-Holst and van der Mensbrugghe 2001; and Monteagudo and Watanuki 2001.

20. Of course, the balance of short-term costs and longer-term benefits and the pattern of economic transformation will be decisively influenced by the provisions and characteristics of the eventual agreement with regard to the treatment of the differences in size and levels of development among participating countries.

21. For Brazilian positions on the FTAA, see Lafer 2001; Barbosa 2001; and Soares de Lima 1999.

22. The incidence of antidumping procedures in countries of the Americas is analyzed by Tavares, Macario, and Steinfatt 2001.

23. For a collection of analyses on the role of services in hemispheric integration, see Stephenson 2000.

24. This is also why some analysts consider the U.S. government's response to the crisis in Argentina to be an important test of Washington's interest and commitment to a hemispheric vision. See Hakim 2002.

25. For an explanation of these benefits, see Salazar-Xirinachs 2001.

26. See also, Schott and Hufbauer 1999 and Schott 2001.

27. The most important concerns refer to the more intensive consultation procedures, in general, and special consultations regarding sensitive agricultural and textile products, the interpretation of the parameters to negotiate labor and environmental issues, and the removal from the Caribbean Basin Trade Partnership Act of 2000 of the possibility of dying and finishing textile and apparel in the region. A major source of concern, the Dayton-Craig amendment, was removed during conference negotiations. The Dayton-Craig amendment would have allowed Congress to veto specific provisions of trade pacts if they changed U.S. antidumping and other trade remedy laws. However, one of the primary negotiating objectives of TPA is to preserve the integrity of those laws.

28. Data from the International Trade Administration, U.S. Department of Commerce. Available at <www.ita.gov/td.industry/otea/usfth/aggregate/h99t06.txt>.

29. The full detail of the methods and modalities approved for the FTAA negotiation can be read in document FTAA.TNC/20, publicly available on the FTAA official web site at <www.alca-ftaa.org>.

30. For a definition of U.S. principal negotiating objectives, see H3009, Division B – Bipartisan Trade Promotion Authority.

31. Aid for trade-related capacity building has recently received renewed attention in the FTAA talks with the adoption by FTAA Trade Ministers in Quito on November 1, 2002, of a hemispheric cooperation program. A number of donors, most notably the Inter-American Development Bank, have mobilized significant additional resources in the past few years. New mechanisms for country/donor coordination and introduction of best practices on trade-related aid and capacity building are also in the process of formulation and implementation by the Tripartite Committee (OAS, IDB, ECLAC). See <http://www.sice.org/TUnit/Seminar/trinidad/conf-tt.asp>.

32. Professor Joseph Nye (2002) argues that getting the objectives of U.S. foreign policy right will require not only overcoming the dispute over multilateralism versus unilateralism in U.S. foreign policy, but a new understanding of the sources of U.S. power and willingness to pursue the national interest, increasingly based on the use of "soft power" and cooperative relationships.

33. "Spaghetti bowl" is a metaphor first used by Jagdish Bhagwati to refer to the complex web of bilateral or regional trade agreements with different tariff reduction schedules, rules of origin, technical standards, and other administrative aspects and their systemic risks and disadvantages in terms of increased transactions costs, administrative costs, and difficulties for business.

34. For a discussion of the evidence, see Krueger 1999; Rodríguez-Mendoza 1999; Burfisher, Robinson, and Thierfelder 2001; Salazar-Xirinachs 2002; and IDB 2002.

35. Many trade experts have argued that the creation of the European Economic Community (EEC) led directly to the Dillon and Kennedy Rounds. Others point to the 1982 shift to regionalism by the United States as having been instrumental in persuading the EU and developing countries to launch a new round. The WTO (1995) argues that the failed Brussels Ministerial in December 1990 and the spread of regional integration agreements after 1990 were major factors that led to eliciting the concessions needed to conclude the Uruguay Round. In early 2001, many expressed concern that the new Bush Administration would give priority to the FTAA and not to a new WTO round. This provided an additional incentive for the European and Japanese calls for a new round in Davos in early 2001 and throughout the year.

36. See also Hoekman 2001.

37. The dilemmas and opportunities in some of these areas are analyzed by contributions to this volume.

REFERENCES

Aggarwal, Vinod, and Ralph Espach. 2001. "Diverging Trade Strategies in Latin America." Paper prepared for the conference, Regionalism and Transregionalism in the Americas: Comparing Trade Strategies, September 24, 2001. Washington, D.C.: Woodrow Wilson International Center.

Barbosa, Rubens. 2001. "The FTAA That Is in Brazil's Interest." *Gazeta Mercantil*, November 5.

Birdsall, Nancy, and Augusto de la Torre. 2001. *Washington Contentious: Economic Policies for Social Equity in Latin America.* Washington, D.C.: Carnegie Endowment for International Peace and Inter-American Dialogue.

Burfisher, Mary E., Sherman Robinson, and Karen Thierfelder. 2001. "The Impact of NAFTA on the United States." *Journal of Economic Perspectives* 15: 1 (Winter): 125-144.

Cooper, Richard N. 2002. "Growth and Inequality: The Role of Foreign Trade and Investment." In *Annual World Bank Conference on Development Economics 2001/2002*, eds. Boris Pleskovic and Nicholas Stern. Oxford, UK: World Bank-Oxford University Press.

Devlin, Robert, and Ricardo Ffrench-Davis. 1999. "Towards an Evaluation of Regional Integration in Latin America in the 1990s." *The World Economy* 22: 2 (March).

Devlin, R., and A. Estevadeordal. 2000. "What's New in the New Regionalism in the Americas?" Mimeo. October.

Diao, Xinshen, E. Díaz-Bonilla, and S. Robinson. 2001. "Scenarios for Trade Integration in the Americas." Paper presented at the Conference on Impacts of Trade Liberalization Agreements on Latin America and the Caribbean, November 5-6, 2001, Washington, D.C. Inter-American Development Bank and Centre d'Etudes Prospectives et d'Information Internationales.

Dollar, David, and Aart Kraay. 2000. *Growth Is Good for the Poor.* Washington, D.C.: Development Economics Research Group, World Bank.

Doha Development Agenda. 2001. "Ministerial Declaration." Paragraph 29.

The Economist. 2002. "Has Latin America Lost Its Way?" March 2-8.

Estevadeordal, A., J. Goto, and R. Sáez. 2000. *The New Regionalism in the Americas: The Case of MERCOSUR.* Working Paper 5. April. Buenos Aires: INTAL-ITD.

Estevadeordal, A. 2000. "Negotiating Preferential Market Access — The Case of the North American Free Trade Agreement." *Journal of World Trade* 34: 1 (February).

Ethier, Wilfred J. 1998. "The New Regionalism." *The Economic Journal* 108: 449 (July).

Feinberg, Richard. 1997. *Summitry of the Americas: A Progress Report.* Washington, D.C.: Institute for International Economics.

Finger, Michael. 2001. "Implementing the Uruguay Round Agreements: Problems for Developing Countries." *The World Economy, Global Trade Policy.* Special Issue.

Franco, Patrice. 2000. *Towards a New Security Architecture in the Americas: The Strategic Implications of the FTAA.* Washington, D.C.: Center for Strategic and International Studies.

Frankel, Jeffrey, and David Romer. 1999. "Does Trade Cause Growth?" *The American Economic Review* (June).

Gaviria, César. 2001. "Integration and Interdependence in the Americas." In *Toward Free Trade in the Americas*, eds. José M. Salazar-Xirinachs and Maryse Robert. Washington, D.C.: The Brookings Institution Press/General Secretariat of the Organization of American States.

Hakim, Peter. 2002. "Aid to Argentina: Strings Attached." *Washington Post*, March 5.

Harrison, Lawrence. 1997. *The Pan-American Dream: Do Latin America's Cultural Values Discourage True Partnership with the United States and Canada?* New York: Basic Books.

Hoekman, Bernard, and Michel Kostecki. 2001. *The Political Economy of the World Trading System*. 2d ed. Oxford, UK: Oxford University Press.

Hoekman, Bernard. 2001. *Strengthening the Global Trade Architecture for Development: The Post Doha Agenda*. Washington, D.C.: The World Bank and CEPR. November.

Hufbauer, Gary, Jeffrey Schott, and Barbara Kotschwar. 1999. "U.S. Interests in Free Trade in the Americas." In *The United States and the Americas: A Twenty-First Century View*, eds. Albert Fishlow and James Jones. New York, London: W.W. Norton and Company.

Hufbauer, Gary, and Jeffrey Schott. 1999. "Whither the Free Trade Area of the Americas?" In *The World Economy: Global Trade Policy 1999*, eds. Peter Lloyd and Chris Milner. Oxford, UK: Blackwell Publishers.

Inter-American Development Bank (IDB). 2002. *Beyond Borders: The New Regionalism in Latin America: Economic and Social Progress in Latin America, 2002 Report*. Washington, D.C.: IDB.

Irwin, Douglas, and Marko Tervio. 2000. *Does Trade Raise Income? Evidence from the Twentieth Century*. National Bureau of Economic Research Working Paper Series No. 7745. <http://www.nber.org/papers/w7745>.

Jones, Charles I. 2000. *Comments on Rodríguez and Rodrik, Trade Policy and Economic Growth: A Sceptic's Guide to the Cross-National Evidence*. Macroeconomics Annual. National Bureau of Economic Research. Cambridge, Mass.: MIT Press. <www.stanford.edu/-chadj>.

Kissinger, Henry. 2001. "Brazil's Destiny: An Obstacle to Free Trade?" *Washington Post*, May 15.

Klenow, P., and A. Rodríguez-Clare. 1997. "Economic Growth: A Review Essay." *Journal of Monetary Economics* 40(3): 597-618.

Krueger, Anne. 1999. *Trade Creation and Trade Diversion Under NAFTA*. National Bureau of Economic Research Working Paper Series No. 7429. Cambridge, Mass.

Lafer, Celso. 2001. "Brazil at the Inter-American Dialogue." Speech by Ambassador Celso Lafer, Minister of Foreign Affairs of Brazil. Washington, D.C., March 1.

Lawrence, Robert. 1997. "Preferential Trading Arrangements: The Traditional and the New." In *Regional Partners in Global Markets: Limits and Possibilities of the Euro-Med Agreements*, eds. Ahmed Galal and Bernard Hoekman. London: Centre for Economic Policy Research.

The Leadership Council for Inter-American Summitry. 2001. *Advancing Toward Quebec City and Beyond*. Policy Report III. Coral Gables, Fla.: The Dante B. Fascell North-South Center at the University of Miami.

Levine, Ross, and David Renalt. 1992. "A Sensitivity Analysis of Cross-Country Growth Regressions." *American Economic Review* 82 (September): 942-963.

Mace, Gordon, Louis Belanger, and contributors. 1999. *The Americas in Transition: The Contours of Regionalism.* Boulder, Colo.: Lynne Rienner Publishers.

Monteagudo, Josefina, and M. Watanuki. 2001. "Regional Trade Agreements for MERCOSUR: The FTAA and the FTA with the European Union." Paper presented at the Conference on Impacts of Trade Liberalization Agreements on Latin America and the Caribbean. Washington, D.C.: Inter-American Development Bank and Centre d'Etudes Prospectives et d'Information Internationales, November 5-6.

Moran, T.H. 1999. *Foreign Direct Investment and Development.* Washington, D.C.: Institute for International Economics.

Naim, Moisés. 1999. *Fads and Fashion in Economic Reforms: Washington Consensus or Washington Confusion?* IMF Conference on Second Generation Reforms. < http://imf.org/external/pubs/ft/seminar/1999/reforms/Naim.HTM>.

Nye, Joseph. 2002. *The Paradox of American Power.* New York: Oxford University Press.

Ocampo, José Antonio. 1998. "Beyond the Washington Consensus: An ECLAC Perspective," *Cepal Review,* No. 66. < www.eclac.org>.

Oxfam. 2001. *Eight Broken Promises: Why the WTO Isn't Working for the World's Poor.* Oxfam Briefing Paper No 9.

Perroni, Carlo, and John Whalley. 1994. *The New Regionalism: Trade Liberalization or Insurance?* National Bureau of Economic Research Working Paper Series No. 4626. Cambridge, Mass.

Prusa, Thomas J. 1999. *On the Spread and Impact of Antidumping.* National Bureau of Economic Research Working Paper Series No. 7404. Cambridge, Mass. October.

Robert, Maryse. 2001. "Free Trade Agreements." In *Toward Free Trade in the Americas,* eds. José M. Salazar-Xirinachs and Maryse Robert. Washington, D.C.: The Brookings Institution Press/General Secretariat of the Organization of American States.

Robinson, Sherman, and Karen Thierfelder. 1999. *Trade Liberalization and Regional Integration: The Search for Large Numbers.* TMD Discussion Paper 34. January. Washington, D.C.: Trade and Macroeconomics Division (TMD), International Food Policy Research Institute (IFPRI).

Rodríguez-Clare, Andrés. 2002. "Comment." In *Annual World Bank Conference on Development Economics 2001/2002,* eds. Boris Pleskovic and Nicholas Stern. Washington, D.C.: World Bank-Oxford University Press.

Rodríguez-Mendoza, Miguel. 1999. "Dealing with Latin America's New Regionalism." In *Trade Rules in the Making: Challenges in Regional and Multilateral Trade Negotiations,* eds. Miguel Rodríguez-Mendoza, Patrick Low, and Barbara Kotschwar. Washington, D.C.: Organization of American States/The Brookings Institution Press.

Rodríguez, Francisco, and Dani Rodrik. 2000. *Trade Policy and Economic Growth: A Skeptic's Guide to the Cross-National Evidence.* <http://ksghome.harvard.edu/drodrik.academic.ksg/skeptic1299.pdf>.

Rodrik, Dani. 1999. *The New Global Economy and Developing Countries: Making Openness Work.* Policy Essay No 24. Overseas Development Council. Baltimore: The Johns Hopkins University Press.

Rodrik, Dani. 2001a. "Development Strategies for the Next Century," paper presented at CEPAL's Seminar on Development Theory at the Dawn of the Twenty-First Century, in commemoration of the 100th anniversary of the birth of Raul Prebisch, Santiago, Chile, August 28-29. < www.eclac.org>.

Rodrik, Dani. 2001b. *Development Strategies for the Next Century*. Cambridge, Mass.: Harvard University Press. <www.eclac.org/prensa/noticias/comunicados/6/7616/DaniRodrik29-08.pdf>.

Roland-Holst, David, and D. van der Mensbrugghe. 2001. "Regionalism versus Globalization in the Americas: Empirical Evidence on Opportunities and Challenges." Paper presented at the Conference on Impacts of Trade Liberalization Agreements on Latin America and the Caribbean, November 5-6. Washington, D.C.: Inter-American Development Bank and Centre d'Etudes Prospectives et d'Information Internationales.

Sachs, Jeffrey, and Andrew Warner. 1995. *Economic Reform and the Process of Global Integration*. Brookings Papers on Economic Activity 1: 1-118.

Sala-i-Martin, Xavier X. 1997. "I Just Ran Two Million Regressions." *American Economic Review* 87 (May): 178-183.

Salazar-Xirinachs, José M. 2001. "The FTAA Process: From Miami 1994 to Quebec 2001." In *Toward Free Trade in the Americas*, eds. José M. Salazar-Xirinachs and Maryse Robert. Washington, D.C.: The Brookings Institution Press/General Secretariat of the Organization of American States.

Salazar-Xirinachs, José M. 2002a. "Proliferation of Sub-Regional Trade Agreements in the Americas: An Assessment of Key Analytical and Policy Issues." *Journal of Asian Economics* 13: 2 (March-April).

Salazar-Xirinachs, José M. 2002b. "Key Issues for Developing Institutional and Human Capacity in Trade Policy." Remarks at OAS-IDB-ECLAC Conference on Trade Related Capacity Building: Conference and Donor Workshop. Trinidad and Tobago, May. <http://www.sice.oas.org/TUnit/Seminar/trinidad/conf-tt.asp>.

Salazar-Xirinachs, José M., Theresa Wetter, Karsten Steinfatt, and Daniela Ivascanu. 2001. "Customs Unions in the Western Hemisphere." In *Toward Free Trade in the Americas*, eds. José M. Salazar-Xirinachs and Maryse Robert. Washington, D.C.: The Brookings Institution Press/General Secretariat of the Organization of American States.

Salazar-Xirinachs, José M., and Maryse Robert, eds. 2001. *Toward Free Trade in the Americas*. Washington, D.C.: The Brookings Institution Press/General Secretariat of the Organization of American States.

Schott, Jeffrey. 2001. *Prospects for Free Trade in the Americas*. August. Washington, D.C.: Institute for International Economics.

Soares de Lima, Maria Regina. 1999. "Brazil's Alternative Vision." In *The Americas in Transition: The Contours of Regionalism*, eds. Gordon Mace, Louis Belanger, and contributors. Boulder, Colo.: Lynne Rienner Publishers.

Steinfatt, Karsten. 2001. "Preferential and Partial Scope Agreements." In *Toward Free Trade in the Americas*, eds. José M. Salazar-Xirinachs and Maryse Robert. Washington, D.C.: The Brookings Institution Press/General Secretariat of the Organization of American States.

Stephenson, Sherry, ed. 2000. *Services Trade in the Western Hemisphere: Liberalization, Integration, and Reform*. Washington, D.C.: The Brookings Institution-OAS.

Stephenson, Sherry. 2001. *Multilateral and Regional Services Liberalization by Latin America and the Caribbean.* OAS Trade Unit Studies No. 9. March. Washington, D.C.: OAS. <http://www.sice.oas.org/tunit/pubinfoe.asp#tustudies>.

Stiglitz, Joseph. 1998. "More Instruments and Broader Goals: Moving Toward the Post-Washington Consensus," 1998 WIDER Annual Lecture, Helsinki, Finland. < http://www.wider.unu.edu/publications/publications.htm>.

Tavares de Araujo Jr., José, Carla Macario, and Karsten Steinfatt. 2001. *Antidumping in the Americas.* OAS Trade Unit Studies No. 10. March. Washington, D.C.: OAS. <http://www.sice.oas.org/tunit/pubinfoe.asp#tustudies>.

Weintraub, Sidney. 2000. *Development and Democracy in the Southern Cone: Imperatives for U.S. Foreign Policy in South America.* Washington, D.C.: Center for Strategic and International Studies.

Whalley, John. 1996. *Why Do Countries Seek Regional Trade Agreements?* National Bureau of Economic Research Working Paper Series No. 5552. Cambridge, Mass.

Williamson, John. 1997. "The Washington Consensus Revisited," in *Economic and Social Development into the XXI Century*, ed. Louis Emmerij. Baltimore: The Johns Hopkins University Press/IDB.

Winters, L. Alan. 1999. "Regionalism vs. Multilateralism." In *Market Integration, Regionalism and the Global Economy*, eds. R. Baldwin, D. Cohen, A. Sapir, and A. Venables. Cambridge, UK: Cambridge University Press.

Wolf, Martin. 2001. "Broken Promises to the Poor." *Financial Times*, November 21.

World Bank. 2000. *Trade Blocks.* A World Bank Policy Research Report. Oxford, UK: Oxford University Press.

World Bank. 2002. *Global Economic Prospects and the Developing Countries: Making Trade Work for the Poor.* Washington, D.C.: The World Bank.

World Trade Organization (WTO). 1995. *Regionalism and the World Trading System.* Geneva: WTO Secretariat.

Chapter Two

ECONOMIC INTEGRATION IN THE SOUTHERN CONE: CAN MERCOSUR SURVIVE?

Roberto Bouzas

INTRODUCTION

O ver the last 15 years, the Argentine and Brazilian trade regimes have undergone significant transformations. Following the accession to power of the liberal-oriented governments of Carlos Menem (Argentina) and Fernando Collor de Mello (Brazil) in the early 1990s, unilateral trade liberalization deepened markedly in the Southern Cone. Unilateral trade policy reform was stimulated and reinforced by multilateral commitments. In effect, the conclusion, in 1993, of the Uruguay Round negotiations of the General Agreement on Tariffs and Trade (GATT) carried significant implications for the region, not only in the realm of market access conditions for goods, but also for a broader range of disciplines previously not subject to binding international scrutiny, such as trade in services, protection of intellectual property rights, and trade-related investment measures.

The more liberal trade policy environment, fostered by unilateral and multi-lateral liberalization, proved supportive of more substantive regional integration agreements. Although the history of preferential liberalization in the Southern Cone is a long one, the decade of the 1990s proved particularly fruitful in terms of substantive commitments and heightened trade interdependence. In a relatively short period of time, the Southern Common Market (Mercado Común del Sur — MERCOSUR), formed by Argentina, Brazil, Paraguay, and Uruguay, eliminated tariffs on all trade except automobiles and sugar and agreed to and partially implemented a common external tariff (CET). By past Latin American standards, these achievements were remarkable.

After an initial bright start in 1991, however, MERCOSUR experienced mounting difficulties. Nontariff barriers remained largely untouched, and enforcement of the CET was more difficult than expected. The so-called "deepening" agenda that involved issues such as services trade and government procurement, also made scant progress. After nearly a decade of rapid increase in trade interdependence and intraregional trade liberalization, MERCOSUR reached a critical point in the late 1990s. The political environment soured, trade restrictions multiplied, and the CET became largely symbolic. The macroeconomic crisis that shocked the region after the East Asian financial meltdown led to a sizable devaluation of the Brazilian currency in 1999, followed by the collapse of the Argentine currency board in 2001. These adverse macroeconomic conditions greatly aggravated MERCOSUR's woes, but the fundamental determinants of its performance are deeper than the macroeconomic turmoil.

This chapter provides a summary account of the record of MERCOSUR during the 1990s and of its main determinants. This stylized account is intended to explain the underlying incentives and obstacles to further economic integration in the Southern Cone. The first section of the chapter provides a summary account of the performance of MERCOSUR since the signature of the Treaty of Asunción on March 1991. The second section offers a stylized review of the factors that help account for performance. The third section briefly discusses four fallacies that pervade the present policy debate on the future of MERCOSUR. A fourth and final section assesses the prospects of MERCOSUR in light of Argentina's and Brazil's new administrations.

An Overview of MERCOSUR's Performance

The state and performance of MERCOSUR in the 1990s can be summarized by examining three indicators: 1) the evolution of economic interdependence, 2) the effectiveness of the policy and regulatory process, and 3) the way that differences in interests and perceptions were processed by domestic politics.[1] Whereas the intensity of economic interdependence can be measured by quantitative indicators, the effectiveness of the regulatory process and the way that differences in interests and perceptions are processed by the domestic polities can only be grasped by qualitative observation.

The intensity of economic interdependence can be partially measured by indicators such as the ratio of intraregional to total foreign trade or the ratio of intraregional trade to gross domestic product (GDP). Economic interdependence is a proxy indicator of the intensity of regional spillover effects. Although closer interdependence caused by trade discrimination may not be welfare enhancing when, for example, it is the result of net trade diversion, a preferential trade arrangement that does not stimulate increased interdependence is unlikely to be meaningful to its members. In contrast, increased interdependence will create stronger incentives to cooperate and to manage growing cross-border spillovers.

The effectiveness of the policy and regulatory process is critical for a process of regional integration to move forward (indeed it is critical for any public policy). Effectiveness can be measured by the "relative enforcement gap," that is, by the wedge that exists between policy decisions (commitments) and implementation. Although implementation will always lag behind decisions, a meaningful preferential trade arrangement will be incompatible with an ever widening "relative enforcement gap." Should that gap become too wide, the credibility of the regional decision-making process will collapse and make the regional integration process irrelevant, in the sense that regulations will have no material effect on the behavior of economic agents. In the Latin American experience of regional integration, there have been plenty of agreements that were only partially implemented and became gradually irrelevant.

The way that differences in interests and perceptions are processed by the domestic polities (what we have called the "politicization bias") is important because it gives indications of the cooperative or conflictive nature of the regional game. The "politicization bias" tries to capture the way that the polities of member states deal with their natural differences and conflicting interests. Negative politicization will predominate when differences, including technical ones, are "captured" and exacerbated by the domestic political process, thus leading to polarization and raising the costs of compromise. But the politicization process can also show a positive bias when, for example, overriding political incentives lay the ground for constructive compromise.

These three indicators are not enough to capture all facets of the performance of MERCOSUR since its inception. Yet, they can offer a stylized account of it. By organizing time according to alternative combinations of this set of indicators, the history of MERCOSUR can be classified into three distinct phases: 1) the 1991-1994 "transition period" to the customs union, 2) the 1995-1998 period of rising interdependence and low regulatory efficiency, and 3) the post-1998 crisis (see Table 1).

Table 1. The First Decade of MERCOSUR: A Stylized Account

Variables Period	Interdependence	"Relative enforcement gap"	"Politization bias"
1991/1994	Rising	Low	"Positive"
1995/1998	Rising	High and rising	"Neutral"
1998/?	Falling/Stagnant	High and rising	"Negative"

Source: Created by author. Please note that as of fall 2003, the situation had not changed since 1998.

The "Transition Period" (1991-1994) Toward a Customs Union

The Treaty of Asunción christened the period scheduled to conclude on December 31, 1994, as the "transition period" toward the customs union. During this period, intraregional trade flows increased rapidly, deepening interdependence, particularly between MERCOSUR's two largest trading partners, Brazil and Argentina. In a period of just four years, the intraregional exports to GDP ratio and the intraregional exports to total foreign trade ratio increased by more than 60 percent. By opening up economies and enabling geographical proximity to work, unilateral trade liberalization was a decisive factor behind regional interdependence. But trade preferences also played a significant role (Frankel 1997). During this period, economic interdependence increased significantly throughout the region.

MERCOSUR's founding charter included three major commitments. The first one was to put in motion a trade liberalization program that consisted of automatic and across-the-board tariff cuts. That program should be implemented in a period of four years (Paraguay and Uruguay had an additional year to comply). The second commitment was the adoption of a CET as of January 1, 1995, when the customs union would start to be implemented. The third commitment, at last, had no specific deadline and simply stated the target to coordinate macroeconomic and sector policies. By the end of the transition period (1994), MERCOSUR had achieved a significant lowering of tariff barriers —100 percent preferences over most favored nation (MFN) tariff rates for nearly 85 percent of the tariff schedule — and it had also agreed on a CET. No progress had been made, however, in the coordination of macroeconomic and sector policies.

In just four years, MERCOSUR made more progress toward intraregional trade liberalization than in the previous three decades. By January 1995, only a handful of sensitive products still paid positive import duties, but member states had agreed on an automatic calendar to eliminate all tariffs by January 1, 2000, at the latest.[2] The two "special sectors" (sugar and motor vehicles) that were transitorily excluded from intraregional free trade should, by the end of this decade, also be covered by the general disciplines.

By the end of 1994, MERCOSUR member states had also agreed on a CET and drafted a customs code. The conflicting interests that emerged from divergent national protection structures were accommodated through a compromise that maintained national tariff rates subject to automatic convergence schedules for a limited number of sensitive items, such as those included in national exception lists, capital goods, and information and telecommunication products (Olarreaga and Soloaga 1998). By January 1995, MERCOSUR had made little progress in addressing the issue of nontariff barriers (NTBs). It was also still far from being an effective customs union. However, relative to the typical Latin American regional integration process, it showed a modest "relative enforcement gap."

The transition period was not free from clashes of interest among member states. Most visibly, these were caused by rising Argentine bilateral trade deficits with Brazil, as the currency board fixed the nominal exchange rate of the peso to the US dollar. But these conflicts were typically addressed through a cooperative and accommodating approach. Many examples can be cited in this period, such as the acceptance on the part of other MERCOSUR member states of the increase in Argentina's statistical import tax surcharge from 3 to 10 percent at the end of 1992 (a levy contrary to MERCOSUR's rules) and the Brazilian official decision to purchase oil and wheat from Argentina to reduce bilateral trade imbalances.[3] Instead of widening the divide between conflicting national interests, during this initial period, policy decisions aimed to bridge that gap through a combination of flexibility and compromise, in an example of what we have called a "positive politicization bias."

On balance, therefore, the transition period was quite successful, at least when compared with past experience. This positive record prepared the way for an optimistic view of the prospects of regional integration in the Southern Cone for the remainder of the decade of the 1990s. Unfortunately, optimism diminished as the decade proceeded.

Rising Interdependence and Falling Regulatory Efficiency (1995-1998)

The period from 1995 to 1998 was one of contrasts. During these years, regional economic interdependence continued to rise, but regional regulatory and policy processes became increasingly ineffective. The sustained expansion of intraregional trade and investment flows in the context of growing regulatory inefficiency was interpreted by some analysts as an indication of the strength of market forces pushing toward regional economic integration. In this view, higher regional interdependence was, to a large extent, the result of a natural partnership detached from policy decisions. Yet, the increasing difficulties involved in tackling some of the policy issues that confronted MERCOSUR (such as NTBs) and the reluctance of member governments to upgrade institutions and decision-making procedures led to an ever expanding list of unfinished business. Ultimately, this widening "relative enforcement gap" damaged the credibility of rules and policy-making organs alike.[4]

During the period from 1995 to 1998, the ratio of intraregional to total foreign trade and the ratio of intraregional exports to GDP increased by nearly 50 percent. Intraregional investment also rose remarkably, leading to an unprecedented boom in intraregional foreign direct investment (FDI). Yet, this increase in interdependence occurred in parallel with an ever widening "relative enforcement gap." Member states successfully implemented the agreed-upon tariff cuts for sensitive products, but sugar and motor vehicles remained subject to special rules and were excluded from intraregional free trade. More important, very little progress was made in the area of NTBs, which remained largely intact.

Implementation of common trade policies also advanced only partially. The CET was plagued by a growing number of exceptions, and the customs code eventually proved unenforceable. As a result, all traded goods remained subject to rules of origin, thus inhibiting one of the major benefits of a customs union over a free trade area — the free circulation of goods. Following the free trade agreements that were successfully concluded with Chile and Bolivia, MERCOSUR's collective negotiations with the Andean Community and Mexico broke down, resulting in new perforations of the CET (Bouzas, da Motta Veiga, and Torrent 2003).

The "deepening agenda" of *Agenda Mercosur 2000*, agreed upon in December 1995 in Montevideo, also failed to make progress. The only major achievement was the signature of a Services Trade Protocol in 1997, the congressional ratification of which is still pending (hence, it is still not in force). The Services Protocol established free trade in services to be reached in a period of 10 years after ratification and convened annual rounds of negotiations. After three rounds of negotiations, member states have undertaken liberalization commitments that are only modestly beyond those already undertaken under the General Agreement on Trade in Services (GATS).[5] Member countries also agreed upon common procedures for safeguards, antidumping, and countervailing duties, but they all failed to be adequately enforced.

From an institutional perspective, the major innovation of the 1995-1998 period was the creation of a MERCOSUR Trade Commission in charge of administering common trade policy instruments. However, the Trade Commission was rapidly overloaded with the management of intraregional trade disputes rather than with the enforcement of common trade policies. Despite mushrooming trade conflicts, the dispute settlement mechanism (DSM) remained dormant until 1999.[6]

As far as "politicization" was concerned from 1995 through 1998, the rising number of conflicts that split member states apart were dealt with in a less cooperative manner than during the transition phase. National governments tried to prevent polarization, usually through the direct engagement of the presidents in what came to be known as "presidential diplomacy." As clashing interests and perceptions became more frequent, vocal, and visible, the recourse to direct involvement of the presidents became more and more costly and, over the medium term, ineffective. Divergences multiplied not only in the economic arena, but also in the realm of foreign policy and international bargaining strategies, such as the stance to be adopted in negotiations toward a Free Trade Area of the Americas (FTAA). The scope of negative politicization significantly widened following the regional negative repercussions of the East Asian financial crisis.

In summary, this second phase stands out as one of contrasts. While regional economic interdependence continued to rise at a rapid pace, the regulatory process gradually lost credibility. Moreover, the cooperative approach that characterized the administration of conflict during MERCOSUR's early years, when political commitment was at a peak, gradually gave way to growing polarization and rifts. The deteriorating external environment that prevailed after 1997, specifically the crisis in East Asia, the Russian default, and falling terms of trade, simply made matters worse.

Since 1998, Crisis or Disintegration?

The January 1999 maxi-devaluation of the Brazilian real is conventionally referred to as a turning point in the recent history of MERCOSUR. This is an overstatement because the factors that account for the disappointing performance of MERCOSUR are more fundamental than the Brazilian devaluation alone (similarly, for the collapse of the currency board in Argentina).

One facet of the disappointing performance of MERCOSUR since 1998 has been the significant contraction of economic interdependence. During 1999, intraregional trade flows fell in absolute terms by more than 25 percent, while the ratio of intraregional to total foreign trade returned to the levels recorded in 1995. Intraregional trade flows recovered by 17.6 percent in 2000, but only reached levels recorded in 1996. The ratio of intraregional to total foreign trade, in turn, remained constant at the same level of 1995. At the end of 2001, the ratio of intraregional to total foreign trade stood at 18.2 percent, still significantly below the 25 percent peak recorded in 1998.[7]

Falling regional trade interdependence was, to a large extent, the result of adverse macroeconomic trends (falling aggregate demand) but also a consequence of explicit policy decisions. Argentina entered into a protracted economic recession in 1998, only to be aggravated by the downturn of the Brazilian economy and the sharp devaluation of the real in 1999. Less than two years later, the Argentine currency board collapsed, engulfing the country in its deepest recession in history (real output fell by 11 percent in 2002). These adverse macroeconomic trends depressed intraregional trade and investment flows through the conventional real and financial transmission channels (Heymann 1999). But intraregional trade was also hard hit by ad hoc trade relief measures, materialized in new nontariff barriers and officially sponsored or tolerated private sector "orderly marketing arrangements." Unable to raise tariffs or enforce safeguards, the member states most severely hit by the Brazilian devaluation got hold of a variety of NTBs. The Argentine crisis gave new opportunities for exceptional measures to be applied by the smaller countries (Paraguay and Uruguay).

The recourse to ad hoc and unilateral trade measures to isolate countries from negative external shocks was also an indicator of the growing regulatory ineffectiveness of MERCOSUR. In such a negative context, common trade policies and the "deepening" agenda gradually lost substance. The implementation of the CET experienced significant reversals, such as Argentina's unilateral tariff changes for capital goods and consumer products in 2001.[8] In sum, during this latest phase, not only the pre-existing backlog in implementation remained untouched, but it was significantly expanded in number and scope. The institutional machinery of MERCOSUR continued to produce meetings and regulations, but most of them had little effect on economic agents. The result was a deepening credibility crisis.[9]

During this phase, the growing number of conflicts that plagued the relationship between MERCOSUR member states was also subject to negative politicization. The conflicts created by the contrasting monetary and exchange rate regimes of Argentina and Brazil after the devaluation of the real were probably the most vocal and contentious, but they were by no means the only ones that occurred. In effect, the differences that emerged during the previous period in other policy areas, such as foreign policy and international trade bargaining strategies, deepened remarkably.

The coming to office of new administrations in Argentina and Brazil in 2003 raised new expectations that the most critical issues in MERCOSUR's agenda could be dealt with in a more collaborative and effective manner. The two new governments have emphasized that they consider MERCOSUR a key component of their countries' foreign trade strategies. They have also been vocal as to the priority that MERCOSUR will receive. However, although a renewed political commitment is a necessary condition for reinvigorating MERCOSUR, it is by no means sufficient by itself.

ACCOUNTING FOR MERCOSUR'S PERFORMANCE

The general background of MERCOSUR is one of structurally low and asymmetric interdependence among its member states. This is the counterpart of large differences in the size of the economies and the degree of openness. While Paraguay and Uruguay are two small and open economies highly vulnerable to regional events, Brazil is a continental and relatively closed economy with comparatively modest regional interdependence links. Although the regionwide ratio of intraregional to total foreign trade increased considerably in the 1990s (from 11 percent in 1991 to 21 percent in 2000), its absolute value is still low by European Union or even North American Free Trade Agreement (NAFTA) standards. A relatively low level of economic interdependence means that the functional demands for coordination are modest. In such circumstances, the costs of foregone national policy discretion and lost flexibility must be weighed against limited gains accruing from enhanced interstate coordination.

Moreover, since regional economic interdependence in MERCOSUR is highly asymmetric, the net benefits of lost flexibility and discretion as a result of policy coordination will be heterogeneously distributed among partners. This means that they will not face equivalent incentives to coordinate. While for the smaller partners the loss of policy discretion may be an acceptable price to be paid for better control of negative spillovers, for the larger ones, particularly for Brazil, the incentives to resign policy flexibility will be much more modest. This pay-off matrix will also constrain MERCOSUR's larger member states, again particularly Brazil, from supplying the public goods required for regional integration to proceed.

But low and asymmetric regional interdependence in MERCOSUR is a structural factor, the nature of which has not changed significantly in the last decade, despite the increase experienced by intraregional trade and investment flows. Therefore, the degree of interdependence cannot by itself account for the contrasting performance of MERCOSUR in the decade that followed the signature of the Treaty of Asunción. In this section, three factors that can help to explain the cycle of progress and stagnation experienced by MERCOSUR in the 1990s and its current impasse will be discussed and briefly analyzed. These factors are 1) the national revealed policy preferences, 2) the nature of the negotiating agenda, and 3) the external environment (see Table 2).

Table 2. Accounting for MERCOSUR's Contrasting Performance

Variables \ Phase	Revealed national policy preferences	Content of the policy agenda	External environment
1991/1994	Macro diverge/ Micro converge	Border barriers (tariffs) and agreement on common trade policies	Positive
1995/1998	Macro converge/ Micro diverge	Non-border barriers, NTBs, implementation of common trade policies	Worsening
1998/?	Macro/Micro diverge	Non-border barriers, NTBs, implementation of common trade policies	Negative

Source: Created by author. Please note that as of fall 2003, the situation had not changed since 1998.

Revealed National Policy Preferences

Engagement in a process of economic integration assumes the existence of a potential for mutual gains. The materialization of mutual gains may be facilitated by shared interests (vis-à-vis nonmembers), similar perceptions or visions of the world, and convergent revealed national policy preferences. Although member states may not share the same motivations for economic integration, these cannot be mutually inconsistent. Provided they are not, reaching a satisfactory compromise among parties who do not share fully identical interests, perceptions, and revealed policy preferences requires a negotiation that must be crafted by politics. Political leaders must also take care that this compromise is dynamically adjusted to new circumstances in order to maintain commitment over time. The nature of the bargain may change with new and unforeseen domestic and external circumstances, which will demand a continuous search for compromise.

During the decade of the 1990s, the revealed economic policy preferences of MERCOSUR member states showed periods of partial convergence and wide divergence.[10] On aggregate, throughout the 1991-1994 period, microeconomic policy preferences converged but in the context of widely divergent macroeconomic policies. In effect, after two hyperinflationary episodes at the turn of the decade, Argentina stabilized its macroeconomy through the enforcement of a nominal peg and a currency board. This rigid monetary regime severely limited the discretion of the Central Bank. Constrained in its ability to monetize deficits, the federal government was left with no other option but to raise public sector revenues through taxation, privatization, and borrowing in international financial markets. The new policy mix helped to reduce inflation sharply and to stimulate aggregate domestic demand, but at the cost of a real appreciation of the local currency. At the same time, however, the Brazilian government was enforcing a "crawling peg" (small exchange rate devaluations at relatively short intervals) in an environment suffering from high inflation and a fragile fiscal position.

Despite these divergent macroeconomic policies and performances, however, microeconomic policy choices were largely convergent: structural reform, deregulation, and privatization became words of the day in Argentina as well as Brazil. Although the Argentine and Brazilian governments differed in the details of their microeconomic policies, they converged remarkably around market-friendly interventions. This was most visible and decisive in the realm of trade policy, where unilateral trade liberalization provided fertile ground for lowering barriers to intraregional trade.

The period from 1995 to 1998 was also one of partial policy convergence. But this time, in contrast with the "transition phase," convergence occurred on the macroeconomic policy realm in parallel with a growing wedge in microeconomic policies. In effect, after the Real Plan (*Plano Real*), Argentina and Brazil experienced de facto convergence on macroeconomic, particularly exchange rate policies. This shift, however, coincided with a growing divide over prevalent microeconomic regimes. While the Argentine government continued its policy of limited government intervention, based on ideological preferences and institutional constraints, Brazilian central and local authorities gradually moved toward more active sector and horizontal policies, such as the automotive regime for the northern and northeastern regions and more aggressive supply of development and export finance (da Motta Veiga 1999). These divergent paths of public sector intervention proved particularly conflictive because member states failed to agree on how to treat the distortions created by public sector aids.[11]

During most of the third and most critical period, 1999-2000, the divide on revealed economic policy preferences was all-encompassing because Argentina and Brazil displayed divergent preferences both in the macro- and microeconomic spheres. The devaluation of the real in January 1999 brought de facto macroeconomic convergence to an abrupt end. The shift toward a floating exchange rate regime in Brazil, while Argentina struggled to maintain its currency board, confirmed a widening gap in macroeconomic policy preferences and laid the basis for open bilateral rift. In December 2001, the currency board collapsed, and Argentina moved to a floating exchange rate regime as well, bringing national exchange rate policies more into line. However, by that time the credibility of MERCOSUR was clearly at stake. As far as microeconomic policy instruments were concerned, the Brazilian government continued its policies of horizontal activism. During the latest phase of the currency board, in turn, the Argentine government joined in implementing targeted interventions to compensate temporarily for the negative effects on price competitiveness of the fixed exchange rate. Ad hoc interventions and the lack of a mechanism to discipline or regulate public sector aids led to mounting conflict and resentment.

Macroeconomic turmoil and subsidy competition brought the issue of enhanced coordination and harmonization to a leading place in the regional policy agenda. However, initiatives aimed at macroeconomic coordination remained, at best, formal. President Menem, who raised the issue of a common currency in 1998, tabled the proposal as a euphemism for regional "dollarization" rather than as a step toward regional macroeconomic coordination and eventual monetary unification. The idea was plainly rejected by Brazilian officials. In 2000, after the devaluation of the real, MERCOSUR member states agreed on indicative targets for a set of macroeconomic indicators. These, however, were rapidly rendered obsolete by the deepening Argentine crisis. Although the abandonment of the currency board and the devaluation of the Argentine peso in January 2002 removed one major obstacle to enhanced macroeconomic cooperation, the economic crisis and the instability that followed created a context not conducive to heightened economic cooperation.

The Changing Content of the Negotiating Agenda

During the early stages of MERCOSUR, the policy and regulatory agenda remained largely concentrated on the removal of tariffs and other border barriers to trade ("shallow integration"). The Act of Buenos Aires (*Acta de Buenos Aires*), signed by the Argentine and Brazilian governments in 1990 and adopted by MERCOSUR in the Treaty of Asunción, was very effective in this endeavor because it adopted a linear, automatic, and across-the-board tariff-cutting program. This program involved a major change in the focus and procedures for preferential trade liberalization, as compared with the past, as it shifted emphasis from a positive to a negative list approach. Consequently, intraregional trade liberalization moved forward at a rapid pace.

However, by the mid-1990s, the very success of MERCOSUR's tariff-cutting exercise had brought new policy issues to the forefront. With most tariff barriers removed or subject to automatic schedules for elimination, the negotiating agenda shifted toward the more complex issues of identifying and removing nontariff restrictions and nonborder barriers to trade. It is well known that NTBs and nonborder restrictions pose tough challenges to trade liberalization, due to their lack of transparency, their sensitivity to the quality of enforcement, the blurred border-line between legitimate and trade-obstructing regulations, and the limited consensus about the optimal degree of policy harmonization that should be enforced. This led to a more complex and conflict-prone negotiating agenda.

The adverse macroeconomic environment that prevailed after the East Asian crisis made this agenda more relevant because one of its effects was to fuel a battery of new, ad hoc trade restrictions. Consequently, MERCOSUR not only failed to make progress on its unfinished business, but it faced an ever expanding inventory of questionable practices that led to more market fragmentation in a context of reduced credibility. In this environment, it was simply natural that the more demanding issues of common trade policies and "deepening" would lose touch with reality.

As discussed earlier, the agreement on a common trade policy, particularly a CET, in the mid-1990s was facilitated by the convergence of national trade policy regimes (unilateral liberalization) and a flexible approach that materialized in long transition periods for sensitive products and sectors. While the CET largely replicated the structure of protection of Brazil, long transition periods served to smooth the conflicts of interests created by heterogeneous national protection and production structures.

However, implementing common trade policies proved to be far more demanding than agreeing on them. On the one hand, implementation required a degree of positive integration that assumed not only shared interests and preferences, but also equivalent institutional capabilities. On the other, as common policies were the result of a transaction between different interests and perceptions in an environment characterized by large asymmetries, their stability partly depended on dynamic trade-offs that failed to materialize as the integration process evolved.[12]

In summary, as the easy phase of tariff elimination was completed in the mid-1990s, MERCOSUR's negotiating agenda shifted toward more complex matters that require deeper coordination and more national policy restraint. This nonborder agenda was, per se, more complex than traditional border issues and demanded more convergence in preferences and institutional capabilities, as well as a higher degree of "positive" integration. Thus, the lack of progress in the harmonization of NTBs was compounded by a growing divide on the CET, which surfaced dramatically in 2001 when Argentina unilaterally abandoned the CET for a large number of items. Although MERCOSUR organs waived Argentina's unilateral step a few months later, the credibility of the regional integration process suffered one more blow, precisely at a time when the group was engaged in collective negotiations in the FTAA process and with the European Union.

The External Environment

The record of MERCOSUR during the 1990s cannot be properly understood without taking into account the changing external environment. The two external factors that stand out as the most influential are the state of international financial markets and the pace and credibility of the negotiations toward a Free Trade Area of the Americas (FTAA).

The state of international financial markets has no straightforward relationship to regional economic integration. However, it has been a key factor shaping the performance of MERCOSUR. During the initial 1991-1995 phase, liquid international financial markets played the role of lubricant for regional economic integration. Abundant external finance relaxed one major constraint on economic growth and, thus, helped to reduce the typical conflicts created by growing bilateral trade imbalances and economic adjustment in a slow-growth context. In a context of financial liquidity and economic expansion, trade liberalization was made more palatable and the financing of current account deficits easier.

These favorable conditions, temporarily reversed during the Tequila Crisis of December 1994 and early 1995, changed radically after the 1997 East Asian crisis. Economic growth suffered following the drying out of external finance in the late 1990s, making trade liberalization more conflict-prone and placing the lowering of trade deficits as a major objective, even through the enforcement of "beggar-thy-neighbor" policies. This environment was not conducive to further economic integration and trade liberalization, whether preferential or unilateral, and explains to a large extent the step backward in trade liberalization policies throughout the region.

The second external factor to be considered is the pace and credibility of FTAA negotiations. In the early 1990s, announcements of NAFTA, the Enterprise for the Americas Initiative (EAI), and a proposed FTAA at the heads of state Summit of the Americas, in Miami in December 1994, all contributed to raise the "defensive" incentives behind regional integration, as perceived by MERCOSUR member states and particularly by Brazil. It was not by chance that the Buenos Aires Charter, which adopted an automatic mechanism for trade liberalization, was signed in mid-1990, just a few months after Mexican and U.S. authorities publicly acknowledged that they were engaged in negotiations toward a free trade agreement. By the same token, it was not fortuitous that the pace and commitment to reach a settlement on the CET peaked just prior to the Miami Summit.

This perceived pressure relaxed during the second half of the 1990s, following the U.S. administration's failure to secure fast-track negotiating authority from Congress. This damaged the credibility of U.S. negotiators and reduced the incentives to consolidate an effective negotiating coalition in MERCOSUR. In particular, it reduced the incentives of Brazil to commit more fully to the customs union and to pay the costs of a benign leadership at critical times. If it is true that MERCOSUR was seen, particularly by the Brazilian government, as a strategic instrument to improve its international bargaining position, more credible FTAA negotiations would have enhanced the perceived net benefits of enforcing an effective customs union. By 2002, when the Bush administration obtained fast-track negotiating authority (renamed trade promotion authority — TPA) from

Congress, it already seemed quite clear that FTAA negotiations would lead, at best, to a "light" hemispheric trade agreement. By that time, MERCOSUR was already in a state of disarray.

FOUR FALLACIES AND THE PRESENT POLICY DILEMMAS OF MERCOSUR

I have argued that the current impasse of MERCOSUR and the open debate over its prospects as a customs union are the results of a set of factors that include divergent interests and perceptions, an increasingly complex negotiating agenda, and an adverse external environment. The negative consequences of this set of factors, however, could be ameliorated through adequate political bargaining. But this has so far failed to materialize.

The accession to office of two new governments in Argentina and Brazil in 2003 creates a propitious opportunity to make a reassessment of where member states want MERCOSUR to be taken. Presidents Luiz Inácio Lula da Silva of Brazil and Néstor Kirchner of Argentina have both reaffirmed a commitment toward regional integration and have underlined the high priority that their administrations will assign to MERCOSUR. This renewed political commitment and the rebuilding of the foundations of a common endeavor will be necessary conditions to revitalize the process of regional integration. However, politics by itself will not do the trick. MERCOSUR needs to adopt rules and procedures to make integration effective. In this context, four common fallacies help to distract attention from the present policy dilemmas of MERCOSUR.

Fallacy # 1: MERCOSUR Is an "Imperfect" Customs Union

The concept of an "imperfect" customs union, used so frequently to characterize MERCOSUR, assumes that a "perfect" customs union exists. However, these notions are static and lack practical policy relevance. Rather than these ambiguous notions, what seems more important to characterize a customs union is whether its member states are effectively moving toward a unified trade policy and a single customs territory. This is essentially a dynamic process. As long as the movement toward a unified customs territory is credible and effective, a customs union can include exceptions, convergence calendars, and special treatment for smaller economies.

When the record of MERCOSUR is analyzed in detail, it is fair to conclude that progress toward a customs union has been modest or even nonexistent. The CET agreed upon in 1994 has been implemented only partially, there have been a growing number of exceptions (many of them unilateral), and the customs code is still not being enforced. In addition, member states have made practically no progress toward implementing common trade disciplines vis-à-vis third parties. The necessary institutional and organizational machinery to negotiate with third parties (such as in the FTAA or with the European Union) also remains quite underdeveloped.

Defining MERCOSUR as an "incomplete" customs union thus helps very little to understand the state and condition of the regional integration arrangement. In practice, MERCOSUR has made very little progress toward becoming a unified customs territory, has advanced very little in shaping a common negotiating agenda with third parties, and has quite a high number of items of "unfinished business" concerning intraregional trade liberalization. If these issues are not explicitly addressed, it will be difficult for MERCOSUR to design a policy agenda to extricate it from its current impasse.

Fallacy # 2: MERCOSUR Cannot Move Forward due to National Constitutional Impediments

It is frequently argued that MERCOSUR member states display constitutional asymmetries that make deeper regional integration impossible. In particular, while Argentina and Paraguay have constitutions that establish the supremacy of international over domestic law, in the cases of Brazil and Uruguay the effects of an international treaty can be modified through a domestic legislative act. According to some observers, this asymmetry is revealed in the Brazilian government's reluctance or inability to increase its commitment and move faster toward regional integration.

Pointing out a constitutional constraint certainly looks intimidating. However, it does not help to clarify the mechanisms that may be used to make compatible Brazilian and Uruguayan constitutional precepts and effective regional integration procedures. There are legal and political mechanisms that can help to avoid or reshape the obstacles put in place by dualist legal schemes, as widely demonstrated by the European experience. In fact, this type of conflict (much deeper and more "supra-national" than that of MERCOSUR) also emerged in the context of the process of European economic integration, but it was addressed through formulas designed to cope with its effects. The real obstacle to deeper and more effective economic integration in MERCOSUR is not constitutional but political. There are formulas that can help to make the rule-making process more effective, but these are not adopted because of political rather than constitutional constraints.

Fallacy # 3: The Paralysis of MERCOSUR Is the Result of the Macroeconomic Crisis

As mentioned before, since the devaluation of the real in 1999, the macroeconomic crisis of the region has been the preferred explanatory factor for the weakening of MERCOSUR. Naturally, the process of regional economic integration has suffered from a negative macroeconomic environment, but this is not enough to account for its present state. As we have argued in the previous sections, MERCOSUR showed significant weaknesses prior to the macroeconomic crisis, many of which concerned the effectiveness of the rule-making process. Indeed, during the period of macroeconomic de facto convergence between 1995 and 1998, MERCOSUR accumulated the largest "relative enforcement gap."

If the current crisis of MERCOSUR is attributed to the macroeconomy, then the demand for macroeconomic coordination becomes a prerequisite for reinvigorating the process of economic integration. Yet, moving toward macroeconomic coordination will demand deeper and more stringent conditions than enforcing a free trade area or even a customs union. Those who demand that policymakers accomplish macroeconomic coordination as a prerequisite for restoring the vitality of MERCOSUR draw the policymakers' attention away from less demanding initiatives that could actually help to increase the intensity of bonds between or among countries and gradually raise the incentives for deeper coordination.[13]

Fallacy # 4: The "Trading" MERCOSUR Should Be Replaced by a "Political" MERCOSUR

As a process of economic integration among developing nations, MERCOSUR is and should be led by politics. In this respect, the identification of shared and complementary interests by political leaders is a necessary condition for the process to move forward. However, this strategic convergence — a political construct — must be given a practical agenda. The emphasis on politics, and particularly foreign policy, as a substitute for trade convergence is not akin to the historical experience of other successful economic integration initiatives.

The existence of strong economic interdependence is a prerequisite for successful regional integration. This usually involves dealing with an agenda focused on trade policy issues, as has been the case of European integration. Emphasizing the need to focus on politics rather than on trade matters, as has become commonplace in MERCOSUR, risks becoming an appeal for rhetoric rather than substance. MERCOSUR faces a thorny technical and institutional agenda that needs to be addressed. That agenda includes prosaic issues such as the enforcement and eventual renegotiation of the CET; the removal of NTBs that constitute unfair obstacles to intraregional trade, such as import permits; the adoption of mechanisms to cope in an orderly manner with the effects of macroeconomic shocks; the adoption of common negotiation strategies vis-à-vis third parties (both in the FTAA process and with the European Union); and an increase in the effectiveness of the rules-making process, which may demand more automatic mechanisms for the "internalization" of regulations. This agenda is full of "grey" issues, but all need to be addressed effectively if the impasse is to be left behind.

CAN MERCOSUR SURVIVE?

Regional integration cannot proceed without the provision of certain collective goods. But doing so generally involves a cost. Making sure that the glue that holds together the partners to a regional integration agreement is solid and lasting requires a long-term, strategic view that may involve trade-offs with other short-term priorities. In this sense, MERCOSUR has suffered from a significant leadership gap. While Argentina has traditionally been reluctant to accept Brazilian regional preeminence, the largest South American country has frequently been more focused on its own internal problems rather than on acting as a regional, benign hegemon. The modest commitment of Brazil to act as the benign leader of MERCOSUR may be considered to be the result of an unattractive pay-off matrix, partly derived from size asymmetries and even frustration over expected, as yet unrealized gains and trade-offs.

Moreover, in the medium term, even "willingness to lead" may not be enough. A benign hegemon also needs resources to make leadership effective. But resources are scarce and must be allocated among alternative uses. Resources to exert effective leadership may not even be at hand. For example, had Brazil been able to provide an anchor for regional macroeconomic stability and a focal point for convergence, the monetary and exchange rate instability — and the ensuing conflicts — that have dominated the regional economic scene during the late 1990s and culminated in the 1999 devaluation of the real and the collapse of Argentina's currency board in December 2001 could have been significantly minimized.

Keeping MERCOSUR together as a customs union will demand a significant investment of political energy. Torn apart by internal differences over the structure of protection and other domestic policy and international bargaining preferences, overburdened by a complex negotiating agenda, and negatively affected by the adverse external environment, member countries may find that their common endeavor is too demanding for the existing capabilities and structure of incentives. We argued in this chapter that the financial crisis in Argentina, as well as the devaluation of the real in 1999, worsened the prospects of regional economic integration. But the determinants of MERCOSUR's performance are deeper.

MERCOSUR displays significant problems in the realm of implementation of commitments. One area in which these problems have been most evident is the enforcement of trade disciplines that affect intraregional trade, where the subsistence of unilateralism has been a relatively low-cost policy option. In practice, unilateralism has been stimulated by an approach that enshrined flexibility and a case-by-case focus, as opposed to the enforcement of rules and preestablished procedures. Structural instability (macroeconomic volatility) contributed to making things worse, widening the scope and reasons for unilateral action, but it has not been the main factor behind unilateralism.

During its short life, MERCOSUR has made intensive use of diplomatic resources, of which so-called "presidential diplomacy" has been a major example. However, the regular intervention of top political authorities, combined with poor implementation mechanisms, enshrined the preservation of national policy discretion as a rule. The inadequacy of this approach worsened as the regional integration agenda grew more complex and demanded a deeper pooling of national sovereign resources. The obstacles to moving forward effectively with this deeper agenda translated into a "broadening" of the issues addressed at the negotiations and a parallel multiplication of normative acts, the majority of which were usually not enforced. This "broadening" of the negotiating agenda led to a loss of focus and a "normative inflation" that amplified the stock of unfinished business and further damaged MERCOSUR's credibility.

Whether MERCOSUR member states will abandon (in practice) the target of building a customs area is not a minor issue for domestic as well as external reasons. At this time, the "imperfections" that pervade MERCOSUR's common trade policies are numerous. There are a large number of exemptions to the CET (many of them discretional), and member states are far away from anything that may resemble a transition toward a "free circulation of goods." These issues, which have been under discussion for years, have shown very limited signs of progress toward being resolved.

If MERCOSUR is to survive as a relevant economic integration process, its effectiveness and credibility will have to be significantly enhanced. In this context, the improvement in the macroeconomic outlook appears to be a necessary but not a sufficient condition. The revitalization of MERCOSUR will critically depend on a new "regional contract" that lays renewed foundations for a regional partnership and reshapes common objectives and shared targets. This will demand a deep revision of the role of Brazil and of its readiness and ability to provide constructive leadership. It will also require the end to opportunistic behavior on the part of the smaller partners, especially Argentina.

NOTES

1.   For a more thorough discussion, see Bouzas (2002).

2.   Paraguay and Uruguay were given one additional year to complete tariff-cutting commitments.

3.   Brazil was a natural market for Argentine wheat, but Argentine exporters suffered from the competition of developed countries' subsidized exports. Similarly, Brazil had traditionally purchased oil in the Middle East but shifted its supply sources to Argentina, following an official decision by Petrobras (the Brazilian state oil company) and the deregulation of the energy sector in Argentina.

4.   For a detailed account of MERCOSUR's institutional performance, see Bouzas and Soltz 2001.

5.   For a detailed analysis, see Bouzas, da Motta Veiga, and Torrent (2003).

6.   For a detailed discussion of dispute settlement in MERCOSUR, see Bouzas and Soltz 2001.

7.   Data Intal 3.1 database.

8.   In March 2001, the Argentine government unilaterally raised tariff rates on consumer goods and eliminated all import duties on capital goods, breaking apart from the CET. A few weeks later, the Common Market Group temporarily waived Argentina's CET obligations.

9.   In the year 2000, member states announced an ambitious "re-launching agenda," characterized by a lack of focus and implementation procedures. Shortly after, the "re-launching process" drifted away under the weight of Argentina's economic collapse.

10.   The analysis focuses on Argentina and Brazil because their policy choices carried most of the weight in MERCOSUR.

11.   The issue of distortions to investment location was particularly divisive in the case of the automobile industry. For a discussion of the extent and treatment of policy and structural asymmetries in MERCOSUR, see Bouzas (2003).

12.   The inducements for the smaller partners to accept a suboptimal CET from the standpoint of their production structures may have been the expected gains from better and more stable access to the large Brazilian market. However, as Brazil proved reluctant to resign its policy discretion on market access conditions, one of the dynamic payoffs implicit in the initial deal failed to materialize, thus altering the perceived net benefits of the transaction. This, in turn, reduced the incentives for smaller partners to comply.

13.   It is remarkable, for example, that MERCOSUR has no formal mechanism to cope with the effects of intraregional trade flows due to unforeseen macroeconomic shocks. In effect, since 1994, MERCOSUR has had no safeguard mechanism in force, allegedly under the argument, largely supported by the Brazilian government, that such a mechanism would be incompatible with a customs union!

REFERENCES

Bouzas, Roberto, and Hernán Soltz. 2001. "Institutions and Regional Integration: The Case of MERCOSUR." In *Regional Integration in Latin America and the Caribbean: The Political Economy of Open Regionalism*, ed. Víctor Bulmer-Thomas. London: Institute of Latin American Studies (ILAS) Series.

Bouzas, Roberto. 2002. "MERCOSUR Ten Years After: Learning Process or Dejà-Vú?" In *Paths to Regional Integration: The Case of MERCOSUR*, ed. Joseph S. Tulchin, Ralph H. Espach and Heather A. Golding. Washington, D.C.: The Woodrow Wilson Center for International Scholars (WWCIS).

Bouzas, Roberto. 2003. "Mechanisms for Compensating the Asymmetrical Effects of Regional Integration and Globalization: The Case of MERCOSUR." Paper presented at the seminar, "Confronting the Challenges of Regional Development in LAC," IDB Governors' Meeting, Milan, March.

Bouzas, Roberto, Pedro da Motta Veig, and Ramón Torrent. 2003. "In Depth Analysis of Mercosur Integration, Its Prospects and the Effects Thereof on the Market Access of EU Goods, Services and Investment." Observatory of Globalization, University of Barcelona. <http://mkaccdb.eu.int/study/studies/32.doc>.

da Motta Veiga, Pedro. 1999. "Brasil en el MERCOSUR: Política y Economía en un Proyecto de Integración." In *MERCOSUR. Entre la Realidad y la Utopía*, ed. Jorge Campbell. Buenos Aires: CEI-Nuevohacer.

Frankel, Jeffrey. 1997. *Regional Trading Blocs*. Washington, D.C.: Institute for International Economics.

Heymann, Daniel. 1999. "Interdependencias y Políticas Macroeconómicas: Reflexiones sobre el MERCOSUR." In *MERCOSUR. Entre la Realidad y la Utopía*, ed. Jorge Campbell. Buenos Aires: CEI-Nuevohacer.

Olarreaga, Marcelo, and Isidro Soloaga. 1998. "Endogenous Tariff Formation: The Case of Mercosur." *The World Bank Economic Review* 12 (2, May): 297-320.

Chapter Three

MEXICO: EXPORT PROMOTION, NORTH AMERICAN FREE TRADE AGREEMENT, AND THE FUTURE OF NORTH AMERICAN ECONOMIC INTEGRATION

Gustavo Vega-Cánovas

INTRODUCTION

L ike many other developing countries in the mid-1980s, Mexico adopted a growth strategy based on export promotion as a means of surmounting the debt crisis, which had exploded at the beginning of that decade, and of recovering sustained economic growth. By adopting this new development policy, Mexico implemented an extraordinary program of macro- and microeconomic reforms that transformed the Mexican economy from being highly protected, with pervasive participation of the state, into an economy open to international markets, thus transferring the initiative to the private sector.

With this new, more open economy, Mexico shifted away from specialization in the production of raw materials and mining products, mainly oil, and moved toward becoming an economy that supplied manufacturing exports of increasing sophistication and complexity. At the same time, Mexico diversified its sources of foreign exchange.

In the 1990s, Mexico also negotiated a series of free trade agreements, the most important of which was the 1994 North American Free Trade Agreement (NAFTA) with Canada and the United States, which helped Mexico make strong inroads in the international market. By 2001, Mexico was ranked thirteenth among the most important exporting nations in the world and nineteenth among importing ones — Mexico had turned into the most important exporting and importing country in Latin America. Foreign trade became a vital factor for the economy as a source of raw materials, industrial inputs, and capital goods, as well as for its overall economic growth and welfare. Likewise, in spite of having experienced the most dramatic financial crisis in its history between 1994 and 1995 (even though the Asian financial crisis unleashed by the 1997 Thai devaluation raised questions about the viability of emerging markets), Mexico experienced robust rates of economic growth throughout the second half of the 1990s and was the preferred host economy for foreign direct investment (FDI) in Latin America after Brazil.[1]

This chapter evaluates the role of trade liberalization and NAFTA in the achievement of economic development in Mexico since the 1980s. It is argued that trade liberalization, in general, and NAFTA, in particular, have helped Mexico become a successful exporter of manufactured products and an attractive location for FDI. Trade liberalization and NAFTA have also made important contributions to Mexico's financial recovery and economic growth during the 1980s and 1990s. These contributions are highlighted by exploring not only economic performance since trade liberalization and NAFTA went into effect, but also by considering the domestic and global environment that Mexico confronted in the mid-1980s and final half of the 1990s.

This chapter also addresses the policy opportunities and dilemmas Mexico currently faces in its trade policy as a result of the recent changes in the international environment, in particular, the effects of the September 11, 2001, attacks on the United States. The events of 9-11 have forced Mexico to look for a closer economic and security relationship with the United States to ensure that closure of the Mexico-U.S. border does not occur again, as it did after 9-11. This closer relationship, which so far covers borders matters, should also be expanded to include a program for Mexican migrant workers and the legalization of immigrant workers already living in the United States, both necessary steps in the overall economic integration of North America. Some recommendations are made regarding the type of immigration agreement that could satisfy security concerns and facilitate further deepening of economic integration in North America.

TRADE POLICY: FROM IMPORT SUBSTITUTION TO EXPORT-LED GROWTH

Mexico's decision to adopt an export-oriented policy resulted from a number of internal and external factors. From the early 1950s to the early 1980s, Mexico, like most countries in Latin America, employed a growth strategy based on import substitution that emphasized growth of the internal market. The import substitution industrialization (ISI) model delivered results during the 1950s and 1960s; however, it began to stumble in the 1970s due to persistent inefficiency resulting from a protected industrial structure. Moreover, industrial growth did not match the demand for new jobs required by Mexico's labor force.

By the early 1980s, Mexico had become dangerously dependent on oil for its revenues. The 1982 collapse of international oil prices made it impossible for Mexico to service its foreign debt, which by then had reached almost US$100 billion. Mexico's debt crisis not only threatened its economy, but also the stability of the international financial system. Mexico was forced to negotiate a rescue package with the International Monetary Fund (IMF) that emphasized fiscal and monetary stringency, deregulation, privatization, and liberalization of trade and investment policies.

Trade liberalization started in 1983 with a moderate unilateral reduction of import tariffs and a gradual elimination of official prices, quotas, licenses, and import permits. In 1986, Mexico became a member of the General Agreement on Tariffs and Trade (GATT), and its maximum tariff was bound at 50 percent, down from 100 percent (Story 1986; Torres and Falk 1989). In 1987, Mexico went even further in unilateral liberalization when it set the highest import duty at 20 percent. These policy decisions were consistent with the Economic Solidarity Pact (Pacto de Solidaridad Económica), a corporatist arrangement that incorporated business and labor. The pact aimed to stabilize the economy by reducing inflation, an objective shared by business and labor. It also helped legitimize difficult economic policy choices, such as trade opening.

By 1994, Mexico's highest import tariff was at 20 percent, and its import schedule was substantially simplified. Almost all import licenses disappeared, and restrictions on foreign investment were eliminated for most industries and substantially reduced for many others.[2] The dismantling of policy instruments that had granted protection to Mexico's industries transformed the economy into one of the most open among developing countries;[3] it also helped to change the composition of merchandise trade during this period. In 1985, raw materials and mining products made up 62.4 percent of total exports, of which the most important was crude oil. Starting in 1986, this proportion began to decrease until, in 1993, it reached a level of 19.6 percent, of which oil was 14.2 percent. At the same time, manufacturing exports grew every year from 1986 to 1993, showing a trend toward the production of more complex goods in terms of design, production, and commercialization.

Mexico's structural reforms also made it the darling of foreign investors. Few predicted anything but a promising future for the Mexican economy. In 1994, annual inflation was down to 7 percent from 160 percent in 1987. Between 1987 and 1994, real gross domestic product (GDP) grew by 23 percent, after a decline of 8 percent between 1981 and 1987, and real wages increased by close to 20 percent, after having plummeted 30 percent between 1981 and 1987. The government's fiscal deficit, which in the early 1980s was as high as 15 percent of GDP, declined to 2 percent in 1994. Debt restructuring also strengthened the confidence of national and international investors in the Mexican economy, and until 1993, capital inflows reached unprecedented high levels (Kehoe 1995, 141).

Despite these positive indicators, however, there were signs of weakness and vulnerability in Mexico's economic foundations. Since 1989, Mexico had been accumulating growing current account deficits that reached $29.7 billion by 1994, 6.8 percent of GDP. The semifixed exchange rate had caused real appreciation of the currency since 1991 and had undermined competitiveness in the context of liberalized trade and widened the current account deficit. Critics questioned the model's sustainability and suggested a devaluation was needed. However, the Mexican government rejected such criticism and argued that devaluation would ignite inflation and damage international confidence. Besides, foreign capital inflows were enough to finance the current account deficit, and growth of imports, which were mainly composed of capital goods and inputs, were making the Mexican economy more competitive over time.

Subsequent events proved otherwise. A series of domestic and external developments led to a collapse of the currency in December 1994 and what was subsequently called the "peso crisis of 1995." In addition to Mexico's Chiapas uprising and highly publicized political assassinations, rapid growth in the United States caused the Federal Reserve to raise interest rates, which made U.S. securities far more attractive to international investors than investments in Mexico (Kessler 1998). The cumulative result of domestic, political, and international economic events was a dramatic reduction of foreign capital inflows. Nominal interest rates increased substantially. To prevent further interest rate increases, the government expanded domestic credit and converted short-term, peso-denominated government liabilities known as CETES or *cetes* (Certificados de la Tesorería de la Federación or Federal Treasury Certificates), which were falling due to dollar-denominated bonds, known as *tesobonos*. As noted by several analysts, by late 1994, capital flight out of Mexico had depleted foreign exchange reserves and made further defense of the peso unsustainable (Naim and Edwards 1997).

MEXICO'S NETWORK OF FREE TRADE AGREEMENTS

During the 1990s, Mexico became an active player in international trade. It sought to maintain an agenda of trade liberalization that served to open markets for its exports and to attract productive investment. While Mexico had undertaken a unilateral trade and liberalization policy during the 1980s to recover macroeconomic stability, negotiations with its main trading partners were needed to reap the full benefits of openness. Because its development strategy relied heavily on exports, market access was essential.

At the multilateral level, Mexico participated in the Uruguay Round of GATT, largely to counteract global protectionist trends. Later, World Trade Organization (WTO) membership granted Mexico a clear and transparent set of rules for its export activities, reducing the likelihood of unilateral trade restrictions. For Mexico, WTO membership contributed to the durability, stability, and predictability of its liberalization reforms.[4] GATT/WTO commitments diminished Mexico's ability to use economic instruments, such as subsidies or production and export requirements, to promote industrialization (GATT 1994).

However, Mexico's most important strategy has been the negotiation of bilateral free trade agreements. During the 1990s, Mexico negotiated a series of free trade agreements with its most important trading partners and pursued a strategy of "aggressively dismantling its trade barriers" with other Latin American markets (Schrader 1999). Mexico's network of free trade agreements provides a high degree of credibility and permanence to the domestic policy reforms undertaken since the mid-1980s and reassures private investors that Mexico will not revert to economic isolation.[5]

Mexico's first comprehensive free trade agreement was NAFTA, which served as a model for the negotiation of free trade agreements with countries in Latin America and beyond. Mexico's strategy is to become a trade hub, where producers can take advantage of preferential access to a large number of markets.

THE NORTH AMERICAN FREE TRADE AGREEMENT

Without a doubt, the most important of Mexico's free trade agreements is NAFTA. In 1990, the Mexican government announced its intention to negotiate a free trade agreement with the United States, a path-breaking decision that challenged all previous conceptions of United States-Mexico relations.[6] Mexico's decision to negotiate NAFTA resulted from the following combination of international and domestic factors: the 1989 Canada-United States Free Trade Agreement, the scarcity of foreign capital outside North America, the emergence of regional economic blocs,[7] and the limited potential for the multilateral trading system under the Uruguay Round of GATT (del Castillo and Vega 1995; Lustig, Bosworth, and Lawrence 1992).

Mexico pursued a free trade agreement with the United States to promote and secure access to its most important market and to contest U.S. protectionist practices, which had impeded access to competitive exports in the past. In addition, trade integration with a rich country like the United States would yield benefits beyond trade efficiency by stimulating FDI and encouraging technology transfers. Given the lack of domestic savings and high level of foreign indebtedness, Mexico saw foreign capital investment as an indispensable financial resource for its productive activities.

NAFTA is the first reciprocal free trade treaty among two industrialized countries and a developing one. It is based on principles of equality and full reciprocity, in spite of vast asymmetries. (The size of the Mexican economy, for example, is just 5 percent that of the United States.) NAFTA created the second largest free trade area in the world, with almost 400 million people and one-third of world GDP (around US$8 trillion). NAFTA also seeks to encourage investment in member countries, especially direct investment in plants and equipment, and to further the integration of the three North American countries through changes in institutions that will facilitate cooperation via procedures to expedite the resolution of disputes. NAFTA also includes supplemental cooperation agreements designed to encourage protection of the environment and improve and enforce labor laws in the region.

STRUCTURAL CHANGE IN MEXICO SINCE THE 1980S

Mexico has undergone a strong process of structural change since it decided to open its economy. Table 1 shows the performance of the Mexican economy during successive periods, beginning with the administration of President Miguel de la Madrid, who initiated the opening of the economy (1983-1988). This period was followed by the term of President Carlos Salinas de Gortari (1989-1994), the peso crisis of 1995, and the period of successful stabilization and growth during the tenure of President Ernesto Zedillo (1995-2000). Information about the first years of the administration of President Vicente Fox is also included.

Macroeconomic Overview

The changes that have taken place in the Mexican economy before and after NAFTA can easily be seen. Although Mexico suffered a devaluation and financial crisis in 1995, only one year after NAFTA went into effect, the crisis was not caused by free trade. The high current account deficit, which reached $29.7 billion in 1994, or 6.8 percent of GDP, was instead caused by heavy overvaluation of the peso exchange rate because the currency had been used since 1989 as an anchor to bring

Table 1. Economic Performance by Periods 1983-2001 ($ million)

	1983-88	1989-94	1995	1996-2000	2001
GDP (annual growth %)	1.1	3.9	-6.2	5.5	-0.3
GDP in manufacturing (annual growth %)	2.3	3.5	-4.8	6.4	-3.9
Manufacturing employment (annual growth %)	0.9	-1.2	-8.9	2.5	-4.3
Trade balance ($bn annual average)	7.0	-12.2	7.1	-2.9	-9.9
Exports (annual growth %)	16.7	12.2	30.6	16.0	-4.8
Imports (annual growth %)	12.0	19.1	-8.7	19.3	-3.5
Manufactured exports ($bn annual average)	7.3	33.3	66.6	109.7	141.3
Current account balance ($bn annual average)	1.8	-10.7	-1.6	-11.6	-17.4
Foreign direct investment ($bn annual average)	2.3	4.6	9.5	11.8	27.7
U.S. GDP (annual growth %)	4.4	2.4	2.7	4.1	1.2
Foreign debt, end of period ($bn)	101.8	153.6	176.5	173.7	172.2

Source: INEGI, U.S. Department of Commerce, and Ecanal.

inflation down. NAFTA undoubtedly accelerated trade growth in 1994 and, thus, indirectly helped to precipitate the balance-of-payments crisis. But such a crisis would have occurred in any event, as the economy had accumulated considerable distortions from the overvalued peso.

Free trade was, however, crucial to Mexico's quick recovery after 1995, as Table 1 shows. High import growth in 1994 caused the external deficit to rise from -(minus)$23.4 billion to -$29.7 billion; when the peso was adjusted downward, the deficit fell dramatically. There was unprecedented growth in exports, from $51.9 billion in 1993 to $166.4 billion in 2000, which helped overcome this crisis within a short period of time. The current account deficit fell to -$1.6 billion in 1995 and rose only to -$2.3 billion in 1996.

As a result, for the first time in more than 30 years, Mexico saw a reduction in its external current account deficit, even in the presence of high import growth, which was on average 19.3 percent per year from 1996 to 2000. The current account deficit was only -$11.6 billion on average and never exceeded -$18 billion, including the year 2001, when exports to the United States fell to -5 percent. The low current account deficit meant that the economy could grow faster than before without suffering balance-of-payments crises, as had been the case from the 1970s through 1994.

Exports of goods and services jumped from 19.4 percent of GDP in 1985 to 32.8 percent in 2000. Employment in manufacturing, not having grown for 15 years, grew 2.5 percent per year from 1996 to 2000, only interrupted in 2001 by the U.S. recession. Another significant change was that as Mexico became more integrated with North America, in 2001 its economy adjusted downward following the U.S. recession, avoiding an expansion of domestic demand when exports were flat.

Since 1995, Mexico has had a floating exchange rate, which became validated as the appropriate regime, for it allowed Mexico to adjust smoothly to external shocks from the Asian and Russian crises of 1997-1998. The floating exchange rate has been responsible for much of the success of Mexican exports and for the control of the trade deficit within manageable limits.

Privatization was another important change in the macroeconomy, for Mexico had a very large and inefficient state-owned sector, engaged in steel, fertilizers, hotels, banks, insurance, telephones, and many stakes in manufacturing industries. The state withdrew from all of these industries. Privatization was a sound policy because it reduced the size of the state and budgetary transfers. But clearly one problem was that many privatizations during the term of Salinas lacked transparency and ended up in bankruptcies after the peso devaluation in 1995.

New privatization projects are now focused on electricity, gas, and a new regime for toll roads. President Fox, however, who had to contend with the negative experiences of the 1990s, especially the high cost of rescuing banks that had been privatized, must assure the Congress and the public that his administration will not repeat past mistakes and vices before it obtains broad support for privatizations.

FOREIGN DIRECT INVESTMENT

Table 1 shows that FDI jumped after NAFTA was established, which led to major changes in ownership across sectors and transformed Mexican companies into more efficiently run firms by changing the way management operated. FDI was an average of $4.6 billion per year during 1989-1994 and almost tripled to $11.8 billion during 1996-2000. It reached a peak of $27.7 billion in 2001.

Apart from the greater flows of capital and technology, FDI has led to qualitative improvements in corporate governance, an area until recently ignored by Mexican regulators. That is, for the first time, regulations were issued in 2001 establishing rules for the conduct of boards of directors and for the protection of minority rights (*Indice del Diario Oficial de la Federación*, 2001, "Ley del Mercado de Valores").

NAFTA has been instrumental in making Mexico more attractive and secure for foreign investors because they know that the free trade regime is permanent, removing a possible cause for uncertainty. The agreement also amplifies the size of the potential market to investors operating in any of the three countries.

NAFTA contains a precept guaranteeing national treatment status to any investor from the region investing in any of the three countries. Moreover, in practice, it has helped create a climate more propitious to relaxing restrictions, as foreign investment is more capable of maneuvering across economic activities, which the public gradually saw as an opportunity for more jobs and higher incomes. In 1995, the first foreign banks were permitted to increase their equity shares in Mexican banks to acquire control, and gas distribution was open to private investors. Later on, most of the banks were acquired by foreign investors.

The positive effects of FDI have become clear across sectors of activity. The modernization of management and work standards has been visible in all banks acquired by foreigners. The contribution of foreign partners to modernizing management of family-owned businesses has also been substantial. In many of the largest public firms, professional managers are now more prominent than they were in the early 1990s, while boards of directors are much more active. Investors, for their part, demand greater information on companies' operations.

Under NAFTA, foreign capital flows to Mexico have revitalized older sectors and created new ones. Foreign investment has contributed to the establishment of state-of-the-art plants that are internationally competitive. Three industrial sectors that stand out — automobiles, electronics, and textiles — which represent core sectors from traditional, heavy, and high technology industries, have become more dynamic and competitive since the agreement became effective in 1994.

Sectors that have not received the same kind of capital inflows have not enjoyed the same kind of success. For example, Mexico's agriculture sector has shown mixed results under NAFTA. A dynamic export-oriented agribusiness sector coexists with a traditional self-subsistence agriculture sector. The uneven performance of agriculture reveals what NAFTA really is — an agreement to reduce tariff barriers and promote trade and investment flows — and the limits to what it can deliver. NAFTA is only an instrument that creates opportunities for growth in certain economic sectors; it is not a solution for transforming the entire economy.

LABOR MARKETS

NAFTA increased industrial and services employment, offsetting losses of jobs in farming. In those sectors where employment increased, output increased at a faster rate so that productivity is considerably higher than it was before NAFTA. This explains why there has been a steady increase in real wages, which continue to catch up with higher wage levels in North America.

Nevertheless, wages increased from very low levels, after major macro crises wiped out almost one-half of their purchasing power in the early 1980s. In the more recent period of 1998 to 2001, wages have shown a steady upward trend, despite fluctuations in output and employment (Instituto Nacional de Estadística Geografía e Informática — INEGI).

Labor productivity in the manufacturing industry, measured crudely as the ratio of output to employment, grew 38 percent during the 1980s until 1990, that is, by 3.3 percent per year. From 1990 to 1993, this growth accelerated to 6.4 percent, and from 1993 to 2001, it slowed down to 4.8 percent (Ramírez De la O 2000).

NAFTA has been a major catalyst for the increase in productivity, which has been highly correlated with exports (Ramírez De la O 1998). But even with such improvements in productivity, labor markets in Mexico are still much less flexible than in North America. Workers continue to enjoy heavy protection against shedding (layoffs) or relocation; collective labor contracts contain a myriad of uneconomic or costly conditions for companies; and measures to reduce employment are, in practice, extremely difficult to implement. In 2001, the combination of the U.S. recession and a strong peso exchange rate led some multinational firms in manufacturing to close down operations for the first time in many years, blaming high labor costs (Luhnow 2002). In fact, this is one cause for the fall in manufacturing employment of -3.9 percent last year.

SECTORAL DEVELOPMENTS OF NAFTA

Table 2 shows the dramatic increase in exports from Mexico, from $41 billion in 1990 to $51.9 billion in 1993 (8.1 percent per year) and $166.4 billion in 2000 (15 percent per year from 1990 and 18.1 percent from 1993). On this measure, the post-NAFTA period recorded most of the growth in exports.

Table 2. Total Exports of Mexico and Selected Manufactures ($ million)

	1990	1993	2000
Exports	**41,046**	**51,886**	**166,424**
Crude Oil	8,921	6,485	14,884
Manufactures	**29.062**	**42,500**	**146,439**
Textiles	1,291	2,770	12,512
Chemicals	1,830	2,558	5,971
Glass	258	673	1,561
Steel	938	1,399	2,983
Transport Equipment	12,876	14,514	51,143
Electrical, Electronics	7,022	14,032	49,156

Source: Bank of Mexico, "Indicadores del Sector Externo," various years.

Table 3 shows that imports recorded a similarly high increase, so that the link between export and import growth became accentuated.

Table 3. Total Imports of Mexico and Selected Products ($million)

	1990	1993	2000
Imports	**41,579**	**65,367**	**174,480**
Agriculture	2,265	2,393	4,855
Manufactures	**28,341**	**61,568**	**165,221**
Textiles	1,706	3,525	10,035
Chemicals	2,929	4,855	11,425
Plastics	785	3,404	9,277
Steel	1,628	3,312	7,653
Transport Equipment	13,821	16,770	44,497
Electrical, Electronics	7,265	12,511	44,744

Source: Bank of Mexico, "Indicadores del Sector Externo," various years.

The Auto Sector

The auto sector has been NAFTA's most dynamic sector. Mexico's exports (see Table 2), which designate the auto sector as "transport equipment," jumped from $12.8 billion in 1990 to $14.5 billion in 1993 and $51.1 billion in 2000.

Mexico's export drive started before NAFTA came into force in 1994 but did not truly accelerate until after NAFTA was established.

The automotive industry plays a crucial role in the economies of Mexico, Canada, and the United States in terms of exports, employment generation, and technological and industrial development. Thus, it is not surprising that the automotive sector was singled out as particularly sensitive during the NAFTA negotiations. From the Mexican perspective, the sector is not only the largest exporter and importer of manufactured goods, but it is also a prime example of the kind of intra-industry trade NAFTA was designed to boost. Free trade allows firms that sell to the entire North American market to relocate their production facilities among NAFTA countries to minimize costs and take full advantage of specialization and economies of scale.

The auto industry in Mexico has taken full advantage of trade and investment policies established under NAFTA. It has gone through a restructuring process that has enabled it to increase competitiveness and to integrate successfully into the North American and world auto market.

The automotive industry has contributed to growth and job creation. Although the 1995 peso crisis had a devastating effect on Mexican auto production, with domestic sales falling by 80 percent, NAFTA made it possible for the industry to recover with remarkable speed. Vehicle production and auto parts production represent 2 percent of Mexico's GDP and more than 11 percent of Mexico's manufacturing GDP. The auto industry accounts for 20 percent of Mexico's total exports and 22 percent of total manufacture exports (INEGI).

Production jumped from 1.055 million units of cars and trucks in 1993 to 1.854 million in 2001, an annual growth rate of 7.3 percent. Exports of cars and trucks were 493,194 and 1.382 million, respectively, which represents growth of 13.8 percent per year from 1993 through 2001. Domestic sales of vehicles jumped from 576,025 to 918,835 units, growing 6 percent per year from 1993 to 2000, despite the deep recession in 1995, when sales plummeted -69 percent followed by only a mild recovery (INEGI).

Employment in manufacturing in the auto industry reached 313,157 workers in 1993, rising to 432,733 in 2001, a 4.1 percent increase per year. Comparing this figure with that of output growth, it can be inferred there was an annual increase in productivity per worker of 3.1 percent per year. While employment levels for vehicle producers only rose mildly from 1993 to 2001, employment in the auto parts sector increased by 4.8 percent per year (INEGI), significantly higher than the increase of 2.6 percent per year recorded for the entire manufacturing sector, as was shown in Table 1.

Under NAFTA, the Mexican auto industry has become highly integrated with its Canadian and U.S. counterparts, so that vehicles made in Mexico have a high U.S. and Canadian content. Trade in automotive products has consequently exploded. U.S.-Mexico trade in vehicles and auto parts expanded from $14.6 billion to $47.1 billion between 1993 and 2000. Almost 25 percent of U.S. auto parts imports come from Mexico.[9] Around 90 percent of Mexico's vehicle exports are sold in the U.S. market, 6 percent in Canada, and 3 percent in Germany. Mexico has become the second largest export market, after Canada, for both U.S. vehicles and auto parts. In 2000, U.S. car exports to Mexico totaled $4.3 billion (USITC 2001).

Mexico, largely as a result of NAFTA, is now the eighth largest global producer of cars and fifth largest for trucks. The good performance of the auto industry makes it key for future integration with North America. Moreover, the Mexican government is keen to create conditions to attract more FDI and is in close consultation with the auto industry regarding taxes and other factors that affect costs and prices. The next few years will see greater commitments by the government to facilitate expansion and productivity growth in this industry.

The Textile and Clothing Industry

A major goal for Mexico during NAFTA negotiations was to gain improved access to the U.S. market for its textile and clothing products through full elimination of tariffs and multilateral fiber agreement (MFA) quotas. Prior to NAFTA, the so-called "Special Regime" enabled Mexican apparel assembled from U.S. fabric to benefit from flexible quotas and the application of U.S. tariffs only on the non-U.S. value added (in other words, "round trip" U.S. fabric was free from duty). Intensive utilization of the Special Regime by Mexican exporters established the basis for a fast growing garment industry and created many jobs for low-skilled workers. Under NAFTA, immediate elimination of MFA quotas, coupled with substantial cuts in exceptionally high tariffs as NAFTA entered into force, extended the gains achieved under the Special Regime. Benefits were also extended to Mexican fabric producers, who became qualifying suppliers under the complex NAFTA rules of origin.[10]

After eight and one-half years under NAFTA, performance of the Mexican textile and clothing industry bears out initial expectations. In 1995, the Mexican industry suffered from the collapse of the domestic economy. Like the auto industry, it was able to export its way to recovery thanks to preferential market access. After a sharp 6-percent decline in 1995, the industry grew by 15, 10, and 5 percent in 1996, 1997, and 1998, respectively (Sistema de Información Empresarial Mexicano 2000).

In 2000, Mexico's textile and clothing industry exported $11 billion, contributing more than 6.5 percent of Mexico's total exports. Two-way Mexico-United States trade in textiles and clothing increased from $4.1 billion in 1993 to $15.3 billion in 2000 (Sistema de Información Empresarial Mexicano 2000). In 1998, Mexico became the leading supplier of textile and clothing products to the United States, displacing China.[11] Significantly, Mexico has also become the largest market for U.S. textile products.[12] Today, Mexico's textile and clothing industry includes almost 1,200 *maquiladora* (assembly) plants, employing close to 286,000 workers.

The Electronics Industry

The electronics industry, in a fashion similar to the automotive and textile/clothing sectors, became a major export player for Mexico as a result of trade and investment opening promoted by NAFTA. Mexico has established itself as the main trading partner for the United States in electronics, surpassing such key players as

Japan, Canada, Taiwan, Korea, and Singapore. In 2000, both Mexican exports of electronics to the United States and U.S. exports to Mexico amounted to about $34 billion in each direction. Electronics trade between Mexico and Canada rose from $210 million in 1993 to $773 million in 2000. Zero tariffs and a stable investment climate are behind these trade statistics (Parliament of Canada, *Partners in North America*, Chapter 2, 2002).

NAFTA has encouraged Mexican production of sophisticated electronic products that go beyond mere assembly, with significant research and development now conducted in Mexico (Carrillo and Hualde 1997). The 1970s stereotype of low-cost, labor-intensive assembly no longer characterizes the new generation of electronics production (Lowe and Kenney 1999).

Some 570 *maquiladora* plants now operate in the electrical and electronics sectors, representing almost 12 percent of the total number of *maquiladora* plants in Mexico. In 2000, these firms employed approximately 350,000 workers, an increase of 80 percent over 1993 levels (Secretaría de Economía, "Mexican Maquiladora Industry," June 2002).

The trade and investment story for electronics, as for autos, textiles, and clothing, finds firms repositioning themselves through mergers, acquisitions, and greenfield (new plant) investments and restructuring their chains of supply. The result is far deeper integration of the North American economies. The rewards for Mexico have been higher productivity in favored sectors, a strengthened position in the world economy, and booming intra-industry trade.

The Agriculture Sector

Compared with its strengthening of the manufacturing sector, NAFTA has had quite different effects upon Mexico's two-tier agriculture sector: a booming agribusiness sector coexists with a self-subsistence, backward, and traditional sector. While the agribusiness sector has increased its exports as a result of improved market access into the United States and Canada, the traditional sector has been unable to take advantage of NAFTA's benefits in terms of investment and increased production.

Agriculture accounts for less than 5 percent of Mexico-United States trade. While trade in this sector has grown, export dynamism is concentrated among fruit and vegetable producers in northern and western Mexico, who have access to credit and have traditionally been quite competitive. These producers do not engage in traditional Mexican subsistence agriculture, which is heavily concentrated in the central and southern parts of Mexico. The dichotomy between subsistence *ejido*-type production and export-led agriculture pushed the government to introduce a variety of domestic support policies that side-step NAFTA, so that the Mexican peasantry's livelihood could be sustained.[13]

Regional Effects of NAFTA

Exports and investment have been the leading forces of growth in Mexico for the past five years. Both are closely linked to NAFTA, but for similar reasons their effects have been uneven across regions.

The main driver behind exports and manufacturing activity has been the northern region, especially the border. South of the border, the industrial area north of Mexico City, Guadalajara, Monterrey, and Aguascalientes have seen growth in industrial activity and in exports. These regions are all located in the northern corridor from the center of Mexico to the northeast and in the western region of Guadalajara, where foreign firms in electronics have proliferated in recent years.

Regional disparities have increased since NAFTA came into effect because the south of Mexico has not attracted as much activity as the north. This problem has been aggravated by budget constraints, preventing the government from investing in infrastructure and social services. Lack of opportunities in the south, while exports and activity have grown in the north, have resulted in large flows of migrants from southern states to the northern border area; nearly all of these people eventually travel into the United States illegally.

The relatively high growth experienced in the north has placed additional pressures on public infrastructure and social services, leading in some instances to extremely poor environmental conditions, a lack of water, and a dearth of other public services in northern cities. With this in mind, President Fox's government announced an ambitious plan, called Plan Puebla-Panama, to invest in infrastructure and connect southeastern Mexico with Central America through more roads, telecommunications, and seaports. This plan, however, depends entirely on the successful integration of Mexico with North America. But can successful integration with North America be maintained and enhanced in light of recent events in the United States, particularly the attacks of September 11, 2001? In the next section, the significance of the 9-11 attacks for the future of Mexico-United States economic relations is discussed.

NAFTA, SEPTEMBER 11TH, AND THE NEED FOR SECURE, OPEN BORDERS

History shows that stunning events can force a new perception of the world and a new set of policies. In 1941, Japan's attack on Pearl Harbor forced the American public to follow President Franklin Roosevelt's lead, abandon the entrenched post-World War I policy of isolationism, and adopt a new policy of active engagement in world turmoil. In 2003, the tragic events of September 11, 2001, are still being debated in the United States. President George W. Bush has called for a global war on terrorism, based on a new doctrine of preemptive strikes and the creation of a new Department of Homeland Security with extensive powers. How these initiatives will play out remains to be seen. But the same openness that fosters economic integration is evidently a great source of vulnerability. Thus, the United States has begun to adopt an array of new policies to make its domestic territory and its borders more secure.

For Canada and Mexico, the new U.S. security policies had immediate and shocking implications. On September 11, 2001, the U.S. authorities took a number of immediate measures at the country's north and south borders. U.S. Customs went into a high level of alert, which still exists (Level One: sustained and intense inspection). For several days thereafter at border areas, automobile traffic was delayed for several hours, and commercial traffic for up to 12 to 15 hours. Just-in-time manufacturers, particularly auto companies and Mexican goods exporters, were in crisis. By some estimates, unexpected shutdowns due to parts shortages cost automakers up to $25,000 per minute in lost production. Cross-border retail shopping and tourism plunged. The U.S. Customs Service beefed up its staffing along the border and introduced legislation to triple the number of agents. The Immigration and Naturalization Service (INS) announced plans to introduce an entry/exit system by 2003 at airports and seaports and at the 50 largest land entry points by 2004. This system would require visitors, including those from Mexico, to have their names recorded every time they enter and leave the country.

As these measures were adopted, Mexico's choices seemed to narrow between either taking a leap toward deeper integration and being "inside the U.S. tent" or seeing the bilateral border re-erected and being left outside. Debates about deeper integration predated September 11, as did work to negotiate new initiatives that would allow more Mexican migrant workers into the United States and legalize workers already living in the United States, but the range of possibilities changed that day. Deeper integration became a matter of national security; if Mexico wanted to preserve openness, it had to pay more attention to security.

Longer term, the impact of a permanent increase in border transaction costs acts like a tariff, particularly on Mexican and Canadian goods entering the United States. For example, the higher cost of exports causes U.S. customers to switch to cheaper domestic and alternative foreign suppliers. Mexico's exchange rate depreciates, as the demand for Mexican pesos declines and more expensive imports undermine Mexican living standards. The higher costs of moving people, goods, and services also erodes Mexico's productivity performance. Another longer-term impact could be the reconsideration of plans to invest in Mexico by countries like Japan and those in the European Union. Increasingly, such countries can be expected to head for the United States with new investments. Why invest in Mexico or Canada if border delays are to be a permanent factor in the other North American markets? Diversion of such investment would also undermine Mexico's productivity growth.

Mexico is not alone in its dilemma. Increased border security raises transaction costs around the world. Some estimates put the aggregate increase in transaction costs at 1 to 2 percentage points. If these costs become permanent, some way will have to be found to offset the increase, for example, by negotiating — in the WTO or the Free Trade Area of the Americas — an across-the-board reduction in industrial tariffs of an equivalent or greater amount.

Mexico's response, after a period of uncertainty and delay, was to negotiate a Border Partnership Action Plan with the United States (U.S. Department of State 2001a). This accord is similar to the one signed on December 11, 2001, by the United States and Canada on Smart Borders.

The Mexico-U.S. Border Partnership Action Plan, signed on March 21, 2002, aims to achieve the following three objectives: to secure infrastructure, the flow of people, and the flow of goods. The securing of infrastructure aims to

... conduct a joint survey of ... [the] ... border to identify bottlenecks that impede the movement of goods and people . . . to develop integrated infrastructure investment plans ... and to conduct security assessments of critical infrastructure and take steps to protect them from terrorist attacks (U.S. Department of State 2001b).

The securing of the flow of people, in turn, aims to

... develop and implement technology systems at ports of entry to speed the flow of bona-fide travelers; to cooperate to identify individuals who pose threats to . .. [both] societies before they arrive in North America and to coordinate efforts to deter smuggling of third-country nationals and establish a joint U.S.-Mexico Advanced Passenger Information Exchange System (U.S. Department of State 2001b).

Finally, the securing of the flow of goods aims to

. . . implement technology-sharing programs to place non-intrusive inspection systems on cross-border rail lines and high-volume ports of entry; develop and implement technology systems to increase security at all points of the supply chain that link producers and consumers and to expand partnerships with the private sector to increase security of commercial shipments (U.S. Department of State 2001b).

In other words, all of these measures aim to "move the border away from the border," by fast-tracking precleared travelers at border points; employing integrated border enforcement teams staffed by the two countries with common objectives and integrated actions; using internet-based measures to simplify border transactions for small- and medium-sized enterprises; and encouraging infrastructure investment to improve access to border crossings through, for example, new highway bypasses that avoid congested downtown streets, along with a smart handling of goods and people at crossings. These are all sensible measures to secure an open border for goods and services. However, there are a number of sensitive measures that relate to the movement of people that are still undefined. Many measures will speed the cross-border movement of business travelers. Even permanent resident cards have been contemplated, including a biometric identifier, which is a system that identifies a person by means of reading the retina of the eye.

These measures will also undoubtedly increase confidence that people from third countries coming to North America do not have malicious intentions. But what is not clear from the Border Partnership Action Plan is the treatment to be given to Mexican migrant workers. Within this category, there are two groups: 1) those who already reside in the United States, a group whose number reached between 3 million and 4.5 million in the last decade (Pastor 2001; Camarota 2001); and 2) those who will come to the United States to work in the future. All that was mentioned when the Border Plan was announced by Presidents Fox and Bush in Monterrey, Mexico, was that the Cabinet-level migration group should continue negotiating this issue as directed in previous meetings between both presidents in Guanajuato and Washington, D.C. (Presidents Bush and Fox 2002). In these meetings, both presidents committed to a "grand bargain" in immigration flows from Mexico that seeks 1) alternatives to legalize or regularize migrants who already reside in the United States and 2) the adoption of a more liberal approach for those who will come to work in the United States in the future.

The question, however, is whether the "grand bargain" approach is still a viable initiative after the events of 9-11. For Mexico, no doubt, immigration is an issue that has to form part of the Border Partnership Action Plan. The Mexican government considers the legalization of immigrant workers a matter of human rights and social justice — and a necessary step in the economic integration of North America. In terms of economic benefits, legalization will help ensure that the Mexican economy receives a growing flow of worker remittances, which now run about $8 billion a year (U.S-Mexico Migration Panel 2001). The legalization of millions of Mexicans working in the United States, moreover, will improve their economic prospects and enable many to return to Mexico as successful entrepreneurs.

On the U.S. side, feelings are equally strong. Some Americans flat out oppose any increase in immigration. More immediately, the 9-11 attack and the subsequent deterioration of the U.S. economy put a damper on discussions of a "grand bargain" that began in the U.S. administration and Congress in the fall of 2001. The fact that many of the terrorists overstayed their visas cast a huge shadow over any legalization initiative.[14] The recession and rising unemployment gave fresh impetus to groups that opposed the opening of the border to migrant workers. According to a 2001 poll, many U.S. citizens grew more apprehensive after September 11 about what they perceive as weak border controls and voiced stronger support for enforcing immigration laws.[15]

What does this imply for a grand bargain on undocumented immigration and the concept of a Border Partnership Action Plan? The shifting political landscape in the United States has superimposed security concerns on top of the already difficult economic issues wrapped up in immigration policy. Any deal on immigration will need to enhance the security climate in comparison with the current regime.

What kinds of assurances could an immigration agreement provide that satisfy both security concerns and facilitates the creation of a secure border? The place to start is with the ongoing flow of migrant workers arriving in the United States. When the current recession gives way to a stronger economy, the United States should take up Fox's challenge, put forward shortly before the 9-11 attacks, to enlarge substantially the annual quota of Mexicans legally authorized to enter the United States on temporary (but renewable) work permits. In recent years, legal immigration from Mexico to the United States has numbered about 130,000 to 170,000 people annually (U.S. Department of Justice 2002). Illegal immigration numbers are, of course, speculative, but the INS places the annual average at about 150,000 between 1988 and 1996 (U.S. Immigration and Naturalization Service 2001).[16]

The way to tackle the flow problem is to start with an expanded number of legal visas, say, to 300,000, from Mexico annually. (This would amount to an increase of approximately 130,000 to 170,000 legal visas per year.) Additional visas should be issued on a work skill basis, including unskilled workers, not on a family reunification basis, which is the dominant test for current visas. However — and this is where security is underlined — to obtain a temporary work permit, the Mexican applicant would have to undergo a background check designed to avert security threats. Once inside the United States, temporary permit holders periodically would need to inform the INS, electronically (with the biometric identifier) or in person, of their address and place of employment. Permit holders could renew their permits as long as they were employed a certain number of months, say eight months, in each rolling 12-month period, had no felony convictions, and reported regularly to the INS. They could apply for U.S. citizenship after a certain number of years (for example, a cumulative five years as temporary permit holders). In the meantime, they should accumulate public social security and Medicare rights, as well as any private health or pension benefits because they will be paying U.S. taxes for these benefits.

Coupled with this substantial, but closely regulated, increase in temporary work permits, the United States and Mexico should embark on a joint border patrol program to reduce the flow of illegal crossings. The program should include features such as enhanced use of electronic surveillance, ineligibility for a temporary work permit for three years after an illegal crossing, and short-term misdemeanor detention (perhaps 30 days) in Mexico following an illegal crossing. No border patrol program will eliminate illegal crossings, but a joint program, coupled with a substantial temporary work permit initiative, could reduce the flow.

That leaves the very difficult question of perhaps 4 million undocumented Mexicans living and working in the United States. There is no magic solution. The foundation for my tentative suggestions is the proposition that nearly all of these people have made permanent homes in the United States, and they are not going to pick up their lives and return to Mexico. Under a set of appropriate circumstances, therefore, they should be granted residence permits with eligibility for citizenship. Appropriate circumstances would encompass the following two components: a threshold relating to illegal crossings and standards for individual applicants.

Proposal for a Resident Permit Program

- The resident permit program would be launched when the presidents of the United States and Mexico could jointly certify that the annual rate of illegal crossings does not exceed 50,000 persons. This would entail a reduction of more than two-thirds in illegal crossings estimated in recent years. The resident permit program would be suspended in years when the presidents could not make this certification.
- Individual eligibility would require evidence that the person resided in the United States prior to the announcement of the program. Otherwise, eligibility standards would parallel those for temporary work permits discussed earlier.
- An applicant for a residence permit who could provide satisfactory evidence of residence in the United States prior to the announcement of the program would not be subject to deportation (whether or not he or she met other eligibility requirements), as long as the applicant periodically reported a place of residence to the INS and committed no felony after the issuance of the residence permit.

- Holders of residence permits would be immediately eligible for public social security and Medicare benefits, as well as private health and pension benefits. They could apply for citizenship after five years.

CONCLUSIONS

This chapter analyzes the role that export promotion and NAFTA have had in the achievement of economic development in Mexico since the 1980s. It posits that export of manufactures and the rationalization and integration of industry that NAFTA has promoted at the regional level have made important contributions to Mexico's financial recovery and economic growth in the 1980s and 1990s and has allowed the Mexican economy to remain stable in the years 2001 and 2002, despite disruptions at the international level. The chapter highlights those contributions by exploring Mexico's economic performance since trade liberalization went into effect and by considering the domestic and global environment that the country confronted in the mid-1980s and final half of the 1990s. While the chapter recognizes the significant contributions of export promotion and NAFTA to financial recovery and economic growth, it also identifies the challenges that Mexico still faces in the near future. Export promotion and NAFTA have not bridged the gap that separates a two-tier agriculture sector, where a booming agribusiness sector coexists with a self-subsistence, backward, and traditional sector. Regional disparities have also increased after NAFTA was adopted, and the south of Mexico has not attracted as much activity as the north. This problem has been aggravated by budget constraints, preventing the government from investing in infrastructure and social services. The lack of opportunities in the south contrasts with growing exports, and activity in the north results in large flows of migrants from southern states to the northern border and eventually to illegal entry into the United States. In any case, tackling pending social problems will require continuing and enhanced integration with North America.

This chapter also highlights the policy opportunities and dilemmas Mexico faces in the near future if it is to continue to benefit from an export promotion policy and, particularly, North American integration. Up to 2001, Mexico's foreign trade policy was guided by a policy of trade diversification, which led Mexico to become a member of GATT in 1986 and a founder of the WTO in 1994, while signing FTAs with 32 countries across the Americas, Europe, and the Middle East. Despite this policy, Mexico saw its trade and financial flows concentrated more and more in the U.S. market as a result of the implementation of NAFTA. In 2002, close to 90 percent of Mexico's trade was with the United States, while more than 72 percent of outside FDI came from its northern neighbors.

The unexpected events of September 11, 2001, however, changed the way Mexicans and Americans viewed their relationship. Suddenly, access to the United States was closed. U.S. Customs went into a level of high alert that still exists. Just-in-time manufacturers, particularly auto companies and Mexican goods exporters, were in crisis. Cross-border retail shopping and tourism plunged. Upbeat talk of opening borders was replaced by more somber talk of homeland defense and security perimeters.

As new measures were adopted, Mexico's choices seemed to narrow between the following two options: either take a leap toward deeper integration and be "inside the U.S. tent" or see the bilateral border re-erected and be left outside. Deeper integration became a matter of national security; if Mexico wanted to preserve openness, it had to pay more attention to security. Mexico's response, after a period of uncertainty and delay, was to negotiate with the United States a Border Partnership Action Plan that was announced by the two countries in March 2002.

The Border Action Plan's main goal is to "move the border away from the border" by fast-tracking precleared travelers at border points; employing integrated border enforcement teams staffed by the two countries with common objectives and integrated actions; instituting Internet-based measures to simplify border transactions for small- and medium-sized enterprises; and increasing infrastructure investment to improve access to border crossings through, for example, new highway bypasses that avoid congested downtown streets along with a smart handling of goods and people at crossings. These are all sensible measures to secure an open border for goods and services. They will also necessarily imply a high degree of policy harmonization in a variety of areas.

The Border Plan, however, left an issue undefined that the Mexican government has shown a particular interest in negotiating with the United States since 2001, namely, the treatment of Mexican migrant workers already residing in the United States and handling of those who will come in the future. The Mexican government would like to negotiate an expanded program for Mexican workers and obtain a commitment from the United States to legalize those immigrant workers already residing in the United States as a matter of human rights and social justice — and as a necessary step in the economic integration of North America. The question, however, is whether such legalization is still a viable initiative after the events of September 11.

This chapter argues that the shifting political landscape in the United States has imposed security concerns on top of the already difficult economic issues wrapped up with immigration policy, and any deal on immigration will need to enhance the security climate in comparison with the current regime. This study outlines a possible immigration agreement that both satisfies security concerns and facilitates the creation of an open border.

NOTES

1.   Despite the sharp fall in gross national product (GDP) in 1995 as a result of the financial crisis, by 1996, GDP grew 5.2 percent and more than 4 percent in 1997. While almost every major economy in the world experienced an economic slowdown in 1998, Mexico's grew by 4.8 percent, the second highest rate among the 15 largest economies. In 1999 and 2000, the growth rates were 3.8 and 6.9 percents, respectively (Federal Reserve Bank of Dallas 1999; Bank of México Indicadores del Sector Externo 2000 and 2001).

2.   In 1984, Mexico began lifting restrictions on foreign ownership by changing the administrative regulations and guidelines of the 1973 Law to Promote Mexican Investment and to Regulate Foreign Investment. This law had empowered the Foreign Investments Commission (Comisión Nacional de Inversión Extranjera — CNIE) to waive restrictions on foreign investments when it deemed foreign participation to be in the public interest. Following the 1989 changes, the CNIE granted automatic approval for investment projects in "unrestricted industries" when investments met guidelines designed to promote foreign trade and to create jobs outside major industrial areas such as Mexico City, Guadalajara, and Monterrey. By 1993, according to GATT's Trade Policy Review, the CNIE had approved 98.4 percent of the investment projects that it had reviewed since 1989. In December 1993, a new Foreign Investment Law was enacted. This new law did away with most of the restrictions incorporated in the 1973 law. The impact of the 1989 regulatory changes is evident in the increase in foreign investment during that period. More impressive, however, than the increase in FDI was the surge in portfolio investment. In 1989, the CNIE and the National Securities Commission were authorized to approve trust funds through which foreigners could buy equities issued by Mexican firms without acquiring shareholder voting rights. Foreign investors were attracted to the Mexican stock market by the large returns available. Between 1991 and 1993, Mexico was able to offset its substantial current account deficit with substantial inflows of foreign capital. (General Agreement on Tariffs and Trade 1994; Kehoe 1995, 147).

3.   Openness of the economy, measured as the ratio of trade (the sum of exports and imports) in goods and nonfactor services to GDP, increased from 33 percent in 1985 to 38 percent in 1993 (Bank of México Indicadores del Sector Externo 1994).

4.   GATT's Uruguay Round was the eighth round of multilateral trade negotiations. The Uruguay Round comprises 28 agreements signed by 128 countries. The agreements entered into effect on January 1, 1995, and were the result of the most ambitious and comprehensive effort of multilateral trade liberalization.

5.   In early 2002, Mexico was the only Latin American country that had Free Trade Agreements (FTAs) with two major world markets — the United States and the European Union — and numerous FTAs with Latin American countries (Bolivia, Colombia, Costa Rica, Chile, El Salvador, Guatemala, Honduras, Nicaragua, and Venezuela, and ongoing negotiations with Ecuador and Panama). It also has signed a FTA with the European Free Trade Association and another with Israel.

6.   NAFTA was not the first attempt at promoting economic integration between Mexico and the United States. Under the 1942 U.S. Reciprocal Trade Agreements Program,

Mexico and the United States entered into a bilateral agreement that lasted only until 1950. Later in 1980, Ronald Reagan proposed the creation of a North American common market as a presidential campaign issue. Given Mexico's historical suspicions about excessive U.S. influence in domestic affairs, the project did not go forward; in 1981, a rather ineffective Joint Commission on Trade and Commerce was established instead. Later on and consistent with Mexico's outward orientation, arrangements leading toward Mexico-U.S. economic integration included the 1985 Bilateral Understanding on Subsidies and Countervailing Duties, the 1987 Framework Agreement on Trade and Investment, and the 1989 Understanding Regarding Trade and Investment Facilitation Talks. Attraction of U.S. capital and access to the U.S. market were the basis for Mexico's involvement in international trade negotiations with the United States.

7.   Out of concern to diversify export markets and reduce excessive dependence on the U.S. market and in order to attract foreign investment, President Carlos Salinas de Gortari made a trip to Europe in 1990. After the World Forum annual meeting in Davos, Switzerland, he realized that the 1989 revolutions in the former Soviet bloc countries had increased competition for foreign capital on the continent; Mexico was both geographically and politically far from European interests (Mayer 1998).

8.   NAFTA provisions will only be fully implemented in the year 2003, when the specific levels of local content and export requirements for manufacturers of autos in Mexico and the conditions for importing foreign vehicles based on sales in the Mexican market, as provided in the 1989 Auto Decree, are eliminated.

9.   Among the main auto parts that the United States buys from Mexico are wire harnesses, auto stereos, auto body parts, speedometers, engines, and air conditioning parts. For its part, Mexico buys from the United States engines, wheels, seat parts, and auto stereos. A similar type of integration has occurred between the Mexican and Canadian automotive sectors.

10.   NAFTA stipulates that no new quotas in the textile and clothing sector may be imposed except under specific safeguard provisions. Moreover, some products that do not meet NAFTA's rules of origin may still qualify for preferential treatment up to a "tariff preference level" or up to a specified import level, which is negotiated between the three countries (Hufbauer and Schott 1993).

11.   Mexico's main textile and clothing exports to the United States are denim products, knit fabric, synthetic fabric, trousers, T-shirts, sweaters, and underwear.

12.   Approximately 75 percent of Mexico's clothing production incorporates U.S. fabric. (Kurt Salmon Associates Capital Advisors 1999).

13.   This is the case of the Program for Direct Support for Mexican Producers, which delivers cash payments to guarantee a minimum income for 2.9 million farmers who sow 14 million hectares of basic crops (Yunez-Naude, Antonio 2002, 6-7). Note: *ejido* means land that peasants can use or exploit but not sell.

14.   According to some analysts, the events of September 11, 2001, shifted the immigration discussion from legalizing illegal migrants toward cracking down on them (Brownstein 2001).

15.   In a national poll conducted after September 11 by John Zogby for the Center for Immigration Studies in Washington, D.C., some three-fourths of Americans said that the government was not doing enough to control the border, and nearly as many said that it should greatly increase the resources devoted to enforcing immigration laws (Brownstein 2001).

16.   Steven Camarota estimates that total legal and illegal immigration from Mexico averaged about 400,000 annually between 1998 and 2000. By implication, his figures suggest that illegal immigration was running over 200,000 annually in recent years (2001).

REFERENCES

Bank of Mexico. Various years. "Indicadores del Sector Externo." At <http://www.banxico.org.mx/>.

Brownstein, Ronald. 2001. "Green Light, Red Light." *The American Prospect* 12:21 (November).

Bush, George W., and Vicente Fox. 2002. "The Monterrey Compromise." Joint Statement by the Presidents of the United States and Mexico. March 22. Monterrey, Mexico. At <http://www.state.gov/p/wha/rls/rm/8948.htm>.

Camarota, Steven A. 2001. *Immigration from Mexico: Assessing the Impact on the United States.* Paper No. 19 (July). Washington, D.C.: Center for Immigration Studies.

Carrillo, Jorge, and Alfredo Hualde. 1997. "Third Generation In-Bond Assembly Plants: The Case of Delphi-General Motors." *Comercio Exterior* 47: 9 (September).

Del Castillo, Gustavo, and Gustavo Vega-Cánovas. 1995. *The Politics of Free Trade in North America.* Ottawa, Canada: Centre for Trade Policy and Law.

Economic Analysis for Company Planning (Ecanal). Various years. Various statistics. At <http://www.ecanal.com.mx/>.

General Agreement on Tariffs and Trade. 1994. *Trade Policy Review: Mexico.* Geneva, Switzerland: General Agreement on Tariffs and Trade.

Federal Reserve Bank of Dallas. 1999. "The Mexican Economy." Federal Reserve Bank of Dallas, El Paso Branch.

Hufbauer, Gary Clyde, and Jeffrey Schott. 1993. *NAFTA: An Assessment.* Washington, D.C.: Institute for International Economics.

Indice del Diario Oficial de la Federación. 2001. "Ley del Mercado de Valores," June 1.

Instituto Nacional de Estadística Geografía e Informática (INEGI). Various years. Various statistics. At <http://www.inegi.gob.mx/>.

Instituto Nacional de Estadística Geografía e Informática (INEGI). Various years. *Encuesta Industrial Mensual. Indicadores del sector manufacturero.* At <http://www.inegi.gob.mx/>.

Kehoe, Tim. 1995. "A Review of Mexico's Trade Policy from 1982 to 1994." In *The World Economy Global Trade Policy 1995*, eds. Arndt Sven and Chris Milner. London: Blackwell Publishers Limited.

Kessler, Tim. 1998. "Political Capital: Mexican Finance Reform under Salinas." *World Politics* 51: 1 (October): 36-66.

Kurt Salmon Associates Capital Advisors. 1999. *Textile Transactions and Trends. Perspectives on Mergers and Acquisitions in the Textile Industry.* Newsletter (Summer).

Lowe, Nichola, and Martin Kenney. 1999. "Foreign Investment and Global Geography of Production: Why the Mexican Consumer Electronics Industry Failed." *World Development* 27 (8): 1427-43.

Luhnow, David. 2002. "Tire Industry Hits the Skids." *Wall Street Journal*, March 4.

Lustig, Nora, Barry P. Bosworth, and Robert Z. Lawrence, eds. 1992. *North American Free Trade: Assessing the Impact.* Washington, D.C.: The Brookings Institution.

Mayer, Frederick W. 1998. *Interpreting NAFTA: The Science and Art of Political Analysis.* New York: Columbia University Press.

Naim, Moisés, and Sebastian Edwards. 1997. *Mexico 1994: Anatomy of an Emerging-Market Crash.* Washington, D.C.: Carnegie Endowment for International Peace.

Parliament of Canada, Partners in North America. Advancing Canada's Relations with the United States and Mexico. *Report of the Standing Committee on Foreign Affairs and International Trade.* December 2002. At <http://www.parl.gc.ca/infocomdoc/37/2/fait/studies/report/faitvp03-E.htm>.

Pastor, Robert. 2001. *Toward a North American Community: Lessons from the Old World for the New.* Washington, D.C.: Institute for International Economics.

Ramírez De la O, Rogelio. 1998. "The Impact of NAFTA on the Auto Industry in Mexico." In *The North American Auto Industry under NAFTA*, eds. Sidney Weintraub and Christopher Sands. Washington, D.C.: Center for Strategic and International Studies.

Ramírez De la O, Rogelio. 2000. "What Has Changed in the Performances of Employment and Wages in Mexico after NAFTA?" *Incomes and Productivity in North America. Papers from the 2000 Seminar.* Washington, D.C.: Commission for Labor Cooperation.

Schrader, Esther. 1999. "Mexico Learns Lesson Well in Pursuit of Trade Accords; Exports Pacts Similar to NAFTA May Hinder Clinton's Push to Form 34-Nation Free Trade Area of the Americas." *Los Angeles Times*, September 14.

Secretaría de Economía, Government of Mexico. 2002. "Mexican Maquiladora Industry Heading Towards Recovery," NAFTA Works, Vol. 7, Issue 5 (June). At <www.naftaworks.org>.

Sistema de Información Empresarial Mexicano. 2000. *NATFA Works: For the Textiles and Apparel Industry.* Sectoral Fact Sheet. At <http://www.naftaworks.org/Publications/Industrial/industrial.html>.

Story, Dale. 1986. *Industry, the State and Public Policy in Mexico.* Austin: University of Texas Press.

Torres, Blanca, and Pamela S. Falk, eds. 1989. *La Adhesión de México al GATT. Repercusiones Internas e Impacto sobre las relaciones México-Estados Unidos.* Mexico City: El Colegio de México.

U.S. Department of Commerce. Various years. Various statistics. At <http://www.commerce.gov>.

U.S. Department of Justice. 2002. *Legal Immigration. Fiscal Year 2000.* Annual Report Number 6. Office of Policy and Planning — Statistics Division. January.

U.S. Department of State — Office of the Press Secretary. 2001a. "Smart Border: 22 Point Agreement — U.S.-Mexico Border Partnership Action Plan." Fact Sheet. Washington, D.C.: The White House. At <http://www.state.gov/p/wha/rls/fs/8909.htm>.

U.S. Department of State — Office of the Press Secretary. 2001b. "Specific Measures that Compromise Joint Action Plan with Mexico." Fact Sheet. Washington, D.C.: The White House. At <http://www.state.gov/p/wha/rls/fs/8910.htm>.

U.S. Immigration and Naturalization Service. 2001. *Illegal Alien Resident Population.* At <http://www.ins.usdoj.gov/graphics/aboutins/statistics/illegalalien/>.

U.S. International Trade Commission (USITC). 2001. *The Year in Trade.* At <http://www.usitc.gov/>.

U.S.-Mexico Migration Panel. 2001. *Mexico-U.S. Migration: A Shared Responsibility.* Washington, D.C. and Mexico City: Carnegie Endowment for International Peace and Instituto Tecnológico Autónomo de México.

Yunez-Naude, Antonio. 2002. *Lessons from NAFTA: The Case of the Mexican Agricultural Sector (Final Report for the World Bank).* At <http://www.worldbank.org>.

PART II

COPING WITH FINANCIAL INSTABILITY

Chapter Four

MEXICAN AND OTHER RECENT LATIN AMERICAN FINANCIAL CRISES: HOW MUCH SYSTEMIC, HOW MUCH POLICY?

Sidney Weintraub

INTRODUCTION

The spate of financial meltdowns the world witnessed in the 1990s began with the Mexican experience of 1994-1995, followed by the financial crisis in Thailand in 1997 that quickly spread to other countries in East Asia. However, focusing on Latin America, the next major crisis unfolded in Brazil in 1998-1999, triggered in part by the Russian bond default and the collapse of long-term capital management (DeLong and Eichengreen 2001). Argentina was hit hard by the effects of the Brazilian crisis, mainly by the large currency devaluation, and has been suffering from economic problems ever since and going through a dramatic default as of December 2001.

Each of these financial-economic crises had distinct precipitating events. The causes were rooted in the international financial system itself, in the contagion that was evident between a Russian default and a Brazilian crisis, and in economic policies of each of the countries. There were political antecedents based on each country's history, practices, and habits of government. This chapter will not provide detailed descriptions of the meltdowns as they proceeded, but instead will try to sort out the policy failures from the systemic shortcomings.[1] This cannot be an exercise in precision because domestic policy and systemic circumstances are intertwined; in fact, much domestic economic-financial policy is determined by an evaluation of what the global market will allow.

The analysis that follows is based on an assessment of how much weight should be given to systemic causes for the crises and how much to domestic policy actions. Put differently, the question that lies behind this evaluation is the following: Was there scope for domestic policy to counteract, at least to some extent, the systemic shocks? The focus will be on the three large Latin American countries most severely affected by financial breakdowns — Mexico, Brazil, and Argentina.

In each case, authoritarian or military regimes gave way to democracy during the 1980s and 1990s. Each country reduced its high import barriers over the past decade, Mexico more than the others. All were part of regional economic integration agreements, the Southern Common Market (Mercado Común del Sur — MERCOSUR) for Brazil and Argentina and the North American Free Trade

Agreement (NAFTA) for Mexico. Privatization of state-owned enterprises was substantial in each country. And each country received financial support from the international community, assistance that was vital in helping Mexico and Brazil recover from their shocks, but was less valuable in this respect for Argentina, although future support is possible (even likely) in the ongoing critical situation in Argentina.

Other chapters in this volume deal with the paths of economic opening and insertion into the world economy of the different countries of Latin America. This chapter highlights the fact that economic changes were accompanied by serious crises in the three countries with the largest economies. Economic restructuring involved much pain in the three countries — and the suffering still has a long way to go before the economic problems are resolved in Argentina.

MEXICO

S ince 1976, Mexico has had recurring currency crises, almost unerringly connected with changes in government leadership. This is known in the country as the "*sexenio* (six-year term) curse" (Heath 1999). After six years of financial mismanagement, each president in turn apparently wished to leave a clean slate for his successor and devalued the peso to compensate for the inflation-driven currency overvaluation during his six-year term in office. The 1994 version of this devaluation occurred three weeks after President Carlos Salinas de Gortari left office. He did not wish to take the blame himself and, as the crisis played out, he could later argue that the problem was in the way President Ernesto Zedillo, who followed him in office, handled the devaluation. The "*error de diciembre*" ("error of December"), as Salinas phrased it, is now part of Mexican economic and political lore. This repetitive curse cycle was broken in the transfer from Zedillo to President Vicente Fox, from a president of the Institutional Revolutionary Party (Partido Revolucionario Institucional — PRI) to one from the National Action Party (Partido de Acción Nacional — PAN).

Is the curse broken? Here's what Jonathan Heath thinks: "... [I]f we can avoid a crisis in 2000 [which Mexico did, after his words were written] that may still be considered the exception and not the emergence of a new rule." (Heath 2000, 105)

In 1987, before he left office, President Miguel de la Madrid set up a form of incomes policy which he called a *pacto de solidaridad* (solidarity pact), under which the government, labor, and business agreed to refrain from inflationary actions by moderating expenditures, limiting wage demands, and avoiding excessive price increases. This corporatist technique of addressing issues was congenial to the authoritarian political practices that had existed in Mexico. When the *pacto* policy was adopted, there was an initial large currency devaluation, designed to undervalue the peso enough so that future inflation did not have to be incorporated fully in the crawling exchange rate that Mexico used. The idea was to reduce inflation enough over about a *sexenio*, so that whatever overvaluation did occur could be corrected by productivity increases. This practice of using the exchange rate as the anchor for combating inflation was not unique to Mexico. The problem there, as in other countries that have adopted this technique of inflation moderation, is that the process lasted much longer than its useful life. When Mexico finally was forced to devalue the peso in December 1994, the manner in which this was done was decided at a *pacto* meeting. Therein lies a tale of undue influence of self-interested nongovernmental actors over a decision that had a profoundly adverse effect on the entire population.

The public sector deficits that were the main cause of inflation in Mexico during the 1970s and which, in turn, brought on the cursed currency devaluations, were policy failures. The *pacto* technique for dealing with inflation was a policy action, one that fit in with Mexican practices. The world financial system was involved because Mexico had to decide how to value its currency in relation to other currencies, essentially in relation to the U.S. dollar. Mexico, based on its own analytical and national proclivities, chose what was essentially a fixed rate, a band within which the peso could fluctuate, coupled with a modest daily crawl of depreciation insufficient to compensate fully for the steady real appreciation of the peso. The band was protected by intervention in the currency market. This was a policy decision driven essentially by domestic politics but influenced by conventional systemic thinking of the time.

It is best at this point to home in on the year 1994 in Mexico, when both the systemic and the domestic policy aspects were simultaneously in play. The problems of the previous years were fiscally driven, and the policy imperative for 1994 was to eliminate this shortcoming by tight fiscal policy, as well as to decide what to do about the increasing overvaluation of the Mexican peso. The government, in 1994, boasted about its fiscal stringency, about achieving a balanced budget. However, the reality was different. Off-budget credits outstanding of Mexico's development banks were 3 to 4 percent of gross domestic product in 1994, which had an effect no different from that of a deficit in the financial budget itself. This, arguably, could have been coincidence, but this hypothesis does not pass the credibility test. The Mexican economy had been declining coming into the presidential election year 1994 and the penchant to spend for political victory was too deeply ingrained. Just to highlight this point, the public sector deficit in the last year of the de la Madrid government, which preceded that of Salinas, was 9.3 percent of the gross domestic product (GDP). Salinas promised not to use the budget this way; however, the extra expenditures did not cease but instead moved off budget.

Another antecedent that had a large part of its denouement in 1994 was in the policy of the Bank of Mexico, Mexico's Central Bank. Mexico's commercial banks had been nationalized at the end of 1982 as one of the senseless departing measures of then President José López Portillo. He blamed the banks for complicity in the capital flight then taking place, despite the fact that government policy created the conditions under which rational people tried to protect their assets. Why stay in pesos if there is a near certainty that the peso will be devalued? The devaluation did take place before López Portillo left office. The banks were reprivatized in 1991 and 1992 at high prices, well above book value. Many buyers turned out to be less than scrupulous managers, and the timing and the high prices were unfortunate. Projections of economic growth, the basis for the high prices paid, turned out to be optimistic. Consequently, interest rates charged were steep in order to maximize profits, nonperforming loans skyrocketed, and eventually the banks had to be rescued. The relevant aspect for this discussion of national policy leading to the crisis is that the Bank of Mexico felt constrained in its monetary policy in 1994, out of fear of further aggravating what turned out to be a major banking debacle in any event.

Once again, every phase of the banking fiasco — from the nationalization, to the reprivatization, to the influence on monetary policy, to the rescue by buying off the bad loans and converting private debt into public debt — was determined by policy and not by anything inherent in the international financial system. When Mexico entered into NAFTA, it made few concessions to allow foreign banks to operate fully in Mexico. This policy was changed after the meltdown, when it became clear that foreign banks would add to the stability of Mexico's financial structure. The policy to favor Mexican owners was another aspect of policy based on politics and ingrained nationalism. Today, in contrast, foreign banks play a large role in Mexico.

One aspect of policy that deserves considerable attention was the handling of Mexico's public debt, particularly foreign borrowing. The most common instrument used for government borrowing prior to 1994 were treasury certificates, best known in Mexico by the abbreviated name of *cetes* or CETES (Certificados de la Tesorería de la Federación) and denominated in pesos. In the latter part of 1993, when there was uncertainty over whether NAFTA would be approved by the U.S. Congress, Mexico increased the issuance of a debt instrument whose very name has since become infamous in the country — that is, *tesobonos*. These were treasury bonds of relatively short duration, denominated in pesos like the *cetes*, but indexed to the dollar. For all practical purposes, therefore, they were dollar obligations.

The sale of *tesobonos* increased consistently during 1994. On December 20, the day that the peso band was widened (in effect, a devaluation that could not be controlled), the amount of *tesobonos* outstanding was slightly more than $20 billion, and the level of Mexico's foreign reserves was $10.5 billion. As an aside, one day later, on December 21, the reserve level dropped to $5.8 billion — that is, Mexico tried to maintain the 15 percent devaluation implicit in the band widening and squandered $4.7 billion in reserves by its interventions — and on December 22, the peso was allowed to float. (This point will be revisited later because it says much about policy in relation to the world financial system.) In short, Mexico had run out of reserves to meet its *tesobono* obligations and discovered, to its dismay, that it could not refinance these. The problem was brought on by policy failure. However, the inability to deal with the repayment of debt was largely systemic; perhaps the better word is rational. There is a world process of capital flows that is merciless in shunning countries seen as bad risks. Bad policy did Mexico in, and a ruthless process of portfolio capital outflows did not let Mexico find its way out. This, with all of the related details omitted, is what led to the massive U.S. and International Monetary Fund (IMF) rescue package early in 1995. The United States was fearful of the fallout of an unrescued Mexico on its own financial structure.

When Mexican authorities gathered on December 20, 1994, to discuss how to deal with the exchange-rate problem and the related issue of outstanding *tesobono* debt and availability of foreign reserves, it did so in a manner that was unlike the way authorities deal with exchange-rate changes in most countries — or unlike the way

Mexico would have dealt with the problem in a pre-*pacto* environment. Not only were government representatives there, but labor and representatives of the private sector, including banks, were present, too. Going into the meeting, the action favored by the head of the Central Bank and the minister of finance was to allow the peso to float. To most economists, that was the logical next step. The conventional systemic thinking, by then, had moved against adjustable pegs in the conviction that they were unsustainable in a crisis. Most economists would have liked to envelop any devaluation in a wider program of budgetary measures, monetary discipline, wage stringency, and the like, but the preparation for such actions had not been taken in advance. For this, both the new finance minister and the old one who had just left office barely three weeks before could be blamed.

What happened instead at the *pacto* meeting was that the representative of the banking sector favored raising the ceiling of the exchange-rate band (the most depreciated level) by 15 percent in relation to the dollar. He was an interested party, which understates the inconsistency, and should not have been there, but this was a *pacto* meeting — the then finance minister later defended his presence on these grounds. President Ernesto Zedillo, who was out of the city, was called and gave his consent to lifting the band. As indicated above, all hell broke loose the next day. The predictable turned into tragedy. This array of decisions was politics mixed with preference for special interests.

Why didn't the previous finance minister and his president take the necessary exchange-rate action on their watch? Several reasons were given: the markets must first be prepared for a change; a sudden change would cause havoc; and the action could wait until the New Year. The deeper answer surely is politics once again: Salinas did not want devaluation on his watch. And politics is policy (the words are synonymous in Spanish). There was a systemic element, namely, the fear that any devaluation would stimulate the kind of market reaction that did, in fact, occur after December 20, but an earlier devaluation could have been carried out when Mexico's economic situation was relatively strong. In addition, the corollary steps could have been put into place in a less frenetic atmosphere.

Mexico did face some severe shocks in 1994 that were overlaid on the policy atmosphere. The year started with the rebellion of the Zapatista Army of National Liberation in the state of Chiapas. This did not cause any financial turmoil. On March 23, the presidential candidate of the PRI, Luis Donaldo Colosio, was assassinated. This did bring on a fall in reserves of some $10 billion over the following month. Later in 1994, on September 28, José Francisco Ruiz Massieu, the secretary general of the PRI, was assassinated. Kidnappings of prominent persons increased. These events, coming like plagues throughout the year, undoubtedly raised the level of anxiety inside and outside Mexico. At times of high uncertainty, it is not surprising that nationals try to move their assets to safe locations, and the evidence, as later presented by analysts at the IMF, proved that this is exactly what occurred. And foreign investors stood back for a while to evaluate the situation. These shocks cannot be ascribed to policy or to the financial system. They just happened, and they aggravated an already complicated situation.

The U.S. Federal Reserve raised the federal funds rate six times during 1994 to deal with the inflationary situation in the United States, which must have affected the management of financial policy in Mexico. This is systemic, in that Mexico cannot escape the monetary actions of its large neighbor on which it depends heavily for capital flows and credits. There is no systemic cure for this kind of contagion. If the Mexican economy were fully dollarized and, therefore, part and parcel of policy actions taken by the Federal Reserve, Mexico would still have to live with the fallout.

There are other systemic aspects to what happened in Mexico in 1994. Most significantly, the ease of communications and the rapidity with which capital can be moved into and out of Mexico facilitated the crisis. It is not evident that the crisis could have been averted if funds could not have been moved so quickly, but there might then still have been a crisis played out in slower motion. The ability to move funds quickly is part of the world system, and there have been suggestions for putting a ratchet or brake on the movement of short-term capital. Chile for a time put a tax on the inflow of short-term capital (of up to one year) and this apparently helped to lengthen the maturity of Chilean borrowing. James Tobin[2] has suggested a tax on capital movements. Malaysia restricted capital movements at the time of the Asian crisis in 1997 without any apparent damage to its economy.

Had there been such a brake, would this have helped? It is unclear that a Tobin tax, instituted globally on all forms of capital transfers, would have slowed capital movements to Mexico, unless the tax were high enough to remove the interest incentive of the hot money. A Chilean-type tax would almost surely have slowed the short-term capital inflows (the *tesobonos*), but would have done nothing to stem the outflows once the devaluation occurred. The problem with these counterfactual scenarios is that the Mexican authorities, banks, and businesses depended on these inflows. This dependence grew out of the Mexican economic-financial framework established in the years that preceded the eruption of the crisis.

These are some of the issues that the world financial community has been trying to deal with in altering the "architecture" of the system. The bailout of Mexico in early 1995, which was led by the United States and the IMF, and in which many other countries participated, raised another vexing issue that has since grown in financial circles, that of moral hazard. There are many who believe that the moral hazard issue — the rescue of investors who sent money to Mexico to earn high profits — is so serious that similar rescue packages should be shunned. This, essentially, is the position taken by the Meltzer Commission (Report of the International Financial Institution Advisory Commission 2000), but when the Bush administration in its early days had to deal with the situation in Argentina, it, too, supported a bailout despite early statements of misgiving. At some point, Argentina will need another and more significant bailout, and it is most likely that the IMF and the United States will be pressured to participate in this. (The IMF and the United States, as this is written, have been avoiding a rescue until Argentina presents a credible recovery plan.)

The Mexican rescue package worked in the sense that it permitted Mexico to pay its *tesobono* and other debts (although some elements of debt still linger, especially related to the rescue of Mexican banks), restore growth after one year of grotesque hardship in 1995,[3] and repay the money lent to it by the United States and the IMF. What is more important, once a country gets into the mess that Mexico did?

To stand on principle and avoid moral hazard, or to shorten the period of hardship by facilitating economic recovery? The international effort today is to try to bail in (as opposed to bail out) the banks and other investors when a rescue is mounted, but the techniques to do this are not self-evident.

The conclusion that emerges as to whether the Mexican crisis was ignited more by self-imposed policy decisions, based in large degree on political considerations, or by shortcomings in the international financial system is that the main culprit was policy. Earlier policy decisions set the parameters for the actions of 1994. Mexico chose its own exchange-rate policy. It used *tesobonos* on its own initiative to the almost complete exclusion of other credit and reserve measures. Its fragile banking structure, which impeded vigorous monetary action to deal with the economic-financial situation, was a construct of successive Mexican actions. The use of off-budget development banks to stimulate the economy was led by the Mexican authorities. The decision not to act earlier on the exchange rate was taken by Mexican policy leaders. The shift from the Central Bank preference of floating the peso to raising the band on December 20 was an official Mexican decision.

The international system permitted Mexico to take these actions. The system facilitated capital inflows and was powerless to slow down outflows at a time of trouble. It was within Mexico's power to put a damper on interest-sensitive capital inflows but, in fact, Mexico sought them. Mexico had to live with the consequences of U.S. interest rate increases, and there is no evident cure for this dependence on the policies of an economically powerful neighbor.

BRAZIL

The antecedents to Brazil's 1998-1999 crisis were similar in many respects to those that confronted Mexican policymakers in 1994, but there were also differences. Brazil had an overvalued and essentially fixed currency, reserves were run down to maintain the peg, and the budget was in deficit. Brazil also had a growing current account deficit. The twin deficits, fiscal and balance of payments, meant that Brazil's need to import capital was substantial. Brazil received large inflows of foreign direct investment (FDI) but needed other flows as well, including portfolio capital. Brazil, in other words, was in no position to put a tax on the inflow of short-term capital, as Chile did.

The elements of the Brazilian problem, as laid out by two Brazilian economists, were the following: an investment boom fueled by debt, high leverage of commercial banks, growing short-term obligations of private firms and banks, and a fixed exchange rate in a context of a growing current account deficit (Averburg and Giambiagi 2000).

One of the more complete analyses of Brazilian macroeconomic and structural policies is that of Edmund Amann and Werner Baer (2000). Their main conclusion is that fiscal adjustments were constantly postponed under the Real Plan, so much so that government credibility gradually vanished. The international crises of 1997-1998 then accelerated the Plan's endgame. Public debt rose, as did interest rates. The failure to reform civil service pensions was a contest between the bureaucracy, which was allied with the Congress, and the government, and the bureaucracy-Congress won. Over the period leading up to the crisis itself in 1998-1999, Brazil's share of world trade declined.

Brazil's political party structure is chaotic. Seventeen parties were represented in the 513-member Chamber of Deputies in early 2000, and only eight parties had more than 30 members. The 81-member Senate had nine parties (Gordon 2001, 154). To say that the Brazilian legislature is fractious is a monumental understatement.

Brazilian fiscal, trade, and legislative difficulties were clearly made in Brazil. However, these homegrown problems worsened from contagion by the Asian crisis. Adjustments were made after 1997, and the fiscal situation improved somewhat in 1998, as did the real value of the exchange rate, but the adjustments were far from adequate.

The Russian default in August 1998 hit Brazil hard. This was systemic, in that the Russian problems led investors to withdraw funds from Brazil and other emerging countries. There were many reasons for the default's widespread effect, such as the need for investors to cover positions, but there was also uncertainty regarding policies of countries that had serious but uncorrected problems. There was a clear fear on the part of investors that Brazil might default on its debt or, more likely, further depreciate the *real* and decrease the value of their investments. By September 1998, Brazil had lost $30 billion of its foreign reserves in only 50 days. In contrast, it took Mexico almost one year, 1994, to lose reserves approaching that amount and force a devaluation of the peso (Weintraub 2000).

Brazil, however, was not yet ready to make a substantial devaluation of the *real*. Instead, on the eve of the general elections, the authorities opted to seek help from the IMF. Their request was granted, with a credit of 600 percent of quota, and the United States, Japan, the World Bank, and the Inter-American Development Bank (IDB) provided more or less similar absolute dollar amounts in November. The total credit made available was $30.4 billion, which was more than the $18.5 billion the IMF loaned Mexico in the 1995 bailout package, but less than the total $50 billion line of credit provided to Mexico from all sources in the package (IMF *Survey,* September 2002). The reforms promised by Brazil were considerable: mainly a strong fiscal adjustment and tight monetary policy with sky-high interest rates, and these were generally met.

The exchange rate was not touched. This can be explained by the fact that Brazil was coming into an election. There was much criticism by financial experts at the time that the IMF was trying to prevent a crash, using large sums of money, but leaving out the core of the problem. For a while, the prevention program worked. Fernando Henrique Cardoso was reelected; country risk levels fell, as did interest rates. But the euphoria did not last. In December 1998, the fractious Brazilian Congress did not approve all of the provisions in the IMF agreement with the government. Then, in January 1999, the Governor of Minas Gerais, Itamar Franco, called for a default on the state's debt to the federal government.

Those who were skeptical about the IMF agreement were proved correct. Brazil's reserve losses hemorrhaged — at $1 billion per day in early January. The Central Bank president was replaced, and Brazil adopted a currency band system, in effect seeking a controlled devaluation of 9 percent. It took two days to demonstrate the inadequacy of this measure. Shades of the Mexican experience — the attempt to control the extent of devaluation was to widen the band. Brazil's currency was allowed to float on January 15, 1999. At first, there was overshooting of the depreciation to as high as 2.16 *reais* to the dollar, but the rate settled at about 1.65 *reais* to the dollar within a few weeks (*Financial Times*, daily market reports).

Additional details could be provided, but the picture as to the roles of policy and the world system in contributing to the Brazilian 1998-1999 crisis is clear enough. Brazil left itself vulnerable to the external shocks that came, especially from Asia and then Russia. In many ways, this is inherent in the Brazilian economic structure because of the great reliance on capital inflows, which come when investors are confident in Brazilian policy. Inflows do not come when there is doubt about the efficacy and sustainability of policy. The country's fractured political system only adds to uncertainties. The fact that the governor of Minas Gerais defaulted on his state's debt payment to the federal government at a moment of great delicacy in the international financial structure was difficult for non-Brazilians to fathom. Mexico did not float its peso at a calm moment, but instead waited until the crisis erupted in December 1994 — because the PRI did not want to disturb the electorate before a presidential election. In a similar manner, Brazil fought hard and squandered large amounts of foreign reserves but resisted a currency float in order not to disturb a presidential election.

Policy decisions were dominant in bringing on the financial crisis in Brazil, but there also were international systemic features. The most significant is the contagion inherent in the current financial architecture. Developing countries, even those as significant as Brazil, tended to be lumped together. But it is hard to see what architecture can be devised to convince investors to act against what they see as their interests. Why throw money at a country where the risk is high? Why not wait out the storm — or get out of the storm as soon as possible? The call between the systemic or domestic policy causes of the Brazilian crisis is closer than in the Mexican case because of the contagion from the Russian default, but the conclusion is the same. Brazil left itself vulnerable to the kind of contagion that occurred, and this was a national policy decision.

ARGENTINA

Argentina actually suffered multiple crises during the 1990s, first early in the decade and then again starting in 1999. As this is written in 2003, the economic-political situation is unclear, and many decisions must be made in the near future. These presumably will be made by President Néstor Kirchner and his administration. The current period of uncertainty will be discussed later in this section.

Argentina's inflation in 1990 reached more than 2,300 percent, and the population obviously yearned for some relief. This came in 1991, when the Economy Minister, Domingo Cavallo, introduced Argentina's convertibility system precisely to choke off the inflation. The peso was set at a value of one dollar, backed by dollar reserves equal to the monetary base. This permitted exchange of pesos for dollars on a one-to-one basis. A currency-board system was put in place that severely limited the money-creating powers of the Central Bank.

The system worked — for a time. Inflation came down and remained low until the peso devaluation, and GDP grew sharply by an annual average of 5.8 percent between 1991 and 1998. But then problems began to emerge. The current account deficit rose to 4.2 percent in 1998, and fiscal deficits were quite consistent from 1995 on. Indeed, the size of these deficits was hidden from public view by the use of off-budget accounts. This created problems in an economy that was essentially dollarized, in that the public debt to finance the twin deficits — fiscal and current account — was mostly in foreign currency and is not being serviced. Public foreign debt is about $140 billion. Kirchner's government will have to negotiate a rescheduling with creditors. The Argentine private sector also accumulated substantial dollar debt, so much so that there was much fear that devaluation would devastate many businesses, unless they were bailed out. Many private contracts within Argentina, such as mortgages and car payments, are expressed in dollars. The risk premium Argentina had to pay to borrow in external markets was extremely high; the actual figure varies regularly, but in mid-December 2001, before the devaluation, it was 33 percent, almost six times as high as that of Mexico and double that of Brazil (*Financial Times*, daily market reports). In essence, the political risk premium was so high that the Argentine government could not really borrow in foreign markets. The markets lived for about a year with almost daily discussion of whether Argentina would have to default on its foreign debt, despite Herculean, and eventually unsuccessful, efforts to avoid this. In the end, Argentina did default.

One additional troubling feature should be mentioned. Even during the good years of the mid-1990s, when GDP growth was substantial, Argentine unemployment remained high, in the range of 12 to 15 percent of the economically active population. It has since peaked up to 25-plus percent as the economy continues to weaken (CEPAL 2002). Looking back, the convertibility measure was a masterstroke. It eliminated inflation and permitted Argentine families — at least those not affected by unemployment — to live normal lives and not have to run to spend their paychecks before prices rose too much in the course of the next hour or so. The stability this afforded also provided much stimulus for economic growth. The low inflation was extremely popular, which explains the reluctance to tinker with the exchange rate.

However, looking back at what has happened since 1999, the evidence is that the rigidity of convertibility, in concert with the limited monetary flexibility of the currency board structure, lasted too long. Diehard advocates of a hard peg, especially those who believe that Argentina should go even further and officially dollarize the economy, will dispute this. The overvaluation of the Argentine peso was brought about largely by the appreciation of the U.S. dollar, to which the peso was tied. The advantage of full dollarization would be to rule out a peso devaluation, as there would be no peso to devalue, but the disadvantage is that Argentina's monetary fate would be decided by the U.S. Federal Reserve, exactly as it was under the currency board.

Argentina not only had the rigidity of convertibility, but it entered into what it hoped would become deep economic integration with Brazil. Under MERCOSUR,

Argentina's exports to Brazil increased dramatically and reached about one-third of total exports. Then came the Brazilian devaluation of 1999, and the incompatibility of the two exchange-rate systems became manifest. As one economist put it, Argentina then discovered the error of tying its economy to a larger, but poorer, country (Elizondo 2001). Not only have Argentina's exports to Brazil diminished, but many Argentine producers moved their plants to Brazil to take advantage of the cheaper costs there.

When Cavallo returned as economy minister in 2001, he took a number of measures to avoid both outright devaluation and debt default. These included convincing the legislature to pass a law to alter the backing of the monetary base from dollars to a 50-50 mixture of dollars and euros when the two currencies reached equal value; using this dollar-euro average value for export purposes, which amounted to a partial devaluation; removing duties on capital goods imports and raising them on consumer products, in violation of the common external tariff of MERCOSUR; engineering at high interest cost a megaswap of relatively short-term to longer-term debt; instituting a monthly zero-deficit policy; obtaining further credit from the IMF; and then the ultimate blow, allowing only $1,000 of withdrawal from bank deposits each month. None of this worked (Krauss 2001). Indeed, the evidence is the reverse. Cavallo was brought back into government because of his reputation as the miracle man of the early 1990s, only to gain a new reputation for futile arrogance before he was forced to resign in December 2001.

Argentina's recession began in 1999 and worsened as Brazil's currency depreciated further in 2001, making the mismatch between the Argentina exchange rate structure and the Brazilian more evident then ever. The economy showed signs of growth in early 2003, but this was partly illusory because government debts are not being serviced.

The dismal economic situation, coupled with what was seen as the ineptitude of the government, led to the resignation of President Fernando de la Rúa in December 2001. There were several ineffectual interim presidents. President Eduardo Duhalde had to govern in a state of daily uncertainty. Except for a modest IMF credit of $2.98 billion in January 2003, to help Argentina pay its arrears to the IMF, the IMF and Argentina have been at loggerheads (IMF Press Release, January 2003). Argentina has defaulted on its government debt and the peso, which was disconnected from the dollar, was then trading between 3.2 and 3.4 pesos to $1. By mid-2003, the rate had strengthened to close to 3 pesos per dollar. In short, the political-economic picture in Argentina is wretched — a long, arduous, painful debt workout lies ahead. The primary responsibilities of the Kirchner administration will be to balance domestic political imperatives to ease hardships on the Argentine population and to meet IMF demands for fiscal stringency.

The Argentine case is unlike that of Mexico and Brazil, in that it is not a crisis that can be overcome within a relatively short time. It has similarities with the Brazilian case, however, in that the fallout from external events (the Asian and Russian collapses for Brazil and the Brazilian devaluation in the Argentine case) was a precipitating cause of what followed. Much more important, the three cases all share the reality that their own policies, over many years, made them ultravulnerable to internal and external shocks.

The systemic aspects of the Argentine case are an extension of the country's own structure. Argentina, even more than Mexico and Brazil, was highly dependent on capital inflows. When these slowed down, ceased, or became inordinately expensive because of internal political and economic events, serious economic problems were created. Architectural changes in the international monetary system can do little to correct this structure. Argentina, like Brazil, is not a major trading country; its exports are about 10 percent of GDP, but its relatively small internal market cannot compensate for the low level of exports. The essential problems that Argentina must confront are homegrown, and they are gargantuan.

Argentina's failure to alter its convertibility system in good times, when the economy was growing sharply, is understandable. Why discard a structure that is working? Many outside experts, including those from the IMF, also opposed devaluation out of fear of the consequences on the repayment of official and private debt. Thus, there have been mitigating circumstances in Argentina's case, even more so than in Brazil. Yet, each country is responsible for its own policies, and Argentina chose the policies that drastically weakened its economy. Now with the devaluation, Argentine exports have become more competitive. The current finance minister believes this and proposes to adopt a policy of export-led growth. If this works, this may ease the recovery once Argentina devises a program that meets the demands of external lenders (primarily the IMF). However, the central issue for the foreseeable future is to deal with the economic, political, and social chaos that exists, without aggravating the country's external problems.

President Kirchner's intentions are unclear. He has been ambiguous about the relative weights he will assign to job creation and its fiscal implications, as opposed to meeting the conditions requested by the IMF and the demands of foreign creditors. The agreement reached with the IMF in early September 2003 is only an initial step in the recomposition of Argentina's external relations.

CONCLUSIONS

The following conclusions emerge from the three cases:
1. The crises in the Mexican and Brazilian cases became publicly apparent suddenly, but each was years in the making. Argentina's crisis was played out over many years in what appeared to be slow motion.
2. The countries themselves largely made the policies that led to the crises, although there were systemic problems that aggravated these decisions.
3. Politics and historical conditioning were as much, or more, the driving forces of these mistaken or inadequate policies as economics.
4. There is something to the moral hazard argument: that is, each country felt it would be rescued from its errors by somebody — the United States, other industrial countries, the IMF, or a combination of all of the above.
5. The world system contributed to the outcomes in the sense that capital movements are global, near instantaneous, and merciless when countries' weaknesses are observed.
6. These are known realities and must be taken into account when policies are put in place.

The conclusion of this examination is that international systemic realities played a role in each of the financial-economic crises examined, more so in the Brazilian and Argentine cases than in the Mexican, but the policies put in place at home were the overwhelming cause of the hardships suffered. What these three examples demonstrate is that reconciling Latin American countries' insertion into the world economy with domestic political realities is not easy, because each country's political situation limits its flexibility in making economic policy decisions.

NOTES

1.   I have given a blow-by-blow account of the Mexican breakdown in Sidney Weintraub, 2000, *Financial Decision-Making in Mexico: To Bet a Nation* (London: Macmillan; and Pittsburgh: University of Pittsburgh Press).

2.   The late James Tobin, 1981 winner of the Nobel Prize in economics, was a professor at Yale University. See <http://cowles.econ.yale.edu/archive/people/tobin/tobin_ynr.htm>.

3.   The hardship was mitigated modestly for some in Mexico by the increase in exports to the United States in 1995, facilitated by the existence of NAFTA and Mexico's depreciated exchange rate. Nevertheless, the year 1995 was a horrible one for most middle- and lower-income Mexicans.

REFERENCES

Amann, Edmund, and Werner Baer. 2000. "The Illusion of Stability: Brazilian Economy Under Cardoso." *World Development* 28 (10): 1805-1819.

Averburg, André, and Fabio Giambiagi. 2000. "The Brazilian Crisis of 1998-1999: Origins and Consequences." Textos para Discussão 77, Planning Area, Economics Department, Central Bank Economic Studies Department (DEPEC).

Comisión Económica para América Latina y el Caribe (CEPAL). *2002. Balance Preliminar de las Economías de América Latina y el Caribe, 2002.* Santiago: CEPAL. <http://www.cepal.org/>.

DeLong, Bradford, and Barry Eichengreen. 2001. "Between Meltdown and Moral Hazard: The International Monetary and Financial Policies of the Clinton Administration." Paper prepared for a conference on the economic policies of the Clinton administration, Kennedy School of Government, Harvard University, Cambridge, Mass., June 26-29.

Elizondo Mayer-Serra, Carlos. 2001. "La Tragedia de Argentina." *Reforma*, July 20.

Financial Times, daily market reports, various years.

Gordon, Lincoln. 2001. *Brazil's Second Chance: En Route toward the First World.* Washington, D.C.: The Brookings Institution Press.

Heath, Jonathan. 1999. *Mexico and the Sexenio Curse.* Washington, D.C.: Center for Strategic and International Studies (CSIS). Also published in Spanish in 2000. *La Maldición de las Crisis Sexenales.* México, D.F.: Grupo Editorial Iberoamérica.

International Financial Institution Advisory Commission. 2000. *Report of the Chairman, Allan H. Meltzer.* Submitted to the U.S. Congress and U.S. Department of the Treasury. March 8.

International Monetary Fund (IMF). 2002. *Survey* 31: 17, September 16. <www.imf.org/imfsurvey>.

IMF Press Release. January 2003. "IMF Approves Transitional Stand-By Credit Support for Argentina." No. 03/09. <http://www.imf.org/external/np/sec/pr/2003/pr0309.htm>.

Krauss, Clifford. 2001. "Economy's Dive Dazes Once Giddy Argentina." *New York Times*, September 30.

Weintraub, Sidney. 2000. *Financial Decision-Making in Mexico: To Bet a Nation.* London: Macmillan; and Pittsburgh: University of Pittsburgh Press.

Chapter Five

ALTERNATIVES TO COPE WITH FINANCIAL INSTABILITY IN LATIN AMERICA

Sylvia Maxfield

Financial and exchange rate crises are likely to remain part of the Latin American landscape for years to come. These two types of crises are often linked. Deterioration of bank balance sheets hints of broader national economic problems and rising risk for investors. National and foreign investors begin to withdraw funds from the country. They sell assets denominated in the national currency and demand hard currency. Fears of national currency devaluation build because sellers outweigh buyers. Because financial institutions often have foreign currency-denominated liabilities, potential for devaluation portends further balance sheet deterioration. A vicious cycle is under way.

While financial instability has been particularly pernicious in Latin America, financial crises have left no continent untouched in the past 25 years. The "miracle" countries of Asia were not immune, nor were Great Britain or the United States. Financial crises have indiscriminately afflicted countries with fixed exchange rates, floating exchange rates, considerable state control of financial markets, and more liberal approaches to financial regulation. Marx-inspired economists see financial crises as an inevitable feature of capitalism.

Even so, Latin America seems to have suffered more than its share of financial crises in the past several decades. No doubt, aspects of the international environment, such as International Monetary Fund (IMF) actions or exchange rate arrangements, contributed to Latin American financial woes. But recent history also shows that Latin American countries can do relatively little to change international circumstances. The modest policy proposals in this chapter focus on measures within reach of most Latin American countries today. While internationally renowned economists debate the future of the IMF at world summits and in the opinion pages of the *Financial Times*, there are policy choices Latin American officials might consider reinforcing or adopting anew in efforts to reduce the probability and severity of future financial crises.

This chapter discusses four policy arenas. All four are interconnected. Progress and effectiveness in one arena hinge on efforts in other areas. The first of these is managing national capital structures through capital account regulations and innovative incentive structures for private corporations. A second, and related, policy area is local financial market deepening, encouraged through pension fund reform and regulation. At its simplest, the goal in both of these cases is to discourage mismatch in the term and currency denomination of national financial liabilities and assets. For example, if a country's income and assets are denominated in local currency, heavy foreign currency borrowing is a risk if the country's foreign currency earnings are volatile. Careful consideration of multiple financial options and structures should govern public and private finance in Latin America. Latin American governments should demand more creative financial engineering from their financial advisers and large investment banks.

A third policy area is institution building, specifically, prudential supervision of financial institutions, encouraging public ownership, and enforcing strict disclosure requirements, all of which should also help limit the extent of financial crises in Latin America. Public scrutiny creates incentives for sound corporate finance, a lesson that needs to be relearned in the United States.

Conduct of macroeconomic policy is a fourth important arena in the fight against financial instability. Countercyclical macroeconomic policy practices, common in the industrialized world, have eluded Latin American governments, to their detriment. Coping with financial crises would be easier if governments could save in boom eras to build a cushion for bad times. This would help Latin American governments break away from macroeconomic policy patterns that tend to accentuate, rather than dampen, economic growth cycles. In good times, Latin American governments often pursue loose fiscal policies, while they tighten policies in economic downturns. A simple, if partial, remedy is greater use of fiscal stabilization funds.

MANAGING INTERNATIONAL CAPITAL FLOWS

As is evident in the stylized description of financial and exchange rate crises, a common culprit is "volatile" capital. Volatile capital crosses national borders quickly and massively. Table 1 (below) illustrates the volatility of private capital flows into Latin America. Inoculation for financial crises hinges in part on policies that respond to the problem of large, cross-border capital flows.

But capital is a broad term, and overall capital flows are not likely to recede. Policymakers need to think about the costs and benefits of different kinds of capital and about mechanisms to encourage a particular composition of capital flows and stocks. Restrictions can include many different policies, covering taxes, price, or quantity restrictions or outright prohibition on international purchase and sale of financial assets. Capital controls can be employed for different purposes, such as temporarily halting outflows in the case of Malaysia in 1997 or biasing the long-term composition of inflow as Chile attempted in the 1990s.

Table 1. Purposes of Capital Controls

Purpose	Strategy	Example
Generate Revenue	Control **outflows** to permit higher inflation with fixed exchange rate and keep domestic interest rates low	Most belligerents during WWI, WWII
Government Guidance of Credit Allocation	Restrict **outflows** to permit government price setting in banking system	Japan 1960s-1980s, many developing countries
Correct Balance of Payments Deficit	Control **outflows** by reducing demand for foreign assets without deflationary monetary policy or devaluation; allow higher inflation	U.S. interest rate equalization tax 1963-1974
Correct Balance of Payments Surplus	Control **inflows** to reduce foreign demand for domestic financial assets without expansionary monetary policy or revaluation, allows lower inflation	German policy mid-1970s
Prevent Potentially Volatile Inflows/ Financial Destabilization	Restrict composition of capital **inflows** to limit amount that can leave during crisis	Chilean tax 1991-98
Prevent Real Currency Appreciation	Restrict **inflows** instead of expansionary monetary policy	Chilean tax 1991-98
Restrict Foreign Investment	Restrict specific type of **inflows** to protect import-competing sectors	Mexican foreign investment restrictions

Source: Christopher J. Neely, 1999, "An Introduction to Capital Controls," *Review* 81, 6: Nov./Dec. (St. Louis: Federal Reserve Bank of St. Louis), 13-30.

Temporary controls on outflows rarely succeed (Eichengreen et al. 1999). In fact, capital controls rarely succeed in shaping the overall volume of capital flows out of or into a country (Neely 1999; Reinhart and Montiel 1999). But a few countries have explicitly aimed to shape the composition of capital inflows by prohibiting certain types of flows, imposing deposit requirements, or instituting a financial transactions tax (Budnevich and Le Fort 1997). The goal is generally to limit short-term credits in the overall pool of capital inflows.

The composition of national capital structures has shifted in the past decade with bond financing, equity financing, and foreign direct investment (FDI) growing relative to private and multilateral bank financing. Latin America leads the way among other developing country regions in bond finance (see Table 2).

Table 2. Composition of Capital Flows to Latin America

A. Composition of External Debt, 1999 *(in percentages)*

	Asia	Latin America	Central Europe	Africa and Middle East
Bank Loans	39	33	39	42
Bonds	17	46	29	11
Non-bank Trade Credits	6	3	15	19
Multilateral and Bilateral Loans	37	18	16	27

Source: Joint BIS-IMF-OECD-*World Bank Statistics on External Debt*. Available at <www.oecd.org/dac/debt>.

B. Debt vs. Equity Financing to Latin America, 1970-1999 *(in percentages)*

	Debt/GDP	Equity/GDP		Debt/GDP	Equity/GDP
1970	9	5	1990	22	5
1975	17	5	1995	20	7
1980	25	5	1999	17	16
1985	27	4			

Source: International Monetary Fund, 2001, *International Capital Markets*, August; Bankim Chadha et al., 2001, International Monetary Fund, "Emerging Market Financing," *Quarterly Report* II: (3, August): 1-2.

The problem with portfolio investment is "contagion" or "herding." These are circumstances where investors sell a particular country's stocks or bonds en masse. In the case of herding, facts or rumors about a potential change in asset values start a massive sell-off. Contagion is a situation that occurs when capital suddenly flows out of a country because of something that has happened elsewhere. A classic example of contagion is when the hint of poor economic performance in one developing country, such as Mexico, starts a sell-off in all developing countries. This may occur because investors lack information and assume if one developing country is in trouble, risk must be rising in all similar countries.

To avoid these problems, some countries, including Chile and Colombia in Latin America and others outside the region, have adopted policies aimed at increasing FDI relative to short-term and portfolio flows. As will become clearer below, FDI is a healthier form of international financing not because it is "bolted down," but rather due to the lower risk of currency or maturity mismatch inherent in FDI. If a foreign company buys machinery for a Latin American subsidiary, the machine is "bolted down." But the company's treasury may use the machine as collateral to contract a domestic bank loan (Hausmann and Arias 2000). Latin American officials must walk a fine line between encouraging FDI with minimal regulation of their operations, while asking foreign direct investors to use local currency finance.

Initial research suggests that controls on the composition of capital inflows may successfully shift the composition of flows in favor of foreign direct investment (Reinhart and Montiel 1999). Chile successfully used an "unremunerated reserve requirement" that skewed capital inflows toward longer-term investments. Investors had to deposit a varying percentage of the amount of their investment with the Central Bank at no interest. In some cases, investors could choose between this deposit and simply paying a fee up front to the Central Bank. Between 1991 and 1998, these reserves averaged 2 percent of Chilean gross domestic product (GDP) annually. Making this form of international capital control work requires very active management by the Central Bank. The Chilean Central Bank frequently made minor revisions to its international capital control policies. The Chilean Central Bank stresses that the impact of capital control measures tends to be short-term and that policy innovation must keep pace with financial innovation to make such policies effective over the longer term.

Another way to analyze problems relating to capital flows is through the lens of the corporate finance approach. Corporations seek sources of borrowing whose expense varies inversely with their revenues. The first step in this process is to evaluate the weight of different kinds of risks to their business. These risks might be currency risk, real interest changes, commodity price shifts, or declining growth or inflation, among others. The most appropriate form of corporate financing varies with the salience of different risks. If currency risk is a major threat to the business model, the corporation should eschew foreign currency borrowing and raise capital through local currency borrowing or equity issuance. If national growth is especially sensitive to commodity price changes, the country would be wise to issue commodity-price indexed bonds. Michael Pettis uses the terms "correlated capital" and "inverted capital" to synthesize this logic. The carrying costs of correlated capital rise when a major business risk rises. The carrying costs of inverted capital are not affected by an increase in key business risks (Pettis 2001).

The ideas and terminology of the corporate finance approach are slightly complex, but several policy recommendations stand out. Beyond eschewing short-term capital, this approach, like the volatility literature, suggests countries actively seek to manage the composition of capital inflows. The volatility approach tends to elevate FDI in the hierarchy of salutary to demonic capital flows. Pushing beyond the volatility literature, the corporate finance approach argues for creativity in developing country finance. Latin American governments should push their financial advisers harder to design innovative inverted finance mechanisms. They should also consider incentive schemes for private corporations operating in their countries that seek and sustain inverted finance structures.

The corporate finance approach highlights the value of local currency borrowing for businesses sensitive to local interest rates, currency risk, or inflation. But local currency borrowing requires robust domestic credit and corporate bond markets. While domestic credit markets in Latin America are emerging to varying degrees from the "financial repression" of the import substitution period (1960-1980s), robust domestic corporate bond markets are still a long way off for most countries in the region.

This section has highlighted two ways Latin American countries might seek to guide the composition of capital inflows. First, they might actively manage taxes on international capital flows as Chile did in the 1990s. Second, Latin American governments might push the financial advisers and corporations operating within their borders to develop innovative "inverted" financing structures.

DOMESTIC FINANCIAL MARKET DEEPENING

To the extent that financial volatility stems from countries taking on too much foreign currency-denominated debt, substituting local for foreign currency borrowing is a good idea.[1] But small, inefficient local currency financial markets limit local currency options. Several factors have stymied local currency credit and capital market growth in Latin America.

An important feature of import substitution industrialization policies was government intervention in local credit markets. Governments intervened to try to channel credit toward favored (import competing) industries. Ceilings on interest rates that banks could offer depositors kept credit scarce. Typically, the government also imposed very high reserve requirements on banks. Together, these policies restricted bank lending. But the government also imposed ceilings on loan interest rates. Banks had to lend at rates well below the market-clearing rate, which would have been high, given overall credit scarcity. The government exploited bank weakness by offering banks advantages for lending to government-specified sectors and for government-targeted purposes. These advantages included lower reserve requirements or lower discount rates. Latin American governments did not invent this system. The French and Japanese governments followed similar policies in the 1960s and 1970s.

One aspect of local financial market deepening is increased financial intermediation by banks. This means banks take in more deposits and make more loans. Another aspect of financial deepening is increased volume of transactions in local bond and stock markets. But generalizing across financial crises of the past decade reveals an unfortunate story of financial liberalization gone awry, partly because of simultaneous domestic and international financial liberalization. Trouble starts when the government lifts controls on local credit markets and simultaneously allows the private sector freedom to raise capital internationally. Local interest rates are likely to rise to reflect the relative scarcity of local capital. The local markets will suddenly be awash with foreign capital inflows attracted by high returns. Banks previously guided by the government must now practice credit analysis. But after years of government control, banks in this situation cannot effectively evaluate risk. Historically in these circumstances, banks booked far too many high-risk loans. As a consequence, the financial reform literature now recommends undertaking domestic financial reforms and institutionalization of prudential and supervisory bank regulation reforms before putting into place policies that facilitate increased international financial integration. In other words, this literature coincides with the recommendation, at least temporarily, to control international capital flows.

There are other ways to facilitate financial market deepening in Latin America. Privatization of pension fund management has boosted local bond and stock markets. Together, bond and stock markets constitute a country's capital markets. Bank lending activity occurs in the credit market. Financial deepening refers to growth of both local credit and capital markets. Most countries in Latin America have transferred pension fund management from the government to the private sector. Together with restrictions on foreign investment, this pension fund privatization created instant demand for local stocks and bonds. Governments often restricted pension fund investments for the following two reasons: to make them captive buyers of local securities and to ensure prudent management. The Mexican government prohibits pension managers from investing in local stocks or foreign securities. As of 2001, in Chile and Argentina, pension funds could hold up to 16 and 17 percent, respectively, in foreign securities. The amounts under pension fund management are large. Assets under management throughout Latin America in 2001 amount to $175 billion or 18 percent of GDP (IMF 2001).

Privatized pension funds have boosted local bond markets in particular, becoming large holders of local currency-denominated government bond issues. Governments have helped by announcing bond auction schedules and buying back illiquid issues, both measures that improve market liquidity. On several occasions prior to the financial collapse in late 2001, Argentine pension funds played a stabilizing role in the financial crisis by buying government debt. In 2000, the government of Argentina planned to meet 78 percent of that year's government finance shortfall by tapping local investors, including pension funds. Argentina saw its share of domestic debt relative to total public debt increase from 23 percent at year-end 1997 to 36 percent at year-end 2000 (IMF 2001, 45). Pension funds tend to be long-term investors because they must match the maturity of their investments to the maturity of their liabilities (retirement fund payouts). Pension funds help deepen local financial markets by creating a base of long-term national investors.

Obviously, the overall macroeconomic environment also facilitates or hinders local financial market deepening. As Ricardo Hausmann notes so colorfully, countries that have committed "original sin" and suffer serious bouts of repeated price instability and currency weakness face unbounded challenges building a framework for financial stability. For example, many Latin American countries face financial sectors that are increasingly dollarized. While selling a soft currency asset (when you sign a loan agreement, you are "selling" the bank a note in return for cash) is attractive, buying it is not. In several Andean countries, individuals can only finance a home purchase with a dollar-denominated mortgage because there is little or no liquidity in local currency financial assets. This kind of de facto dollarization is different from official dollarization. De facto dollarization occurs when country rules permit individuals and businesses to choose between local and foreign currency-denominated assets and when fear of devaluation is rampant. In some circumstances, there are synergies between dollarization and local financial market deepening. Official dollarization may be a plausible policy response to the dilemma of weak domestic financial markets and recurring financial/exchange rate crises (Hausmann 1999). Former Argentine President Carlos Menem explored the idea of officially converting his country's national currency to the dollar in the late 1990s. But he could not do so without support from the U.S. government and Federal Reserve Bank. U.S. officials were unable and unwilling to cooperate in what would have been a massive exchange of pesos for dollars. In a world where prevailing wisdom holds that the only viable exchange rate regimes, especially for crisis-prone countries, are the hardest possible fixed rate (dollarization is a hard fix) or floating rates, Menem's dollarization idea might have saved Argentina from its most recent financial collapse.

As Table 3 shows, financial market deepening is progressing unevenly across Latin America. Chile has reached levels of equity market capitalization relative to GDP that is comparable to the G-4 countries. Argentina, Chile, and Colombia saw modest increases in capital market size from 1980 to 1995. Mexico stands out for fairly rapid stock market growth. The data show an incomplete story for Venezuela. In that country, the stock market grew rapidly through 1995 but has shrunk considerably during Hugo Chávez's administration. Chile and Mexico also stand out for their increases in long-term debt, an indicator of credit market deepening. While neither country has attained G-4 levels of long-term lending, the rate of growth between 1980 and 1995 was high. Mexico's 1995 exchange rate and financial crisis wiped out much of this gain. Other countries in the region have witnessed relatively little growth in long-term lending. By the measure of total bank deposits to GDP in 1999, Chile and Brazil stand out, while Venezuela fares poorly. Numbers for Mexico show the lingering impact of the bank crisis.

Table 3. Indicators of Financial Market Deepening in Latin America
(in percentages)

A. Ratios of Stock Market Capitalization over National GDP (%)

Equity/GDP	1980-1985	1985-1990	1991-1995
Argentina	0.0	0.1	0.2
Brazil	0.2	0.2	0.3
Chile	1.1	2.0	1.1
Colombia	0.3	0.2	0.4
Mexico	0.0	0.1	0.6
Peru	<.05	<.05	<.05
Venezuela	0.3	1.0	1.4
G-4 (average)	0.7	1.4	1.0

Table 3. —*continued*

B. Long-Term Debt Outstanding over GDP (in %)

	1980-1985	1985-1990	1991-1995
Argentina	Not avail.	0.0	0.3
Brazil	0.2	0.1	0.4
Chile	1.3	1.9	3.2
Colombia	0.2	0.2	0.5
Mexico	0.0	0.4	2.3
Peru	0.0	0.1	0.4
Venezuela	0.7	1.9	0.3
G-4 (average)	4.8	6.8	7.6

C. Bank Deposits and Assets over GDP (in %)

	Argentina	Brazil	Chile	Colombia	Mexico	Peru	Venezuela	US
Deposits 1999	45	92	71	49	34	40	22	NA
Assets 2001	54	55	97	NA	30	36	6	66

D. Borrowing from Domestic Banks over GDP (in %)

	Argentina	Brazil	Chile	Colombia	Mexico	Peru	Venezuela
1995	20	31	53	18	37	16	9
2000	23	30	67	19	12	26	10

Sources: Statistics were compiled by the author, based on data from the IMF, International Financial Statistics, <www.imf.org/external/bopage/arindex.htm>; and the Bank for International Settlements, *The Banking Industry in the Emerging Market Economies: Competition, Consolidation and Systemic Stability,* BIS Papers No. 4, August 2001, <http://www.bis.org/publ/bispap04.htm>.

In the second half of the 1990s, bank mergers and foreign purchases of domestic banks have helped spur financial deepening throughout the region. Over the long-term, foreign investment may help promote efficient management practices, while mergers help banks reach sectoral economies of scale. Foreign banks' share in total bank asset ownership is up to 40 percent from 10 percent in the mid-1990s (Hawkins and Mihaljek 2001, 48). Spurred by the banking sector collapse after 1995, foreign investment in Mexican banks rose dramatically between 1997 and 2001. Brazil and Colombia underwent increased merger activity. Brazil experienced 38 mergers in the 1997-1999 period, up from eight in the prior six years, while Colombian banks completed 11 mergers in 1997-1999, compared with only three in the prior six years (Hawkins and Mihaljek 2001, 40).

Financial sector performance in Latin America falls well short of G-4 and even other emerging market regions. The record of domestic financial market growth in emerging market countries is promising. Including the Latin American region, emerging market countries have seen domestic credit and bond financing almost triple since 1995, while foreign credit and bond financing has remained virtually constant (IMF 2001, 45). But credit to the private sector as a percentage of GDP is less than 35 percent in Latin America, while it is almost twice that level in Southeast Asia and exceeds 100 percent in highly industrialized countries (Hausmann 1999, 3).

In an effort to build domestic financial markets over the near term, Latin American governments might consider reinforcing existing or nascent plans for pension fund privatization, concomitant with regulations requiring those funds to become active investors in their national capital markets. Over the longer term, macroeconomic policy and institutional weakness still hinder financial market deepening. These topics are discussed in the next two sections. The following section addresses institutional requisites for coping with financial instability.

INSTITUTION BUILDING

Institutional capacity is a requisite of financial stability in the following two areas: bank supervision and regulation and creditor/shareholder rights. Building capacity to supervise and regulate banks for financial stability involves creating rules and then building enforcement capacity. But this "helping hand" view of bank supervision is controversial. Overzealous bank lending has played a role in numerous Latin American bank crises. However, contrary to conventional wisdom, recent research suggests that the best supervision promotes private monitoring rather than extensive government control. The goal of supervision should be to prevent excessive bank risk taking. Supervisory authorities need to disseminate key rules for bank health. These include international accounting standards, capital adequacy directives, and disclosure requirements. Disclosure and accountability are key components of policies to promote private monitoring. If disclosure is high, market pressures should bring international standards to bear without extensive government intervention.

Banks need to keep books according to internationally understood accounting practices. For example, bank practices regarding past-due loans vary with significant consequences for financial system health. The key issue is how many months past due a loan is when it is shifted from the category of a performing to a nonperforming asset. The higher the value of a bank's nonperforming assets, the greater the reserves a bank must put aside to maintain capital adequacy. Banks can hide problem loans and avoid increasing reserves by keeping past-due loans in the performing asset category. But whether the government should try to enforce these accounting rules or create mechanisms to encourage private sector monitoring is open to question. Private monitoring should function well if a large percentage of top banks are rated by international credit agencies, if an external audit is required, and if directors are legally liable for misleading information.

Reporting requirements are an important category of financial supervision. Rules governing how loans are contracted constitute another important arena for supervision and regulation. The goal is rules that encourage quality lending through careful evaluation of customers' creditworthiness. Can this be accomplished through market pressure or is direct government prescription required? One controversial issue is "insider" lending. Corporate conglomerates crossing the financial and industrial sectors are common in Latin American history. One view is that conglomerate banks tend to lend to other enterprises within the group, eschewing rigorous credit evaluation. Some countries restrict intragroup lending; a few others have tried to prevent cross-ownership of bank and nonbank business. Detailed research on Mexico shows that related loans are 33 percent more likely to default than unrelated ones (La Porta, López-de-Silanes and Zamarripa 2001). But Barth et al. scrutinize a 100-country survey for evidence that restricting "insider" lending improves bank health and find none (Barth et al. 2001).

Whatever the costs of insider lending, few could argue against policies encouraging banks to predicate lending upon careful credit evaluation of the potential borrower. This task is easier for banks if there are local credit research companies. In India, for example, World Bank programs promote domestic for-profit credit research agencies. Subsidiaries of the major U.S. credit rating agencies, Moody's and Standard and Poor's, operate in the big Latin American markets. Entry of foreign banks from advanced industrial countries is also helping to encourage the practice of credit evaluation and other forms of private sector monitoring.[2]

The correct degree of policy emphasis on improving government enforcement capabilities is another controversial issue in light of the debate between those who see regulation as a helping hand and those who see it as a grabbing hand. Proponents of the helping-hand view would look at measures of supervisory authority, such as codified supervisory powers/independence or supervisor turnover/salary relative to private bankers.

Table 4 draws on World Bank data to indicate cross-national variations in Latin American financial regulation. Policy strongly encourages private monitoring in Argentina, Brazil, Chile, and El Salvador. Policy creates fewer incentives for private monitoring in Bolivia, Guatemala, and Venezuela, with several important countries such as Mexico excluded for lack of data. Government supervisory authority, measured by legal code, is high in Brazil, Peru, and Venezuela and lower in Bolivia, Chile, and Mexico.

Table 4: Indicators of Financial Supervision

A. Private Monitoring Incentives

	Certified audit required	Consolidated financial statement	Director liability	Deposit insurance	% top 10 banks rated by intl. agency	Aggre-gate*
Argentina	Yes	Yes	Yes	Yes	100	8
Bolivia	Yes	No	Yes	No	20	7
Brazil	Yes	Yes	Yes	Yes	100	8
Chile	Yes	Yes	Yes	Yes	50	8
El Salvador	Yes	Yes	Yes	Yes	90	8
Guatemala	Yes	No	Yes	Yes	0	5
Mexico	Yes	Yes	Yes	Yes	NA	NA
Venezuela	Yes	Yes	Yes	Yes	34	6

*The numbers in the last column (Aggregate) represent an index ranging from a low of 0 (little private monitoring incentive) to a high of 11 (high private monitoring incentive). These figures were updated by the author in September 2003 from World Bank data. See <www.worldbank.org/research>.

B. Government Supervisory Authority*

	Argentina	Brazil	Bolivia	Chile	El Salvador	Mexico	Peru	Venezuela	US
Codified Supervisory Power	12	15	11	11	12	10	14	14	14
Supervisor Tenure (years)	6.3	15	6.2	NA	6	NA	13	5	8

*The Government Supervisory Authority Index runs from a low of 0 to a high of 18.

Source: James R. Barth, Gerard Caprio, Jr., and Ross Levine. 2001. *The Regulation and Supervision of Banks Around the World.* (Washington, D.C.: World Bank Group.) Available at <www.worldbank.org/research>.

A very different set of institutional issues involves creditor rights. Bankruptcy and reorganization laws make creditors vulnerable and limit financial market deepening in this way. An example is that many countries fail to put a neutral, court-appointed individual in charge of business reorganization once bankruptcy is apparent. Obviously, creditors can be hurt if management continues in place once bankruptcy is apparent. Other issues include whether creditors' consent is required for reorganization and creditors' access to disposition of securities or proceeds from disposition of corporate assets (La Porta et al. 2000; Galindo 2001). Among Latin American countries, creditors are in the worst situation in Argentina, Colombia, Paraguay, and Peru where a firm can easily declare itself in reorganization or bankruptcy, stop paying creditors, and continue to maintain business ownership and operational control.[3]

Institutional lacunae also hinder stock market growth in Latin America. Trading and trade settlement procedures are antiquated, and legal protection for minority shareholders is weak. Rarely is stock ownership of a publicly traded company evenly disbursed across a large number of investors. Controlling shareholders dominate ownership of most publicly traded companies, but legislation offers varying degrees of protection for minority shareholders. Important issues include whether one share equals one vote, whether voting rules favor minorities through proportional representation or other mechanisms, how easy it is to call a shareholder meeting, and whether minority shareholders are offered preemptive rights to purchase new issues. Based on these criteria and others (La Porta et al. 2000), an index of shareholder rights in Latin America has been created. By this measure, Argentina and Chile do an excellent job protecting minority shareholders, while Colombian, Mexican, Uruguayan, and Venezuelan law offers little assurance for minority owners. Colombia and Peru fall in between the two extremes. An important policy recommendation for financial deepening, particularly stock market growth, is to revise legislation guiding corporate governance.

Coping with financial volatility requires institution building in two important arenas: government monitoring and private monitoring. Although controversy surrounds research on the effectiveness of extensive government monitoring, government policy should, at the least, encourage private monitoring. This places emphasis on disclosure requirements such as a certified external audit. Furthermore, disclosure requirements are more likely to be followed when bank directors are liable for publication of misleading information. Beyond improved monitoring laws, guaranteeing creditor protection through clear bankruptcy guidelines will help foster credit market growth. Similarly, revising corporate governance rules to protect minority shareholders — as was done recently in Chile and Brazil — should spur stock market development.

COUNTERCYCLICAL MACROECONOMIC POLICY

A final set of policies for coping with financial instability in Latin America encompasses measures to break the cycle of procyclical macroeconomic policy that has consistently been part of the financial crisis story. Theoretically, financial markets are meant to help smooth consumption across time. When income falls, financial markets provide income-supplementing resources. But for Latin America, financial markets have not provided opportunities to smooth consumption or investment. International financial shocks and tight macroeconomic policy occur simultaneously, aggravating the boom-bust cycles rather than smoothing them out. Latin American governments hit by international shocks tend to turn all macroeconomic policy dials to contractionary settings. Central banks raise interest rates to try to stem capital outflows, and fiscal authorities contract their macroeconomic policies.

Latin American policymakers can tackle this problem in several ways, although the greatest need and opportunity for change lies on the fiscal policy front. Latin American fiscal policy exhibits a costly perversity. Public spending tends to expand in good times and contract in bad. Highly industrialized countries pursue cautious fiscal policy in booms and expand spending or cut taxes during downturns (IDB 1997, 104). Private behavior also follows this trend. Savings fall in boom times. Political economists offer several interesting explanations for this trend, suggesting it is more or less amenable to correction. Lane and Tornell (1998) build a model with a procyclical or countercyclical equilibrium outcome driven by whether or not the economy is dominated by large economic groups. Procyclical macroeconomic policy is a bigger problem in countries with large business conglomerates. The story they tell using deductive reasoning modeled mathematically is plausible, given the business history of Latin America. Over time, stock market growth and improved legal protection for shareholders should help break the economic stranglehold of large groups.

In the meantime, governments can try to ameliorate procyclicality through other policy measures. Policy should create mechanisms that spur buildup of precautionary fiscal surpluses during economic upswings. Fiscal flexibility is key to coping with financial volatility. But few countries ever have fiscal flexibility when they need it. In 2001, for example, Brazil had little fiscal flexibility, and Brazilians paid an economic and political price as the region slid deeper into recession. Of course, building and sustaining a fiscal surplus is no easy task. The toughest obstacles are political.

Tax reform has long been on the Latin American policy agenda, and some countries have made more progress than others. Needless to say, tax reforms to strengthen public finances would help Latin America cope with financial volatility. However, there are two more limited fiscal policy initiatives on which Latin American governments might focus their attention. These are creating budget stabilization and/or commodity stabilization funds.

Commodity stabilization schemes aim to promote fiscal flexibility through mandatory precautionary savings funds for use during commodity price declines. Chile and Venezuela, the two countries in Latin America that depend on one commodity, oil, for more than 20 percent of their export earnings, both have such schemes. Mexico depends on oil for a much smaller portion of export earnings but has also legislated a stabilization fund. Other countries in the region are relatively heavily dependent on one commodity export and should consider such funds. These countries are Colombia, Peru, Ecuador, Paraguay, and all the Central American countries.

All but five states in the United States have budget stabilization funds. These are precautionary savings funds that state governments expand during periods of strong revenue growth for use when revenues dip. Latin American governments seeking pragmatic measures to help in the war on financial instability might consider using their limited political capital to seek legislative approval for new or expanded stabilization funds.

CONCLUSION

Short of changing the international environment, this chapter suggests that Latin American governments might look in four areas for modest, feasible measures to cope with financial instability. These are international capital management, financial deepening, financial institution building, and countercyclical fiscal policy. Governments might actively discourage short-term capital inflows by charging a fee or "tax" for short-term investments, as Chile did in the 1990s. They might create positive incentives for financial innovation leading to lower risk sovereign and corporate finance. Governments might demand more financial creativity from the large banks that earn fees from business with Latin American governments and corporations. Latin American officials might consider reinforcing or expanding pension fund privatization, while requiring pension funds to invest partially in domestic financial instruments. Latin American policymakers might also explore ways to increase private financial monitoring through disclosure requirements. They might encourage investment and orderly crisis resolution through bankruptcy guidelines and minority shareholder protection. Finally, this essay stresses the value of fiscal stabilization funds to provide macroeconomic flexibility in the face of international financial shocks. There are no easy answers to Latin America's history of financial volatility or to that of all market-based financial systems, for that matter. Recognizing powerful political realities at the international level hinders large-scale changes in international financial markets and governance. Also mindful of national circumstances militating against substantial change in the politics of policymaking, this essay has focused on relatively modest but, hopefully, politically feasible proposals for chipping away at the mountain of financial volatility that blocks Latin America's road to economic, political, and social development.

NOTES

1.   There is some debate about the relationship between the impact of financial intermediation, or deepening, on economic growth. Studies of growth see a positive correlation, while studies of financial crises see financial intermediation as a precursor to financial trouble. Loayza and Ranciere (2002) find that financial intermediation may be negatively correlated with financial stability and growth in the short term but positively correlated over the longer term.

2.   The IMF and World Bank have initiated international financial "health checks" designed to discourage excessive risk taking. The Financial Sector Assessment Program (FSAP) is meant to help prevent financial crises by identifying financial sector weaknesses quickly enough for remedial action to forestall financial collapse (Aninat 2001).

3.   A separate institutional issue bearing on creditors' incentives are laws regarding collateralization. Creditors are often more willing to lend if the borrower offers a form of collateral as a guarantee to the creditors in case of default. In specific Latin American countries, law often restricts use and appropriation of collateral.

REFERENCES

Aninat, Eduardo. 2001. "Developing Capital Markets in Latin America." Speech prepared for the Inter-American Development Bank Conference on Capital Market Development. Washington, D.C., February 5.

Barth, James R., Gerard Caprio, Jr., and Ross Levine. 2001. *The Regulation and Supervision of Banks Around the World.* Washington, D.C.: World Bank Group. Available at <www.worldbank.org/research>.

Budnevich, Carlos, and Guillermo Le Fort. 1997. *Capital Account Regulations and Macroeconomic Policy: Two Latin American Experiences.* Santiago, Chile: Central Bank of Chile. Available at <www.bcentral.cl/Estudios/DTBC/06/06/htm>.

Chadha, Bankim, and IMF staff team. 2001. International Monetary Fund, "Emerging Market Financing." *Quarterly Report II:* (3): 1-2.

Eichengreen, Barry. 1999. "Ties Need Not Bind." *Milken Institute Review* (March): 13-16.

Galindo, Arturo. 2001. "Creditor Rights and the Credit Market." Annual Meeting of the Board of Governors, Inter-American Development Bank. Santiago, Chile, March 16.

Hausmann, Ricardo. 1999. "The Exchange Rate Debate." *Latin American Economic Policies* 7: 1-4.

Hausmann, Ricardo, and Eduardo Fernando Arias. 2000. "Foreign Direct Investment: Good Cholesterol?" Paper prepared for the Annual Meeting of the Board of Governors of the Inter-American Development Bank. New Orleans, March 26.

Hawkins, John, and Dubravko Mihaljek. 2001. *The Banking Industry in the Emerging Market Economies.* Basle: Bank for International Settlements (BIS) Papers No. 4.

Inter-American Development Bank (IDB). 1997. *Latin America After a Decade of Reforms.* Washington, D.C.: IDB.

International Monetary Fund (IMF). 2001. *International Capital Markets.* Washington, D.C.: IMF, August.

La Porta, Rafael, Florencio López-de-Silanes, and Guillermo Zamarripa. 2002. *Related Lending.* National Bureau of Economic Research (NBER) WP No. 8848. Available at <www.papers.nber.org/papers/w8848>.

La Porta, Rafael, Florencio López-de-Silanes, Andrei Schleifer, and Robert Vishny. 2000. "Investor Protection: Origins, Consequences." *Journal of Financial Economics* 58 (1): 1-25.

Lane, Philipp R., and Aaron Tornell. 1998. *Why Aren't Savings in Latin America Procyclical?* Harvard Institute for International Development (HIID) Discussion Paper No. 642.

Loayza, Norman, and Romain Ranciere. 2002. *Financial Development, Financial Fragility, and Growth.* Central Bank of Chile Researh Paper No. 145. Available at <www.bccentral.cl/estudios>.

Neely, Christopher J. 1999. "An Introduction to Capital Controls." *Review* 81 (6): Nov./Dec. St. Louis: Federal Reserve Bank of St. Louis, 13-30.

Mishkin, Frederic S. 2001. "Financial Policies and the Prevention of Financial Crises in Developing Countries." Paper prepared for the NBER Conference on Economic and Financial Crises in Emerging Market Countries. Woodstock, Vt., October 19-21.

Pettis, Michael. 2001. *The Volatility Machine.* Oxford: Oxford University Press.

Reinhart, Carmen M., and Peter J. Montiel. 1999. "Do Capital Controls Influence the Volume and Composition of Capital Flows?" *Journal of International Money and Finance 18 (4): 619-635.*

PART III

ACCUMULATING HUMAN CAPITAL

Chapter Six

WHAT HUMAN CAPITAL POLICIES CAN AND CANNOT DO FOR PRODUCTIVITY AND POVERTY REDUCTION IN LATIN AMERICA

Suzanne Duryea and Carmen Pagés[1]

INTRODUCTION

The structural economic reforms introduced in Latin America during the end of the 1980s and beginning of the 1990s brought deep and, in many cases, unpleasant adjustments under the promise of better living conditions for all. However, by the end of the 1990s, those expectations had not been fulfilled. Job creation was slow, unemployment rates steadily increased during the decade, and poverty declined only modestly. Social unrest and opposition to further reforms are on the rise (Lora and Panizza 2002). It is quite clear that substantial improvements in living conditions must be achieved if the reforms initiated in the 1990s are to be maintained.

At the same time, there has been a growing sense of disenchantment with the outcome of the reforms in developed countries and in the international institutions that funnel resources for development. While some proposals call for a reversal of the policies of the 1990s, others propose a new agenda of policy tools that emphasize poverty reduction, education, and good governance as fundamental development goals (Birdsall and de la Torre 2001). As a sign of the new times, in the year 2000, world leaders of 189 states met at the United Nations Millennium Summit and set forth a series of ambitious international goals to be achieved by the year 2015. The millennium goals set targets to reduce poverty to half of its early-1990s level, eradicate extreme poverty and hunger, and achieve universal primary education. These commitments indicate that the pendulum of foreign economic policies is slowly shifting toward social agendas, since the completion of these goals not only relies on faster economic growth, but also on more social spending, including health and education. These new goals impose opportunities and constraints on the policy menu of governments as they direct resources to education, health, and other social policies at the expense of resources for other objectives. The expectation is that these investments will bring about rapid improvements in living conditions.

This chapter assesses the role that human capital policies play in improving economic conditions in the region, particularly for the poor. The focus is on human capital policies because of all social policies, the lack of education, both in terms of qualifications and broad abilities, is repeatedly noted as one of the main factors behind the unsatisfactory economic and social performances of Latin America. In testimony to the U.S. Congress in 2000, the acting USAID administrator for the Latin American and Caribbean (LAC) region, Carl Leonard, stated, "The single most powerful tool for reducing poverty and improving equity in the long run is high quality primary and secondary education." Likewise, the Millennium Development Goals state, "Education is a powerful instrument for reducing poverty and inequality, improving health and social well-being, and laying the basis for sustained economic growth" (MDG).

Education brings new ideas and technologies that foster productivity growth. In turn, new technologies can be adapted to the production process only when workers have the skills and abilities to do so. Raising educational standards is also being increasingly recognized as a critical factor for poverty reduction. Former U.S. Treasury Secretary Paul O'Neill repeatedly asserted that multilateral development banks and international institutions should focus on raising productivity. In testimony to the U.S. Congress in May 2001, he noted that programs that raise workers' labor income are the critical link for reducing poverty.

The level and progress of education in the region are troublesome. Not only are educational levels low, but progress is typically much slower than that attained by the fast growing countries of East Asia. In addition, educational attainment is deeply unequal; large inequalities exist within rural and urban areas, across racial and ethnic groups, and between richer and poorer households. Moreover, although there is scant evidence about the quality of education, what is known suggests that quality is also an area of concern. To improve educational attainment, governments and donors should focus on increasing per student expenditures for education, introducing mechanisms of control and accountability within the education administration and in schools, revising pay and incentives for teachers, and alleviating the liquidity constraints that inhibit poor households from sending their children to school.

However, while human capital reforms can increase the quantity and quality of educated workers in the region, are they enough to lift the incomes and the sense of well-being of the majority of Latin Americans within a 10-year time span? Should policymakers devote substantial resources to education at the expense of resources devoted to other ends? This chapter examines the ability of education directly to lift labor incomes above poverty levels in Latin America and asserts that for many countries, educational interventions have a positive, although limited, potential to increase workers' incomes above the poverty line. In general, the immediate prospects of this happening are dim because 1) progress in raising average schooling levels has been slow, even under the best historical scenarios, and 2) skilled workers require complementary conditions, such as adequate capital, infrastructure, institutions, and cooperative labor relations to be productive. Without these complementary conditions, education generally fails to lift earnings above minimum levels. Moreover, the better the quality of this environment, the larger will be the absolute gains in earnings given by an expansion in education. These findings should not be interpreted as justifying lower expenditures on education. On the contrary, expenditures for education are low in Latin America, relative to other regions in the world, and there is much room for improvement. Investments in education continue to have positive wage returns in most LAC countries. In the long run, a better educated workforce should attract investments in capital and technology. Chapter Seven in this volume demonstrates the continuing need for educational expenditures to be reallocated away from tertiary to secondary and primary levels. The results set forth in this chapter underscore the modest prospects for increases in education to reduce earnings poverty in the short run. The results also caution against placing unrealistically high expectations on education as the sole remedy for low productivity and suggest the importance of factors complementary to education.

The sections that follow

- Explain the relationship between education and productivity;
- Assess education in Latin America relative to other regions of the world;
- Examine how fast education can be expanded;
- Calculate the impact of education expansion in reducing the share of "poor" workers and show that education, by itself, cannot remedy the productivity deficit in the region;
- Explore the reasons behind the limited role of education in reducing the share of poor workers;
- Evaluate the impact of job training policies; and
- Suggest interventions for a high productivity agenda.

EDUCATION AND PRODUCTIVITY

The positive relationship between schooling and higher earnings is well documented in the microeconomic literature for industrialized as well as developing countries. There has been intense discussion regarding whether the earnings of educated workers reflect their inner abilities or instead reflect the increases in productivity associated with education. If the most able workers are the ones who can complete higher levels of education, education may be a way to signal higher ability. If this were an important part of the story, the expansion of education would not necessarily lead to more productivity. However, recent research suggests that higher earnings do indeed reflect that education imparts knowledge and skills that increase workers' productivity (Krueger and Lindahl 2000).

In the 1990s, many researchers attempted to link aggregate schooling measures to national productivity and income. Using cross-country data, most found that the initial level of schooling within countries was linked to subsequent increases in national income. However, not all studies showed strong links between changes in schooling levels and income growth; some studies have found no relationship between changes in education attainment and gross domestic product (GDP) growth (Benhabib and Spiegel 1994). Some even found an empirical link between increases in women's schooling and slowdowns in growth (Pritchett 1996; Barro and Sala-i-Martin 1995). There are a variety of reasons driving inconsistencies in research with aggregate data. One is that it is extremely difficult to collect comparable measures of schooling across countries. For example, the schooling level classified as completed primary in one country may be considered completed first cycle of secondary in another country. Average levels of quality may differ widely. The resulting measurement error would bias the results against finding that aggregate measures of schooling affect income growth. Krueger and Lindahl (2000) found that once corrections are made for errors in measuring years of education, changes in education positively affect GDP growth. Therefore, while the jury is out regarding the best estimation approaches with aggregate level data, both micro- and macroeconomic literature suggest a link between schooling and productivity.

EDUCATION IN LATIN AMERICA

G iven the strong relationship among education, earnings, productivity, and GDP growth found by many studies, it is not surprising that Latin America's deficit in educational attainment has been identified as the leading cause of low income and high poverty rates in the region (IDB 1998, 2001). Low levels of education, deep inequalities, and very poor quality characterize education outcomes in Latin America.

Low Levels of Schooling

Educational attainment in Latin America lags behind that in other regions. Using estimates from the Barro-Lee (2000) data set on education, Table 1 shows the average years of schooling attained by those older than 25 in Latin America was approximately six years in 2000. With averages of more than 11 years in the United States, Canada, and Sweden, attainment in these countries is twice the Latin American average. There is of course much disparity in average schooling levels within Latin America and the Caribbean, with the lowest average attainment in the table found in Guatemala (3.12 years) and the highest in Argentina (8.49 years).

The availability of skilled workers can be proxied[2] by the share of population who have completed at least secondary schooling. Again, using the Barro and Lee (2000) figures shown in Table 1, the percentage of skilled workers in South Korea, Taiwan, the United States, Canada, Japan, and Sweden is at least twice that of the Latin American or Caribbean average. For example, 42 percent of adults age 25 and above in Taiwan have completed at least secondary school, whereas the average for the same age group in Latin America is 22 percent. Among the countries with the lowest share of potential workers with completed secondary schooling are Guatemala, Honduras, Nicaragua, Brazil, and El Salvador, where less than 15 percent of adults have completed secondary school.

Slow Progress

Of particular concern is that not only are attainment levels in the region very low, but progress has been very slow, especially in recent decades. As shown in Table 1, the average years of schooling for those older than 25 in Latin America rose from 3.2 years in 1960 to 4.4 years in 1980 and then to 5.9 years in 2000. Thus, the average years of schooling increased less than one year per decade in the region over the 1960 to 1980 period as well as during the 1980 to 2000 period.

Some countries were more successful than others. For example, Mexico, Chile, Panama, Peru, and Argentina increased their schooling by one year per decade between 1980 and 2000. Others, such as Colombia, Guatemala, Paraguay,

Table 1. Summary Measures of Schooling Attainment Across Countries, Population Age 25 and Older

	Average Years of Completed Schooling				Percentage Completing at least Secondary			
				Change per decade over period of				Change over 1980
	1960	1980	2000	1980-2000	1960	1980	2000	to 2000
East Asia and the Pacific								
South Korea	3.23	6.81	10.46	1.83	8.4	27.6	60.3	32.70
Singapore	3.14	5.52	8.12	1.30	7.7	8.4	23.8	15.40
Taiwan	3.32	6.37	8.53	1.08	8.8	22.6	42.0	19.40
Thailand	3.45	3.77	6.10	1.17	2.2	5.2	15.4	10.20
Advanced Countries								
United States	8.66	11.91	12.25	0.17	35.4	76.9	71.7	-5.20
Canada	8.37	10.23	11.43	0.60	34.4	53.4	64.9	11.50
Japan	6.87	8.23	9.72	0.75	21.7	29.7	41.4	11.70
Sweden	7.65	9.47	11.36	0.94	25.9	51.1	66.0	14.90
Latin America								
Argentina	4.99	6.62	8.49	0.94	8.3	14.7	30.1	15.40
Bolivia	4.22	4.00	5.54	0.77	13.2	12.9	20.4	7.50
Brazil	2.83	2.98	4.56	0.79	6.0	7.7	13.8	6.10
Chile	4.99	5.96	7.89	0.97	13.1	18.8	30.9	12.10
Colombia	2.97	3.94	5.01	0.54	5.8	10.9	18.5	7.60
Costa Rica	3.86	4.70	6.01	0.66	5.1	12.8	23.3	10.50
Ecuador	2.95	5.40	6.52	0.56	4.0	15.5	27.0	11.50
Guatemala	1.43	2.34	3.12	0.39	1.5	4.4	8.6	4.20
Honduras	1.69	2.33	4.08	0.88	2.2	4.6	12.5	7.90
Mexico	2.41	4.01	6.73	1.36	2.9	10.5	24.6	14.10
Nicaragua	2.09	2.86	4.42	0.78	3.9	7.5	13.7	6.20
Panama	4.26	5.91	7.90	1.00	6.7	19.8	35.9	16.10
Paraguay	3.35	4.64	5.74	0.55	3.8	10.6	17.5	6.90
Peru	3.02	5.44	7.33	0.95	6.7	20.8	35.2	14.40
El Salvador	1.70	3.30	4.50	0.60	2.5	6.9	14.3	7.40
Uruguay	5.03	5.75	7.25	0.75	10.0	13.0	21.8	8.80
Venezuela	2.53	4.93	5.61	0.34	3.7	16.2	22.0	5.80
Latin America Average	**3.20**	**4.42**	**5.92**	**0.75**	**5.85**	**12.21**	**21.77**	**9.56**
Caribbean								
Dominican Republic	2.38	3.36	5.17	0.91	1.5	7.2	19.2	12.00
Barbados	5.22	6.84	9.11	1.14	5.7	12.7	25.6	12.90
Jamaica	2.46	3.60	5.22	0.81	2.1	6.4	15.2	8.80
Trinidad and Tobago	4.19	6.60	7.62	0.51	4.2	6.9	17.3	10.40
Caribbean Average	**3.11**	**4.57**	**6.19**	**0.81**	**3.38**	**8.30**	**19.33**	**11.03**

Source: Robert J. Barro and Jong-Wha Lee, *International Data on Educational Attainment: Updates and Implications* (CID Working Paper no. 42), Harvard University.

and Venezuela, grew at a dismal rate. This is particularly troubling because some of these countries were already among the worst performers in 1980.

Large Inequalities

Differences across income, area of residence, and race in educational outcomes remain a challenge for Latin America. Figure 1 shows that on average across 18 countries, children from the poorest 30 percent of households are less likely to be attending school than children from the richest 20 percent of households. The gaps are most pronounced in the early years, at ages 6 and 7, and then again after age 12. For example at age 6, 90 percent of children from the relatively higher income households attend school, while only 73 percent of children from the poorest households do. At age 16, the gap is over 30 percentage points. There are also large inequities between rural and urban areas. The 2001 study by the Partnership for Educational Revitalization in the Americas (PREAL) reports differences in enrollment between urban and rural areas of more than 30 percentage points, while in Nicaragua they exceed 50 percentage points.

Figure 1. School Attendance Rates by Per Capita Household Income Decile Average across 18 Countries Based on Household Surveys circa 1999

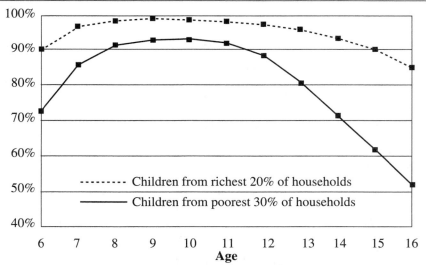

Source: Duryea and Pagés (2002) based on individual household surveys.

The scarce available data suggest that inequity persists across racial and ethnic groups as well. Using information on self-reported race and ethnicity information from household surveys, Figure 2 shows that indigenous children are less likely to be attending school than nonindigenous children during the first two years of primary school. In Brazil, Afro-Brazilian children are slightly less likely to be attending school compared with their white counterparts.[3] Although the gaps in attendance are much smaller in Brazil and Peru, they do not bode well for equity among future workers because differences tend to be magnified with age, as children who start school at later ages are more likely to quit school earlier.

However, one notable development is that the traditional gender gap in schooling is no longer an issue in most countries in the region. Girls are receiving as much schooling as boys except in specific regions of Latin America, such as Guatemala, rural Bolivia, and rural Mexico. Again, the 18-country average is instructive of overall tendencies. Whereas women born before 1950 tended to have almost one year of schooling less than their male counterparts, women born in 1980 have completed almost one-half of a year more schooling than men (Duryea, Edwards, and Ureta 2001).

Figure 2. Attendance Rates by Race and Ethnicity, First Two Years of School

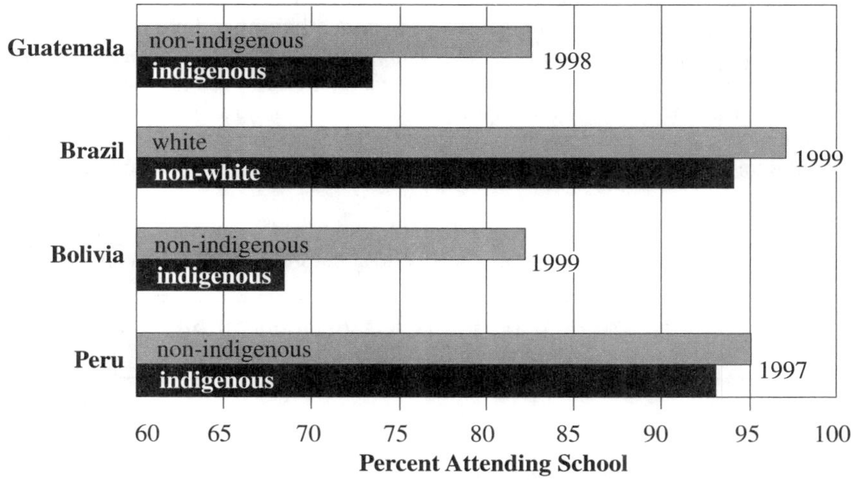

Source: Duryea and Pagés (2002) based on individual household surveys.

Poor Quality

There are very few measures of schooling quality available for Latin America, but available data suggest that the quality of schooling in the region is very low. Only a few countries participate regularly in internationally comparable achievement tests, making comparisons across countries and regions very difficult. However, on the few occasions when a Latin American country has participated, students performed below other countries, particularly relative to those in East Asia.[4] Colombia and Mexico participated in the International Mathematics and Science Study in 1996. Colombia ranked 40th out of 41 countries, and Mexico refused to release the results. Similarly, Chile participated in the same test in 1999 and finished 35th out of 38 countries, below any other participating Asian, Eastern European, and Middle Eastern countries. Moreover, the only test that so far allows comparing countries within Latin America — although it is not comparable to other countries outside the region — indicates that most countries would achieve even lower levels in internationally comparable tests. In 1998, the Latin American office for United Nations Educational, Scientific, and Cultural Organization (UNESCO) developed the first regionally comparable test in the subjects of language and mathematics.[5] The results indicated that Chile was among the best performers in the region (after Cuba and Argentina in math scores and after Cuba, Argentina, and Brazil in language). The Dominican Republic, Venezuela, Honduras, and Peru were the lowest performers in both math and language tests.

Although it is not clear what is causing such failures in education, four culprits have been identified. They relate to the low level of per student expenditure in education, the lack of mechanisms of control and accountability in most education systems, the inadequate pay for teachers, and the liquidity constraints and other barriers that drive parents to take their children out of school.

First, most countries in the region do not spend enough on education. Thus, while expenditure on education as percentage of GDP is higher in Latin America than in South or East Asia (although lower than in other more developed regions), education per student remains very low. Thus, expenditures do not reflect the fact that in the region populations tend to be young and, therefore, a relatively large part of the population is of school age. Once these demographic differences are accounted for, Latin America spends less per student (as proportion of GDP per capita) than any other region in the world, with the exception of sub-Saharan Africa (see Figure 3).

The second factor contributing to failures in LAC education is that educational systems lack mechanisms of control and accountability at all levels. In many

**Figure 3. Public Expenditure in Education per Student
(as % GNP per capita)**

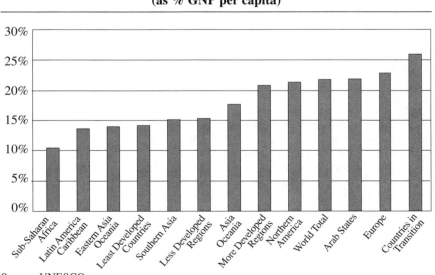

Source: UNESCO.

countries, education authorities do not have the mechanisms and technological systems to collect relevant information regarding the number of schools, number of students per school, teachers per school, projected needs in each geographical area, and other such statistics. Moreover, there are very few built-in incentives to produce high-quality teaching or, in some instances, even to show up for work. For example, while teachers are (informally) evaluated by students, parents, and school directors, teachers' pay and other incentives are usually determined by the Ministry of Education or local Education Secretary. Teachers' performance (or even attendance) is hardly monitored. When it is, there are no rewards or penalties associated with performance. In addition, in most cases school budgets are directly allocated by the government without leaving much scope for directors, parents, or teachers to allocate resources in ways that are conducive to better education outcomes. Moreover, because resources are allocated independently of school outcomes (generally as a function of the number of teachers) there are neither positive reinforcements nor negative feed back associated with school outcomes. Finally, all countries lack a set of standards that clearly define what student should know at each school level and what constitutes excellent, average, and poor performance.

Third, teachers are also victims of poor educational systems. In many countries, they finish formal training without the required skills. In others, candidates without the required qualifications are appointed as teachers. Often, when teachers are administered the same tests given to their students, they achieve only slightly higher grades than the students. Although this is not the case in all countries, low teachers' pay remains a problem. Even so, teachers' wages amount to the largest item in education budgets, and investments in textbooks, computers, and other education inputs remain very low.

Fourth, poor and disadvantaged families face important financial constraints that force them to take children out of school. Even if they realize the market value and the importance of education, they often depend on income earned by their children to meet short-run needs.

How Fast Can Education Be Expanded?

As measures that track average years of schooling for the adult population change very slowly, because only a few people change their schooling between periods, it is instructive to examine educational progress across generations, using individual records from household survey data. Table 2 contains information for 18 countries in Latin America and the Caribbean, and four non-LAC countries. The evolution of educational attainment across birth cohorts indicates that no country grew faster than two years across decades. For example, persons born in 1975 in Venezuela had on average 9.0 years of schooling, whereas the generation born one decade before, in 1965, had an average of 8.6 years of education. For the region as a whole, between 1955 and 1965, the increase in schooling was less than one additional year per decade. Indeed, educational progress has slowed by almost half a year per decade for those born from 1965 to 1975. The LAC as a region, plus the individual countries of Peru, Bolivia, Ecuador, El Salvador, and Dominican Republic, have progressed at the fastest rate over cohorts born from 1955 to 1975, at a rate of 1.2 years per year. Although these patterns are discouraging, it is important to acknowledge that while East Asian countries progressed faster, the

Table 2. Mean Years of Completed Schooling by Birth Cohorts

(Three year moving averages)

	Survey	Born in 1935	Born in 1945	Born in 1955	Born in 1965	Born in 1975	Change 1955-1965	Change 1965-1975	Change 1935-1975
Argentina*	1998	8.16	9.03	9.96	10.55	11.02	0.59	0.47	2.86
Bolivia	1999	3.79	5.52	6.24	7.45	9.07	1.20	1.62	5.27
Brazil	1999	3.36	4.56	6.14	6.97	7.43	0.84	0.45	4.07
Chile	1998	6.80	8.18	9.83	10.70	11.46	0.87	0.76	4.66
Colombia	1999	3.99	5.46	6.99	7.75	8.59	0.76	0.83	4.59
Costa Rica	1998	5.34	6.08	8.13	8.41	8.45	0.28	0.04	3.10
Dominican Rep.	1996	4.17	5.59	7.36	8.73	8.97	1.38	0.24	4.81
Ecuador	1998	4.35	6.14	7.99	9.33	9.41	1.33	0.08	5.06
Guatemala	1998	2.23	3.27	3.94	4.65	5.66	0.71	1.01	3.44
Honduras	1999	2.17	3.30	4.66	5.86	6.29	1.20	0.43	4.12
Mexico	1998	4.26	5.30	6.87	8.29	9.03	1.41	0.75	4.77
Nicaragua	1998	2.35	3.21	5.30	5.92	6.17	0.62	0.24	3.82
Panama	1999	6.74	8.10	9.45	10.08	10.49	0.63	0.41	3.75
Peru	2000	5.65	7.44	8.58	9.54	10.92	0.96	1.39	5.28
Paraguay	1998	3.86	5.12	6.35	7.72	7.89	1.37	0.17	4.03
El Salvador	1998	3.01	3.79	5.73	7.02	7.76	1.29	0.74	4.75
Uruguay*	1998	6.86	8.24	9.72	10.36	10.47	0.64	0.10	3.60
Venezuela	1999	4.66	6.64	7.96	8.59	8.95	0.62	0.36	4.28
LAC Average circa 1998		**4.54**	**5.83**	**7.29**	**8.22**	**8.78**	**0.93**	**0.56**	**4.24**
Taiwan	1996	5.31	7.73	9.94	11.75	12.55	1.81	0.80	7.24
Thailand	1998	3.81	4.94	5.72	6.75	8.29	1.03	1.54	4.48
USA	1998	12.22	13.05	13.33	13.19	12.80	-0.14	-0.39	0.58
Korea	1997	6.62	8.68	10.26	11.63	12+	1.37	na	5.38**

Source: Authors' calculations for household survey data. Data for Korea was taken from *UNESCO Statistical Yearbook*, 1997.

* Surveys cover urban areas only.

** The mean years for cohorts born in 1975 was not available; 5.38 is the increase in mean schooling across cohorts born in 1935 to 1970.

maximum increase observed across a decade is below two years of schooling. This suggests that changing the distribution of education across a 10-year period is a fundamentally difficult endeavor.

Quantifying the Effect of Education on Poverty

What if one does not accept the maximum observed increase in schooling in East Asia as a natural limit for improvements in LAC? If the region managed to make significant changes in schooling within a decade, how might productivity be expected to change? What is the expected reduction in the share of workers with low wages or "poor" workers? In Suzanne Duryea and Carmen Pagés (2001), we examined this question by estimating the expected changes in wages associated with changes in education. In this chapter, the main findings and conclusions of this research are summarized, and readers are referred to our technical paper for additional information.

Economists tend to associate wages with productivity. This is because standard economic theory predicts that in sufficiently competitive labor markets, workers' wages will be equal to workers' contribution to productivity. We therefore refer interchangeably to workers' earnings and workers' productivity. Although a more direct measure of productivity, such as total-factor productivity, would be more desirable, this measure requires obtaining data on capital stock and other inputs, which for developing countries are difficult to obtain and unreliable.

To assess how changes in education affect productivity and, in particular, the share of workers that have very low incomes (and therefore are expected to belong to poor households in per capita income terms), a productivity threshold was defined that can be compared across countries. We consider a worker to have "low productivity" if he or she earns less than US$1 per hour in his/her primary job.[6] The one-dollar threshold has been adjusted in each country to reflect differences in the cost of living by adjusting for purchasing power parity (PPP). We use this definition of "low productivity" because of its simplicity and because it is meaningfully related to the moderate poverty measure.[7]

We used individual wage data from males ages 30 to 50 in urban areas, gathered from the most current household surveys of 12 countries, to compute our measure of low wages.[8] It can be noted from Figure 4 that, although our individual-based measure of low wages is not a perfect proxy for the poverty status of the household, there is a strong relationship between our measure of low wages and other per capita measures of poverty, such as the "moderate poverty" indicator. The latter measure is computed by aggregating all incomes from all sources within a household and dividing by household size.

Figure 4. Moderate Poverty and the Percentage of Low Paid Workers

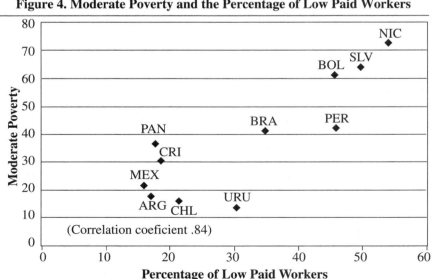

Source: Duryea and Pagés (2002) and Székely (2001).

Figure 5. Percentage of Workers in Sample Earning below $1 an hour/PPP

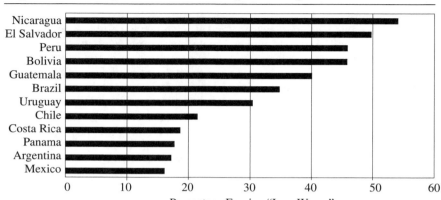

Percentage Earning "Low Wages"

Source: Duryea and Pagés (2002) based on individual household surveys.

Note: Purchasing power parity = PPP.

Figure 5 shows the share of low-paid workers among urban males, ages 30 to 50, for 12 countries in the region. For this sample, over 45 percent earn less than the US$1 threshold in Nicaragua, El Salvador, Peru, and Bolivia, while fewer than 25 percent have hourly earnings below $1 in Chile, Costa Rica, Panama, Argentina, and Mexico.[9] These figures suggest that in the Latin American region, wages, and — to the extent that wages reflect productivity — productivity levels are very low, at least for a large share of workers. It is interesting to note that, in general, the share of low-paid workers is higher in countries with poor educational attainment, and it is lower in countries with higher levels of schooling. An exception to this rule is Peru, a country with higher than average educational attainments and a high share of low-paid workers. Why has Peru, with its outstanding educational progress, not reduced the share of low-paid workers? Moreover, can an expansion of schooling reduce the high shares of low-paid workers in the region?

To assess how an expansion in education will affect productivity and, in particular, the share of workers who have very low incomes, we simulated the results of making secondary school universal. That is, we computed what would be the effect on incomes and the share of "poor" workers if all workers who in the late 1990s had completed less than secondary school have their schooling raised to completion of secondary school. It should be noted that this simulation ignores the possible reduction in the wage returns to secondary school caused by an increase in the supply of skilled workers. Additionally, this approach ignores the indirect routes by which more education may increase GDP, such as improvements that might occur through reductions in fertility and increases in foreign direct investment (FDI). We interpreted this simulation as revealing an upper limit of the scope for the change in education to affect hourly wages directly in the short run. Table 3 shows the baseline shares of low-paid workers (column 1) and the estimated reduction in that rate (column 2) as a consequence of the change in schooling. While the share of poorly remunerated workers falls by over one-half in Brazil, Mexico, and

Table 3. Simulation Results: Urban Male Workers Ages 30-50

Country	Year	(1)	(2)	(3)	(4)	(5)	(6)	(7)	(8)
Argentina	1999	17.00	13.00	3.53	0.60	4.60	39.96	54.09	11.42
Bolivia	1999	45.62	45.93	35.33	3.31	6.29	61.84	69.43	36.66
Brazil	1999	34.80	13.72	2.32	4.42	7.79	31.20	42.45	11.91
Chile	1998	21.38	11.38	1.17	2.02	4.91	42.86	55.65	16.27
Costa Rica	1998	18.55	14.17	3.12	2.12	6.12	52.38	63.31	17.52
Guatemala	1998	39.92	16.55	8.12	4.68	8.68	49.65	59.02	22.52
Mexico	1998	15.89	6.67	1.51	3.27	6.58	42.75	55.14	15.89
Nicaragua	1998	53.96	36.16	17.30	3.94	7.35	53.38	61.91	28.98
Panama	1999	17.64	10.76	2.22	1.98	4.88	48.11	63.42	14.39
Peru	2000	45.83	40.39	18.17	1.23	3.82	31.51	45.83	9.10
El Salvador	1998	49.63	42.67	15.97	3.89	7.12	46.36	59.53	19.08
Uruguay	1998	30.35	24.38	9.85	2.95	6.21	30.35	45.51	9.34

(1) Percent of workers earning "low wages" (baseline)
(2) Percent earning "low wages" if all have completed secondary
(3) Percent earning "low wages" if all have completed 4 years of college
(4) Education effort to achieve results in 2 years of education
(5) Education effort to achieve results in 3 years of education
(6) Percent earning "low wages" if country assigned median "underline conditions"
(7) Percent earning "low wages" if country assigned minimum "underline conditions"
(8) Percent earning "low wages" if country assigned maximum "underline conditions"

Source: Duryea and Pagés (2002) based on individual household surveys.

Guatemala, in four countries — Bolivia, Peru, El Salvador, and Nicaragua — 30 percent or more still earn below the threshold. Even in Uruguay, almost 20 percent of the workers still qualify as "low productivity," according to our measure. Taking the average across countries, the percentage of low-paid workers falls by about one-third or from 33 to 23 percent.

Although such a reduction is impressive and encouraging, it is useful to consider the extraordinary effort that is required to achieve this effect. Column 4 in Table 3 reports the education effort required to give every worker at least secondary education. Education effort is defined as the increase in the average years of schooling under the simulation.[10] In some countries, such as Argentina, Chile, Costa Rica, Panama, and Peru, this increase could be achieved in two decades if current progress were maintained in the future or in one decade if the education progress attained the levels achieved in Southeast Asia. In others, however, the required education progress is huge. In Brazil, it is necessary to increase average years of education by at least four years, which at their historical rates of progress would require another 40 or 50 years!

Can incomes be lifted above the low-wage threshold merely by increasing education? To answer this question, we performed a second simulation, addressing an even more outlandish counterfactual: "How would the share of workers earning less than $1 an hour change if all workers with less than four years of tertiary schooling were to have their schooling raised to that level?" Column 3 in Table 3 reports the results of this exercise. Overall, the percentage of poorly remunerated workers falls by 20 percentage points, from 33 to 10 percent. Nonetheless, over 15 percent of the workers earn wages below the poverty threshold in Bolivia, Peru, El Salvador, and Nicaragua. These partial equilibrium simulations only measure the direct effects of education on wages, ignoring indirect effects, such as the ability of higher average levels of schooling to attract foreign capital or the reduction in the wage returns of schooling as the supply of higher schooling increases. Still, we hope that the straightforward calculations inject some healthy skepticism into the political arena, which envisions rapid changes by 2015.

What Limits the Effect of Education?

The results presented in the previous section highlight that a tangible expansion in education can bring increases in productivity and earnings and reductions in poverty. However, they also showcase that expansions in education alone will not lift everyone's productivity and earnings above poverty levels. It is important to understand what limits the effect of education, not only because it allows more realistic assessments of the impact of education, but also because it yields interesting insights about how expansions in education can be made more effective.

In order for expansions in education to have a large effect on individual incomes, the effect of every additional year of education on wages (the so-called "wage returns to education") has to be large. Despite widespread failure in the

Table 4. Returns to Education, Experience, and Other Factors: Urban Male Workers Ages 30-50

Country	Year	(1)	(2)	(3)	(4)	(5)	(6)	(7)
Argentina	1999	17.00	10.40	0.05	0.08	0.17	0.22	0.48
Bolivia	1999	45.62	9.72	0.05	0.03	0.13	0.18	0.44
Brazil	1999	34.80	7.03	0.12	0.15	0.22	0.18	0.28
Chile	1998	21.38	10.88	0.07	0.12	0.24	0.09	0.50
Costa Rica	1998	18.55	9.83	0.06	0.06	0.19	0.14	0.54
Guatemala	1998	39.92	7.32	0.08	0.13	0.14	0.17	0.37
Mexico	1998	15.89	9.17	0.07	0.10	0.15	0.18	0.55
Nicaragua	1998	53.96	7.39	0.09	0.13	0.15	0.10	0.30
Panama	1999	17.64	10.96	0.06	0.08	0.16	0.10	0.51
Peru	2000	45.83	11.10	0.10	0.09	0.15	0.09	0.24
El Salvador	1998	49.63	8.67	0.05	0.08	0.20	0.20	0.29
Uruguay	1998	30.35	9.63	0.09	0.09	0.15	0.22	0.31

(1) Percent of workers earning "low wages" (baseline)
(2) Average years of completed schooling
(3) Returns to primary*
(4) Returns to secondary*
(5) Returns to tertiary*
(6) Returns to 5 years of experience
(7) Hourly earnings of a worker without schooling or experience (in PPP-adjusted $)

* Return is the percentage increase in hourly wage for an additional year of schooling.

Source: Duryea and Pagés (2002) based on individual household surveys.

Table 5. Percentage Earning "Low Wages" by Education Levels: Urban Male Workers Ages 30-50

		All Education Levels	Primary	By Education Level Secondary Complete	Four or More Years of Higher Ed.
Argentina	1999	17.00	15.32	7.54	5.66
Bolivia	1999	45.62	65.70	41.30	17.60
Brazil	1999	34.80	47.40	15.70	2.70
Chile	1998	21.38	38.90	16.80	2.40
Costa Rica	1998	18.55	30.60	14.70	2.20
Guatemala	1998	39.92	29.81	8.56	0.33
Mexico	1998	15.89	27.70	5.10	1.00
Nicaragua	1998	53.96	71.00	43.50	14.00
Panama	1999	17.64	33.20	15.10	2.70
Peru	2000	45.83	72.80	48.10	19.00
El Salvador	1998	49.63	69.20	35.90	6.30
Uruguay	1998	30.35	28.37	18.16	8.09

Source: Duryea and Pagés (2002) based on individual household surveys.

quality of education and poor results obtained in internationally comparable exams, in Latin America, the percentage increase in earnings associated with one extra year of primary, secondary, or tertiary education is quite high. Table 4 presents the estimated wage returns to an additional year of education across countries.[11] In our sample of countries, the median return for one year of primary is 7 percent, while the median return for secondary and tertiary schooling are even higher (9 and 16 percent, respectively).[12] As a comparison, Alan Krueger and Mikael Lindahl (2000) report average wage returns to schooling across all schooling levels between 3 percent in Sweden, 6 to 7 percent in Canada, 9 percent in the United States, and 13 percent in Austria.

However, large wage returns as a result of schooling are only a necessary, but not a sufficient, condition for education to have a large effect on earnings. Indeed, even when more educated workers earn higher wages, returns of schooling are measured in percentage rates. This implies that the final impact on absolute wages depends upon the base to which that percentage applies. As Latin American workers without education or skills earn very little, a relatively large increase in their wages (in percentage terms) due to additional education may still leave the worker with very low wages. This explains why a large percentage of educated workers earn wages below poverty levels. Table 5 reveals that in Bolivia, 46 percent of workers with secondary education and 18 percent of workers with four years of university education earn very low wages. These percentages are similarly high in Nicaragua and Peru. In contrast, in Mexico only 5 percent of workers with a secondary education and 2 percent of workers with university schooling are poor, according to our measure. The proportions of low-paid workers with high levels of schooling are also relatively low in Argentina and Costa Rica.

The hourly wages of workers without education or experience are a reflection of the productivity that unskilled workers are able to obtain with other factors of production, such as physical capital, utilities, and telecommunications, or public goods such as institutions or infrastructure. Therefore, the hourly wages reflect the "quality" of the institutional and economic scenario in which workers live and produce. Moreover, the better the quality of economic and institutional conditions for production, the higher the increase (in absolute terms) in earnings produced by an expansion in education. Column 7 of Table 4 reports this measure across countries in LAC. Perhaps, not surprisingly, countries such as Argentina (in 1999), Mexico, and Chile show larger values than countries such as El Salvador or Peru. It is also notable that in all cases, the hourly earnings of workers without education or experience are below our individual "poverty" line. In some countries, like Argentina, workers are nearer the $1 per hour earnings threshold than in others, but the "poverty gap" is still very large.

While our simulations have considered the impact of an increase in the quantity of schooling, we have made no reference to the effects of the quality of schooling. What is the role of improvements in the quality of education in increasing earnings and reducing poverty? Quantifying the scope for improvements in the quality of schooling is an extremely challenging task. In the absence of a standardized measure, attempts to measure the impact of quality of schooling on wages typically consider a reduction in the number of pupils per teacher, an increase in the education of teachers, or an increase in the per-pupil expenditure on education. Jere R. Behrman and Nancy Birdsall's seminal work (1983) finds that an increase in the schooling of teachers by region in Brazil increases the wage returns to schooling. For South Africa, Anne Case and Motohiro Yogo (1999) find that a reduction in class size by five pupils increases wage returns to schooling by 1 percent. In their synthesis of the literature on the quality of schooling, David Card and Alan Krueger (1996) suggest that a 10 percent increase in school spending per pupil is consistently associated with a 1 to 2 percent increase in subsequent earnings. The range of quality found in the region suggests that improving quality can hasten increases in wages but again in a modest manner. For example, wage returns to secondary school in Chile are only 25 percent higher than in Peru, even though these countries are at the two extremes of the range of results in the UNESCO exams. It is clear from these estimates that while better quality of education will deliver higher earnings, the magnitudes involved will not be sufficient to lift a large share of workers out of poverty.

JOB TRAINING

Human capital policies can also take the form of job training. However, there is intense discussion regarding whether public training policies can increase earnings and reduce poverty in the region because 1) around the world there is little evidence that public training programs translate into large wage returns, and

2) Latin American training policies have been particularly ineffective. Although there are innovations in Latin America that are worth examining and that can bring interesting results, the fundamental problem is that it is very difficult to remedy educational shortcomings with short-term vocational training. The wage returns are likely to be small; the best option probably is to give adults the opportunity to go back to school.

A recent study by the Inter-American Development Bank (IDB 2001) shows that a significant percentage of firms provide on-the-job training for their workers. This is particularly so for firms that are undergoing major investments or technological changes. However, the relevant questions pertain to whether disadvantaged workers benefit from these investments and whether on-the-job training is capable of remedying learning deficits. The IDB study shows that in all countries, technicians, supervisors, and skilled workers are much more likely to receive on-the-job training than unskilled workers, suggesting that investing in such workers commands higher returns. These results also suggest that employer-financed, on-the-job training is not likely to do much to improve the productivity of low-skilled workers. The question is whether public policy in the region can perform that role.

Evaluations of public training programs suggest that for workers without basic skills, job-training programs are not cost effective. Wage returns as results of job-training programs tend to be particularly low (on the order of one-fifth of wage returns that result from schooling) for disadvantaged male workers and somewhat higher for women. Instead, studies tend to find that the wage returns resulting from formal adult education tend to be similar to the returns for young-age schooling (Krueger and Lindahl 1999). These findings suggest that rather than providing remedial, short-term training to highly unskilled workers, resources can be better allocated by extending adults' formal education. They also suggest that because formal education and job training tend to be complementary rather than substitutive, workers who benefit from extended adult education will also benefit from more employer-financed job training.

In Latin America, training policy has been channeled through public training institutes, funded by a training levy or tax (1 to 2 percent of payroll) and administered by the government with the participation of employers and workers. Vocational education/training programs began in Brazil in the 1940s and then expanded in the late 1950s and 1960s to Columbia, Venezuela, Peru, Costa Rica, Chile, and Ecuador. During the 1970s, a new generation of these training institutions emerged in Paraguay, Honduras, Brazil, Guatemala, and Panama. With a few exceptions, public training systems have suffered from the same lack of control and accountability mechanisms as educational systems. Operated as public monopolies, the systems have lacked discipline to manage human resources. Instructors are poorly trained and poorly paid, and have limited experience in the private sector. Administrative costs have consumed almost the totality of operational budgets, while investments have been kept to a minimum. In addition, public training systems have lacked incentives to adapt the course subjects and contents to ever changing labor market needs. Contents have been excessively formal and classroom-based, without sufficient firm-based experience. Moreover, middle- or highly-skilled workers have been more likely to attend than low-skilled workers. As a consequence, the public training institute model does not appear to deliver high-quality training to unskilled workers. An evaluation for Colombia found that the impact of training on wages is lower for trainees who attended public relative to private institutions; however, the difference in wage returns could be attributed to the greater motivation and higher learning abilities of private sector trainees.[13]

Summarizing, there is evidence that firms undertake investments in on-the-job training for their most skilled workers, while leaving behind workers with little formal education. Evaluations of public training programs suggest that training unskilled workers, particularly older workers, is not cost effective. Instead, evaluations suggest that scarce public resources would be better spent devising policies that bring unskilled adult workers back to school.

WHAT LIES AHEAD

Latin American governments face the challenges and opportunities brought by pressing conditions at home and ambitious international goals. Although the objectives of the two constituencies seem to go in the same direction — to improve the distribution of wealth and the living conditions of all — the choice of instruments and policies with which to pursue these aims is not obvious. In addition, while the millennium goals emphasize social spending, players in international capital markets and debtors may focus on workers' wage returns from education. A way to reconcile these conflicting objectives is to focus on productivity growth. Low productivity is the main source of low competitiveness in Latin America (IDB 2001). In order to speed up productivity growth, public policy needs to address Latin American educational shortcomings. However, a policy based solely on educational investments is not likely to bring a substantial reduction in poverty. To boost the effects of education reforms, Latin American policymakers should also identify which other policies are required if skilled workers are to be productive. Some of the options are considered in the following section.

Quality, Quantity, and Equity of Schooling in the Region

Though education by itself has a limited effect on improving productivity, increasing the level and quality of education remains one of the main challenges of the region. If Latin American countries want to overcome their educational deficits, public expenditure per student should rise. Increasing the amount of resources directed to education is already a priority in countries under the highly indebted poor countries (HIPC) initiative, but it should be made a priority in less indebted countries as well.[14] The opportunity brought by more favorable demographic conditions should not be wasted. Thus, as the general population ages and the school-age population declines, per student investments can be increased even if total expenditures on education remain constant. These additional resources per capita can finance higher pay for teachers and increased investments in books, computers, and other educational inputs.

However, increasing per student expenditure is not likely to bring substantial gains in education without parallel reforms aimed at improving the control and accountability mechanisms in educational systems. For this to occur, it is necessary to improve management within the education administration. It is also necessary to transfer authority and resources from the ministries and local education departments to school directors and parents. Such a transfer would enable important decisions regarding teacher recruitment, teacher evaluation, and resource allocation to be made progressively at the school level. At the same time, it would be necessary to implement learning standards and monitor the performance of schools and students relative to those standards and to other countries. Finally, schools should be made accountable for decisions. Transfers to schools should be made dependent both on the characteristics of the students and the communities they serve — awarding more resources to poorer and disadvantaged communities — and on their progress in achieving educational standards. Additionally, demand-side constraints should be addressed with programs that provide financial relief to poor families with children of school age.

Not all countries need start from square one. Indeed, there are a host of unique solutions being employed in the region. As far as improving control and accountability mechanisms, some countries, particularly in Central America, have experimented with giving more autonomy to schools, although in most cases, these efforts have only applied to new or rural schools (PREAL 2001). This is the case of the Educo schools in El Salvador.[15] In other countries, like Nicaragua, school autonomy is being extended at the national level. Although it is quite early to have conclusive results, the available evidence shows that giving more authority to parents and school directors increases teachers' attendance and punctuality, as well as the interaction of teachers with parents. It also suggests that school autonomy increases learning, as measured by scores on math and language exams. Unique solutions are also being implemented to address demand-side constraints. Conditional cash-transfer programs targeted to the poorest families are showing encouraging results. This is the case of the Oportunidades Program, in Mexico, or the Bolsa-Escola, in Brazil, in which low-income families receive a cash transfer if they comply with the program requirement to send their children to school regularly.

Another promising area for policy is adult education. Although providing adult education has been a low priority in most countries, research suggests that bringing adults back to school can be effective in increasing productivity (particularly, when compared with the results of public job training targeted at unskilled workers). Latin American governments should devise ways to bring adults back to school. Examples include issuing tax credits to employers that provide the time or resources for employees to attend school or giving tax relief to adult workers who enroll to finish their formal schooling.

QUALITY OF THE ECONOMIC AND INSTITUTIONAL ENVIRONMENT

While expanding the coverage and improving the quality and equity of education are important development goals, the simulations reported in a previous section make clear the shortcomings of productivity-growth and poverty-reducing strategies that are based solely on human capital development. The newly emphasized focus on education might be a hindrance for productivity growth if abiding by international educational goals does not allow governments to expand expenditures in areas complementary to education. Thus, while education can increase the earnings of a person relative to the earning of someone who does not have education, educated workers will not be able to use their skills productively if the economic and institutional environments in which they live and work are not sufficiently "fertile." This is why without simultaneous investments in the institutional and economic environment, the productivity and earnings of a large share of the population will not be lifted above poverty levels any time soon.

To assess the importance of these other environmental factors, two additional simulations were done. First, we asked how much the share of workers with very low earnings would decline if countries could instantaneously achieve the economic and institutional conditions of Mexico, the country with the best "underlying" conditions in the sample, as measured by the earnings of a person without education or labor market experience. Second, we computed what would be the share of low-paid workers in countries such as Argentina or Mexico if they were to have the quality of the economic and institutional conditions of Peru, the lowest in our sample.

Columns 7-8 in Table 3 show the results of changing the quality of the economic environment. Column 7 shows the percentage of low-paid jobs that would result if workers in all countries worked with the economic and institutional conditions of Peru. The results are quite remarkable. Under Peruvian conditions, the percentage of low-paid jobs in countries such as Argentina, Mexico, or Panama would increase to more than 50 percent. This comparison illustrates that Peru has a relatively lower share of low-paid workers, given its underlying conditions as a consequence of its high investment in education. In contrast, the share of poor workers would decline substantially in most countries if countries had the underlying conditions of Mexico. Peru's share of low-paid jobs would drop dramatically from 46 to 9 percent, while El Salvador's share would decline from 49 to 20 percent (see Table 3, Column 8).

The simulation results demonstrate that improving the economic and institutional environments can bring substantial increases in productivity and reductions in poverty. Moreover, expansions in education will have larger effects on income when they occur in countries with better underlying economic and institutional conditions. The relevant question is how should countries go about improving these conditions, and what are the magnitudes involved? In Duryea and Pagés (2001), we attempted to answer some of these questions by examining the statistical relationship between the hourly income of a noneducated worker (that is, our measure of the underlying conditions of a given country) and different variables that are expected to affect those conditions. Among the variables that we analyzed were labor relations and regulations; financial development; degree of technological innovation; physical infrastructure variables; and institutional variables.

LABOR RELATIONS AND REGULATIONS

L abor relations and regulations affect productivity in multiple ways. By defining the set of rules that govern employment, labor relations can be conducive to high motivation, effort, and productivity, or instead, can promote low morale and poor outcomes. In Latin America, labor market regulations alter labor relations by shifting the balance of power between employers and employees. In many instances, by banning forms of labor relations that are not acceptable, government regulations level the playing field and improve workers' welfare. In others, however, governments simply fuel the fire between labor and management by restricting forms of payment that align the objectives of the firm with the objectives of workers, such as profit or revenue-sharing, or by interfering in conflict resolution and being partial to employers or employees. The available evidence suggests that the quality of labor relations in Latin America is poor. According to the *World Competitiveness Workbook 2000*, of the six countries of the region included in a sample of 47 countries worldwide, two ranked among the countries with the most hostile labor relations, while the four others were in the median or below (International Institute for Management Development 2000). Moreover, the 1997 *Latinobarómetro*, an opinion survey covering the urban areas of 17 countries in the region, suggests that a wide majority of the respondents mistrust employers and think that relations between employees and employers are poor. In addition, a large majority of respondents think that success in life does not depend on hard work, but rather on connections. Given this state of affairs, employers, employees, and governments should invest in promoting more cooperative and productive labor relations. This could be achieved by removing legislative constraints to high-performance pay schemes, facilitating permanent venues for dialog between employers and employees, and educating managers and workers' representatives in conflict resolution and management of human resources.

FINANCIAL DEVELOPMENT

D espite intense financial liberalization and improvements in financial supervision, access to capital remains tight in the region. The *World Business Environment Survey*, an opinion survey addressed to firms worldwide, suggests that the limited access to capital is one of the biggest constraints to productivity and growth in Latin America (World Bank 1999). The available research suggests that in order to expand access to credit, public policy should concentrate on creating a stable economic environment, preserving low inflation rates, promoting better creditor rights, and expanding registry services.[16] It should also continue improving the quality and independence of financial supervision.

TECHNOLOGICAL INNOVATION AND ADOPTION

G rowth theory emphasizes the role of new technology adoption and development as the engine of productivity and growth. However, in Latin America, the rates of technology innovation and adoption are below the world average (World Economic Forum 2000; IDB 2001). Improving educational attainments in the region will help boost innovation, which in turn will foster more productivity. However, promoting an environment conducive to innovation is also fundamental. This requires laws that address clear intellectual property rights as well as institutions and resources to enforce them. It also requires financial institutions specialized in start-ups and venture capital.

PHYSICAL INFRASTRUCTURE

Poor infrastructure continues to be a barrier to productivity growth in Latin America. There are too few roads, and most are in very poor condition. Sea transport is hampered by the inefficiency of ports (IDB 2001). Utility prices, particularly electricity, and the price of phone calls remain high despite intense restructuring and privatization. Limited competition and poor regulation have turned public monopolies into private ones. In the near future, governments should improve the technical capabilities and the independence of regulatory agencies. They should also limit the monopoly power of large firms by further opening the market to competition.

SOCIAL INFRASTRUCTURE

Robert E. Hall and Charles I. Jones (1999) denominated the set of institutions, regulations, and laws that make economic transactions possible as "social infrastructure." Kaufmann et al. (1999) assembled quantitative measures of social infrastructure in the areas of political stability, quality of the government, quality of the regulatory framework, rule of law, and control of corruption. These indicators suggest that Latin America ranks significantly lower than other Organization for Economic Cooperation and Development (OECD) and Southeast Asian countries. Hall and Jones (1999) and Duryea and Pagés (2001) find these variables to be highly associated with productivity per worker and earnings. While some of this association may be due to reverse causation, because richer countries can afford better institutions, there is some evidence of causality running from institutions to earnings. Therefore, efforts devoted to improving the quality of the institutional environment in any of these areas can provide large payoffs. As an example, Duryea and Pagés (2001) report that improving the quality of the Peruvian institutions to the level achieved in Chile would achieve a reduction in poverty equivalent to the one attained with 2.71 extra years of college education, or 4.3 extra years of secondary education. This is a remarkable gain because, assuming that education progress continues at the current rate and the returns of education remain constant, achieving this expansion in education would take between 30 and 45 years.

MACROECONOMIC MANAGEMENT

A factor not included in the estimates reported in Duryea and Pagés (2001) but that will likely have a substantial effect on productivity, wages, and poverty is the quality of macroeconomic management. In a new set of estimates, some evidence was found that in a cross section of Latin American countries, the incomes of noneducated workers (our measure of the quality of the economic environment) are negatively correlated with the average inflation rate of the past 20 years. These results suggest that in countries where government deficits have been repeatedly financed via inflation, the overall level of wages is lower regardless of education levels. It is worth mentioning that variables such as the average government or current account deficits over the period 1980-1999 were not correlated with our measure of the quality of the economic environment. This suggests that it is not so much the (average) level of the deficits that matters, but the inability of countries to finance them by issuing domestic or foreign debt.

CONCLUSIONS

The economic reforms of the 1990s have not delivered substantial improvements in the living conditions of the vast majority of people in Latin America. Governments are faced with raising popular discontent and the pressing need to show tangible results in the short run. This chapter assesses the effects on productivity and poverty of one of the most popular prescriptions for achieving sustainable gains in economic conditions: improving the educational attainment of the population. The level, progress, and equity of Latin American education have been reviewed, and it was found that education is underfunded and lagging behind other fast-growing regions. However, our analysis also suggests that development policies cannot be solely based on education. Thus, while education can have a positive impact by lifting workers' productivity and incomes, our results underscore the modest prospects for increases in education to reduce earnings poverty in the short run. To achieve substantial change, investments in other complementary policies should be pursued as well. Some of the policy options identified by the results include expanding the provision of basic infrastructure, creating the conditions for cooperative labor relations, providing a stable and fertile environment for innovation, sustaining a prudent macroeconomic management, and investing in improving the institutions and government regulations that prevent diversion of resources away from productive uses.

NOTES

1.   We thank Lisa Lynch for her helpful comments on a preliminary version of this chapter. We also wish to thank Werner Hernani for outstanding research assistance and Reyes Aterido for editorial assistance. The content of this chapter reflects the opinions of the authors and does not represent an official position of the Inter-American Development Bank or its Board of Directors.

2.   "Proxied" is commonly used to mean "very imperfectly measured" by the use of another variable.

3.   Primary school officially starts for children at age six in Peru and Bolivia and at age seven in Brazil and Guatemala. The Afro-Brazilian category includes children who were identified by the respondent in the household as *preta* (black) or *parda* (brown).

4.   For more information on schooling quality in Latin America, see PREAL 2001.

5.   Laboratorio Latinomericano de Evaluación de la Calidad de la Educación. 1998. *Primer Estudio Internacional Comparativo*. UNESCO. Noviembre.

6.   All results are computed from the income of the primary job. However, except when otherwise mentioned, our results do not differ much when we use a more comprehensive measure of income including all jobs.

7.   Thus, considering that the average worker in the region works an average of 44 hours per week and shares his or her income with two dependents, earnings of less than PPP$1 result in a per capita household income of less than PPP$2 per day, a standard measure of moderate poverty.

8.   We focus on males from ages 30 to 50 in urban areas because hourly earnings are less likely to be contaminated by factors such as the urbanization rate of the country and selection into the labor force.

9.   The derivation of the $1 PPP nominal currency cutoff per household survey can be found in the technical appendix.

10.   Unlike the change in the share with completed secondary schooling, the change in the mean is less dependent on the initial distribution of education and, thus, a better indicator of "education effort."

11.   See Duryea and Pagés (2001) for a description of the methodology used to estimate wage returns to schooling in Latin America.

12.   Properly speaking, these coefficients do not measure returns but wage effects because, in order to capture returns of education, one should subtract forgone earnings and other costs of education.

13.   See the evaluation by Carlos Medina and Jairo Nuñez, 2000, *The Impact of Publicly Provided Job Training in Colombia*, Latin America Research Network Working Paper R-391 (Washington, D.C.: IDB).

14.   The HIPC is an initiative of the International Financial Institutions to reduce the external debt of highly indebted and poor countries. By means of this initiative, countries agree to expend a large share of the forgone debt service for education and other social expenditures.

15.   For a description of the nature and the results of different experiences of school autonomy in Latin America, see Espinola (2000).

16.   See Galindo (2001) and Galindo and Miller (2001) for an assessment of the importance of creditor rights and credit registries in the supply of credit.

REFERENCES

Barro, Robert J., and Jong-Wha Lee. 2000. "International Data on Educational Attainment: Updates and Implications." Harvard University, Cambridge, Mass. February. Manuscript.

Barro, Robert, and Xavier Sala-I-Martin. 1995. *Economic Growth.* New York: McGraw-Hill.

Behrman, Jere R., and Nancy Birdsall. 1983. "The Quality of Schooling: Quantity Alone Is Misleading." *American Economics Review* 73: 928-46.

Benhabib, Jess, and Mark Spiegel. 1994. "The Role of Human Capital in Economic Development: Evidence from Aggregate Cross-Country Data." *Journal of Monetary Economics* 34: 143-174.

Bils, Mark, and Peter Klenow. 2000. "Does Schooling Cause Growth?" *American Economic Review* 90 (5): 1160-1183.

Birdsall, Nancy, and Augusto de la Torre. 2001. *Washington Contentious: Economic Policies for Social Equity in Latin America.* Washington, D.C.: Carnegie Endowment for International Peace.

Case, Anne, and Motohiro Yogo. 1999. *Does School Quality Matter: Returns to Education and the Characteristics of Schools in South Africa.* National Bureau of Economic Research (NBER) Working Paper No. 7399.

Card, David, and Alan Krueger. 1996. "School Resources and Student Outcomes: An Overview of the Literature and New Evidence from North and South Carolina." *Journal of Economic Perspectives* 10 (4): 31-50.

Duryea, Suzanne, Alejandra Cox Edwards, and Manuelita Ureta. 2001. "Women in the LAC Labor Market." Paper presented at the Annual Meeting of the Inter-American Development Bank. Santiago, Chile, March 16.

Duryea, Suzanne, and Carmen Pagés. 2001. *Achieving High Labor Productivity in Latin America: Is Education Enough?* mimeo. Washington, D.C.: Inter-American Development Bank.

Espinola, Viola. 2000. "Autonomía escolar: Factores que contribuyen a una escuela más efectiva." Discussion Document. Operational Department Region I. Washington, D.C.: Inter-American Development Bank.

Galindo, Arturo. 2001. *Creditor Rights and the Credit Market: Where Do We Stand?* Research Department Working Paper No. 448. Washington, D.C.: Inter-American Development Bank.

Galindo, Arturo, and Margaret Miller. 2001. "Can Credit Registries Reduce Credit Constraints? Empirical Evidence on the Role of Credit Registries in Firm Investments Decisions." Inter-American Development Bank. Research Department. Washington, D.C. Paper prepared for the "Towards Competitiveness: The Institutional Path" seminar, Santiago, Chile, March 16.

Hall, Robert E., and Charles I. Jones. 1999. "Why Do Some Countries Produce So Much More Output per Worker than Others?" *The Quarterly Journal of Economics* 114 (1, February): 83-116.

Inter-American Development Bank (IDB). 1998. *Facing Up to Inequality in Latin America.* Washington, D.C.: Inter-American Development Bank (IDB).

IDB. 2000. "Reverse Gender Gaps in Schooling." *Latin American Economic Policies Newsletter 12* (Third Quarter). Washington, D.C.: Research Department, Inter-American Development Bank.

IDB. 2001. *Competitiveness: The Business of Growth.* Washington, D.C.: Inter-American Development Bank.

International Institute for Management Development. 2000. *World Competitiveness Yearbook.* Available at <http://www.imd.ch/wcy >.

Kaufmann, Daniel, Aart Kraay, and Pablo Zoido-Lobatón. 1999. *Governance Matters.* World Bank Policy Research Department Working Paper 2196.

Krueger, Alan, and Mikael Lindahl. 2000. *Education for Growth: Why and For Whom.* NBER Working Paper No. W7591.

Latinobarómetro. 1997. *Opinión Pública Latinoamericana. Chile.* Corporación Latinobarómetro. Available at <http://www.latinobarometro.org>.

Leonard, Carl. 2000. "Written Testimony." House International Relations Committee Subcommittee on Western Hemisphere. June 28. Available at <http://wwwa.house.gov/international_relations/107/65971.pdf>.

Lora, Eduardo, and Ugo Panizza. 2002. *Structural Reforms in Latin America Under Scrutiny.* Research Department Working Paper No. 470. Washington, D.C.: Inter-American Development Bank.

Mammen, Kristin, and Christina Paxson. 2000. "Women's Work and Economic Development." *Journal of Economic Perspectives* 14 (4, Fall): 141-64.

Medina, Carlos, and Jairo Nuñez. 2000. "The Impact of Publicly Provided Job Training in Colombia." Unpublished Document.

Millennium Development Goals (MDG). Available at <http://www.undp.org.mk/mdg/mdg.htm>.

PREAL. 2001. *Lagging Behind: A Report Card on Education in Latin America.* Santiago, Chile: Partnership for Educational Revitalization in the Americas.

Pritchett, Lant. 1996. *Where Has All the Education Gone?* World Bank Policy Research Department Working Paper No. 1581. Washington, D.C.: The World Bank.

Rodrik, Dani. 1999. "Democracies Pay Higher Wages." *Quarterly Journal of Economics* 114 (3, August): 707-38.

Székely, Miguel. 2001. *The 1990's in Latin America: Another Decade of Persistent Inequality, but with Somewhat Lower Poverty.* Research Department. Working Paper No. 454. Washington, D.C.: Inter-American Development Bank.

U.S. Treasury Press Release. 2001. PO376. May 15.

UNESCO. 1997. *Statistical Yearbook, 1997.* Paris: UNESCO.

UNESCO. 1998. *Primer Estudio Internacional Comparativo.* Laboratorio Latinomericano de Evaluación de la Calidad de la Educación. Noviembre. Paris: UNESCO.

UNESCO. 2000. *World Education Report.* Paris: UNESCO.

United Nations. 2000. *A Better World for All.* Paris: UN.

World Bank. 1999. *World Business Environment Survey.* Available at <http://www.worldbank.org/privatesector/ic/resources/index.htm>.

World Economic Forum. 2000. *The Global Competitiveness Report.* Geneva: World Economic Forum.

Chapter Seven

EDUCATION POLICY REFORM IN LATIN AMERICA: NEW OPPORTUNITIES, OLD CONSTRAINTS

Wendy Hunter

Few issues generate greater consensus than the idea that education is decisive for the promotion of both growth and equity in developing countries (Psacharopoulos 1995; World Bank 1993). Well-targeted educational investments play a critical role in increasing a country's gross national product (GNP) as well as in alleviating poverty and reducing inequality. For this and related reasons, the educational component of human capital, the focus of this chapter, is now widely recognized by policy analysts and decisionmakers as a key area for reform.

The spectacular rise of many East Asian economies in the postwar period and the crucial role that strong, basic public schooling played in boosting the export capacity of those countries lend strong empirical justification to these reform efforts. A number of recent studies confirm the importance of sizable public allocations to education, health, and other social services for the productivity of these economies (Mingat 1998; Mundle 1998; Rao 1998). The availability and quality of education in the advanced countries of East Asia have been critical in creating a more productive, flexible, and technologically adept workforce. These factors have also contributed vitally to lowering economic inequality, which itself can have a positive and independent impact on growth (Birdsall and Sabot 1997, 1).

As developing countries become more integrated with global markets, their competitiveness will depend ever more on the skills and knowledge levels of their workers. Latin America's openness to global market forces has increased markedly in the last two decades. While many regions of the world have become more integrated with global markets, few have undergone as rapid and thorough a transformation as Latin America. The effect of this change has been twofold. It has heightened policymakers' and business leaders' awareness of the need to expand the knowledge and skill base of Latin American populations. By increasing the demand for skilled labor, recent economic reforms have raised the private returns to human capital investment and generated interest among business elites for improving public education (Birdsall, Londoño, and O'Connell 1998, 41). Economic openness has also widened wage and income gaps among workers, based on their relative education and skill levels (Stallings and Peres 2000, 126-129). Education has become a fundamental element of the social and economic policies of many governments in the region. Policymakers are now debating the amounts, levels, and kinds of schooling required by present and future labor forces.

Testimony to the recognized linkage between education and economic competition in an era of globalization are the increasing efforts being made by Latin American governments to spend a greater percentage of their social budgets on education (Kaufman and Segura 2001). Moreover, recent years have witnessed efforts by governments, private businesses, and experts in multilateral lending agencies to create incentives for students and workers to develop specialized knowledge or training in areas related to a country's economic profile and potential. In this connection, whereas the World Bank used to focus almost exclusively on expanding coverage for general primary and secondary education, it has begun to commission analyses to determine what educational priorities should be in relation to market possibilities and to make provisions for vocational programs that can feed directly into the productive process (Gajardo 1999). Also, more than ever, Latin American governments have begun to give priority in their scholarship choices to university students who choose to specialize in areas with strong developmental or market potential. Indeed, the connection between programs to develop human capital and foreign economic policy has begun to converge in a region that, until recently, paid scant attention to this link.

Domestic efforts to improve education have been strongly supported by global and regional initiatives. "Education for All," the 1990 United Nations-sponsored conference in Jomtien, Thailand, crystallized the normative commitment among the international community to the universal provision of basic schooling, an event and platform frequently invoked by developing world governments seeking to realize this goal and to legitimize the resources they dedicate to it (Iguiñiz 2000). In the first hemispheric summit held in Miami in 1994, educational issues were among many themes debated by heads of state and governments. By the time of the Santiago Summit in 1998, the coverage and quality of education stood out as one of four central commitments that all parties agreed to, the others being free trade, democracy, and human rights (Gajardo 2000).

While Latin American governments have certainly not heeded all recommendations of the multilateral banks regarding the education sector, the tendency is toward conformity with the general lines of neoliberal social policymaking that the banks are pursuing. Beyond the fact that many economists and experts in Latin American education ministries share the same educational formation and socialization as their counterparts within the banks and, hence, tend to agree with these general principles, the economic resources that the banks make available are vital for the creation of new programs and initiatives. In most countries, upward of 80 to 90 percent of the education budget goes to pay operating costs. Bank loans provide a certain incentive for governments to follow international tendencies in education reform. In short, notwithstanding some of the macroeconomic problems within the region induced or aggravated by globalization, the current international climate is generally one propitious for undertaking efficiency and equity-oriented education reforms.

This chapter suggests, however, that the prospects for education reform are not uniform across all issues. The current climate opens a window of opportunity for some reforms more than others. This chapter argues that the current international climate of ideas favors decentralization in the administration of primary and secondary education much more than it does redistributive financial reforms in higher education.

THE STATE OF LATIN AMERICAN EDUCATION

The strong interest that many Latin American governments are taking in education as an economic strategy is relatively new. Ensuring high-quality public education, with the partial exception of developments at the university level, has historically not been a central concern of most governments in the region. As a result, education achievement levels in Latin America are poor by most measures. Although levels of illiteracy are low relative to many other developing regions and the gender gap is relatively small,[1] Latin America's record in education leaves much to be desired. The differences with East Asia are especially striking. Progress has been weaker for Central America than for South America on the whole.[2] On average (with wide variations across countries), half of the students who begin primary school do not finish the sixth grade. This compares with completion rates for primary school of 95 percent in Korea and Malaysia and more than 80 percent in Sri Lanka and Thailand. Only one of three children in Latin America attends secondary school, as compared with more than 80 percent in Southeast Asia, and many Latin American children who enter secondary school do not finish (PREAL 1998, 6).

Repetition rates, usually associated with inadequate learning, in Latin America are extremely high, indicating that the general quality of the education provided is poor. Roughly half of all students fail the first grade, and nearly one third repeat whatever grade they are in. These high rates of repetition are demoralizing to students and place a big burden on public finances.

International comparisons reflect the poor performance of Latin American schools. The vast majority of Latin American countries choose not to participate in worldwide tests, but evidence from the small number of countries that have participated indicates that educational progress, even in the more affluent Latin American countries with better developed education systems, such as Chile, Costa Rica, and Colombia, lags far behind not only the industrialized countries of North America and Europe (Arnove 1997, 83) but also behind countries such as Indonesia, Thailand, and Singapore (Wolff 1998, 1-4; PREAL 1998, 6). In this connection, particularly in light of its per capita income, Latin America's human capital accumulation is weak compared with other regions, especially in education. On average, Latin American workers have nearly two years less schooling than workers in other countries at similar levels of income (PREAL 1998, 6).

Not only is the quality of education in Latin America generally low, but its provision is highly inequitable. This contributes greatly to income inequality in the region. Educational inequities are strikingly apparent when schooling rates for disadvantaged and higher income groups are compared. The poor are less likely than more affluent sectors to complete primary school and are far less inclined to enter and finish secondary school, let alone to attend public universities. Even in a country as equitable as Costa Rica, only 72 percent of the poorest 40 percent completed primary education, as compared with 99 percent of the most affluent (Grindle 2000b, 3). Virtually all families with the resources to send their children to private primary and secondary schools do so. Their poor counterparts have no choice but to enter into the public system. Students from private schools score significantly higher on achievement tests than those who attend public schools (PREAL 1998, 8). Living in a rural area is another source of inequality. Children who live in the countryside are the least likely to attend school at any level. They are especially at a disadvantage at the secondary level. Ethnicity and race create further divisions. Children of indigenous and African backgrounds enjoy less education than their poor white counterparts. According to a report by PREAL (2001, 9-10), school attendance among indigenous children in Bolivia and Guatemala is nearly 10 to 15 percent below that of their nonindigenous peers even as early as the first two years of schooling. Historically, public spending patterns have reinforced these inequalities by concentrating resources on the middle class (in considerable part through the substantial resources allocated to higher education) and on urban areas. Little attention has been paid to addressing the inequities within the system.

THE POLITICAL DIFFICULTY OF MAKING EDUCATION REFORMS

While the 1990s gave rise to numerous efforts by Latin American governments to improve the quality of education provided in their countries, political resistance has plagued many of these efforts. In fact, one source reports that "while many countries have expressed a strong commitment to improving education and have undertaken reforms to make schools better, results have been slow in coming" (PREAL 2001, 5). At the most general level, "education is intensely political because it affects the majority of citizens, involves all levels of government, is almost always the single largest component of public spending, and carries public subsidies that are biased in favor of the elite" (Fisk 1995). More specifically, recent reform efforts have suffered from many of the factors common to "second generation reforms." These are summarized well by Joan Nelson in *Reforming Health and Education* (1999, xiiii).

In contrast to many macroeconomic or financial reforms, there is far less apparent urgency in instituting education reforms. While wide-ranging actors agree that the quality of educational services needs to be improved, education deficits rarely take the form of an acute crisis that compels politicians to act decisively and be willing to absorb the political costs of reform. Along these same lines, the improved productivity gains that ensue from making investments in education are long and slow in coming. Hence, faced with a wide variety of demands that, if addressed, would make a more immediate impact on the country's economic welfare, public officials are often tempted to put education reforms on the back burner and expend their political capital elsewhere.

Making matters more difficult is the fact that there is no blueprint or technical consensus model for reforming education (or health). The basic merits versus drawbacks of certain models or policies are hotly disputed. Poor or nonexistent data on the results of given reforms, together with the difficulty of clearly linking given outcomes to specific policies or programs, makes these disputes difficult to resolve on a factual basis. This opens the way for and reinforces the interest-based intervention of politicians and interest groups.

Further inhibiting politicians from spearheading and supporting reforms over the long term is the strong opposition that many reform proposals provoke from powerfully organized and influential groups, such as teachers' unions and education bureaucracies. Privileged service users, such as university students who enjoy highly subsidized education and politicians who have used education for patronage purposes, stand to lose as well from some of the reforms currently being contemplated. Even state and local governments may object to some aspects of the service delivery that reforms might induce them to perform. Relative to these highly organized groups, the potential beneficiaries of reform — namely, school children, their parents (typically from lower socioeconomic strata), local communities, and some individual teachers — are politically weak and unorganized.

The long timetable necessary for adopting and implementing educational reforms further slows down their enactment. Political conflicts over social sector issues often do not cease after reforms are approved but are "recast and re-fought at both national and local levels, often diluting or derailing the reforms" (Nelson 1999, xiii). The mere fact that education reform bills must go through the congress distinguishes them from some of the economic measures passed by emergency decrees in the recent past. Moreover, the actual impact of educational reforms depends in no small measure on the motivation of the direct provider — classroom teachers, in this case. In effect, this means that the reforms enacted must have at least some support among this group to have their desired impact.

A final factor impeding improvements in education stems from the weakness of external pressures, for instance, from international financial organizations, for education reform. As Javier Corrales (1999) notes, although external pressures for education reform are at an all-time high, they are still weaker than pressures for economic reform. There are no hard and immediate sanctioning mechanisms for noncompliance. As Wendy Hunter and David S. Brown (2000) note, the World Bank has tried to promote certain educational policies with equity and efficiency enhancement in mind. The policy change it has advocated most strenuously to Latin American governments concerns dedicating more resources to basic schooling (primary and secondary) and less to higher education. Despite great efforts on the part of the Bank to promote this shift, most Latin American governments have not significantly altered their spending patterns in such a direction.

THE CURRENT CONTEXT:
NEW OPPORTUNITIES AND OLD CONSTRAINTS

Does the current conjuncture, one marked by a coincidence of democratization and market reforms, provide any windows of opportunity for education reform and the building of human capital? As stated above, at the most general level, market reforms have heightened recognition among policymakers of the importance of having a skilled and educated work force for the sake of economic competitiveness. More concretely, the current conjuncture has given impetus to and facilitated one major type of reform — decentralization. But at the same time, it has done far less to promote other reform initiatives, such as the attempt to institute tuition charges at the university level in order to take pressure off the public budget. Reform efforts to decentralize have, on the whole, met with greater success than attempts to have university students pay a higher share of costs. Excessive administrative and financial centralization, as well as highly subsidized higher education (especially the more it displaces investments for more basic schooling), are among the most frequently cited policies and practices in need of reform. The remainder of this chapter will be devoted to illustrating the window of opportunity that current economic and political developments have opened up for decentralization efforts to unfold. I will contrast this to the difficulty Latin American governments have experienced in instituting tuition charges at public universities, where the obstacles and contrasts that pertained in the past still apply.

EFFORTS TO DECENTRALIZE HIGHLY CENTRALIZED SYSTEMS

The historically highly centralized administration of education in many Latin American countries and the partially overlapping phenomenon of political clientelism are commonly understood to have hurt the quality of elementary and secondary education in the region. In Latin America's highly centralized systems, national ministries of education governed over major policy issues, such as curricula, teacher training standards, textbook selections, and routine matters alike, such as conflicts between an individual teacher and his/her supervisor, funds to buy school supplies, and missing shipments of textbooks. Centralization was reinforced by national control over school financing. For example, in 1996, of 15 primary education systems in Latin America, all but one received 65 to 100 percent of its financing from national governments, and nine countries had no provision for state or municipal financing of education (Grindle 2000b, 4).

The highly centralized nature of education planning and administration, especially in the broader context of poverty and underdevelopment, contributed to other problems associated with poor social services, such as low levels of parental and community involvement. Centralization meant that there were few activities and programs even available for parents to influence. Low levels of transparency, accompanied by a lack of responsiveness and accountability on the part of public officials, also tended to characterize the highly centralized education systems of Latin America.

In this connection, high centralization was often accompanied by efforts on the part of national level politicians to use education resources politically. Indeed, many governments have traditionally relied on education systems as mechanisms of political clientelism and cooptation. Governments typically appoint people to top-level positions in ministries of education as a way to reward political supporters or to "park political allies whom they wish to promote" (Corrales 1999, 9). Similarly, teaching positions are frequently awarded on the basis of political favoritism to individuals totally unequipped to teach. Money is spent on highly visible projects for which politicians can reap political credit, such as school buildings, but these are less essential to learning than other items. Education funds that are channeled through presidents and governors often end up in districts where their political allies reside, not in the areas of greatest need. Not coincidentally, the budget set aside for primary education has tended in many countries to follow the trajectory of other ministries that are well-known bastions of pork barrel, such as transportation and agriculture (Ames 1987).

Yet, by the 1990s, most Latin American countries adopted some form and degree of decentralization in the planning, financing, and delivery of social services, including education. Prominent among these are Argentina, Bolivia, Brazil, Chile, Colombia, El Salvador, Mexico, Nicaragua, Uruguay, and Venezuela. Responsibilities for decisionmaking, revenue raising, and the carrying out of operations from the central government to lower level authorities began to be transferred to lower levels of government or to schools themselves.[3] In the most far-reaching cases, states, municipalities, school principals, and school boards were given responsibility for the hiring, promotion, and disciplining of teachers. Besides lowering the fiscal burden of the central government, decentralization was intended to enhance the efficiency and quality of educational services. The hope was that decentralizing reforms would allow parents to work for better schooling and, partly by creating greater transparency in the allocation and use of resources, make state and local politicians more responsive to the citizenry (Burki et al. 1999). To the extent that decentralization may be defined as a situation in which "public goods and services are provided by the market in response to the express preferences of individuals" (di Gropello 1999, 156), decentralization is a central element of neoliberal social policy. By the mid- 1990s, organizations such as USAID and UNESCO had joined the World Bank in promoting decentralization, including school autonomy.

A wide range of Latin American countries of different sizes, political leanings, and financial endowments underwent some form and degree of decentralization in the 1980s and 1990s. Notwithstanding the tremendous variation among decentralizing experiences (countries differ considerably in which decisionmaking powers have been decentralized and who has received those new powers), the administration of educational services in most countries has undergone some deconcentration, delegation, or even devolution of power. The prevalence of decentralizing reforms stands in striking contrast to the paucity of successful reform efforts aimed at instituting higher tuition charges at public universities. Yet, the veritable wave of decentralization that swept across the region in the 1990s is surprising in light of the number and power of the forces that could be expected to oppose such reform, especially when compared to the potential beneficiaries of reform.

First of all, it is noteworthy that so many national political leaders would want to transfer power downward and allow states, municipalities, and even schools to have independent sources of revenue and to control decisions about matters ranging from school infrastructure to the hiring of personnel.[4] In this light, decentralizing education might be seen as "audacious" (Grindle 2000a). National level politicians, especially presidents, might want to unburden the central government of responsibilities, and they might expect to receive some diffuse credit for enacting decentralization as a modernizing change (Grindle 2000a, 7-8). However, any efficiency gains ensuing from decentralization would take a while to materialize and be visible only in the long term. In any case, they would not offset the loss of patronage national level politicians would suffer.

Decentralization also threatens the power and privileges of bureaucrats in national education ministries. With the exception of small numbers of top technocrats, most bureaucrats are not rewarded for innovation. And those entrusted with carrying out decentralizing reforms stand to lose resources and influence, perhaps even their jobs, as decisions, personnel, and resources get transferred outward. Moreover, central bureaucrats are well positioned — by withholding financial resources from local organs — to undermine local support for decentralization (Corrales 1999, 13).

Considering the interests of teachers' unions toward decentralization adds a further layer to the puzzle. Central bargaining gives teachers more uniform collective strength over salaries, working conditions, and related protections and benefits than they would otherwise have. The great fear is that decentralization will fragment union strength and reduce the leverage of teachers' unions. In fact, many strikes have been mounted to protest the prospect of decentralization.[5] Largely due to their size and national representation, teachers' unions have sometimes been able to take over personnel functions of the ministries of education, appointing, assigning, and promoting teachers, often on the basis of patronage relationships. They have also delivered teachers over to national political machines (Grindle 2000b, 4). Decentralization threatens to reduce these practices. As far as individual teachers go, it opens up the possibility of exposure to more evaluation, especially by immediate superiors or parents.

In looking at the possible bases of support for reform among politicians, it is noteworthy that subnational politicians, governors and mayors, were not particularly strong or consistent advocates of decentralization, especially initially. Decentralization can hurt regional and municipal governments that do not have the financial or human resources to assume added obligations. In this connection, in certain countries, for example, Venezuela and Colombia, subnational politicians only accepted responsibility for school systems after the central government agreed to finance the improvement of these systems before handing them over.

In most cases, the potential societal beneficiaries of reform — parents, students, local communities, and individual teachers who could gain more input into questions about resource and personnel management and even curriculum matters — did not actively mobilize in favor of decentralization. And even when they did, their organizational power and coalition strength were diffuse and did not begin to match that of the detractors of reform, especially in light of the relatively low socioeconomic standing of most parents whose children attend public primary and secondary schools in the region.

In light of the many political obstacles associated with decentralizing reforms, it is remarkable that the impetus for them has been so strong and sustainable over time. The widespread implementation of decentralization becomes even more curious upon considering that the objective record regarding the welfare benefits of decentralization are, in fact, quite mixed, as the chapter by Kent Eaton in this volume suggests. Numerous studies suggest that there is no hard evidence that decentralization enhances educational achievement or performance (Hanson 1997, 14-15;

Fisk 1996). In any case, the benefits of decentralization seem no more compelling than those of other reforms, such as recovering greater costs from students in higher education. Moreover, the devolution of authority, especially in the context of underdevelopment, carries real dangers as well. Foremost among these are the scant technical capacity that exists in many areas and the possibility that decentralization can exacerbate regional inequalities. Another apparent difficulty — that local politicians may be equally if not more interested than their national level counterparts in using available funds for visible short-term gains than in using them for educational goals where gains are less immediately apparent — suggests that decentralization is not a remedy for political clientelism. Indeed, decentralization can sometimes extend, rather than attenuate, patronage networks (Manor 1999, 44).

It should be apparent from the above discussion that an analytical framework that focuses strictly on the objective welfare merits of decentralizing reforms or on the interests of actors and their organizational resources falls short in explaining the widespread implementation of decentralization in Latin America. Given the gap left by accounts that revolve around such factors, analysts need to look beyond the immediate concerns of electoral and interest group politics. In the discussion below, the contributions and limitations of several alternative explanatory frameworks are explored. Although each framework makes some contribution to understanding why decentralization has spread throughout the region, ultimately, the conclusion is reached that the broader ideational context provided by democratization and market reforms was critical in opening up a window of opportunity for the initiation and implementation of decentralizing reforms.

Especially after the debt crises of the 1980s, any analysis of why developing countries behave as they do needs to consider the influence of international lenders. One obvious potential source for stimulating and sustaining decentralization in Latin America rests with international financial institutions (IFIs). The World Bank is the most relevant actor as far as education reform is concerned. Given the weak conditionality or sanctioning that exists with regard to social sector reforms, IFIs' influence in this area tends to be exerted via intellectual and material support for reforms where national level support may need bolstering. Indeed, the World Bank has supported decentralizing reforms in a variety of social sectors, including education, especially since the beginning of the 1990s. This is part of a broader adherence to reforms that promote governance and social capital. Yet, the actual timing of educational decentralization in Latin America is somewhat at odds with the World Bank as a key initiator of reform. Many decentralizing reforms in education were well underway in the second half of the 1980s by the time the World Bank weighed in heavily and decisively on the side of decentralization in the early 1990s. Also, if the World Bank were all that powerful in shaping education reform, Latin American governments would have rationalized higher education expenditures more markedly by now. The World Bank has for two decades strongly advocated recovering costs at the university level, partly in order to divert more funds to basic schooling. As alluded to above and illustrated more explicitly in Hunter and Brown (2000), however, the Bank has been relatively ineffective in this regard.

The underprediction of decentralization, based on a consideration of actors and their interests, shortcomings associated with the other frameworks raised above, and positive evidence for a whole other line of inquiry — the contribution of intellectual trends or "fads and fashions" — leads to the proposal of the following: the prevailing political and economic climate of ideas has contributed critically to the implementation and spread of decentralizing reforms in education.[6]

The content of ideas associated with decentralization has widespread appeal at the current time. The antistate implications of decentralization have captured the imagination of a wide array of actors in the region. This antistate sentiment appeals to the neoliberal, market-oriented right as well as to the center left. For the neoliberal right, decentralization evokes notions like competition, being closer to the user, and empowering the consumer. Even the left has lost its long-standing faith in the state as a promoter of economic development and social justice and now stresses the need for active participation by social movements, citizen groups, and non-governmental organizations (NGOs). For the left, decentralization is appealing insofar as it implies the diffusion of political power and is tied up with notions about democratization. The ambiguity or flexibility associated with the concept and practice of decentralization has been important in allowing policymakers to cast decentralizing reforms either in neoliberal language, for example, efficiency and small government, or in the vocabulary of democracy and participation. Former Argentine President Carlos Menem, for instance, initially used the language of neoliberal economics to promote the decentralization of social services. He later recast the same reforms in the framework of popular participation, arguably to better effect.

While the content of an idea is important to the power it assumes, so is its context. Antistate sentiments reached a new high in Latin America in the late 1980s and early 1990s. This period saw the convergence of marketization, a major economic development, with democratization, a major political development. This convergence opened up reform space and provided for the possibility that a confluence of disparate forces could see decentralization as consistent with their own position and to unite under the same banner. Testimony to the importance of context in providing support for decentralization is the fact that technocrats in previous periods, even as recently as the early 1980s, had tried to sell educational decentralization to top political officials, but their efforts met with little political resonance (Grindle 2000b, 8). A new climate of ideas prompted change and has helped to sustain it.

It is one thing to state that an idea gains influence because of its content and context, and quite another to specify the mechanisms by which it is translated into a policy outcome. One way that ideas can lead to policy innovations is through the "mobilization of bias," a phrase coined by E.E. Schattschneider (1969). This notion can help explain how policies that favor seemingly weaker actors can sometimes be enacted. In the case of decentralization, groups whose "objective power" was relatively minimal, for example, progressive intellectuals in the Brazilian state of Minas Gerais who spearheaded what has turned into a regionwide movement for school autonomy,[7] were encouraged to mobilize because of the attractiveness of the idea they espoused. Without being able to use the spirit of the times in their favor, some of the progressive intellectuals who helped launch the movement for school autonomy would have been on weaker ground.

A policy innovation can gather force not only by activating the resources of supporters but also by silencing or immobilizing detractors. Since the mid-1980s onward, to oppose decentralization — either in word or deed — has been to risk criticism of oneself as an opponent of progress. For example, when Argentine teachers went on strike in 1991 to protest President Menem's decentralization initiative, the president's public response was to cast teachers' unions as retrograde elements in the way of advancement. The symbolic politics of decentralization was also put into stark relief recently when former president and former governor of the Brazilian state of Minas Gerais, Itamar Franco, tried to reverse some of the reforms aimed at expanding school autonomy. Franco backed down after a barrage of public criticism was launched to emphasize how "out of touch" he was with the times.

In short, by the 1990s, fewer and fewer public officials would want to be associated with the rejection of decentralizing reforms. The greater the number of public figures and governments in the region that have endorsed decentralization, the more out of step those who have not have seemed. This "herd effect" is essentially about symbolic concerns. The work of Martha Finnemore (1996) suggests how important this kind of symbolism can be to developing countries.

The dense network of exchange involving education experts serves to accelerate any tendency toward herding. The number of international conferences such experts have attended in recent years is impressive. Some of the more political personnel in the ministries attend such conferences as well. These exchanges have not only dispersed technical information on policy trends, which makes it easier to "go with the flow" (in a kind of bounded rationality sense), but they have also reinforced the notion that decentralization is the modern thing to do.

Ideas do appear to have an independent capacity to shape reform outcomes. Yet, at the same time, the use of appropriate strategies in the planning, launching of, and implementation of reforms is also important in whether and to what extent decentralizing reforms come to fruition. The use of such strategies affects whether the window of opportunity provided by the ideational climate and other related triggers is allowed to remain open and available to be taken advantage of. Research by Merilee Grindle suggests that reforms have proceeded most smoothly when certain processes have unfolded (2000a). One of her observations is that the more successful reform leaders have been cautious and deliberate about the timing and strategy for announcing, debating, and approving new education policies. They have also tried to work out a strategy ahead of time for negotiating or confronting opponents, as the case may be. Other authors, such as Carol Graham and Cheikh Kane 1999, underscore the importance of these and related factors for institutional reform in Latin America. For example, they stress the advantages associated with attempting difficult reforms as early as possible in a president's administration. They also note the importance of bundling painful reforms with certain concessions or benefits to opposing stakeholders.

HIGH SUBSIDIES FOR UNIVERSITY EDUCATION

While the current conjuncture provides some hope of reversing historical patterns of centralization in the region, what hope does it offer for addressing the deeply rooted practice of the state being virtually the sole financier of public university education? That issue will now be explored, beginning with a brief description of expenditure patterns in the region.

It is frequently observed that the most obvious problem in Latin America is not with the low resource levels applied to the education sector overall but with their inefficient and ineffective distribution. In fact, the financial expenditures that many Latin American countries allocate toward education as a whole (primary, secondary, and higher education combined) compares favorably with those of some middle income countries that produce far stronger educational results, such as South Korea and Taiwan. A key distinguishing feature of Latin American educational budgets, however, is the size of the shares that go to fund higher education. One of the main differences between high performing East Asian countries and Latin America is the greater priority that the former has placed on primary (and lower secondary) education. On average, 20 percent of the education budget in Latin America for the last two decades or so has been allocated to higher education. This figure is much higher for some countries, such as Brazil (26 percent), Costa Rica (31 percent), and Uruguay (25 percent), than for others (Birdsall, Londoño, and O'Connell 1998, 50).[8] A comparison between Venezuela and Korea, where basic education is regarded as a collective good, reflects the extremes in this regard. Whereas Venezuela allocated 35 percent of its public education budget to higher education, Korea allocated only 8 percent of its budget to postsecondary schooling (Birdsall, Londoño, and O'Connell 1998, 50).

The tuition-free status of most of the region's public universities is part and parcel of this phenomenon. Exceptions to this policy — which include Chile, Colombia, and Mexico's state universities — are few and far between. "Free" university schooling is a subsidy enjoyed by all students regardless of their economic background. By contrast, facilitating East Asia's heavy emphasis on the provision of quality schooling at the lower grade levels is a high dependence on private funding at higher levels of education.[9] The heavy use of private funds for university education (mainly in the form of user fees) frees up money to be used for basic schooling. Private institutions enroll between 50 and 70 percent of all students in upper secondary and higher education in Japan, Korea, and Taiwan. The fee policy also concerns public institutions, where user fees account for roughly 15 to 35 percent of expenditures in such settings (Mingat 1998, 714).

Leading education economists from international financial organizations, such as the World Bank as well as various Latin American organizations, maintain that there should be greater cost recovery from students (the "users") at public universities. The argument is not that Latin American governments should not subsidize their universities at all but that every student need not be subsidized at exactly the same high rate. In addition, mechanisms need to be put in place to encourage more effective use of the funds that universities receive. Growth, as well as equity considerations, motivate this position. A number of important analyses on the rates of return for money spent at different levels of education suggest that poorer countries spend the overwhelming share of their budgets on basic schooling.[10] Saving money at higher levels would facilitate this. Even one or two additional years of early schooling can contribute substantially to a person's economic productivity (World Bank 1991, 57). Basic schooling is thought to be the single area in which public policy can make the largest impact on reducing inequality (IDB 1998, 129).

Circumstances specific to Latin America provide particular justification for reform. The most salient is ample evidence that the students, overwhelmingly of middle- and upper-class origins, who fill the ranks of Latin America's public universities could afford with little difficulty to pay a greater share of the costs of public higher education (González Rozada and Menéndez 2001; Paul and Wolff 1996; Castro and Levy 2000). In the region as a whole, the cost recovery from student fees is only about 7 percent of the per-student cost of higher education. Estimates suggest that the families of most university students could afford to pay closer to 25 to 30 percent of this cost. Beyond the inequitable distributional consequences of the present system, problems associated with the tuition-free aspect of Latin America's public universities include the excessive number of years students take to complete their studies and low rates of graduation. In short, efficiency and equity could be improved by charging greater tuition and/or fees. Selective loans and outright scholarships could be offered to attract talented students from poor family backgrounds who would otherwise not attend institutions of higher education.

What, then, accounts for such high subsidies at the university level? Student groups from the region's public universities have historically defended the tuition-free status of their institutions. Protests in recent years in Argentina, Chile, Colombia, Mexico, and Venezuela show how active, organized, and vocal these groups are. The notion of equal opportunity informs the students' defense of the present system, even though its main beneficiaries are the relatively well off.[11] Faculty and staff who seek higher salaries and resources often join with student groups in defending the status quo. The fact that university rectors are elected (usually by some combination of faculty and students) has made them reluctant to endorse the unpopular proposal of charging greater tuition and fees to supplement state resources.[12] In short, the political difficulties of reforming the present policy reflect an obstacle typical of second generation reforms; such a reform would impose concentrated costs on the more organized and influential group in question, while possibly distributing benefits in a diffuse way among a less influential and vocal population (Corrales 1999, 4; Nelson 1999, xiii). Even the support of the World Bank and domestic technocratic community on the side of change seems to have made little difference in this equation (Hunter and Brown 2000).

Governments are reluctant to be too heavy-handed with student demonstrators, often yielding to their resistance. This is especially true in the new democratic era. A strike that paralyzed the National Autonomous University of Mexico (Universidad Nacional Autónoma de México — UNAM) for nine months (from April 20, 1999, to February 7, 2000) ended with the government negotiating away its initial demands to raise tuition beyond the miniscule amount that students currently pay. Similarly, in Brazil, long-standing discussions to alter the tuition-free status of the country's public universities have come to naught. Instead, the government of Fernando Henrique Cardoso (from 1994 to December 2002) pursued a policy of trying to rationalize higher education spending through a variety of measures, such as linking federal funding to publicly available information on student performance (Puryear 2000, 1). Chile has been the only Latin American country that has managed to institute an extensive policy of cost recovery for its public institutions of higher learning. This policy redirection began under the dictatorship of Augusto Pinochet (1973-1990) and, needless to say, was backed by the threat of extraordinary force. Only about one-third of Chilean total higher education income now comes from the government (Levy 1994, 10). Tuition charges have been one of the ways that Chile has been able to increase the enrollment ratios in secondary school dramatically without a large increase in per-capita expenditure (Morley and Silva 1994, 9).

Indeed, progress has been halting, at best, in the area of higher education reform. A number of governments have tried to introduce changes that would reduce the financial burden that public universities have placed on state resources, yet the charging of tuition or the implementation of tuition hikes where minimal fees are required has remained highly controversial and has generally been avoided. The problem is not only that government subsidies to higher education are costly but also that they are not well used. Many universities are overstaffed and have employees of questionable quality, while good faculty and their programs receive inadequate financing. Many disciplines where the social returns are high, for example, health and agriculture, go underfunded as well (Puryear 2000, 3). Public universities have tended to operate under perverse sets of incentives, so that improvements in productivity and/or quality bring no rewards. Most of the reforms being considered by Latin American governments in the area of higher education contain market-oriented ingredients aimed at "rationalization" or doing more with less. What follows below is a description of some of the reforms that have been attempted by a number of governments in the context of a broader trend toward privatization and neoliberal social policy.

To understand the significance of these reforms, it is instructive to review the way Latin American governments have financed public universities in the past. In most countries, public institutions have been supported by the state through a mechanism of incremental finance based on previous budgets. Annual adjustments or increases in funding have generally come from the political pressures exerted upon governments by professors' unions and student groups, or they have reflected the expansion of the system, as in larger enrollments. As such, public universities have had few incentives for enhancing the quality of their instruction and research or becoming more efficient internally.[13]

Stimulating Private Institutions

In a few countries, led by Colombia, Brazil, and Chile, governments have chosen to restrain growth in the public sector, while favoring the growth of private institutions. While such a policy does represent a savings for the state, it is not problem free. For one, private institutions have great difficulties entering some of the higher-cost fields of higher education, such as medicine and other scientific areas in which public institutions maintain an oligopoly. Also, many of the new private institutions that have been created to absorb growing enrollments in a period of public belt tightening are of substantially inferior quality to their public counterparts. If the general goal is to provide high-quality education, regardless of who pays, such a situation falls short of the mark.

Selective Research and Salary Funding

Many Latin American countries, such as Chile, Colombia, Brazil, Argentina, Mexico, and Venezuela, have by now adopted some type of contractual funding mechanisms for the financing of research activities deemed to be of relevance and of high quality, often a matter of some debate. Similarly, recognized researchers in some countries are entitled to supplementary salaries and other financial incentives. Such a system rewards productive faculty members rather than providing for across-the-board increases. Special merit-based funds, sometimes from sources other than the education ministry, break with the precedent of standardized pay across public institutions, determined mostly according to seniority, a pattern reinforced by union power. The standardized salary structure is at odds with wider market-oriented economic trends. Needless to say, however, a policy of variable salary increases based on evaluations of research is fraught with problems. What counts as good research is often subjective and can even fall prey to political manipulations. Social science investigations whose findings and conclusions call into question the soundness of government policy may be particularly subject to negative discrimination.

Evaluation-Linked Funding

This is another emerging strategy meant to induce institutions of higher learning to meet academic standards and improve upon internal efficiency. Brazil was the first country in the region to institute a performance-linked mechanism for the financing of its graduate programs. It is developing national examinations by subject area that will be used to determine if universities are meeting academic standards and deserve public funding. Similarly, Mexico and Chile have discussed ways to institute mechanisms designed to channel public resources to the most deserving institutions. Needless to say, what the standards should be and what resources should be provided for universities to attain them is a matter of no small controversy.

In sum, a push is underway to bring universities more in line with current political/economic trends in the region. While an optimistic interpretation of current developments might focus on the fact that there are any changes at all taking place in the financing and administration of higher education, change has been incremental at best, and signs of continuity have been marked. On the whole, resistance to reforms has been striking. Insofar as reforms like those described above run counter to the ideals of self-regulation and academic freedom, championed by much of the university community, proposed changes face stiff opposition. Professors reject the notion that better academic work will emerge from market-oriented sanctions and incentives and contend that the state is irresponsibly withdrawing from its historic responsibilities in sponsoring higher education. What Claudio de Moura Castro says of Brazil rings true generally: "Higher education remains the area in which public policy has been most timid and controversial" (2000, 307).

In contrast to what has been described above in the case of decentralization, there is no overarching, compelling idea that advocates of reform in the area of higher education have successfully latched onto. Possible ideational candidates for reforms in higher education are limited. Reformists whose main inspiration for saving public resources at the university level rests in freeing up funding for basic schooling have stressed concepts like redistribution, the public good, and social equity. Yet none of these ideas seems to have the same currency that the ideas promoting decentralization have at the present time. Even many leftist parties, such as the Workers' Party (Partido dos Trabalhadores — PT) in Brazil, do not appear to be moved by the rhetoric of equity enhancement used in the reformist campaign to charge university tuition. As such, interest based/organizational power factors, such as the politically articulate and organized nature of the coalition between university students and their professors, are not counterbalanced or challenged in the way that they sometimes have been with decentralization. No doubt, there is also a class or social dimension at play that further weakens the inhibition of governments to take a strong stance toward university reforms. Those negatively affected by higher education reform are almost uniformly elites (and the children of elites). University professors, perhaps especially from economics and political science/ sociology faculties, often have close ties to presidents and high-ranking members of governments. By contrast, those who have opposed decentralization tend to be from more socially disparaged groups — unions, bureaucrats, and teachers — even though as mobilized interests they can be quite strong.[14]

CONCLUSION

This chapter has compared the following reform efforts toward two policy traditions commonly judged to have impaired educational outcomes in Latin America: a high degree of centralization in the administration, planning, and finance within the education sector; and the lack of cost recovery from users who attend public universities in the region. In the wake of market reforms and heightened pressures on Latin American countries to rise to the demands of global economic competitiveness, public officials have underscored the need to modify both practices. Policy innovations designed with decentralization in mind have met with much greater success than reform proposals aimed at rationalizing spending on public universities. While a conventional political economy focus on actors and their interests and resources is sufficient to explain the scant reform successes in altering the sources of funding for higher education, such an analytical framework cannot explain the impressive wave of decentralization that took place in the late 1980s to 1990s.[15] Many of the analytical frameworks that comparativists rely on are better at explaining why innovation does not happen than why it does. To understand decentralization, we need to look outside the usual frames of reference.

Ideas or intellectual trends supportive of decentralization, complemented by savvy strategies on the part of reformist elites, have played an impressive independent casual role in the promotion of decentralizing reforms in education. The historical moment — one of political and economic change, uncertainty, and even crisis — provided a unique opportunity for specialists to shape the debate about social policy reform. Political elites, especially presidents, felt compelled to do something about a situation whose failings were and continue to be so blatantly obvious. This was the embarrassing condition of basic education in their countries. These political elites were motivated to respond by building institutions that enjoyed a measure of legitimacy, besides providing some hope for improvement. Decentralization was a policy idea that was on the advance, it had been made even more available or accessible by the policy community, and it was ultimately one that politicians latched onto in greater and greater numbers. That this was true even though decentralization would in important ways challenge their control over decisionmaking and patronage resources is striking. Neither the scope nor timing of decentralization is explicable without reference to the ascendance and power of new ideas, coupled with the ability of reformist elites to present the case for decentralization in the most advantageous and appealing light possible. By contrast, financial reform efforts in higher education have been unable to hook onto catchy ideas with enough appeal among relevant interests — politicians, other public officials, relevant stakeholders, and unmobilized publics — to overcome the persistent political obstacles that have characterized the sector in the past.

Given the increasing globalization of policy networks and diffusion of policy proposals, the time is ripe for increased attention to the political salience of ideas. The challenges of researching and writing on this issue are many. For example, it is one thing to note the widespread presence of an idea and assume its connection to policy outcomes and quite another to document and analyze the process by which an idea gets launched, diffused among policy circles, sold to the politicians of a country, and finally implemented. Issues of measurement comprise an entirely different can of worms. Given the promise of exploring the role of ideas, however, these are challenges worth rising to.

Notes

1.   Enrollments in primary schools, literacy, and other measures of basic achievement do not reflect a gender gap in Latin America and the Caribbean. A notable exception with respect to gender equity pertains to countries with large indigenous populations, such as Bolivia and Guatemala, where indigenous girls receive less education than boys, even at the youngest levels.

2.   With the exception of Costa Rica, basic illiteracy rates in Central America are high (36.6 percent for Nicaragua, 33.4 for Guatemala, 29.3 percent for Honduras) and compare poorly with the rest of Latin America. In Nicaragua, El Salvador, the Dominican Republic, and Honduras, fewer than 60 percent of children who start school reach the fifth grade (PREAL 2000, 8-9). High rates of repetition also obtain, reflecting the poor quality of the educational services provided. For example, in four countries of Central America, it takes an average of ten years to complete six years of schooling.

3.   See Burki et al. (1999, chapter 4) for a discussion on the different origins and objectives of decentralization to lower levels of government vs. schools. See Alvarez (2002) on the issue of school autonomy.

4.   Of course, how willing national politicians are to support decentralization depends partly on how parties and alliances are organized across the local, state, and national levels. See Willis, Garman, and Haggard (1999). Politicians' acceptance of reform also depends on their judgement about how it will affect their competitor's access to patronage in relation to their own (Geddes 1994).

5.   In some countries, such as Argentina, the president proceeded with plans to implement decentralization in the face of staunch union opposition. In other cases, such as Mexico, teachers were able to wrest significant concessions in exchange for going along with the reform (Murillo 1999).

6.   Many of the ideas that I draw on in this section were inspired by Peter Hall's (1989) book on Keynesianism.

7.   See Costa et al. (1997) and Barros and Mendoça (1998) for a description and analysis of the Minas reforms.

8.   See also the figures cited by Castro and Levy (2000, 4), who judge this percentage to be even higher.

9.   It is high even compared to the OECD countries.

10.   Of course, once countries have achieved success at this level, it makes sense that they would then go on to allocate more funds to secondary and higher education. See Brown (1999) for a discussion of studies on the rates of return question.

11.   If systems of taxation in the region were more progressive and effective, these subsidies would not have such regressive implications.

12.   The right to elect rectors directly stems from historical efforts to assure and expand university autonomy.

13.   This section draws extensively from Levy (1994, 8-10).

14.   I am grateful to Merilee Grindle for this insight.

15.   I am not claiming that an approach that looks at actors as self-interested and instrumental is irrelevant. Indeed, in the implementation phase of reforms, complex bargaining and renegotiation take place. It appears that politics as usual reasserts itself in that second phase more than during the period of reform initiation and adoption.

REFERENCES

Alvarez, Benjamín. 2002. "Autonomía Escolar y Reforma Educativa." In *Criando Autonomía en las Escuelas*, ed. Partnership for Educational Revitalization in the Americas (PREAL). Santiago: LOM Ediciones.

Ames, Barry. 1987. *Political Survival: Politicians and Public Policy in Latin America.* Berkeley, Calif.: University of California Press.

Arellano, José Pablo Marín. 2001. "La Reforma Educacional Chilena." *Revista de la CEPAL* 73 (Abril): 83-94.

Arnove, Robert F. 1997. "Neoliberal Education Policies in Latin America: Arguments In Favor and Against." In *Latin American Education: Comparative Perspectives*, eds. Carlos Alberto Torres and Adriana Puiggrós. Boulder, Colo.: Westview Press.

Barros, Ricardo Paes de, and Rosane Mendoça. 1998. "The Impact of Three Institutional Innovations in Brazilian Education." In *Organization Matters: Agency Problems in Health and Education in Latin America*, ed. William D. Savedoff. Washington, D.C.: Distributed by The Johns Hopkins University Press for the Inter-American Development Bank.

Birdsall, Nancy, and Richard Sabot. 1997. "Inequality, Savings and Growth in East Asia and Latin America." Inter-American Development Bank and Williams College. Mimeo.

Birdsall, Nancy, and Augusto de la Torre. 2000. "Economic Reform in Unequal Latin American Societies." Prepared for the commission, "Economic Reform in Unequal Latin American Societies," sponsored by the Carnegie Endowment for International Peace and the Inter-American Dialogue, Washington, D.C., May.

Birdsall, Nancy, Juan Luis Londoño, and Lesley O'Donnell. 1998. "Education in Latin America: Demand and Distribution Are Factors That Matter." *CEPAL Review* 66 (December): 39-52.

Brown, David S. 1999. "Reading, Writing and Regime Type: Democracy's Impact on Primary School Enrollment." *Political Research Quarterly* 52 (4): 681-707.

Brown, David S., and Wendy Hunter. 2001. "Democracy and Education Spending in Latin America, 1980-1992." Prepared for delivery at the XXII International Congress of the Latin American Studies Association, Washington, D.C., September, 6-8.

Burki, Shahid Javed, Guillermo Perry, and William Dillinger. 1999. *Beyond the Center: Decentralizing the State.* Washington, D.C.: The World Bank.

Castañeda, Tarsicio. 1992. *Combating Poverty: Innovative Social Reforms in Chile During the 1980s.* San Francisco: Institute for Contemporary Studies.

Castro, Claudio de Moura, and Daniel C. Levy. 2000. *Myth, Reality, and Reform: Higher Education Policy in Latin America.* Washington, D.C.: Inter-American Development Bank and The Johns Hopkins University Press.

Castro, Claudio de Moura. 2000. "Education: Way Behind but Trying to Catch Up." *Daedalus* 129 (2): 291-314 (Spring).

Corrales, Javier. 1999. "The Politics of Education Reform: Bolstering the Supply and Demand; Overcoming Institutional Blocks." *Education Reform and Management Series* 11(1). Washington, D.C.: The World Bank.

Costa, Vera Lúcia Cabral, Eny Marisa Maia, and Lúcia Mara Mandel, eds. 1997. *Gestão Educacional e Descentralização: Novos Padrões*. São Paulo: Cortez Editora and Edições FUNDAP.

Cox, Cristián, and María José Lemaitre. 1999. "Market and State Principles of Reform in Chilean Education: Policies and Results." In *Chile: Recent Policy Lessons and Emerging Challenges*, eds. Guillermo Perry and Danny M. Leipziger. WBI Development Studies. Washington, D.C.: The World Bank.

Di Gropello, Emanuela. 1997. *Descentralización de la Educación en América Latina: Un Análisis Comparativo*. Comisión Económica para América Latina. Serie Reformas de Política Pública 57. Santiago, Chile: CEPAL.

Di Gropello, Emanuela. 1999. "Educational Decentralization Models in Latin America." *CEPAL Review* 68 (August): 155-173.

Finnemore, Martha. 1996. *National Interests in International Society*. Ithaca, N.Y.: Cornell University Press.

Fisk, Edward B. 1996. *Decentralization of Education: Politics and Consensus*. World Bank Series, Directions in Development. Washington, D.C.: The World Bank.

Gajardo, Marcela. 1999. *Reformas Educativas en América Latina. Balance de una década*. Documentos de Trabajo, no. 15 (September). PREAL. Washington, D.C.: Inter-American Dialogue and Corporation for Development Research.

Gajardo, Marcela. 2000. "Participación de la Sociedad Civil en la Iniciativa de Educación de la Cumbre de las Americas." Corporación de Investigaciones para el Desarrollo, Santiago, Chile. Mimeo.

Geddes, Barbara. 1994. *Politicians' Dilemma: Building State Capacity in Latin America*. Berkeley, Calif.: University of California Press.

Goldstein, Judith, and Robert O. Keohane, eds. 1993. *Ideas and Foreign Policy: Beliefs, Institutions, and Political Change*. Ithaca, N.Y.: Cornell University Press.

González Rozada, Martín, and Alicia Menéndez. 2001. "Public University in Argentina: Subsidizing the Rich?" CEDES, Buenos Aires, and the Woodrow Wilson School at Princeton University. Mimeo.

Graham, Carol, and Cheikh Kane. 1998. "Opportunistic Government or Sustaining Reform? Electoral Trends and Public-Expenditure Patterns in Peru, 1990-1995." *Latin American Research Review* 33 (1): 67-104.

Grindle, Merilee S. 2000a. *Audacious Reforms: Institutional Invention and Democracy in Latin America*. Baltimore and London: The Johns Hopkins University Press.

Grindle, Merilee S. 2000b. "The Paradox in Education Reform: Predicting Failure and Finding Progress." Paper prepared for the XXII Latin American Studies Association Congress, Miami, Fla., March 16-18.

Hall, Peter. 1989. *The Political Power of Economic Ideas: Keynesianism across Nations*. Princeton, N.J.: Princeton University Press.

Hanson, Mark E. 1997. "Educational Decentralization: Issues and Challenges." PREAL Occasional Paper Series No. 9. Washington, D.C.: Inter-American Dialogue and Corporation for Development Research.

Hanushek, Eric A. 1995. "Interpreting Recent Research on Schooling in Developing Countries." *The World Bank Research Observer* 10 (2): 227–246 (August).

Hunter, Wendy, and David S. Brown. 2000. "World Bank Directives, Domestic Interests, and the Politics of Human Capital Investment in Latin America." *Comparative Political Studies* 33: 1 (February).

IDB. 1998/1999. *Facing Up to Inequality in Latin America. Economic and Social Progress in Latin America.* 1998-1999 Report. Washington, D.C. Distributed by The Johns Hopkins University Press for the Inter-American Development Bank.

Iguiñiz, Manuel. 2000. "Acceso con equidad." *Peru Hoy: El Perú y las Cumbres Mundiales.* Lima: DESCO: 7–16.

Levy, Daniel C. 1994. "Higher Education Amid the Political-Economic Changes of the 1990s." Report of the LASA Task Force on Higher Education XXV 1: 3–15 (Spring).

Levy, Daniel C. 1995. *La educación superior y el Estado en Latinoamérica. Desafíos privados al predominio público.* México: FLACSO.

Levy, Daniel C. 1994. *La Educación Superior Dentro de las Transformaciones Políticas y Económicas de Los Años Noventa.* Informe del Grupo de Trabajo sobre la Educación Superior de la Asociación de Estudios Latinoamericanos. Buenos Aires: CEDES.

Mainwaring, Scott. 1999. "The Surprising Resilience of Elected Governments." *Journal of Democracy* 10 (3): 101-114 (July).

Manor, James. 1999. *The Political Economy of Democratic Decentralization.* Directions in Development Series. Washington, D.C.: The World Bank.

McGuire, James W. 1994. "Development Policy and Its Determinants in East Asia and Latin America." *Journal of Public Policy* 14 (2): 205-242.

Mingat, Alain. 1998. "The Strategy Used by High-Performing Asian Economies in Education: Some Lessons for Developing Countries." *World Development* 26 (2): 695-715.

Morley, Samuel A., and Antonia Silva. 1994. "Problems and Performance in Primary Education: Why Do Systems Differ?" The Social Agenda Policy Group. Washington, D.C.: Inter-American Development Bank. Mimeo.

Mundle, Sudipto. 1998. "Financing Human Development: Some Lessons for Advanced Asian Countries." *World Development* 26 (4): 659-672.

Murillo, Maria Victoria. 1999. "Recovering Political Dynamics: Teachers' Unions and the Decentralization of Education in Argentina and Mexico." *Journal of Interamerican Studies and World Affairs* 41 (1).

Nelson, Joan M. 1999. *Reforming Health and Education. The World Bank, the IDB, and Complex Institutional Change.* Policy Essay No. 26. Washington, D.C.: The Johns Hopkins University Press/Overseas Development Council.

Paul, Jean Jacques, and Laurence Wolff. 1996. "The Economics of Higher Education." In *Opportunity Foregone: Education in Brazil*, eds. Nancy Birdsall and Richard Sabot. Washington, D.C: Inter-American Development Bank.

Paxson, Christina, and Norbert Schady. 1999. *Do School Facilities Matter? The Case of the Peruvian Social Fund (FONCODES).* World Bank Policy Research Working Papers No. 2229. Washington, D.C.: The World Bank.

PREAL. 1998. *The Future at Stake: Report of the Task Force on Education, Equity and Economic Competitiveness in Latin America and the Caribbean.* Washington, D.C.: Inter-American Dialogue and Corporation for Development Research.

PREAL. 2000. *Task Force on Education Reform in Central America: Tomorrow Is Too Late.* Washington, D.C.: Inter-American Dialogue and Corporation for Development Research.

PREAL. 2001. *Lagging Behind: A Report Card on Education in Latin America.* Washington, D.C.: Inter-American Dialogue and Corporation for Development Research.

Psacharopoulos, George. 1995. *Building Human Capital for Better Lives*. Washington, D.C: The World Bank.

Puryear, Jeffrey M. 1997. *Education in Latin America: Problems and Challenges*. PREAL. Occasional Paper Series No. 7. Washington, D.C.: Inter-American Dialogue.

Puryear, Jeffrey M. 2000. "Increasing Education Spending Is Not Enough: The Challenge Is to Reach the Poor." Prepared for the commission, "Economic Reform in Unequal Latin American Societies," sponsored by the Carnegie Endowment for International Peace and the Inter-American Dialogue, Washington, D.C., May.

Rao, M. Govinda. 1998. "Accommodating Public Expenditure Policies: The Case of Fast Growing Asian Economies." *World Development* 26 (4): 673-694.

República de Chile. 1994. *Compendio de información estadística*. Santiago, Chile: Ministerio de Educación Pública.

Schattschneider, E.E. [1960] 1969. *The Semi-Sovereign People: A Realist's View of Democracy in America*. New York: W.W. Norton & Co.

Stallings, Barbara, and Wilson Peres. 2000. *Growth, Employment, and Equity: The Impact of Reforms in Latin America and the Caribbean*. Washington, D.C.: The Brookings Institution Press.

UNDP. 1999. *Human Development Report*. New York: Oxford University Press.

Willis, Eliza, Christopher da C.B. Garman, and Stephan Haggard. 1999. "The Politics of Decentralization in Latin America." *Latin American Research Review* 34 (1): 7-56.

Winkler, Don R. 1994. "La Educación Superior in América Latina: Cuestiones Sobre Eficiencia y Equidad." Washington, D.C: The World Bank.

Wolff, Laurence. 1998. *Educational Assessments in Latin America: Current Progress and Future Challenges*. PREAL Occasional Paper Series No. 11. Washington, D.C.: Inter-American Dialogue.

World Bank. 1991. *World Development Report 1991. The Challenge of Development*. New York: Oxford University Press.

World Bank. 1993. *The East Asian Miracle: Economic Growth and Public Policy*. Oxford, UK: Oxford University Press.

PART IV

IMPROVING DEMOCRATIC GOVERNANCE

Chapter Eight

THE DILEMMA OF DECENTRALIZATION IN LATIN AMERICA: RISKS AND OPPORTUNITIES

Kent Eaton

The previous chapters in this volume address some of the most salient economic and social policy challenges facing Latin America, as it forges a new set of foreign economic relations in the twenty-first century. The topic of this chapter — decentralization — is a phenomenon that cuts across each of these distinct policy arenas. In fact, it is difficult to think of a policy issue unaffected by decentralization as it is currently unfolding throughout the region. Perhaps the most obvious example comes from the social policies analyzed by Suzanne Duryea and Carmen Pagés and by Wendy Hunter. Decentralization matters for the study of human capital development largely because the sectors that have received much of the attention from decentralizers are precisely the areas of education and health care.

Decentralization also shapes financial policy by complicating the ability of the national government to use countercyclical policies, one of the key areas of policy innovation that Sylvia Maxfield advocates. Likewise, the expansion of subnational borrowing capacity might be considered a further example of the recent domestic financial policy choices criticized by Sidney Weintraub. With respect to trade policy, decentralization clearly affects the integration dynamics evaluated by Roberto Bouzas, José Salazar-Xirinachs, and Gustavo Vega-Cánovas. In this policy arena, the devolution of authority "downward" to subnational actors arguably makes it harder for national policymakers to, at the same time, delegate trade policy authority "upward" to supranational bodies. Whether the net impact of decentralization on each of these policy fields is positive or negative remains a difficult question, one that can be answered only with detailed empirical research. What is clear, however, is that it is no longer possible to understand the terms of most policy conflicts in Latin America without thinking about decentralization.

At first glance, because decentralization essentially rearranges authority within country borders, it may appear to be unrelated to the making of foreign economic policy. Why a chapter on decentralization in a book on foreign economic relations? After all, the forging of economic relationships between countries has traditionally been the exclusive prerogative of policymakers situated at the national level. As Robert Putnam argues, these national policymakers are engaged in a two-level game, negotiating not just with their counterparts in other countries but with a series of domestic constituents as well, some of whom might have subnational identities (Putnam 1988). Thanks to the decentralization of both political and policy authority, however, some of these subnational constituents are now players in their own right. As a result, foreign economic relations have become the prerogative of a multiplicity of actors and negotiators. Some of the examples of these phenomena are quite well known, as in the case of the tax wars that have erupted among Brazilian states eager to attract foreign investment (Zimmermann 2001). But similar trends are underway in less likely places as well, such as in highly centralized Uruguay, where subnational officials acting independently of the national government have used land grants to secure contracts with foreign companies. The cumulative impact of these emerging subnational actors suggests the need to rethink previous models that understood foreign economic relations through the prism of national politics alone.

According to the argument developed in this chapter, decentralization is relevant to the region's foreign economic relations because it directly shapes the two ingredients — democratic governance and market-oriented economics — on which regional economic integration is currently predicated. With respect to democracy, decentralization affects many of the critical governance issues that Ana Margheritis identifies in the Introduction to this volume. For example, reformers often promote decentralization as a change that can increase the effectiveness of the public administration to the extent that voters may have an easier time holding local, as opposed to national, officials accountable. In a less optimistic vein, many observers worry that decentralization may lead to higher levels of corruption by those same officials, who often escape rigorous oversight by either political or civil society actors at the subnational level.

In addition to democratic governance, regional integration efforts in this contemporary period also depend on the continued application of a development model that is much more liberal than the statist approaches that dominated previous approaches to integration (Salazar-Xirinachs, this volume). Although the adoption of this new development model implies policy change on a number of fronts, there are two essential components of the liberal model — the increased dependence on markets to allocate goods and services and the achievement and defense of macroeconomic stability. Recent events in Latin America show that chronic fiscal imbalance, in particular, and macroeconomic instability, in general, can impede the broader process of regional integration and liberalization. Decentralization can have a variety of impacts on fiscal outcomes. For example, the decentralization of governmental responsibilities can help policymakers cut chronic fiscal deficits at the national level. However, the increase in unearmarked tax transfers and the decentralization of authority over spending have threatened to expand consolidated public sector deficits. According to John Sheahan, one possible solution would be to follow the example of most U.S. states, which operate with requirements that total spending must be closely linked to total revenue (that is, they have freedom on all detailed choices but are constrained to overall balance).[1] In the absence of such mechanisms, however, and given strong pressures facing national authorities in Latin America to bail out subnational governments, the decentralization of fiscal authority must be understood as an important possible threat to stability. Thus, decentralization has the potential to impact powerfully the sustainability of both liberal economic policies and democratic governance models. For this reason, decentralization must be central to a discussion of current foreign economic policy dilemmas.

Decentralization is a particularly critical governance topic in Latin America today because it has led to important changes in the distribution of both political and policy authority. With regard to political decentralization, more mayors and governors and a far greater number of municipal councilors and subnational legislators are now elected than at any point in Latin America's past (Burki, Dillinger, and Webb 1999; Dietz and Shidlo 1998). The contemporary period has thus witnessed a dramatic increase in the potential for democratic politics at the subnational level. Hand in hand with this redistribution of political authority have come increasingly contentious political struggles among mayors, governors, presidents, and national legislators.[2] In the area of economic decentralization, these subnational officials are now endowed with much more authority over salient economic policy decisions than they have ever enjoyed before. As a consequence, mayors, governors, and the elected representatives with whom they share power at the subnational level have emerged as actors whose behavior affects both the maintenance of liberalizing policies and the possible adoption of a series of second-stage economic reforms (Naim 1995). A major challenge facing scholars is to integrate these subnational actors more systematically into the study of Latin American political economy.

This important combination of political and economic decentralization holds out enormous opportunities and risks for Latin America, as it pursues a new development model based on freer markets and freer politics. Chief among the opportunities are the chance to deepen democracy by expanding participation in the policymaking process and the possibility of accommodating differences in the services demanded by different subnational regions in an era of export-led growth. With respect to the risks, fiscal decentralization in many countries has threatened the inflation-fighting strategies of actors at the national level, while the decline in the quality of governmental services subsequent to their decentralization in some countries poses further challenges. In navigating these opportunities and risks, Latin American countries have adopted a variety of strategies, with important consequences for the numerous policy dilemmas highlighted in this volume. This chapter proceeds as follows. In the following section, the unique features of the current wave of decentralization relative to past experiences are discussed, and the similar impacts of integration and decentralization on the set of policy tools available to national decisionmakers are highlighted. The next section reviews some of the most salient risks and opportunities associated with the adoption of more decentralized approaches to the distribution of political power and economic policy authority. This allows for, in the third section, a comparative discussion of the decentralizing choices that have been adopted by different countries in the region. According to the two patterns identified in this section, some countries have decentralized quite aggressively, while others have been more tentative in their approach to decentralization. The more aggressive decentralizers, such as Brazil, Colombia, Argentina, and Bolivia, have started to experience some of the promise of decentralization, as reflected in the innovation achieved by some of their subnational governments. At the same time, however, these countries have squarely confronted the risks that decentralization can pose to macro-level stability. In contrast, tentative decentralizers, such as Chile, Uruguay, Venezuela, and Peru have avoided the macro threat by limiting the scope of fiscal decentralization, but at a cost of seriously limiting democratic participation and innovation at the subnational level. The concluding section synthesizes these country experiences and briefly evaluates challenges for future policymakers in the area of decentralization.

DECENTRALIZATION:
WHAT IS DISTINCTIVE ABOUT THE CONTEMPORARY PERIOD?

Economic liberalism and democratic governments are hardly unique to the contemporary period in Latin America, and neither is decentralization. Although the debate over the causes and consequences of decentralization in the 1990s has largely neglected earlier episodes of decentralization, many countries in the region have a wealth of experiences with both the adoption and revocation of decentralizing policies (Eaton 2001a and forthcoming). For example, repeated transitions back and forth between democratic and nondemocratic rule at the national level in Brazil and Argentina were regularly accompanied by waves of decentralization and re-centralization. As far back as 1891 in Chile and 1897 in Uruguay, national politicians adopted forms of decentralization as a possible solution to national political conflicts. Although decentralization is not new in the third wave of democracy, it has played a particularly important role in shaping this most recent wave.

It is the combination of two overarching changes in the constitution and performance of subnational governments that distinguishes the current experience with decentralization from previous experiences. First, subnational officials in the great majority of countries now hold their offices as the result of being elected rather than nominated by national-level politicians. While some countries in the region had experiences with subnational elections that predate the third wave, for most countries the regular holding of elections below the national level is quite new. Second, these same subnational officials are currently being asked to take charge of ever greater types of responsibilities and resources, both fiscal and administrative. Although the assignment of revenues and expenditures to subnational officials is also not entirely new in the region, the size of the revenues and the importance of the expenditures devolved speak to the special significance of decentralization in the contemporary period.

Previously, the following two common patterns prevailed in the region: political decentralization without the decentralization of policy authority and the transfer of substantial policy authority to subnational officials who were not separately elected. According to the first pattern, some countries previously held subnational elections, but the officials elected to these positions were routinely denied significant policy tools. This does not mean that these officials were unimportant, but it does mean that they were largely unable to counter important policy decisions taken at the national level. As Arturo Valenzuela showed for Chile before 1973, mayoral campaigns were hard fought and played an important role in the broader political system, although mayors held little independent control over revenue and expenditure decisions. In Argentina's experience with democratization during the second wave (1945-1955 and 1959-1966), governors and provincial elections played a significant role in the nation's party system and political life

(McGuire 1997), although the pursuit of state-led industrialization in this period led national policymakers to wrest powers from provincial authorities.

According to the second familiar pattern before the third wave, subnational officials were indeed called on to play critical roles in the provision of important governmental services, but these officials typically held their offices at the pleasure of national authorities. At times in Latin America's past, these subnational officials were appointed by democratically elected presidents, and at other times they were appointed by the military authorities who wielded executive powers at the center. In either case, national authorities could transfer expenditure responsibilities to subnational authorities without surrendering their ability to shape decisions in these different categories of expenditure. In the 1980s, for example, General Augusto Pinochet's government dramatically increased the importance of historically insignificant municipalities by giving them control over schools and health care, but he himself retained tight political control over mayors (Martelli 1998). In Peru, former President Alberto Fujimori increased the salience of regional governments in the 1990s, but only after suppressing the use of electoral mechanisms to generate regional authorities. These instances of deconcentration are significant; principal-agent approaches would predict that informational asymmetries and monitoring costs routinely enable subnational agents to escape the political control of their national principals. Deconcentration, however, should not be confused with measures that truly empower subnational officials whose sources of legitimacy are separate from national actors.

The significance of combined political and economic decentralization in contemporary Latin America begs an important question: why have national politicians surrendered authority over revenues and expenditures to subnational officials whom they cannot easily control? Scholars have compiled an increasingly varied set of explanations for this seemingly irrational act. Merilee Grindle underscores the importance of deep crises of political legitimacy in explaining the perplexing support of national politicians for decentralizing policies that limit their own power (Grindle 2000). Kathleen O'Neill explains decentralization as the result of rational calculations by governing parties that perceive their future electoral fortunes to lie at the subnational rather than the national level (O'Neill, forthcoming). In the Mexican case, Victoria Rodríguez argues that decentralization was adopted by the Institutional Revolutionary Party (Partido Revolucionario Institucional — PRI) in an ultimately unsuccessful attempt to regain the legitimacy and credibility that it had lost in the wake of economic and political crises in the 1980s (Rodríguez 1997). Evaluating these rival explanations of the shift toward decentralization in Latin America is beyond the scope of this chapter, which focuses instead on the various consequences of decentralization for the region's foreign economic policies. Nevertheless, it is important to underscore that, even where self-interest on the part of national policymakers explains their support for decentralization, decentralizing measures do, in practice, reduce the set of policy tools available to them in subsequent periods. The ambivalence of these politicians toward decentralization can be clearly seen in their support for some of the recentralizing measures discussed below.

The willingness of national politicians to confer economic policy authority to separately elected subnational actors in the contemporary period is particularly intriguing because national politicians also stand to lose authority relative to supranational authorities via regional integration (Burki 2000). In this sense, decentralization and integration force policymakers to surrender authority in both directions. Just as politicians have been quick to respond to economic problems at the subnational level by recentralizing, so they have responded to economic problems at the supranational level by reclaiming authority for national policymakers. One can identify instances of reneging on both integration and decentralization in the late 1990s, and this development is not surprising, given the extent to which these twin phenomena tend to eliminate national policy tools. On the other hand, one can think of various ways in which downward devolution and upward delegation might be mutually reinforcing. As William C. Smith argues, "centralized authority may be crucial for initiating integration schemes (while) at subsequent stages, when complex coordination and monitoring problems arise, greater subnational autonomy and flexibility may facilitate the sustained implementation of regional integration."[3] Greater policy autonomy for subnational officials in those jurisdictions that lie near national borders may be an especially critical tool in promoting regional integration, although continuing national security concerns arguably complicate decentralization to these very same subnational jurisdictions.

OPPORTUNITIES AND RISKS ASSOCIATED WITH DECENTRALIZATION

The combination of political and economic decentralization holds out enormous opportunities and risks for Latin America, as it pursues a new development model based on freer markets and politics. Many of the significant advantages that decentralization promises to deliver necessarily come coupled with an equally significant set of disadvantages. As discussed in the conclusion of this chapter, certain institutional reforms and timing decisions may attenuate some of the disadvantages and maximize the promised benefits of decentralization. However, in general, the trade-offs inherent are very real and may not be completely avoided through institutional engineering and sequencing. In practice, for example, genuine decentralization requires that subnational officials wield authority over revenues — rarely is it enough merely to give them control over expenditure decisions while keeping revenues centralized. The Chilean case discussed below is an important example of the limits of an approach that allows regional officials to assign specific projects within the general spending categories set by national ministries, while denying them an independent stake in revenues.[4] Without decentralizing revenues, countries cannot take advantage of the various gains in efficiency, local dynamism, and democracy that decentralization can make possible. In contrast, when national authorities do devolve the ability to influence revenue and expenditure decisions, they by definition open themselves up to the macroeconomic threat posed by independently elected subnational officials.

A clear example of this dilemma is the critical question of who sets salaries for government employees at the subnational level. The ability of subnational policymakers to set compensation schedules for bureaucrats and other public sector employees independently is essential for the attempt to foster innovation and reward excellence. Without such authority over teachers and health workers, it is hard to imagine how independently elected subnational authorities in different regions could respond to diverse preferences on the governmental provision of education and health care. This is central to the ability of decentralization to deliver the gains contemplated in theories of fiscal federalism. At the same time, control over salaries for the scores of government employees who have been transferred in recent years from the national to subnational levels remains an important stabilization tool for national governments. Given the recurring need of many of these governments to stabilize their economies throughout the 1990s and the extent to which stabilization continues to depend more on cutting expenditures than increasing revenues, national policymakers are often loath to give up their prerogatives vis-à-vis the setting of salary levels.

The following paragraphs play out in greater detail some of the opportunities and risks associated with decentralization. Although the recent nature of decentralizing changes in Latin America makes it difficult to evaluate the consequences of these changes in anything approaching a comprehensive fashion, it is, nevertheless, possible and useful to distinguish between possible risks and opportunities. This will serve as a baseline for understanding how different countries have responded to these challenges in the actual adoption of decentralizing policies.

Opportunities

In a variety of ways, decentralization can help consolidate the political and economic models on which continued regional integration depends. According to many different scholars, the impact of decentralization on politics alone can take a number of beneficial forms. To the extent that democratic consolidation in Latin America can be furthered by putting into place additional checks on arbitrary actions by national chief executives, political decentralization is a positive development, analogous to the strengthening of legislative and judicial branches at the national level. The ability of elected subnational officials to delimit the authority of elected national officials is an important consideration, one that blends aspects of the horizontal and vertical accountability relations that have recently received much attention in the literature (O'Donnell 1999 and Shugart 2001).[5] Decentralization in this sense may help limit the scope for the type of dramatic policy swings that considerably undermine regional integration and that were common in the region's past, when these checks were inoperative. In many cases, decisions in new democracies to decentralize in the immediate aftermath of the transition took shape as a strategy to weaken the bases of authoritarian rule at the center and to reduce the likelihood of future democratic reversals (Diamond 1999). In other cases, centralizing projects of military regimes encouraged pro-democracy actors to embrace decentralization as the antiauthoritarian reform par excellence (Souza 1997).

In the contemporary period, unlike most previous periods, decentralizing measures have moved beyond the empowering of subnational elected officials and have included explicit attempts to broaden participation by actors traditionally excluded from policymaking (Crook and Manor 1998; Kammeier and Demaine

2000). The goal in many of these cases is not just to shift power from one set of elected officials to another, but rather to make these officials more responsive to a wider set of interests (Schonwalder 1997). In some cases, this takes the form of establishing local consultative bodies made up of civil society groups. In other cases, it involves actually seating representatives of these groups on real decision-making bodies (Blair 2000). The design and implementation of mechanisms to expand the range of actors who can shape policy outcomes deserves our attention because broader participation at the local level may increase support for democracy at the national level. As seen in the cases discussed below, in at least some subnational regions in some Latin American countries, these attempts to broaden participation have experienced important successes.

Beyond the impact on politics and policy-making procedures, decentralization can also have directly positive implications for economic performance in developing countries undergoing liberalization. For the Colombian case, Bell argues that shifting expenditure decisions over schools and hospitals to local governments can free up the central state to concentrate its efforts on other activities, including the opening of the economy (Bell 1998, 99). More important, perhaps, when control over revenues is shifted to subnational actors, governments at this level can begin to play the role ascribed to them by the theory of fiscal federalism; namely, they can begin to differentiate the set of goods and services provided by government (Musgrave 1965). Some scholars argue that citizens in different subnational regions in developing countries do not differ markedly in the level of governmental services they desire (Prud'homme 1995). There are reasons to believe, however, that subnational flexibility makes more sense in the context of a development model that requires firms in different subnational regions to participate aggressively in international markets. One interviewee, Chilean Senator Carlos Cantero, complains that his home region of Antofagasta is not able to offer the types of basic investment incentives that would enable the region to pursue its specific comparative advantages.[6]

Research by Richard Doner and Eric Hershberg suggests that national policymakers can help domestic firms succeed in international markets by transferring authority over a variety of policies to subnational authorities (Doner and Hershberg 1999). According to their argument, deep technological changes reflected in the shift toward post-Fordist production models have put a premium on governmental interventions that can help specific firms insert themselves into niche markets abroad. When mass production in a period of relatively stable technology was the goal, centralized policymaking was adequate, but this is no longer the case. Doner and Hershberg argue that there is an elective affinity between decentralized policymaking and exporting in the contemporary world; local governments are better able to identify the dynamic needs of businesses that must be highly flexible in order to succeed. In a related vein, other scholars have argued that decentralization and federalism facilitate policy innovation by reducing the risks associated with failed attempts to innovate (Rose Ackerman 1980; Breton 2000). Given the premium placed on flexibility and creativity in the contemporary period, the ability of decentralization to lower the costs of policy innovation may be an important consideration.

Risks

Decentralization also poses a series of risks for Latin America, each of which raises questions about the short-term implications of decentralizing policies for the region. Like the opportunities discussed above, these risks can also be grouped according to their political and economic forms.

On the political side, many scholars worry that rather than empower civil society actors who have long been locked out of decision-making channels, decentralization may merely empower authoritarian enclaves at the local level (Fox 1994). The ability of local elites to dominate the bodies that are now being given control over revenues and expenditures is so great that it has led many civil society organizations to consider these bodies illegitimate and to avoid even attempting to participate in them (Schonwalder 2000). In many cases, the types of oversight activities that might detect abuses by policymakers are weaker at the local level than at the national level, and lower income groups have often been able to amass greater associational power at the national level than at the subnational level. According to these scenarios, decentralization not only complicates democratic consolidation, but by worsening clientelism, it may make it very unlikely that local governments will provide the types of specialized services demanded by firms seeking to participate in the world economy.

On the economic side, decentralization can threaten the following two main components of the liberal development model that currently holds sway in the region: macroeconomic stability and a reduction in state intervention. The first has received a great deal of attention in the literature, particularly by analysts working in the international financial institutions (Burki, Perry, and Dillinger 1999; Dillinger and Webb 1999 and 2001). At the heart of this dilemma is the ability of separately elected subnational authorities to behave in ways that sabotage the stabilization goals of national policymakers. Along with areas such as defense and foreign policy, responsibility for economic stabilization is not a governmental attribute that can be decentralized. Independent spending and taxing decisions by subnational authorities, however, can effectively counter stabilizing attempts by national leaders. Most frequently, this has taken the form of high levels of spending by subnational officials at a time when national authorities are trying to rein in expenditure. A related problem is the failure of subnational officials to spend revenue transfers on the expenditures that actually have been transferred, which national authorities tend to compensate for by sending additional revenues to the subnational level in order to prevent interruptions in the provision of basic governmental services (Bird 2000; Saiegh and Tommasi 1999). These interventions play havoc with rational public budgeting and typically have negative conse-quences for national budget deficits (Rodden 2003).

Although the impact on economic stability has caused the greatest alarm, decentralization can inhibit positive economic performance in a number of other ways. First, limited state capacity at the subnational level may lead to real declines in the quality of service delivery in the wake of decentralization. For example, some reports suggest that decentralization has worsened the provision of health care in many Latin American countries (Burki, Perry, and Dillinger 1999, 85). Such findings are worrisome both for their likely disproportionate impact on lower-income groups and because the inability to develop human capital hinders countries from attracting foreign investment. Another negative implication for economic performance is that many decentralization experiments have failed to define and separate adequately the expenditure responsibilities of different levels of government (Arretche and Rodríguez 2000; Souza 1997). In these unspecified environments, decentralization can encourage shirking by different levels of government and may lead to the type of confusion that makes it harder for voters to hold policymakers accountable. A final dilemma posed by decentralization for economic performance arises from the increased practice of automatic revenue sharing. According to many analysts, the need to share revenues from certain taxes with subnational authorities may perversely lead central governments to increase rates on taxes that are not shared, even if these are inefficient (Dillinger and Webb 2001). Thus, revenue sharing may conflict with the attempts of liberalizing governments to make the tax system more neutral by relying on taxes like the value-added tax, which tends to be shared (Eaton 2002). In Brazil, for example, David Samuels shows that former President Fernando Henrique Cardoso's government relied heavily on increasing "contributions" rather than taxes, as the former do not have to be shared with the states (Samuels 2003).[7] According to William Dillinger and Steven Webb, this same set of incentives led the central government in Colombia to enact an inefficient financial transactions tax "precisely because it did not have to put new taxes into the shared pool" (Dillinger and Webb 1999b and 2001).

CROSS-NATIONAL VARIATION IN LATIN AMERICA'S EXPERIMENT WITH DECENTRALIZATION

Although the direction of the shift in the last 20 years toward more decentralized forms of government is beyond dispute in Latin America, there is a great deal of variation in the scope and depth of decentralization within the region (Fukasaku and Haussmann 1995; López Murphy 1995; Willis, Garman, and Haggard 1999; Garman, Haggard, and Willis 2001). In the 1990s, some countries merely returned to more decentralized patterns, while in others, decentralization was a new phenomenon, new at least in the period since the consolidation of the central state in the nineteenth century. There are a number of ways of characterizing cross-national variation within the regional trend toward decentralization. In the paragraphs that follow, the experience of aggressive and tentative decentralizers is contrasted. Not all countries fit neatly into these two categories, and the recent spate of both decentralizing and recentralizing changes in many of these countries makes them "moving targets" that are hard to classify. Countries do, however, tend to cluster at either end of the spectrum, and the distinction between aggressive and tentative approaches provides a useful first cut in thinking through the challenges posed by decentralization. The aggressive decentralizers have begun to benefit from the important advantages made possible by decentralization, but they have also been exposed to its many risks. In countries that have been hesitant to decentralize, the risks are fewer but so, too, are the attendant gains.

Aggressive Decentralizers

It is not surprising that the most important examples of innovation at the subnational level have emerged among the aggressive decentralizers that include Bolivia, Brazil, and Colombia, in particular. In each of these countries, it would be a gross mistake to conclude that traditional clientelist practices no longer pervade politics at the subnational level. Despite this disturbing continuity, however, at least some subnational governments in each country have been able to use their expanded powers to innovate in important ways. Within these three countries, the performance of local governments looks increasingly heterogeneous, with pockets of democracy mixed in with local authoritarian enclaves. Bolivia offers a clear example of the emphasis placed on participation in the contemporary wave of decentralization (O'Neill 2003). In Bolivia, the 1994 Law of Popular Participation set up vigilance committees, composed of representatives of peasant syndicates and neighborhood councils to monitor elected bodies. While these committees in many areas have been unable to alter the behavior of the elites who tend to dominate the elected bodies, there are exceptions. For example, Harry Blair argues that in Cochabamba, the operation of these vigilance committees compelled the building of primary schools in poor neighborhoods, "moving away from its old pattern of building them mostly in the wealthier central area" (Blair 2000, 25). According to Grindle, the participatory drive of Bolivian decentralization is reflected in the strong opposition to decentralizing legislation by the country's unions, who saw that "their preeminent position in representing group interests in the country was threatened by the new law" (Grindle 2000, 121). Grindle concludes that decentralization has resulted in important political changes in Bolivia, encouraging more responsiveness to local needs and increasing the salience of local issues in electoral contests (Grindle 2000, 129).

Stories of innovative subnational governments have likewise emerged in Brazil, despite the striking continuities of rule by traditional elites in many states (Hagopian 1996). Judith Tendler's work on the state of Ceará in Brazil's poor northeast region shows what can happen when reformist subnational authorities decide they can win elections by such innovative practices as "collecting taxes already on the books . . . and insisting that new government employees be hired only through competitive exams" (Tendler 1997, 9). Though innovation by Ceará's reformist governor, Tasso Jereissati, cost him nearly all of his support in the state legislature, his popularity with voters led to the election of his preferred successor. Innovative practices have also taken root in more developed subnational units in Brazil. Most salient here is the establishment of participatory budgeting by the Workers' Party (Partido dos Trabalhadores) government in the southern city of Porto Alegre. Having won the United Nations' Habitat prize for best-governed city, Porto Alegre's open budgeting model has subsequently been copied by governments in other cities, including the conservative government of Recife (Heller 2001).

Colombia is also an important case to be cited. In response to growing evidence of the state's weakened legitimacy, the country's 1991 Constitution adopted such reforms as the *voto programático* (programmatic vote), recall mechanisms, plebiscites, referenda, and public consultations (Bell 1998). Although Bell argues that these institutional changes have been insufficient to change traditional clientelism in the absence of deeper changes in the party system and that clientelism has prevented decentralization from reaching its goals, there are signs of some positive change. One of the most fascinating examples is the case of Pasto, a poor departmental capital on the border of Ecuador. In 1994, the mayoral election in Pasto was won by Antonio Navarro, head of the former guerrilla group M-19 and copresident of the 1991 Constitutional Convention. Due to the limited chances that M-19 would ever have of winning the presidency, a nontraditional politician like Navarro would have been unlikely to secure such a position in the long period when mayors were appointed by presidents. Political decentralization and the victory of Navarro led to a great deal of innovation at the local level. Navarro introduced direct popular participation in the allocation of spending, created the post of independent municipal watchdog (*veedor*), and increased locally generated taxes by 60 percent in real terms in two years (Angell, Lowden, and Thorp 2001, 70). The victory of outsiders and nontraditional politicians in other key cities has also led to positive changes, including the introduction in Bogotá of a system that fights tax evasion by tying property valuation to subsequent sales values (Angell, Lowden, and Thorp 2001, 37).

What is the relationship between decentralization and these examples of innovation? It would be misleading to attribute innovation entirely to the significant fiscal decentralization that has occurred in these countries. One element in the Brazilian and Bolivian cases cited above that is particularly arresting is that some of the subnational units that have been most able to alter traditional politics (Ceará in Brazil and the city of Pasto in Colombia) are among the poorest.[8] As Tendler shows, Ceará produced its turnaround at the same time that federal transfers to the state were declining (Tendler 1997, 9). However, fiscal decentralization may operate as an important facilitating condition for innovation. Endowing municipalities, states, provinces and departments with greater powers can enhance the reelection prospects of reformist officials at the subnational level, making it possible for them to demonstrate that innovative practices lead to real results and electoral victories. Among the set of tentative decentralizers discussed below, innovation clearly can be stymied by the absence of a national framework that shifts significant formal powers to subnational officials.

Although a more radical approach to decentralization has facilitated participation and policy innovation, these more radical approaches also have a negative side. This can be seen most clearly in the extent to which fiscal decentralization challenged the ability of national authorities in Argentina, Brazil, and Colombia to retain control over national budget deficits in the 1990s. In Argentina, the important shift toward decentralization occurred in 1987, when Peronist governors demanded the passage of a revenue sharing law that increased provincial tax transfers to an historical high. According to this change, the federal government was legally obliged to share with the provinces 56.6 percent of the revenues it collected from a broad set of taxes (Saiegh and Tommasi 1999). Although important responsibilities in the health and education sectors were devolved to the provinces in 1991, revenue transfers remained unearmarked for these activities (FIEL 1993). In many cases, transfers from the center were dedicated to patronage activities within provincial bureaucracies, as public employment in the provinces ballooned (Novaro 1996, World Bank 1990). When the success of stabilization efforts in 1991 promised to expand greatly the size of transfers to the provinces, federal authorities sought ways of reasserting control over these transfers (Eaton 2001b). Although fiscal pacts signed in 1992 and 1993 enabled the federal government to cut the percentage of revenues it had to share with the provinces, it purchased support for this measure by guaranteeing to transfer a minimum level of revenues, an agreement that operated like a straitjacket on the government when the economy began to contract later in the decade. That Argentina's collapse has so destabilized the Southern Common Market (Mercado Común del Sur — MERCOSUR) provides powerful support for the contention that foreign economic relations are increasingly being shaped by the design of subnational institutions.

The challenges to macroeconomic stability posed by fiscal decentralization and subnational spending and borrowing decisions are an even more familiar story in Brazil. As in Argentina, the decision to give subnational governments an independent stake in federally collected revenues in the late 1980s contributed to fiscal imbalance in the 1990s. Even more problematic has been the question of subnational borrowing authority, with the federal government bailing out states that prove unable to service the large debts they incur (Dillinger and Webb 1999a). Unlike in Argentina, where the federal government forced subnational governments to use their own revenue transfers to pay back their loans, the federal government in Brazil has faced greater obstacles in placing similar controls on subnational debt. In 1999, irresponsible spending and borrowing decisions by the states triggered a national economic recession, provoking a currency devaluation that threw regional integration efforts into a profound state of crisis. For many countries in the region, the deep instability resulting from the devolution of political and economic power in Brazil has sounded a note of caution in debates over decentralization. Although there is an important disagreement among scholars over the relative success of attempts by the Cardoso administration to re-centralize authority in response to economic crises in the 1990s (Dillinger and Webb 1999a; Montero 2001; Samuels, 2003), the argument that decentralization contributed to these crises is not disputed.

A somewhat similar story can be told for fiscal decentralization and macro-level instability in Colombia, even though a variety of factors distinguish it from the Argentine and Brazilian cases. First, perhaps in keeping with the country's unitary identity and traditions of responsible fiscal management, decentralization agreements retained greater controls for national authorities with respect to how municipal authorities can use revenue transfers (Dillinger and Webb 1999b; Sánchez and Gutiérrez 1995). Second, the contributing role played by subnational fiscal profligacy is less clear in Colombia than in Argentina and Brazil. In Colombia, the emergence of coal and oil as important new exports in the 1980s, in addition to illegal exports, made macroeconomic management far more difficult than when finances were more centralized. It is, thus, more difficult to isolate the impact of decentralization on macrostability (Angell, Lowden, and Thorp 2001). Despite these differences, it is clear that the costs of fiscal transfers placed serious strains on government finances in the 1990s. Loath to be displaced by revenues that are now transferred directly to subnational authorities, legislators in the 1990s came to depend increasingly on a cofinancing system that enables them to claim credit for sending additional funds to their home districts. This discretionary padding of automatic transfers has widened budget deficits and complicated the budgeting process (Dillinger and Webb 1999b).

Tentative Decentralizers

A different set of countries in Latin America has avoided the pitfalls of aggressive fiscal decentralization, but by bucking the trend toward decentralized governance, these countries have necessarily failed to benefit from some of the positive aspects of decentralization.

Consider the cases of Chile, Peru, Uruguay, and Venezuela. The independent spending, taxing, and borrowing decisions of subnational officials have not posed a threat to stability in any of these countries. Due to the limited fiscal powers of subnational officials, the politics of economic stabilization in these countries are fundamentally different than in the cases of more aggressive decentralization. Given the salience of the politics of economic stabilization in the political life of virtually all Latin American countries in the last 20 years, this difference helps explain the relative insignificance of center-local relations among these tentative decentralizers. Chile's experience is particularly important because its moderate and gradual approach to decentralization has made it a model for many developing countries, particularly in contrast with some of the failures of the more radical approaches adopted in Argentina and Brazil.[9] In Chile, widespread commitment to the overarching goal of fiscal stability was achieved much earlier than in other countries in the region and has proved to be especially solid. Consistently, this goal has been articulated as one that is incompatible with the types of decentralization adopted by neighboring countries. As argued by Carlos Ominami, former senator and economic minister, "In Chile, centralized formulation of the budget and equally centralized tax collection have been fundamental for assuring good management of public finances," with the result that "the most fruitful and interesting path to decentralization is a gradually decentralized allocation of sectoral resources defined in the budget" (Ominami 1995, 178). Chilean decentralization in the 1990s has been limited to allowing subnational authorities greater power to assign central revenues to spending projects within the priority areas selected by central ministries (Martelli and Valenzuela 1999).

Subnational officials in Peru have also been restrained. In the literature on the politics of economic stabilization and liberalization, the Peruvian case is often compared with Argentina and Brazil. In each of these three cases, presidents emphasized the importance of securing national fiscal stability through such measures as deep budget cuts, tax reform, and privatization. In each case, fiscal austerity was proposed as the one sure route to lower inflation. In pursuing these policies in Peru, former President Fujimori faced many of the same obstacles as his Argentine and Brazilian counterparts, but the need to share revenue with independently elected subnational authorities was not one of them. All things being equal, the lack of such a system made President Fujimori's job in the 1990s an easier one. Not only did Fujimori not have to share revenues with subnational officials, but his self-coup (*autogolpe*) in 1992 subsequently made it possible for him to remove regional officials and to trim regional powers (Casas 2000).

In the remaining countries in this set, Uruguay and Venezuela, limited experiences with fiscal decentralization have likewise stopped well short of threatening the stabilization tools of national authorities. In Uruguay, although some services have been devolved to regional departmental authorities in the contemporary period, fiscal authority has remained highly centralized, with the central government reserving for itself the right to introduce all new taxes (Nickson 1995, 255). The Broad Front (Frente Amplio) government, led by Tabaré Vásquez in the department of Montevideo, endorsed administrative deconcentration within that department but has not been able to bring about the greater decentralization of fiscal authority from above (Quintana 1992, 17). According to National Party (Partido Nacional [Blanco]) leader Wilson Ferreira Aldunate, in Uruguay, departmental chief executives "have to go begging for resources, and obtain them or not based on the whims of the Economic Ministry" (Partido Nacional 1989, 94). As one high-level bureaucrat in the Budget Office reports, these subnational officials consequently spend about three days of the week in Montevideo.[10]

Although fiscal decentralization has been more significant in Venezuela than in Chile, Peru, and Uruguay, central politicians designed it in ways that limited the autonomy of subnational officials. For example, according to Penfold Becerra, reforms in 1996 increased the shares of value-added tax (VAT) revenues that are reserved for the states, but gave a central government agency called the Intergovernmental Fund for Decentralization (Fondo Intergubernamental para la Descentralización — FIDES) "responsibility to administer and allocate these resources contingent upon the submission and approval of specific earmarked projects . . . by regional and local governments" (Penfold Becerra 2003). On the expenditure side, governors must submit petitions to the Senate that solicit the transfer of sectoral responsibilities to the states and that demonstrate capacity to deliver the services in question (Penfold Becerra 2003). Together, these design features have preserved federal control over stabilization mechanisms in Venezuela, even before the more explicit recentralization attempts of President Hugo Chávez.

Unsurprisingly, the gains associated with decentralization in the areas of innovation and participation have been quite limited in these countries, particularly in Chile and Peru. Chile remains one of the region's most centralized countries in political terms, largely as a result of Pinochet's ability to direct the democratic transition from a position of strength. When Pinochet relinquished power at the national level to former President Patricio Aylwin's Concertation for Democracy (Concertación por la Democracia) government in 1990, neither the local nor regional governments were democratized. Only in 1992 were the two main party blocs able to agree to a series of institutional changes, according to which the right agreed to redemocratize municipal governments in exchange for the partial democratization of the regional level of government introduced by Pinochet (Bland 2003). As a result of this 1992 agreement, regional councilors in Chile are indirectly elected by municipal councilors. To date, then, voters at this intermediate level of government do not directly elect any of their regional representatives, and national policymakers have resisted reforms that would further democratize regional governments. As a consequence, democracy at the subnational level remains much more limited in Chile than in virtually all of the big Latin American countries, significantly reducing opportunities for innovative and participatory policymaking.[11] In their comparative study of decentralization in Chile and Colombia, Angell, Lowden, and Thorp conclude that more dynamic mayors have emerged in Colombia than in Chile because the former have "the power to make real change" and far greater resources than their Chilean counterparts (Angell, Lowden, and Thorp 2001, 219).

Along with Chile, democracy at the subnational level in Peru has suffered from serious constraints. Late in his beleaguered term as President (1985-1990), Alan García proposed and began implementing elections for regional authorities (Schmidt 1989). According to Sung Han Kim (1992), this reform proposal consti-tuted a strategic attempt by García to carve out regional power bases for his American Popular Revolutionary Alliance (Alianza Popular Revolucionaria Ameri-cana — APRA) in anticipation of its almost certain defeat in the 1990 presidential elections. Shortly after the democratization of this level of government, however, President Fujimori's self-coup led to the suspension of these regional elections for the remainder of the 1990s. Only in the new administration of President Alejandro Toledo have discussions resumed over the need to redemocratize this level of government, culminating in the decision in 2002 to reinstitute regional elections. The contrast between Peru's experience and the emergence and strengthening of democratic subnational governments in other countries in the 1990s is instructive.

CONCLUSION

The cross-national differences in decentralization strategies identified in this chapter have important implications for the region's foreign economic policies. National politicians who have been more radical in the decentralization of economic policy authority have directly undermined their own ability to keep regional integration efforts on track. However, where national politicians have resisted endowing subnational actors with real authority, the continued use of highly centralizing development models likewise undercuts the pursuit of an open-borders approach to integration. According to this analysis, neither the aggressive nor the more tentative approach to decentralization is free of problems, and each has elements that would recommend it to would-be decentralizers. From countries that have pursued decentralization more aggressively, one can gain an appreciation of the long-term benefits for democratic policymaking that decentralizing policies can achieve. From countries that have adopted a less comprehensive version of decentralization, one can appreciate the importance of ensuring that national policymakers can continue to play the critical stabilizing roles that only they can play.

Although it is unlikely that the decentralization experiences of Latin Ameri-can countries will ever converge on one model, a central dilemma for policymakers in the future will be to find ways of maximizing the strengths and minimizing the weaknesses of these different approaches. National authorities in the set of aggres-sive decentralizers will have to design mechanisms that defend the viability of stabilizing policy tools without reintroducing too much discretion or complexity in the relations between national and subnational policymakers. In the past, discretion and complexity have been the enemies of genuine decentralization (Manor 1999). Over time in the established democracies, as Dillinger and Webb note, long-standing decentralized public sectors have been able to develop institutions to prevent the sorts of problems seen in Argentina, Brazil, Bolivia, and Colombia (Dillinger and Webb 2001). Policymakers in Latin American countries where decentralization has been more tentative face the opposite challenge. In this set of countries, national authorities need to appreciate that the retention of overly centralized approaches to governance comes at a cost. More to the point, as the region continues to experience regional integration and liberalization, the costs of remaining highly centralized are likely to increase.

Notes

1.   I am grateful to John Sheahan for this distinction and for his comments on this chapter.

2.   Salient examples include the conflict in Argentina between Peronist President Carlos Menem and Fernando de la Rúa when he served as Radical Party (Partido Radical) mayor of Buenos Aires, the debt default by Minas Gerais Governor Itamar Franco that triggered a major economic and political crisis in Brazil for President Cardoso, and the struggles between Cuauhtémoc Cárdenas as Mexico City mayor and the PRI-dominated national government in the late 1990s.

3.   I am grateful to William C. Smith for his insightful comments on this chapter.

4.   Note that this does not necessarily require subnational governments to depend on revenues that they themselves collect from their own taxes, although this is an important indicator of decentralization. When they are automatically distributed according to criteria legislated ex ante, revenue sharing from the center can fulfill this requirement (Manor 1999, 13).

5.   Horizontal accountability refers to relations among chief executives, judges, legislators, ombudsmen, and regulators at the national level. Vertical accountability refers mostly to voters and citizens in their attempts to control the behavior of officials they elected to national office. How subnational elected officials fit into these relationships is not always clear; they would appear to be part of horizontal accountability due to their status as elected officials but may affect vertical accountability as well due to their closer proximity to voters.

6.   Carlos Cantero noted that industrial policy is quite decentralized in many of the countries that are Chile's main competitors, such as Spain and Italy, and that the absence of a similar degree of regional flexibility puts the country at a disadvantage in international markets. Interview with Carlos Cantero, August 22, 2001, Valparaiso.

7.   According to Samuels (2003), an important example of a such a contribution in Brazil is the "Provisionary Contribution on Financial Operations," in effect, a tax that is levied on financial transactions.

8.   Faletti's work on decentralized education similarly finds evidence of surprisingly positive policy performances by lesser-developed subnational jurisdictions. Tulia Faletti, "The Decentralization of Education in Argentina, Colombia, and Mexico" talk at the Roundtable on Decentralization, Princeton University, February 22, 2002.

9.   Personal communication with Fernando Rojas, The World Bank, July 10, 2001.

10.   Interview by author, Montevideo, May 10, 2002.

11.   In the Chilean case, it is perhaps no coincidence that national authorities have been the most hesitant in the region not just about handing greater authority to separately elected subnational authorities, but also in delegating these powers to supranational authorities (for example, the reluctance to join MERCOSUR).

REFERENCES

Angell, Alan, Pamela Lowden, and Rosemary Thorp. 2001. *Decentralizing Development: The Political Economy of Institutional Change in Colombia and Chile*. Oxford, UK: Oxford University Press.

Arretche, Marta, and Vicente Rodríguez. 2000. *Descentralização das políticas sociais no Brasil*. São Paulo: Edições Fundap.

Bell, Gustavo. 1998. "The Decentralised State: An Administrative or Political Challenge?" In *Colombia: The Politics of Reforming the State*, ed. Eduardo Posada-Carbó. New York: St. Martin's Press.

Bird, Richard. 2000. "Transfers and Incentives in Intergovernmental Fiscal Relations." In *Decentralization and Accountability of the Public Sector*, eds. Shahid Burki and Guillermo Perry. Washington, D.C.: Annual World Bank Conference on Development in Latin America and the Caribbean.

Blair, Harry. 2000. "Participation and Accountability at the Periphery: Democratic Local Governance in Six Countries." *World Development* 28 (1): 21-39.

Bland, Gary. 2003. "The Impetus for Decentralization in Chile and Venezuela." In *Decentralization and Democracy*, eds. Alfred Montero and David Samuels. Notre Dame, Ind.: University of Notre Dame Press.

Breton, Albert. 2000. "Federalism and Decentralization: Ownership Rights and the Superiority of Federalism." *Publius: The Journal of Federalism* 30 (2): 1-16.

Burki, Shahid Javed, Guillermo Perry, and William Dillinger. 1999. *Beyond the Center: Decentralizing the State*. Washington, D.C.: The World Bank.

Burki, Shahid. 2000. "From Globalization to Localization." In *Decentralization and Accountability of the Public Sector*, eds. Shahid Burki and Guillermo Perry. Washington, D.C.: Annual World Bank Conference on Development in Latin America and the Caribbean.

Cantero, Carlos. 2001. Interview by author, August 22, Valparaiso, Chile.

Casas, Carlos. 2000. "Peru." In *Línea de Referencia: El Proceso de Descentralización*. Quito: Consejo Nacional de Modernización del Estado.

Crook, Richard Charles, and James Manor. 1998. *Democracy and Decentralisation in South Asia and West Africa: Participation, Accountability and Performance*. Cambridge, UK: Cambridge University Press.

Diamond, Larry, and Svetlana Tsalik. 1999. "Size and Democracy: The Case for Decentralization." In *Developing Democracy*, ed. Larry Diamond. Baltimore: The Johns Hopkins University Press.

Dietz, Henry, and Gil Shidlo. 1998. *Urban Elections in Democratic Latin America*. Wilmington, Del.: Scholarly Resources, Inc.

Dillinger, William, and Steven Webb. 1999a. *Fiscal Management in Federal Democracies: Argentina and Brazil*. Policy Research Working Paper, No. 2121. Washington, D.C.: The World Bank.

Dillinger, William, and Steven Webb. 1999b. *Decentralization and Fiscal Management in Colombia*. Policy Research Working Paper, No. 2122. Washington, D.C.: The World Bank.

Dillinger, William, and Steven Webb. 2001. "Is Fiscal Stability Compatible with Decentralization? The Case of Latin America." Washington, D.C.: The World Bank. Mimeo.

Doner, Richard, and Eric Hershberg. 1999. "Flexible Production and Political Decentralization in the Developing World: Elective Affinities in the Pursuit of Competitiveness?" *Studies in Comparative International Development* 34 (1): 45-82.

Eaton, Kent. 2001a. "Decentralization, Democratization, and Liberalization: The History of Revenue Sharing in Argentina." *Journal of Latin American Studies* 33 (1): 1-28.

Eaton, Kent. 2001b. "Political Obstacles to Decentralization: Evidence from Argentina and the Philippines." *Development and Change* 32 (1): 101-127.

Eaton, Kent. 2002. *Politicians and Economic Reform in New Democracies: Argentina and the Philippines in the 1990s*. University Park, Pa.: Pennsylvania State University Press.

Eaton, Kent. Forthcoming. *Politics Beyond the Capital: The Design of Subnational Institutions in South America*. Stanford, Calif.: Stanford University Press.

Faletti, Tulia. "The Decentralization of Education in Argentina, Colombia, and Mexico." A talk at the Roundtable on Decentralization, Princeton University, February 22, 2002.

Fundación de Investigaciones Económicas Latinoamericanas. 1993. *Hacia una nueva organización del federalismo fiscal en la Argentina*. Buenos Aires: Ediciones Latinomericanas.

Fox, Jonathan. 1994. "Latin America's Emerging Local Politics." *Journal of Democracy* 5 (2): 105-116.

Fukasaku, Kiichiro, and Ricardo Haussmann, eds. 1998. *Democracy, Decentralisation and Deficits in Latin America*. Paris: Organisation for Economic Cooperation and Development (OECD).

Garman, Christopher, Stephan Haggard, and Eliza Willis. 2001. "Fiscal Decentralization: A Political Theory with Latin American Cases." *World Politics* 53 (2): 205-236.

Gonzales de Olarte, Efraín, Teobaldo Pinzás, and Carolina Trivelli. 1995. "Peru." In *Fiscal Decentralization in Latin America*, ed. Ricardo López Murphy. Washington, D.C.: Inter-American Development Bank.

Grindle, Merilee. 2000. *Audacious Reforms: Institution Invention and Democracy in Latin America*. Baltimore: The Johns Hopkins University Press.

Hagopian, Frances. 1996. *Traditional Politics and Regime Change in Brazil*. New York: Cambridge University Press.

Heller, Patrick. 2001. "Moving the State: The Politics of Democratic Decentralization in Kerala, South Africa, and Porto Alegre." *Politics and Society* 29 (1): 131-163.

Kammeier, Hans, and Harvey Demaine, eds. 2000. *Decentralization, Local Governance and Rural Development*. Bangkok: Asian Institute of Technology.

Kim, Sung Han. 1992. "The Political Process of Decentralization in Peru." *Public Administration and Development* 12 (3): 249-265.

King, Desmond, and Gerry Stoker, eds. 1996. *Rethinking Local Democracy*. London: Macmillan.

López Murphy, Ricardo, ed. 1995. *Fiscal Decentralization in Latin America*. Washington, D.C.: Inter-American Development Bank.

McGuire, James. 1997. *Peronism without Perón*. Stanford, Calif.: Stanford University Press.

Manor, James. 1999. *The Political Economy of Democratic Decentralization*. Washington, D.C.: The World Bank.

Martelli, Giorgio. 1998. *Asociación Chilena de municipalidades: historia, desafíos y reflexiones*. A White Paper from the Fundación Friedrich Ebert, Santiago, Chile.

Martelli, Giorgio, and Esteban Valenzuela. 1999. *Propuestas de reformas a los gobiernos regionales para su fortalecimiento y democratización. Documentos de discusión*. Santiago: Friedrich Ebert Stiftung.

Montero, Alfred. 2001. "Decentralizing Democracy: Spain and Brazil in Comparative Perspective." *Comparative Politics* 33 (2): 149-169.

Musgrave, Richard. 1965. *Essays in Fiscal Federalism*. Washington, D.C.: The Brookings Institution.

Naim, Moisés. 1995. "Latin America: The Second Stage Reform." In *Economic Reform and Democracy*, eds. Larry Diamond and Marc Plattner. Baltimore: The Johns Hopkins University Press.

Nickson, R. Andrew. 1995. *Local Government in Latin America*. Boulder, Colo.: Lynne Rienner Publishers.

Novaro, Marcos. 1994. *Pilotos de tormentas: crisis de representación y personalización de la política en Argentina*. Buenos Aires: Ediciones Letra Buena.

O'Donnell, Guillermo. 1999. "Horizontal Accountability in New Democracies." In *The Self Restraining State*, eds. Andreas Schedler, Larry Diamond, and Marc Plattner. Boulder: Lynne Rienner Publishers.

O'Neill, Kathleen. 2003. "Decentralization in Bolivia and Colombia." In *Decentralization and Democracy*, eds. Alfred Montero and David Samuels. Notre Dame, Ind.: University of Notre Dame Press.

O'Neill, Kathleen. Forthcoming. *Decentralizing the State: Elections, Parties, and Local Power in the Andes*. New York. Cambridge University Press.

Ominami, Carlos. 1995. "Chile." In *Democracy, Decentralisation and Deficits in Latin America*, eds. Kiichiro Fukasaku and Ricardo Haussmann. Paris: OECD.

Partido Nacional (Blanco). 1989. *Documentos sobre el proyecto de descentralización y acondicionamiento territorial del Partido Nacional*. Montevideo.

Penfold Becerra, Michael. 2003. "Electoral Dynamics and Decentralization in Venezuela." In *Decentralization and Democracy*, eds. Alfred Montero and David Samuels. Notre Dame, Ind.: University of Notre Dame Press.

Prud'homme, Remy. 1995. "The Dangers of Decentralization." *World Bank Research Observer* 10 (2): 201-20.

Putnam, Robert. 1988. "Diplomacy and Domestic Politics: The Logic of Two-level Games." *International Organization* 43 (3): 427-460.

Quintana Bigolotti, Mario. 1992. *El proceso de descentralización de la Intendencia Municipal de Montevideo*. Montevideo: Asociación de Administradores Gubernamentales.

Rodden, Jonathan. 2003. "The Dilemma of Fiscal Federalism: Hard and Soft Budget Constraints around the World." In *Decentralization and Democracy*, eds. Alfred Montero and David Samuels. Notre Dame, Ind.: University of Notre Dame Press.

Rodríguez, Victoria. 1997. *Decentralization in Mexico: From Reforma Municipal to Solidaridad to Nuevo Federalismo*. Boulder, Colo.: Westview Press.

Rojas, Fernando. The World Bank, July 10, 2001. Personal communication with author.

Rose Ackerman, Susan. 1980. "Risk Taking and Reelection: Does Federalism Promote Innovation?" *Journal of Legal Studies* 9: 593-616.

Saiegh, Sebastian, and Mariano Tommasi. 1999. "Why Is Argentina's Fiscal Federalism So Inefficient? Entering the Labyrinth." *Journal of Applied Economics* 2 (1): 169-209.

Samuels, David. 2003. *Ambition, Federalism, and Legislative Politics in Brazil.* New York: Cambridge University Press.

Sánchez, Fabio, and Catalina Gutiérrez. 1995. "Colombia." In *Fiscal Decentralization in Latin America*, ed. Ricardo López Murphy. Washington, D.C.: Inter-American Development Bank.

Schmidt, Gregory. 1989. "Political Variables and Governmental Decentralization in Peru: 1949-1988." *Journal of Interamerican Studies and World Affairs* 31 (1 and 2): 193-232.

Schonwalder, Gerd. 1997. "New Democratic Spaces at the Grassroots? Popular Participation in Latin American Local Governments." *Development and Change* 28: 753-770.

Shugart, Matthew, Erika Moreno, and Brian Crisp. 2000. "The Accountability Deficit in Latin America." Paper presented at the conference on "Institutions, Accountability, and Democratic Governance in Latin America." The Helen Kellogg Institute for International Studies, University of Notre Dame, Notre Dame, Indiana, May 8-9.

Souza, Celina. 1997. *Constitutional Engineering in Brazil: The Politics of Federalism and Decentralization.* New York: St. Martin's Press.

Tendler, Judith. 1997. *Good Government in the Tropics.* Baltimore: The Johns Hopkins University Press.

Willis, Eliza, Christopher Garman, and Stephan Haggard. 1999. "Decentralization in Latin America." *Latin American Research Review* 34 (1): 7-56.

World Bank. 1990. *Provincial Government Finances.* Washington, D.C.: The World Bank.

Zimmerman, Horst. 2001. "Guerra Fiscal e Federalismo Competitivo." In *Federalismo na Alemanha e no Brasil*, eds. Wilhelm Hofmeister and José Mário Brasiliense Carneiro. São Paulo: Fundação Konrad Adenauer.

Chapter Nine

DEMOCRATIC GOVERNANCE AND THE DILEMMA OF SOCIAL SECURITY REFORM IN BRAZIL

Peter Kingstone

INTRODUCTION

S ocial security is one of the most complex and politically explosive challenges in the so-called "second stage" of structural reforms. In many Latin American countries, the social security system constitutes a critical component of government expenditures. Unfortunately, almost all social security systems in Latin America were in serious trouble by the 1990s. Both current (fiscal) and future (actuarial) deficits in the system can create serious budgetary difficulties. For example, Brazil's social security deficit was almost US$10 billion by 1999. This kind of performance creates enormous strains for developing countries, which are almost by definition dependent on foreign capital inflows. Foreign investors may not know or care much about social security, but its impact on the budget makes domestic policymakers acutely aware of its importance. Poor fiscal performance increases country risk and the cost of capital, while it discourages private investment. Furthermore, declining budgetary performance and failing social security systems can and do result in International Monetary Fund (IMF) and World Bank pressure for reform. Thus, the status of the social security system and the kinds of reforms domestic governments pursue have critical consequences for the foreign economic relations of foreign-capital-dependent developing countries.

Social security is vital, however, on the domestic political front as well. Social security systems provide protection from a series of risks, notably old age. Properly designed, they can draw workers out of the informal sector into the formal sector as well as provide protection to workers in periods of structural economic reforms, such as those induced by neoliberal programs. Thus, social security has the potential to enhance citizenship in societies with high levels of poverty and inequality. Latin American systems, however, have tended to be regressive in their actual functioning (Cruz-Saco and Mesa-Lago 1998). Low levels of contribution and coverage often have coexisted with generous entitlements for well-organized middle- and upper-income groups. The desire to make social security systems financially sustainable and/or more equitable typically pits reform-oriented governments against well-organized, highly resistant political foes. The qualities noted above make social security reform an excellent case for examining the interplay between "policy opportunities" and "policy dilemmas" introduced by Ana Margheritis in this volume's introductory chapter. Analyzing social security reform also offers an opportunity to consider the tension between international pressure for reform versus the demands of democratic governance.

International political economy literature offers two ways of thinking about this issue. First, the literature on international political economy offers a debate on the extent to which globalization, especially financial globalization, closes policy options so that all countries will tend to converge on the same policy set. For some scholars, the greater mobility of capital means that governments have lost autonomy on policy issues (Strange 1996; Cohen 1998; Garrett 1998). Developing countries, in particular, are highly dependent on continuous inflows of foreign capital. Poor performance on economic policy — especially regarding inflation, balance of payments, and budget deficits — discourages private investment flows. Deviating from orthodox prescriptions for policy reform discourages private investment because of the threat it poses to economic performance.

Yet, an alternative perspective points out that economic reforms still play out in domestic arenas, and struggles over reform are still resolved in domestic politics (Armijo 1999). The actual policy-making process is constrained by what governments can pass politically — the "policy dilemma." Governments need to adapt policy solutions to their own contexts, their own ideological profile, and to the problem of building political coalitions in favor of reform (Boix 1998).[1] That process fundamentally alters policy design, even in the face of pressure to conform to an international prescribed policy solution and even if the basic model for reform is defined outside the country.[2]

In a second, related vein, scholars have questioned whether the pressure for conformity arising from the international political economy tends to undermine democratic governance (Teichman 2001; Teichman 1995). International financial institutions and the threat from mobile capital both push governments to adopt specific, prescribed policies whether or not they are politically popular. Thus, the argument goes, governments must insulate technocrats from domestic political pressure and impose economic reforms on society. One factor that helps governments achieve this insulation is the perception of crisis or the "policy opportunity" discussed by Margheritis in this volume's Introduction. Crises lead societies to delegate unusual levels of authority and discretion to the executive (Tornell 1995; Alesina and Drazen 1991; Keeler 1992). Yet, crises produce only limited windows of opportunity (Corrales 1997-1998, 617). Once the crisis passes, the willingness to delegate authority to executives may pass as well. Moreover, a crisis is in the eye of the beholder and its existence, or nonexistence, may be a subjective question defined in the political arena (Knight 1998). The social security case in Brazil is a perfect illustration. The very existence of a crisis, as well as the extent and nature of the problem with social security, was debated in Brazil. Thus, many actors did not wish to concede autonomy to the government precisely out of the belief that the system was not in a dire enough condition.

This policy dilemma — the gap between the necessary and the politically possible — pressures governments to find less-than-democratic means of imposing policy solutions on an otherwise resistant population. In the Latin American case, the problem is an egregious one because many countries already suffer from weak traditions and institutions supporting democratic governance and accountability. A number of works have argued that executives and their technocratic advisors do bargain with organized groups in society, especially business (Teichman 2001; Silva 1996). Those bargains, however, are closed sessions with privileged inter-locutors, not broad-based debates with representation of diverse interests. In the Brazilian case, these concerns about inadequate representation are particularly strong because of the character of the party and electoral systems, which skew representation and policy deliberation strongly in favor of well-organized, narrow, particularist interests (Mainwaring 1999; Ames 2001).

An alternative perspective, however, notes that various economic reforms have enjoyed greater popular support than the discussion above would suggest. Voters making both retrospective and prospective judgments have been willing to bear short-term costs in exchange for promised future benefits (Weyland 1998; Stokes 1996). Politicians have demonstrated an awareness and responsiveness to public opinion. In this view, the economic reform process need not be conducted in an undemocratic manner. Instead, difficult reforms are amenable to inclusive decisionmaking because governments are able to design reforms in ways that create new beneficiaries and, therefore, democratic supporters (Gray-Molina et al. 1999), and governments are able to craft public messages that attempt to sway public opinion. In this way of thinking, difficult economic reforms are no easier or harder to pass than they are in developed democracies, but they are not inherently more undemocratic either.

This chapter argues that Brazilian social security reform is a case of the primacy of domestic politics over international pressures and the capacity for democratic governance, even in the face of both real and perceived pressures from international financial institutions and foreign investors. There is no question that successive Brazilian governments have felt the need to design policy to preserve a steady inflow of foreign capital. Nor is there any doubt that the Cardoso government has relied on procyclical monetary and exchange rate policies to maintain capital inflows, despite their high domestic costs. Nevertheless, Brazil's gradual, incre-mental reform reflects a compromise among alternative domestic views that are consistent with the country's economic and political context.

Opponents of the reform, both principled critics and defenders of narrow, sectoral interests, portrayed the reform as an imposition by foreign capital and related international organizations. They made this case even though international organizations played no active role in the policy process. The government re-sponded by emphasizing the crisis in the system — independent of international opinion — and the pro-equity aspects of the reform. This rhetorical struggle highlights a crucial aspect of market-oriented reforms: opponents use the specter of international agents to discredit reforms. This forces reformist governments into the position of having to choose between carefully (and effectively) making a *domestic* argument for reform or finding ways to impose it. Ultimately, the quality of democratic governance depends on the tactical decisions governments make. Thus, democratic shortcomings may not reflect the forces of globalization at all. Instead, they stem from governments that do not choose democratic means to make the case for reform.

It is argued here that in Brazil, the government of former President Fernando Henrique Cardoso had some success in balancing these competing demands and was able to effect some incremental changes, although well short of what the system needed and still needs. Arguably, the government has done so in ways that cross the threshold of democratic governance, even though they may fall short of some democratic ideal. Nevertheless, a review of the process reveals crucial tactical errors and suggests ways that the government could have been more successful, in terms of the extent of reform as well as democratic governance. Those errors made it easier to portray the reform as a "fiscal adjustment," driven by foreign and domestic capital. This argument strengthened the rhetorical position of opponents of the reform process. As a result, the government was forced to seek out ways of limiting debate of the reform. Limiting deliberation both weakened democratic governance and ultimately limited the extent and the equity-enhancing aspects of the reform.

The chapter makes this case in three sections. The first provides an overview of the social security system to identify both the creation of specific beneficiaries and the problems of the system. The second section reviews the politics of the reform process. The reform process required the Brazilian government to enter into three interconnected struggles within the administration, the legislature, and the realm of public opinion. The third section identifies the reforms that did occur and the issues remaining on the agenda for the future. It also assesses the politics of the reform process and draws lessons for further consideration.

SOCIAL SECURITY STAKEHOLDERS AND THE SOURCES OF IMBALANCE

Brazil's Three Tiered System[3]

B oth the existence of a crisis and the extent of the crisis in Brazil's social security system have been the subjects of significant debate. Some members of the Left have argued that there is no crisis at all, while others have argued that the problems stem mainly from corruption and poor administration. Instead, they have argued that the reform process is driven by the demands of international financial institutions and foreign investors. They have been joined by a host of reform opponents protecting narrow self-interests under the cover offered by more principled critics. There is no question that there were savings to be found in efforts to curtail corruption and improve administration, and it probably would have been politically expedient for the government to focus attention and effort on those areas. Yet, the discussion below demonstrates the following two points: the system was in serious financial condition by the mid-1990s, and there were very clear stakeholders who stood to lose from the reform process, regardless of the system's poor health.

Brazil's pension system is a three-pillared system; at least two of the pillars faced significant fiscal and actuarial threats by the mid-1990s. Prior to the reforms introduced by the Cardoso government starting in 1998, the system's rules had a series of problems affecting the fiscal and actuarial balance. The first pillar was, and remains, a pay-as-you-go system, providing coverage for private sector workers.

The system was mandatory for all nonpublic sector employees with employee contribution rates varying between 8 and 10 percent. Employer contributions, through a variety of payroll taxes, were fixed at 20 percent. The pillar has several main retirement programs, including old age, disability, and length of service. In addition, certain professions had special retirement rules that granted them advantageous benefits (notably earlier retirement). The length of service program was a particular source of concern because of its very high replacement rates (70 to 100 percent) and its permissive, very early retirement rules, though as Cheikh Kane has argued, the concern over the length of service is somewhat misplaced (Kane 1998, 298-299).

As of 1999, this pillar, the General Social Welfare Regime (Regime Geral da Previdência Social — RGPS), managed by the National Social Security Institute (Instituto Nacional de Seguridade Social — INSS), had nearly 27 million contributors, yet covered only 39.9 percent of the eligible working population (MPAS 2001). Low levels of coverage reflected the high rate of migration of workers to the informal sector, especially in the 1990s. Census data (Draibe 2001, 26), showed a decline in the formally registered working population from nearly 60 percent in 1990 to 46.5 percent of the economically active population. For example, according to national census estimates, the RGPS covers only 27 percent of the close to 5.5 million domestic workers in Brazil (MPAS 2001). The set of payroll taxes are a major source of aggravation in the business community, where they are criticized for undermining competitiveness without providing effective social insurance (Kingstone 1999). The high payroll tax burden constitutes an important incentive for employers to move into the informal sector.

Another factor weakening the link between contributions and benefits is that the system pays retirement benefits to rural workers who do not contribute to the system and are able to retire five years earlier than urban workers. As Rosa Elizabeth Acevedo Marin and Gutemberg Guerra (1994) demonstrate, this program has had an important consequence of sharply increasing the income of rural pensioners and has affected social organization in poor rural areas in important ways. Nevertheless, it adds to the problem that the system's contributors do not provide an adequate base to cover liabilities. As a result, the government has had to transfer general tax revenues to cover unfunded liabilities over the course of the mid- to late 1990s.

The second pillar comprises the civil service regime (Regime Jurídico Único — RJU), which is segmented into separate systems for federal, state, and municipal workers with each state and municipality offering its own system with its own rules. Nevertheless, all the civil service regimes face significant financial strains, due in no small measure to exceptionally generous coverage rules. The civil service regime is largely noncontributory, so that liabilities are funded fully or almost fully out of government transfers. The system's generosity, coupled with its noncontributory nature, place enormous financial strains on governments at all levels, with some states in severe situations (for example, Rio Grande do Sul). Excessively generous retirement rules include retirement at very young ages, accumulation of multiple pensions, receipt of pensions while employed elsewhere (and thus receiving pensions as a form of salary complement rather than as social insurance), as well as a 100-percent replacement rate of the salary at the last year of employment (with some workers receiving replacement rates in excess of 100 percent). The end result is that a system with fewer than 4 million active workers among all levels of government (roughly one-seventh the number of contributors in the RGPS) requires expenditures as high as 75 percent of the expenditures of the RGPS. Since the system is noncontributory, almost the entire amount is funded through government revenues. The system's rules encourage a wide array of perverse behavior and are highly regressive in their distributional effects.[4]

More important, the two pillars combined to produce well-defined and well-organized stakeholders in the status quo, regardless of its implications in terms of equity or in terms of public finances and the threats to continued capital inflows. The most important and powerful group were public sector employees who enjoyed strong connections with the principled Left as well as parties in the government base. Their political force constituted the most important aspect of Brazil's policy dilemma, in that their pillar was simultaneously the most serious threat to the financial health of the system as well as the most staunchly defended in and out of Congress.

THE POLITICS OF SOCIAL SECURITY REFORM IN BRAZIL

President Cardoso began his term as president in January 1995. His election benefited from his success in claiming ownership of the Real Plan, which brought inflation down from 25 to 2 percent per month by the vote in October 1994, and by a multiparty, center-right coalition that backed him against leftist rival Luiz Inácio Lula da Silva. Cardoso entered office with three distinct political advantages. First, successful stabilization gave President Cardoso popular support and legitimacy, as well as freedom to focus on policy areas besides stabilization. No prior president in the New Republic began his term with this advantage. Second, the multiparty coalition gave President Cardoso a majority in Congress with, in fact, sufficient votes to pass constitutional amendments that require two-thirds' majorities. Finally, President Cardoso's economic program benefited from the set of important reforms initiated by former President Fernando Collor de Mello (1990-1992). Despite his impeachment on corruption charges, Collor had confronted and overcome powerful resistance to the neoliberal reform program, and his reforms created a base on which President Cardoso was able to build. All three factors gave President Cardoso unprecedented freedom to maneuver within Brazil's fragmented polity. Nevertheless, social security reform proved exceptionally difficult. To reform the system, the Cardoso administration faced three distinct, but interconnected political battles within the administration itself and Congress, and for public opinion.

Bureaucratic Struggles

Bureaucratic struggles within the Brazilian administration mirrored the basic differences between the World Bank-endorsed model and the International Labor Organization (ILO) model. At the heart of the difference between the two models is a choice between equity and universality — afforded by the ILO model — and the full capitalization and privatization of risk model proposed by the World Bank.

The World Bank approach is primarily focused on ensuring full funding for benefits, creating strong incentives for saving, and deepening financial markets through private pension funds. The World Bank position is particularly focused on minimizing the risks of public management error or neglect that stems from the blurring of savings, redistribution, and insurance functions, often driven by political considerations (Cruz-Saco 1998, 16). Additionally, the World Bank position is particularly attractive to foreign investors because of its emphasis on financial sustainability. By contrast, the ILO position is committed to socializing risk as a means to protect the most vulnerable in society. The ILO view accepts a three-pillar approach as well, but with a larger role for public management. Under this view, the distortions, inefficiencies, and actuarial imbalances of collective systems can be addressed without radical reforms and, thus, without threatening the universality of traditional systems.

The conflict manifested in the mid-1990s between technocrats in the Ministry of Social Security and Assistance (Ministério de Previdência e Assisténcia Social — MPAS) and technocrats in the Ministry of Finance, as MPAS officials supported incremental changes to the system while the Ministry of Finance came to support the Chilean reform, the model for the World Bank position.[5] Both ministries mustered support for their positions among organized social groups. The Ministry of Finance officials, for example, drew support from business groups such as the National Confederation of Industry (Confederação Nacional da Indústria — CNI), the Federation of Industry of the State of São Paulo (Federação da Indústria de Estado de São Paulo — FIESP), the Brazilian Bank Federation (Federação Brasileira de Bancos — FEBRABAN), and the National Association of Private, Open Pension Funds (Associação Nacional de Previdência Privada — ANAPP). Business groups expressed concern about the impact of payroll taxes, particularly the elevated employers' contribution, and were supportive of the vastly diminished role of employer contributions in the Chilean model. ANAPP, for its part, stood to benefit from an expansion of fully funded individual accounts, whether mandatory or voluntary. All business and commerce-oriented groups shared international investors' preoccupation with the government deficit (Coelho 1999).

By contrast, MPAS officials counted on support from a variety of worker and pensioner organizations, including the Association of Social Security Auditors (Associação Nacional dos Auditores da Previdência Social — ANFIP), the Federal Revenue Department Auditors' Syndicate (Unafisco Sindical), the Retired Civil Servant and Pensioners' Movement (Movimento dos Servidores Público — MOSAP), the Brazilian Confederation of Pensioners and Retired People (Confederação Brasileira dos Aposentados e Pensionistas — COBAP), as well as the large labor centrals, notably the Syndical Force (Força Sindical) and the Sole Labor Central (Central Única dos Trabalhadores — CUT). These organizations emphasized the problems of evasion and fraud and argued in favor of passing reforms that would only apply to new entrants to the labor force (Pinheiro 1998). It should be noted, however, that the supporting social groups in both camps had their own agendas with significant conflicts among themselves. Thus, the general battle lines between privatizers and universalizers were clear, but there was little agreement on the details among the members of each group. Instead, the conflict was largely waged among technocrats with competing orientations.

Initially, the government proposals presented in 1995 by Reinhold Stephanes, the MPAS minister, had strong privatizing elements to them. The strongest figures in President Cardoso's cabinet were the economists responsible for the Real Plan, in particular Pedro Malan, Edmar Bacha, and André Lara Resende, all figures with important experience in the United States and in international financial institutions and who occupied positions of influence in the Ministry of Finance. The initial proposal sought to unify the private and public sector regimes into one mandatory, contributory, collective system. The proposal called for the extinction of special privileges, accumulation of pensions, retirement based on time of contribution with a minimum retirement age, and a ceiling of five minimum salaries for benefits. (Note that in Brazil, salaries are measured and classified with reference to multiples of the minimum salary. In turn, payments like pensions are linked to the minimum salary level.) Above that threshold, the proposal called for the creation of fully funded individual accounts (Coelho 1999, 133).

Yet, within a short period of time, it became clear that even the modified Chilean model was not politically or financially viable. Stephanes acknowledged the political difficulties in qualifying the reform with the line "if not the necessary, then the possible" (Coelho 1999, 133). Financially, Ministry of Finance officials recognized that Brazil's burgeoning debt, both foreign and domestic, made the World Bank/Chilean approach untenable because of the enormity of the transition costs (Amaro 2000). As a consequence, the internal divisions muted, and the administration opted clearly for an incremental plan focused on financial viability, but preserving the collective approach to funding the system and to socializing risk. The internal compromise emerged as competing bureaucrats confronted the limits of what was politically and technically possible. Thus, neither globalization nor the preferences of international actors played a key role in shaping the conclusion. This compromise, however, was the easiest part of the political struggle.

The Legislative Struggle

Paul Pierson (1994), in his work on pension reform in developed democracies, suggests the following three strategies for reforming social security systems: obfuscation (concealing the costs of the reform or diverting blame), division (pitting opponents against each other), and compensation (paying off losers). It is striking that none of these three strategies contributes to democratic governance. It is also striking that the Cardoso administration's initial tactical approach to reform did not attempt any of three. The government was quite up front and direct about its reform goals and the reasons for them. Stephanes clearly articulated the government's concern about the solvency of the system and made himself available for regular and frequent meetings with members of Congress to explain the financial and actuarial bases of that concern. Nor did the government attempt in any way to shift blame for the problem or the need for reform—an important aspect of obfuscation for Pierson. Similarly, the government did not frame its proposals in ways designed to drive wedges among organized beneficiaries. In fact, the government proposal worked in the opposite direction, unifying all beneficiaries in opposition to the plan. In addition, the government proposed taxing pensions as a way to address financial imbalances, thus bringing retirees directly into a coalition with public and private employees. Finally, the proposal did not offer any form of compensation to affected interests. In fact, its design maximized the effect of imposing clear costs on well-organized interests while conferring only diffuse, long-term benefits. Side payments (*fisiologismo*) are the basic lubricant of the Brazilian political system and, therefore, are an explicit part of any legislative bargaining (Ames 2001). Yet, in this specific case, patronage politics suffered to some extent because the lead minister, Stephanes, was much more a technocrat than a politician.[6] Furthermore, he did not have the political bargaining clout that came from close association with the president.

Interviews with officials from the President's office and from the Leadership of the Government in the Chamber of Deputies suggest that the government simply did not anticipate the intensity of opposition. It did not take long, however, for that intensity to become clear. Piece by piece, members of Congress forced the government to back off specific elements of the proposal. For example, members of the government's base in the Chamber, led by Almino Afonso of the Brazilian Social Democratic Party (Partido da Social Democracia Brasileira — PSDB), began pushing for a gradual, incremental reform and for a phased-in transition (*Jornal do Brasil*, April 1, 1995). The military insisted on the preservation of its special retirement rules, and members of Congress added firemen and military police (Molica 1995). Members of Congress also opposed the government's effort to set a uniform contribution rate of 10 percent and insisted that benefits be capped at 10 minimum salaries rather than the government's proposed five minimum salaries (Célia 1995). The government also entered into negotiations with the CUT in an effort to reach a deal to win backing from the influential labor central.

The government's negotiations proved of little benefit, as voting on key government legislation began in 1996. In a critical defeat, members of Congress blocked a bill to require monthly contributions from public service pensioners. Presented as a critical step to recover solvency in the system, the government lost 306 votes to 124, with 13 abstentions. Of the parties in the government's coalition, only the PSDB, the president's party, voted in favor (44-35). Defections from the Brazilian Democratic Movement Party (Partido do Movimento Democrático Brasileiro — PMDB) and the Brazilian Progressive Party (Partido Progressista Brasileiro — PPB) were enormous, with only 19 votes in favor from the former (49 against) and 10 from the latter (53 against). Subsequently, in March 1996, the government narrowly lost on its constitutional amendment to reform the social security system, as only 294 out of the necessary 308 voted in favor. Again, the defections from the PMDB and the PPB were substantial: 27 members of the PPB and 38 members of the PMDB voted against the bill.

One key reason for the failure, by a variety of accounts from different perspectives, was that the government was remiss in its public campaign (Confidential author interviews, Brasília, June 2001). In one criticism, Jáder Barbalho, the leader of the PMDB in the Senate and a former social welfare minister, called on the government to play a pedagogic role of justifying the constitutional amendments to both Congress and the public (Holanda 1995). Stephanes, however, was left alone for the most part, with little public support from key ministers, such as Pedro Malan in Finance, José Serra in Planning, or even the president himself. Instead, Stephanes was left to explain the reform publicly, typically in relatively technocratic terms.[7]

The government's failure in March 1996 led to a change of tactics. Constitutionally, legislation could only be introduced once per year. If it went down to defeat, legally it was tabled until the following year. The administration, however, wanted to move ahead with the legislation and, therefore, reintroduced the government's proposal, claiming that it differed so dramatically from the bill voted on that it constituted a new piece of legislation. The Chamber of Deputies' leadership then appointed Michel Temer, the leader of the PMDB in the Chamber, as committee reporter to ensure that the PMDB would not defect en masse again. In any event, the government was aware that the same pressures present in the first vote were still active in the Chamber. For example, in a poll of deputies, 80 percent favored maintaining "the acquired social rights" of the 1988 Constitution in the social security system, 49 percent supported limiting public sector benefits to 10 minimum salaries with less than 8 percent supporting the government's declared preference for three or five. Even with respect to establishing a minimum retirement age, 66 percent wanted the minimum set between 50 and 60 years old with only 28 percent supporting an older minimum age (Praxedes and Franco 1996). As a consequence, they had little expectation that the process would produce an acceptable bill. Ultimately, the new constitutional amendment (PEC 33/95) passed in June 1996, but was so watered down that prominent TV newscaster Boris Casoy declared it a "reform of nothing."

The government had expected that result and had done little to prevent it.[8] Instead, the Cardoso administration looked for rapid passage of the bill, which would then move the legislation to the Senate, where particularist and opposition forces were generally weaker and where the government could count more reliably on support of its allies. Legislative procedure worked in the government's favor. The Senate was not obligated to accept or work with the Chamber of Deputies' legislation in any way. Once the Senate passed its version, however, the Chamber was constrained by that version in the second round of deliberation and voting. Thus, the government could hope to recover the main planks of its proposal and then return to the Chamber with a bill less vulnerable to amendment.

In the Senate, Committee Reporter Beni Veras, of the Liberal Front Party (Partido da Frente Liberal — PFL), who was responsible for ushering through the bill was, like Temer in the Chamber, a solid government ally. According to accounts of participants, Veras's office was the center point of the intense political negotiations that took place in the writing of the legislation. Representatives of key interest groups, as well as senators, met regularly and frequently to lobby for the exclusion of articles affecting their own interests. Consistent with complaints in the Chamber, participants reported little active involvement of the government in the process (Confidential author interviews, Brasília, June 2001). Instead, Veras and the new social welfare minister, Waldeck Ornélas (PFL), carried much of the weight of negotiation. Unlike the negotiations in the Chamber, however, the issues were not debated as openly and publicly. The combination of the Senate's less fractious, particularist nature, committed negotiating by Veras and Ornélas, and less public attention resulted in a limited victory for the government.

In October 1997, the Senate passed its version, restoring many of the most polemic issues removed from the Chamber version. These included a restoration of retirees' monthly contributions, a benefits cap stated in nominal values (1200 *reais*), as opposed to multiples of the minimum wage (as well as a reduction in public sector workers retirement benefits at 70 percent of their last wage), a minimum age for both private and public sector employees, "de-constitutionalization" of the benefit calculation for private sector workers, and the end of special retirement regimes for all categories of workers except the military and school teachers (OECD 2001; MPAS 2001). Maintaining these elements in the Senate bill constituted significant victories for the government, though well short of "the necessary."

Final acceptance of the bill still required one more successful pass through the Chamber, where substantial resistance remained to the Senate version. Research carried out by the Interunion Parliamentary Assistance Department (Departamento Intersindical de Assessoria Parlamentar — DIAP) revealed several points of contention, even within the government base (DIAP 1998). Deputies remained hostile to retirees' contributions as well as to efforts to limit public servants' benefits and to establish a cap on benefits disconnected from the minimum wage. Deputies also expressed a desire to design a transition period to protect workers already in the system and to slow the reform process down and subject the reform efforts to further deliberation. The less permissive voting and amendment rules of the second round made it possible for the government to maintain a number of key items in the legislation. However, in the end, the Chamber did eliminate the most contentious issues, notably retirees' contributions and rules limiting public sector workers' benefits. In the final analysis, the government was able to make important changes to the private sector regime. Public sector lobbies succeeded, nevertheless, in protecting some of their most generous privileges.

In addition to the major reform legislation, the government passed a series of complementary laws regulating a variety of issues, including corruption in the social security system, and perhaps most important, establishing new rules for calculating benefits in the RGPS. The new innovation, the "social security factor" (*fator previdenciário*), incorporates actuarial calculations into individual retire-ment benefit determinations.[9] The mechanism creates strong incentives for workers to work longer and, therefore, is considered to be an important benefit to the system's solvency. Also, the introduction of an individualized calculation into a collective contributory system moves in the direction of privatization in the tightening of the link between contributions and benefits. Thus, the longer-term actuarial picture for the RGPS is greatly improved.

The Public Opinion Battle

As noted above, a number of participants on the government side, both in author interviews and in the press, complained about the lack of government effort in the public campaign. The government's lack of effort was rewarded with poor results in public opinion. One survey revealed that 58 percent of the public was uninformed about the major constitutional revision passed by the Senate in late 1997 (IBOPE 1998). Results from 1996, with more visible public discussion of the reform process in the Chamber, were less benign from the government's point of view. For example, in a Brazilian Institute for Public Opinion and Statistics (Instituto Brasileiro de Opinião Pública e Estatística — IBOPE) poll conducted in January

1995, respondents were asked about their opinion of the effects of proposed changes. A majority of respondents believed that the change would be harmful. Respondents were asked to consider the impact on people earning more than five minimum salaries, people earning less than five minimum salaries, people retired for less than three years, and people set to retire within three years. Respondents, regardless of income or education, believed the reforms would hurt individuals in all categories, with only roughly 10 percent reporting "no opinion" (IBOPE 1995).[10]

One year later, an IBOPE poll revealed a further weakness in the government's public campaign. When asked which constitutional reform was the most important one, more people (roughly 5 percent of the total sample) identified social security reform than any other, including agrarian reform. Yet, 70 percent of the respondents claimed not to have an opinion and/or not to have followed the reform process. When pressed on the specifics of key government positions (ending the mandatory, collective contributory model or replacement of time of service with time of contribution), large majorities opposed the government. In the area of the elimination of special retirement regimes, however, a sizable majority supported the government position (IBOPE 1996). This last point is intriguing because it suggests the possibility of mobilizing public opinion behind efforts to attack the special privileges protected by public-sector employees — essentially to use Pierson's strategy of division.

In fact, in interviews with government allies in the Chamber, Senate, and from Minister Ornélas' office, it was repeatedly observed that the government's public campaign (and support for the Ministry's efforts) was inadequate (Confidential author interviews, Brasília, June 2001). The failure to win the rhetorical battle gave cover to defenders of narrow, privileged interests. Opponents of reform framed their criticism in terms of protection of social rights won in the "Constituente" and protection of seniors (os velinhos). Protectors of special retirement regimes and the very loose eligibility requirements and excessively generous benefits for the public sector were able to hide behind this rhetoric. While it is doubtful that this was a decisive factor in the Deputies' resistance, the government's abdication on the rhetorical front made it easier to defend positions that ultimately render the social security system insolvent and that egregiously violate principles of equity.

The government did make some effort to make a public case about the need for reform. They chose, however, to frame the discussion primarily in terms of finances. Both Stephanes' and President Cardoso's public pronouncements included statements about citizenship and equity, but they often were preludes or postscripts to long discussions of the insolvency of the social security system. For the most part, the government's statements correspond to analyses made by external observers, such as the Organization for Economic Cooperation and Development (OECD) or the World Bank. However, framing the argument in terms of finances opens the door to other ways of spinning financial information — witness the "fuzzy math" debate of the 2000 U.S. presidential elections. Opponents in Brazil, for example, Maria Erbênia Ribas, president of the Gaucha Association of Social Security Auditors, pointed to the positive cash flow in the system and the sharp increases in revenues over the 1990s (Ribas 1995). In the midst of the debate on the solvency of the social security system, the Federal Auditing Department (Tribunal de Contas da União — TCU) published a report claiming that the system not only was not in deficit, but was financing other government operations (Quaglio 1995). Critics from the Workers' Party (Partido dos Trabalhadores — PT) and from associations like the ANFIP focused on fraud in the system and argued that cracking down on this corruption was the only adjustment needed, supported by TCU audits demonstrating large-scale fraud (Praxedes and Campos 1996). In fact, a majority of Workers' Party members believed that the whole reform was intended merely as a form of fiscal adjustment (DIAP 1998). Given the complexity of social security, it is extremely unlikely that any government could win a rhetorical battle strictly by arguing the numbers.

Government supporters in the Congress and within the Ministry also complained that the government failed to connect the reforms to important social and political values. A high official from Beni Veras' office expressed the concern that the government had failed to think about the political and symbolic consequences of a number of decisions (Confidential author interviews, Brasília, June 2001). In particular, members of government, when discussing the insolvency of the system, had not differentiated among the different parts and had not acknowledged that their different financial situations undermined the legitimacy of government claims. Similarly, attempting to reform the system without transition rules put government allies in the position of having to engage in the argument about social rights from a weak position. This strengthened the credibility of PT claims that the reform was merely a fiscal adjustment. In an interview in former Minister Ornélas' office, the complaint was raised that the government had made no effort to strengthen the appeal of the reform for average citizens. Most Brazilian pensioners earn the minimum benefit, and, therefore, are unaffected by most reforms. Furthermore, roughly 50 percent of contributors, mostly poor citizens, never draw any benefits because they work until they die. Thus, Ornélas emphasized the need to invest in improving the reputation of the system through better provision of service. Further, he pointed to the clear need to remove the entire social assistance program from the system, as it is purely a redistributive, noncapitalized, noncontributory system.

Yet, the government made little effort to address any of these concerns — all of which were mirrored repeatedly in congressional struggles. In fact, this specific problem is consistent with a generalized failure identified by Timothy Power (2001), namely, the failure of the government to embed its policy positions in clear and important social values. This failure contributed to a reform that fell well short of the "necessary," protected many of the inequities and financial imbalances of the public sector regime, and did little to extend or improve coverage for the millions of inadequately covered Brazilians in both the formal and informal sectors.

CONCLUSIONS: DEMOCRATIC GOVERNANCE AND POLICY DILEMMAS REVISITED

This chapter began with the question of the compatibility of democratic governance and foreign economic relations in Brazilian social security reform. The case points strongly to the primacy of domestic over foreign factors in understanding the complexity of these issues. The Cardoso government felt a considerable need to preserve foreign capital inflows, and the World Bank served as an important source of technical information about reform options. Nevertheless, the issue played out in domestic political arenas, and the policy outcome was shaped definitively — for the good and for the bad — by the process of securing political support for reforms.[11]

The question, then, is whether the act of implementing reforms violated standards of democratic governance. Evaluating democracy is known to be a difficult and inherently normative task, but we might avoid conceptual debates and still evaluate the quality of governance with reference to the following three criteria: deliberation, inclusiveness, and equity. It is argued here that Brazil's social security reform meets the threshold of democratic governance on all three counts. The administration developed technocratic proposals and submitted them to Congress. However, the Congress played a critical role in revising those proposals and responding to the concerns of organized social interests. Government ministers were forced to offer explanations to the Congress and to the public and, thus, were held accountable in important ways for their decisions. The process was also inclusive. Hearings were held formally and informally in the Congress. Organized interest groups, including business people, pensioners, retirees, and private and public sector workers, were allowed a full airing of alternative perspectives on social security reform. Finally, several key reforms had equity-improving qualities because they placed constraints on some of the worst abuses of the system.

Yet, the process fell far short of ideal on all three measures. As discussed above, the public campaign was less effective and extensive than it could have and perhaps should have been. Brazil's extraordinary inequities opened real possibilities for framing the reforms in terms of fairness and citizenship. The government, forced to adopt an incremental approach, might have chosen reforms that fit more consistently with such values. This case contrasts, for example, with the privatization of telecommunications, where the government was able to isolate opponents of reform by mobilizing and benefiting from strong public support (Kingstone 2003). Similarly, the government was able to mobilize political support in favor of equity-enhancing reforms in the education system despite entrenched opposition from well-defined special interest groups.

In addition, the role of the Congress was less deliberative than it appeared to be on the surface. Deputies, in particular, focused on protection of various organized interests, calling for a slow, incremental, deliberative process. Yet, interviews with staff from the Parliamentary Assistance Office make clear that deputies did not avail themselves of the expertise in the Chamber to understand and develop alternative proposals. In fact, only one member of the PT — who took the public position that the system was not bankrupt and all it needed was a crackdown on corruption — sought help in developing alternative positions.

With respect to inclusiveness and equity, the obvious concern is that Brazil's process lived up to the most critical perspectives of the system, such as those articulated by Scott Mainwaring and Barry Ames. In short, the voices heard and included in the process were the same set of privileged interests that typically are heard in Brazilian politics. The vast mass of uncovered or inadequately covered workers had little or no representation. The resulting reform had little to offer them and played into the view that when all was said and done, it was a fiscal adjustment driven by the concerns of foreign investors.

These shortcomings, however, were not the result of foreign pressure. The difficulty of reforming social security (for developed and for developing countries), the weaknesses of Brazilian political parties, and the tactical decisions of the Cardoso government all proved to be far more important explanations of how social security reform progressed than foreign pressure. Ministry of Finance technocrats shared a common perspective with agencies like the World Bank or the OECD, but their sense of the urgency of reform did not emerge because of foreign pressure. Thus, the Cardoso government faced the policy dilemma of needing to have crucial reforms passed by resistant beneficiaries of the status quo — but it was a policy dilemma of domestic origins.

NOTES

1.   Carles Boix, in particular, has made the case that partisan differences continue to matter in the design of policy programs. Regardless of the pressure governments may feel, left-oriented and right-oriented parties design programs in ways that are true to their partisan, ideological proclivities. Another important discussion of continued diversity even in the face of pressure to converge is Suzanne Berger and Ronald Dore, eds., 1996, *National Diversity and Global Capitalism* (Ithaca, N.Y.: Cornell University Press).

2.   Judith Teichman (2001) has charted, in detailed fashion, the links between World Bank officials, in particular, and networks of technocrats, academics, politicians, and business people that have formed around specific policy approaches in Latin America.

3.   Detailed discussions of the many complexities and perversities of the Brazilian pension system can be found in Cheick T. Kane, "Reforming the Brazilian Pension System," in Cruz-Saco and Mesa Lago, 1998; Organization for Economic Cooperation and Development (OECD), 2001, "OECD Economic Surveys: Brazil (preliminary version)," Paris, June; and Ministério da Previdência e Assistência Social (MPAS), 2001, "Reforma da Previdência em um Ambiente Democrático," Brasília, June.

4.   The final pillar is a complementary system of voluntary open and closed occupational pension funds. Closed pension funds, which are primarily run by state-owned enterprises for their own employees, are by far the larger of the two systems within the third pillar, with 2 million participants. Open funds have a poor performance history in Brazil, and their resulting reputation has dampened participation. The largest issue in the third pillar is the weakness of prudential regulation. Improving the complementary regime has the potential to alleviate problems in the RGPS and the RJU, as the funds typically are designed to achieve a fixed replacement rate. Thus, declines in benefits in either the RGPS or the RJU can be offset by increases in the third complementary pillar. Generally speaking, however, it is the first two pillars that urgently require reform.

5.   These alternative positions emerged out of differing ministries and agencies in the Brazilian government. Kurt Weyland (1996, 134-139) has documented the way progressive reformers in the Ministry of Social Security and Assistance (MPAS) developed universalizing proposals in the period leading up to the writing of the 1988 Constitution. These reformers made little headway, as both old guard members of MPAS and Ministry of Finance officials opposed them. Bureaucratic differences became moot, however, once the Constitutional Assembly (Assembleia Nacional Constituente — ANC) took up the matter.

6.   In one interview, for example, Stephanes was contrasted with Minister of Communications, Sérgio Motta, who had both technical and political skills. Motta also had the distinct advantage of particular closeness to Cardoso. Thus, deputies dealing with him knew that his promises would be backed by the president. Stephanes lacked that kind of credibility, coupled with a much weaker ability politically, which limited his effectiveness in legislative bargaining (Confidential author interview with a member of the leadership of the government in the Chamber of Deputies, June 2001).

7.   To wit, see Stephanes' op-ed piece in the *Estado de São Paulo*, "A Caixa-Preta da Previdência" (March 20, 1995), in which Stephanes responded to criticisms of the reform with explanations of the differences between cash flow and operational balance and deficits and surpluses of the system.

8.   Confidential author interview with a member of the leadership of the government in the Chamber of Deputies, June 2001.

9.   The new rules are discussed in MPAS 2001; and OECD, 2001. They are explained in detail in Vinícius Carvalho Pinheiro and Solange Paiva Vieira, 1999, "Reforma da Previdência no Brasil: A Nove Regra de Cálculo dos Benefícios," *Conjuntura Social*, October-December.

10.   Public opinion data is available at the Roper Center, University of Connecticut.

11.   It is important to note, however, that the Brazilian case does not resolve the issue of domestic politics versus international constraints. Brazil's size, inherent attractiveness for foreign investment, and tradition of policy autonomy almost certainly insulate policymakers from foreign pressure (financial and diplomatic) to a greater extent than most Latin American nations. As a consequence, the Cardoso government may have been freer to allow a fuller play of domestic politics than most Latin American nations.

REFERENCES

Alesina, Alberto, and Allan Drazen. "Why Are Stabilizations Delayed?" *American Economic Review* 81 (5): 1170-88.

Amaro, Meiriane Nunes. 2000. "O processo de reformulação da Previdência Social brasileira." *Revista de Informação Legislativa* 37 (148): 49-76.

Ames, Barry. 2001. *The Deadlock of Democracy in Brazil.* Ann Arbor, Mich.: University of Michigan Press.

Armijo, Leslie. 1999. *Financial Globalization and Democratization in Emerging Markets.* New York: St. Martin's Press.

Berger, Suzanne, and Ronald Dore, eds. 1996. *National Diversity and Global Capitalism.* Ithaca, N.Y.: Cornell University Press.

Boix, Carles. 1998. *Political Parties, Growth and Equality: Conservative and Social Democratic Economic Strategies in the World Economy.* New York: Cambridge University Press.

Célia, Vanda. 1995. "Governo quer desconto de 10% em todos os salários." *Correio Brasiliense*, February 21.

Coelho, Vera Schattan P. 1999. "A reforma da Previdência e o jogo político no interior do executivo." *Novos Estudos Cebrap* 55: 121-142.

Cohen, Benjamin. 1998. *The Geography of Money.* Ithaca, N.Y.: Cornell University Press.

Corrales, Javier. 1997-1998. "Do Economic Crises Contribute to Reform?: Argentina and Venezuela in the 1990's." *Political Science Quarterly* 112 (4): 617-644.

Cruz-Saco, María Amparo, and Carmelo Mesa-Lago. 1998. *Do Options Exist?: The Reform of Pension and Health Care Systems in Latin America.* Pittsburgh: University of Pittsburgh Press.

Departamento Intersindical de Assessoria Parlamentar (DIAP). 1998. "Relatório de pesquisa sobre a reforma da Previdência." Brasília: DIAP.

Draibe, Sônia M. 2001. "Social Policy Reform in the Context of Fiscal Adjustment and Democracy Consolidation: The Recent Brazilian Experience." Paper presented at the Conference on Reforming Brazil, Bildner Center for Western Hemisphere Studies, City University of New York, May 15.

Garrett, Geoffrey. 1998. *Partisan Politics and the Global Economy.* New York: Cambridge University Press.

Holanda, Tarcísio. 1995. "Jáder cobra emendas bem justificadas." *Jornal do Brasil*, March 7.

Instituto Brasileiro de Opinião Pública e Estatística (IBOPE). 1995. *Political Survey BR95.* OUT. — 546. Available at the Roper Center, University of Connecticut, Storrs, Conn.

Instituto Brasileiro de Opinião Pública e Estatística (IBOPE). 1996. *Political Survey BR96.* FEV. — 548. Available at the Roper Center, University of Connecticut, Storrs, Conn.

Instituto Brasileiro de Opinião Pública e Estatística (IBOPE). 1998. *Political Survey BR98.* JUL. — 843. Available at the Roper Center, University of Connecticut, Storrs, Conn.

Jornal do Brasil. 1995. "Aliados do Governo já trabalham por mudança gradual da Previdência." April 1.

Kane, Cheikh T. 1998. "Reforming the Brazilian Pension System." In *Do Options Exist: The Reform of Pension and Health Care Systems in Latin America*, eds. María Amparo Cruz-Sace and Carmelo Mesa-Lago. Pittsburgh: University of Pittsburgh Press.

Keeler, John. "Opening the Window for Reform: Mandates, Crises, and Extraordinary Policy-Making." *Comparative Political Studies* 25 (4): 433-86.

Kingstone, Peter. 1999. *Crafting Coalitions for Reform.* University Park, Pa.: Pennsylvania State University Press.

Kingstone, Peter. 2001. Confidential interviews conducted by the author in Brasília, Brazil, June.

Kingstone, Peter. 2003. "Privatizing Telebrás: Institutions and Policy Performance in Brazil." *Comparative Politics* 36:1, October.

Knight, Allan, 1998. "Historical and Theoretical Considerations." In *Elites, Crises, and the Origins of Regimes*, eds. Mattei Dogan and John Higley. New York: Rowman and Littlefield.

Mainwaring , Scott. 1999. *Rethinking Party Systems in the Third Wave of Democratization.* Palo Alto, Calif.: Stanford University Press.

Marin, Rosa Elizabeth Acevedo, and Gutemberg Guerra. 1994. *Trabalhadores Rurais: A Cidadania via Seguridade Social.* Papers do Núcleo de Altos Estudos Amazônicos, no. 28. Belém, Brazil.

Ministério da Previdência e Assistência Social (MPAS). 2001. *Reforma da Previdência em um Ambiente Democrático.* Brasília, June.

Molica, Fernando. 1995. "Militares não abrem mão de atuais benefícios, diz general." *Folha de São Paulo*, April 11.

Molina, George Gray, Ernesto Pérez de Rada, and Ernesto Yañez. 1999. *La economía política de reformas institucionales en Bolivia.* Working Paper R-350. Washington, D.C.: Inter-American Development Bank.

Organization for Economic Cooperation and Development (OECD). 2001. *OECD Economic Surveys: Brazil* (preliminary version). Paris, June.

Pierson, Paul. 1994. *Dismantling the Welfare State? Reagan, Thatcher, and the Politics of Retrenchment.* New York: Cambridge University Press.

Pinheiro, Vinícius Carvalho. 1998. "Instituições Previdenciárias e Modelos de Desenvolvimento no Brasil e Argentina." Master's thesis, Department of Political Science, University of Brasília.

Pinheiro, Vinícius Carvalho, and Solange Paiva Vieira. 1999. "Reforma da Previdência no Brasil: A Nove Regra de Cálculo dos Benefícios." *Conjuntura Social* (October-December).

Power, Timothy J. 2001. "Blairism Brazilian Style? Cardoso and the 'Third Way' in Brazil." *Political Science Quarterly* 116 (4).

Praxedes, Cleber, and Celso Franco. 1996. "Privatização tem pouco apoio, indica pesquisa." *Correio Brasiliense*, March 17.

Praxedes, Cleber, and André Campos. 1996. "Irregularidades prejudicam reforma." *Correio Brasiliense*, June 2.

Quaglio, Silvana. 1995. "TCU diz que Tesouro use dinheiro do FSE para financiar Previdência." *Folha de São Paulo*, April 17.

Ribas, Maria Eugênia. 1995. "A farsa do déficit na Previdência." *Jornal do Brasil*, March 17.

Silva, Eduardo. 1996. *The State and Capital in Chile: Business Elites, Technocrats, and Market Economics*. Boulder, Colo.: Westview Press.

Stokes, Susan. 1996a. "Public Opinion and Market Reforms: The Limits of Economic Voting." *Comparative Political Studies* 29 (5): 499-519.

Stokes, Susan. 1996b. "Economic Reform and Public Opinion in Peru, 1990-1995." *Comparative Political Studies* 29 (5): 544-565.

Strange, Susan. 1996. *The Retreat of the State: The Diffusion of Power in the Global Economy*. New York: Cambridge University Press.

Teichman, Judith A. 2001. *The Politics of Freeing Markets in Latin America: Chile, Argentina, and Mexico*. Chapel Hill, N.C.: University of North Carolina Press.

Teichman, Judith A. 1995. *Privatization and Political Change in Mexico*. Pittsburgh: University of Pittsburgh Press.

Tornell, Aaron. 1995. "Are Economic Crises Necessary for Trade Liberalization and Fiscal Reform?: The Mexican Experience." In *Reform, Recovery, and Growth: Latin America and the Middle East*, eds. Rudiger Dornbusch and Sebastian Edwards. Chicago: University of Chicago Press.

Weyland, Kurt. 1998. "Swallowing the Bitter Pill: Sources of Support for Neoliberal Reform in Latin America." *Comparative Political Studies* 31 (5): 539-568.

Weyland, Kurt. 1996. *Democracy without Equity: Failures of Reform in Brazil*. Pittsburgh: University of Pittsburgh Press.

Chapter Ten

FOREIGN INVESTMENT AND DEMOCRATIC GOVERNANCE IN LATIN AMERICA

Richard Youngs[1]

This chapter focuses on one aspect of the international dimensions of the evolution of Latin American democracy. It seeks to complement other chapters in this volume by suggesting that political considerations need to be incorporated into the analysis of Latin America's foreign economic relations. Its focus reflects a growing recognition among analysts that issues of democratic governance merit greater attention within the study of the economic dimensions of international policies. The chapter's analysis is predicated on the concept of democratic quality. As is well known, despite democracy's undeniable progress in the region since the mid-1990s, most analysts have continued to stress what they see as the poor quality of Latin American democracy. This chapter assesses how democracy's persisting shortcomings relate to the interests of foreign companies. The focus here is on direct rather than portfolio investment, the constraining impact of speculative capital flows on the de facto democratically elaborated policy options of Latin American states having already been widely analyzed and acknowledged. The analysis here confines itself to examining the increasingly lively debate over the relationship between multinationals' activities and political norms. Are foreign direct investors to blame for the poor quality of democracy in Latin America? Have they actively sought such limited pluralism? Or have they been largely marginal to and untouched by the nature of political change in the region? These questions relate to the relationship between democracy and economic reform but — crucially — extend beyond the standard focus on this linkage in so far as they are entwined with international political variables.[2]

In the academic literature, good quality democracy has not been widely seen as imperative or even helpful to international investors. A significant degree of consensus has emerged around the view that businesses primarily seek strong, executive-led governments capable of expediting economic liberalization. In particular, the study of East Asian developmental states has encouraged the conclusion that semi-authoritarianism can provide a sufficiently rules-based economy to protect individual property rights, while guaranteeing stability and control over antimarket elements. Dominant-party regimes, it is suggested, have often provided bureaucratic continuity, an ability to distribute the costs of economic reform widely, and low levels of corruption (Leftwich 1996; Armijo 1999, 38). The strong version of this view has seen international business successfully leading Western support for autocratic regimes whose repression of human rights is seen as being directly to investors' benefit (Hertz 2000). Other critical theorists have placed more stress on the value of "low intensity democracy" to international business: from this perspective, formal democratic transition is seen as strengthening the legitimacy of the state to pursue market reforms, in a context in which many democratic rights remain heavily truncated. In this sense, democracies comprising overweening executive powers, weak legislatures, a supine civil society, the preservation of significant military power, and the limited protection of human rights are seen as being structured specifically to the interests of transnational capital.[3] Taking one step further along this path of reasoning, apparent trends toward a "new populism" in Latin America, limiting democratic processes to the point of rendering them insubstantial façades, have also been interpreted as ways of facilitating pro-business market reforms (Cammack 2000).

A slightly different angle within this broadly skeptical perspective has focused on instrumental tactical postures of the private sector: even where the private sector has switched to supporting political change, this has been seen as representing a tactical shift to back an ascending pro-democracy alliance led by the working class, rather than a positive adherence to the concept of democracy itself (Rueschmeyer, Stephens, and Stephens 1992). Those writing from a more economistic perspective have also most commonly drawn attention to the dangers to economic reform of strong group rights (Olson 2000). Indeed, the mainstream international focus on good governance has been presented as nominally apolitical but can in some senses be seen as backing up the notion that investors have been concerned with only a narrow range of ostensibly technical issues — the political implication of the good governance agenda having been to distinguish a tightly delineated set of issues relating to corruption and policy-making capacities from broader democratic dynamics. From this perspective, attracting increased flows of international investment to Latin America has been seen in terms of the following: reforming financial systems to facilitate higher saving rates and, thus, decrease the region's vulnerability to capital outflows; improving governance structures underpinning trade policy to increase the still low export propensity of foreign affiliates and, thus, ensure that the magnitude of capital inflows is compatible with a more sustainable level of current account deficit; and, drawing from the perceived lessons of the Asian crisis, to strengthen prudential regulation (Held and Szalachman 1998; UNCTAD 1998, 268; CEPAL 1999, 128).

Broader views on the positive value of higher quality democracy have been less prominent. Some well-regarded writers have warned against the dangers of technocratic, decree-based policy-making styles undermining the sustainability of market reforms (Przeworski et al. 1995; Przeworski 1991, 179-187). One architect of the international financial institutions' agenda in Latin America recognized that "suppression is the best way to convince the conspiratorially minded that there is something to hide" and, thus, provoke greater opposition to economic reform (Williamson 1993, 1330). However, comprehensive assessment of any positive linkages between democratic quality and the specific interests of international investors has been conspicuously absent. This chapter suggests that the relationship between political structures and investor interests is, in fact, complex and varied and argues that the significance of broader democratic quality has been unduly neglected.

THE APPEAL OF STATE AUTONOMY

Inward capital flows have expanded significantly, as democracy has become more widespread and more embedded in Latin America. Overall foreign investment in Latin America increased fivefold between 1993 and 1998 (CEPAL 1998, 774). Foreign direct investment (FDI) stock as a percentage of the gross domestic product (GDP) rose from 11.6 percent in 1990 to 18.4 percent in 1995. With the comparable figure still standing at under 5 percent in Eastern Europe, this implied that earlier democratization had benefited Latin America (Hirst and Thompson 1999, 76). The strengthening of regional and global linkages, democracy, and economic reform have widely been seen as mutually enhancing, as a nexus of factors that together have been crucial to foreign investors' focus on Latin America (Phillips 1999).

Conversely, a comparison with East Asia might suggest that the formal adoption of democratic constitutions was not a primary factor. Post-transition Latin America continued to lose ground to the still largely nondemocratic East Asian region. Between 1975-1982, 64 percent of FDI to developing countries went to Latin America, 19 percent to East Asia; by 1990-1998, 37 percent went to Latin America, 52 percent to East Asia (UNCTAD 1999, 118). FDI per capita in East Asia was, by the end of the 1990s, even more significantly ahead of Latin American inflows. Overall levels of transparency have remained lower in Latin America (3.6) than Asia (4.6) (Nunnenkamp 1997, 65), suggesting that the issues of corruption and transparency pertinent to investment decisions are not tightly related to the presence or absence of political democracy. The magnitude of new investment flows to states such as Singapore — with clean but nondemocratic governance — has stood in dramatic contrast to some of Latin America's small, fractious democracies. The Asian financial crisis was the moment when democratic Latin America might have expected to benefit, as investors recognized the problems of autocratic regimes in East Asia and rewarded Latin America for its relatively higher degree of democracy. In fact, by the end of the decade, East Asia was recovering far better than Latin America, including FDI. By 2001, European credit rating services were still ranking most of (nondemocratic) East Asia and even most North African autocracies as more reliable and stable investment destinations than most Latin American states (*El País*, December 11, 2001). Such observations appeared to be consistent with empirical tests showing that, since the 1970s, no direct relationship has existed between economic development and Latin America's degree of "democraticness" (Landman 1999).

More impressionistic evidence suggests that multinationals have not been uniformly dissuaded by good governance problems in Latin America. The familiar complaint of U.S. firms in the 1990s was that, unhindered by any equivalent to the Corrupt Foreign Practices Act, European companies accommodated themselves to bad governance practices in negotiating access to Latin American markets. Siemens, BP, and Renault were all implicated in such cases, but the most notable attention focused on Spanish firms. Spanish companies in particular have openly admitted to benefiting from many procedures seen as problematically opaque to other foreign investors. Spanish investment in Latin America is that which has increased most dramatically. In 1993, Spanish investment in Latin America was still only one-fifth of investment to European Union (EU) states, but by the end of the decade accounted for over one-half of Spanish FDI. In 1998, Spain overtook the United Kingdom as the second largest investor in the region, and in 1999 surpassed the United States as the largest provider of new capital to Latin America. Spanish investors perceived the preeminence of patrimonial decision-making procedures to have given them a competitive advantage relative to companies originating from more rules-oriented cultures — a perception with which Spain's European and North American competitors readily concur. While purely cultural explanations for Spain's growing role in Latin America are unduly simplistic, Spanish investors themselves insist that this has been key to Spain's spectacularly increased presence in the region. Deals involving large companies were often arranged with significant intervention at the highest political level, this being particularly the case with Iberia's various deals and Repsol's purchase of Yacimientos Petrolíferos Fiscales (YPF). Most dramatic were the governmental links of Telefónica's president, given their prominent role in forging political links in Latin America (Youngs 2001). These trends are consistent with the increasing questioning of spill-over between economic liberalization and higher quality democratic governance: patrimonially based processes have often become further embedded as a means of managing the uncertainty of internationalization, rather than being swept away by increased foreign investment.

It has undoubtedly been the case that significant increases in foreign investment have taken place under conditions exhibiting clear limitations on democratic quality. Some trends make it difficult to refute critical perspectives on international actors' influence over Latin American democracy. Across the subcontinent, there was significant continuity in state elites, providing business with a perpetuation of pre-transition access to policy-making structures. Continuing human rights abuses often tempered unrest in a way that was helpful to multinationals' operations. Market reforms were undeniably facilitated in many countries by the docility of legislatures and opposition parties. There have been criticisms of "flexible rules implementation" being used to lighten multinationals' tax liabilities. Limited decentralization assuaged companies' fears over localized instability and the emergence of populist leaders at the local level. Many companies acknowledged that one of their most immediate concerns was for host governments to enjoy, as one manager put it, "an ability to overcome resistance to FDI." The weakness of Latin American civil society has commonly been interpreted as highly beneficial to multinational corporations (MNCs): the strengthening of civil society has most often been advocated as a means of countering the perceived preeminence of foreign capital. Formal democratization might be seen as having simply been tolerated, rather than positively valued, by foreign investors, as globalization has restricted de facto domestic options. Erstwhile critics of economic orthodoxy — Fernando Henrique Cardoso, Carlos Andrés Pérez, Rafael Caldera, Ricardo Lagos, and prominent Argentine members of the Radical Party— did modify their positions.[4] The lack of substantive democracy *between* nations at the international level might, in this sense, be seen as having trumped the uncertainties to investors of democratization *within* individual Latin American states. To the extent that support for democratization simply reflects an adjustment to current political trends, the critic might question whether it will prove an enduring phenomenon.

Some of the Latin American states with the most limited forms of democracy attracted high shares of new investment to the region in the 1990s. Mexico provides a notable example of this. Over the early part of the 1990s, with political liberalization stalled, Mexico attracted 40 percent of all FDI to Latin America. The attraction of Mexico's membership in the North American Free Trade Agreement (NAFTA) appeared comprehensively to outweigh the evolution of internal political structures. NAFTA not only engendered a reorientation of the United States toward Mexico. FDI to Latin American countries became even more strongly attracted toward Mexico, and the latter also became a proportionately more important destination for European investors hoping to gain better access into the U.S. market. Economic liberalization proceeded through privatizations in the early 1990s, prior to political reform being addressed with any degree of real conviction. Indeed, between 1988-1995 the relative scale of privatization in Mexico exceeded that in all other Hispanic Latin American states (IDB 1997, 46). In per capita terms, Mexico was a relatively high recipient of FDI — at US$79, compared, for example, to Brazil's $35. Overall net capital inflows for 1991-1993 were 8 percent of GDP, compared to the Latin American average of 4.7 percent (Griffith-Jones 1996, 128). The fact that the Confederation of Workers of Mexico (Confederación de Trabajadores de México) remained firmly under Institutional Revolutionary Party (Partido Revolucionario Institucional — PRI) tutelage choked off potential opposition to the government's economic reforms. Arguably, this even provided a "transmission belt," facilitating the acceptance of structural adjustment policies among industrial workers, in a way that a more pluralistic party-trade union relationship would have militated against. Successive PRI administrations frequently exceeded formal constitutional limits to push forward with economic liberalization, these being most notable in the privatization of the banking sector. Many judged that Mexico's former President Ernesto Zedillo was able to rebuild alliances successfully with the private sector after the peso crisis through the implementation of further economic liberalization, with political conditions apparently seen as of little pertinence (Bensabat Kleinberg 1999).

If, in Chile, authoritarian control was widely held to have facilitated the most far-reaching economic liberalization and earliest privatization programs in the region, the controlled nature of Chilean democratization has been cited as having facilitated the continuance of these trends: Chile was the highest per capita recipient (at $160) of foreign investment in Latin America during the 1990s (UNCTAD 1999, 116-7). One key utilities investor suggested that Chile's well-regulated market structures comprehensively eclipsed any consideration of remaining "democratic imperfections." Under former President Alberto Fujimori, Peru was one of the region's most extensive privatizers in the 1990s and was widely perceived as a notable success story in attracting new foreign investment. Cuba's opening up to foreign capital from the mid-1990s, including the real estate and banking sectors, appeared to indicate that the absence of even limited, formal democratization was of little import. Indeed, the Cuban regime went as far as offering streamlined procedures for MNCs in export processing zones.

Overall, the distribution of investment flows in Latin America has commonly been seen as related less to institutional variations than to the extent of privatization processes. One manager pointed out that resource constraints forced most investors to enter the Latin American market through initial purchases in one or two countries and, thus, to focus simply on the "ease of market accessibility." FDI for the purchase of existing assets has comprehensively overtaken green-field investment. It is the relatively high pace and reach of privatization in Latin America relative to other developing regions that has been seen as the key to explaining why the region has maintained its share of FDI as much as it has (UNCTAD 1999, 118). Much of the rise in FDI in Latin America was accounted for by a few large privatizations, the sale of YPF to Repsol dramatically pushing up figures at the end of the 1990s, for example.[5] Sales to foreign buyers have often been pushed through by taking legal, democratic procedures at least to their limit: in 2001, a telecommunications contract won by a Swedish company in Nicaragua was, for example, challenged on these grounds by the Sandinista opposition (*Financial Times*, September 5, 2001). Investment analysts are held not to have distinguished to any significant extent between good and bad democratic performers. Rather, they have based their actions on broad perceptions of the whole region, Latin America being seen in overly optimistic terms in the early 1990s and then in overly negative terms at the end of the decade (Lowenthal 2000, 53). In sum, there is much to suggest that foreign investors have not sought a broadening of democratic quality, and that by engaging so heavily and uncritically with low intensity democracies, they have contributed to a perpetuation of poor quality democratic governance. Crucially, some evidence indicates that foreign investors have operated in a way that has succeeded in blocking spill-over from economic reform to higher quality democracy, rather than acting as a conduit for such a supposedly reinforcing link between market and political liberalization.

DEMOCRATIC IMPERATIVES

While the low intensity democracy thesis retained some validity, it fails fully to capture the evolution of developments since the 1990s. Statistics can be read in contrasting ways. Significant increases in FDI have been registered, but flows to Latin America have remained limited, compared to investment in Organisation for Economic Development and Cooperation (OECD) markets — with greater market capacities but also higher quality and more stable democracies. Prominent economists have suggested that, after the one-off boon provided by utility privatizations, broader institutional reforms became necessary to retain foreign investment in the region (Dornbusch 2001). The development of endogenous growth theories has increasingly incorporated institutional variables, pointing to the restrictions on growth and investment incurred by the "political rents" being appropriated by powerful social groups (Korzeniewicz and Smith 2001). While critiques of the prevailing international order have invariably focused on the extent to which the ascendance of multinationals has undermined the "content" of national democracy, this poor quality of democratic governance has, in fact, exhibited features not obviously to the advantage of MNCs themselves.

Low intensity democracy has palpably not sufficed to invest market reforms with greater legitimacy. Latin American reforms have not been carried out in a way that has provided the legitimacy needed to render economic reforms more sustainable. The case for economic reform has not been argued and cognitively won through the democratic policy-making process. Under conditions of truncated democracy, no new ideational social contract has been constructed to underpin market reforms (Tedesco 2001). Limited democracy has clearly not facilitated the creation of a stable and embedded consensus behind the concept of the impartial regulatory state. Support for democracy has declined over the late 1990s; by 2001, the Latinobarómetro poll showed that in 10 Latin American states under 50 percent of the population thought democracy was preferable to any other kind of government. Significantly, this trend has paralleled a similar decline in support for privatization after 1998 (*The Economist* July 28, 2001). It might be said that many Latin American countries have remained caught between two stools: they do not have the kind of high quality democracy capable of investing legitimacy into economic reform; nor do they have the strong, competent, and politically insulated "developmental state" apparatus of East Asia. The poor quality of democratic management has ensured that the principle of open politics is still questioned from both sides of the political spectrum: the right is able to point to a continuing need for better control and stability; the left is able to point out that democracy has remained a sham in terms of the substantive needs of poorer sectors of society.

Where access to foreign capital has been opened up through executive decree and top-heavy governance procedures — often directly contrary to the mandates that gave politicians victory — greater turmoil has invariably subsequently been unleashed. This was the case with the presidencies of Carlos Menem in Argentina, both Pérez and Caldera in Venezuela, Fernando Collor de Mello in Brazil, Abdala Bucarám in Ecuador, and Alberto Fujimori in Peru. In this context, the prospect of backlash against foreign investors has on occasions been perceived with considerable concern. Elements of this backlash have impinged directly upon foreign investors. The perceived opaqueness of deals involving Spanish companies engendered talk in many states of windfall taxes being imposed on the privatization of public utilities. The backlash against market opening has not been entirely unrelated to the paucity of genuinely and comprehensively competitive politics, which has stifled debate and, in some cases, clearly contributed toward instability and unpredictable policy reversals. The same elite autonomy integral to the operation of low intensity democracy has been used as much to limit as to propel economic reform. Closely related to this, the arbitrary nature of much policymaking has often been directly prejudicial to foreign companies: one company manager likened it to a ". . . double edged sword . . . much better when it is working for you, but much worse when it is working against you" (confidential interview with the author). Macroeconomic stability "by whatever means" could not convincingly be seen as a maxim that has optimized investors' interests. If, for example, moves toward dollarization have been elaborated with international investors in mind, in Ecuador and El Salvador they have also engendered the kind of destabilizing backlash viewed with acute concern by MNCs.

Far from being positively beneficial, the social inequalities apparently central to the "disciplining" utility of low intensity democracy have been viewed by many investors with increasing concern. The extent of Latin America's inequalities is regularly suggested to be a prospective danger to democratic stability. Far more than limits to absolute levels of wealth, inequality is itself held to undermine the functioning of democratic institutions, as it permits these to be captured by economic elites and, thus, suffer a progressive decline in legitimacy (Karl 2000, 155). Empirical tests suggest that inequality has some explanatory force in accounting for the region's relatively low share of global FDI, in so far as social order is related to the degree of equity in the distribution of wealth (Figueroa 1998). As one trade organization suggested, such sociopolitical imbalances may not have been a disincentive to MNCs' first entry into Latin America through privatization purchases. However, once foreign companies were present in the market, these imbalances began to be viewed with increasing concern. Some critical analysts themselves suggested that such apparently business-oriented, rather limited forms of democracy would breed instability and the "tragic paradox" of popular classes increasingly supporting a form of autocratic governance once again inimical to the operation of markets (Borón 1995, 216).

Executive-heavy styles of governance have contributed to limitations in the kind of skills, services, and technical capacities sought by foreign investors. A concern frequently raised is that, with executives hoarding so much responsibility for reform processes, there is a dearth of strongly professionalized independent regulatory agencies (Lowenthal 2000, 47). External investors in privatization processes have complained that the regulatory agencies governing the new market structures have been underresourced and weak, as a result of their political partiality and their being run at least in part as political fiefdoms. Even where it is acknowledged that governmental links have been instrumental to privatization deals, concerns have then arisen over the weakness of structures guiding post-privatization operations. At a broader regional level, the adaptability of economic policies has also given rise to concerns. Early optimism that Latin America was held to have reacted more speedily and appropriately than East Asia to the crisis of 1997-1998 (CEPAL 1999, 118), was the exact reverse of investors' own perspectives as the new century commenced. The democratic state's lack of legitimacy has been a major factor in the failure to raise the region's pitifully low tax base: MNCs insist that, increasingly, they seek environments with well-funded services and infrastructure — this often outweighing the priority attached to seeking out low taxation regimes. It has been suggested that decentralization, still much more limited in Latin America than in OECD countries, would enable local levels of administration to vary services more effectively, in accordance with both local needs and the interests of economic agents (IADB 1997, 153). Overall levels of education have been higher in Asia and OECD countries than in Latin America (Nunnenkamp 1997, 68), and European companies insist that the relatively greater attraction of East Asia has much to do with the availability of more skilled and technically apt workers. In richer Latin American states, the provision of education has remained far less evenly distributed. High-profile European pressure groups with prominent business representation have focused on Latin America and have increasingly called for a more equal provision of education, seeing this as the key to providing greater stability and facilitating the region's fuller insertion into the global economy.[6]

It has been increasingly recognized that improvements in good governance, far from being a narrow technical agenda, have been impeded by broader political dynamics.[7] The World Bank and European governments lamented that proposed cooperation on good governance issues was most commonly frustrated by Latin

American elites. Even the World Bank acknowledged that it was increasingly necessary to understand how improvements in commercially related good governance must be predicated upon broader democratic quality. Due to political obstacles, the Inter-American Convention Against Corruption, signed in 1996, has remained toothless, with "follow-up mechanisms" themselves unspecific, agreed only at the Costa Rica summit in 2001. Far from low intensity Latin American democracies meekly seeking to serve the requirements of global capital, U.S. and European strictures on good governance were resisted and rejected as attempts to burden local industry with higher regulatory requirements (*Agence Europe*, May 17-18, 1999; *The Economist*, June 16, 2001). Good governance improvements have been blocked by political elite strategies for retaining domestic patronage networks. While much attention has focused on elite alliances with foreign capital in lubricating privatization deals, on many occasions foreign investors insist they have been excluded from open bidding processes, as assets have been divided up between domestic allies of incumbent governments — such a process integral to the power structures of low intensity democracy. Significantly, many companies themselves, uncertain over such debates, professed to have been influenced by the World Bank's slightly expanded concept of good governance.

While traditionally seen as stronger than in East Asia, the alliances between domestic and foreign capital in Latin America have been hindered by the nature of domestic capital's political insertion (Payne and Bartell 1995; Whitehead 2000, 75). Local businesses are not judged by international investors to have been strong allies in pushing for improvements in the rule of law and governance structures. The fixes common to executive-heavy policymaking in the region are, in most sectors, perceived by MNCs to favor domestic political allies over outsiders. As one business organization insisted, the prevalence of a general political culture predicated upon a "know-who" rather than a "know-how" logic has been a major obstacle that many potential new entrants to the Latin American market have in common. Even if large privatization deals have often been politically linked, the paucity of rules-based cultures has ensured that the presence of small and medium-sized investors has remained limited. The fact that foreign investment has been so heavily concentrated in a relatively small number of large-scale investments — Spanish FDI in utilities, German investment through two or three firms in the automotive sector, the United Kingdom's massively increased presence solely through Vodafone's recent expansion into Latin America — suggests that patrimonial styles of governance have been a significant barrier to a more regularized, low-level penetration by foreign capital beyond self-contained, politically conditioned, enclave activities.

This range of concerns has been particularly prominent in a number of specific cases. In Mexico, after the heavy foreign investment of the early 1990s, many foreign companies gradually began to view the PRI's political hegemony with increasing concern. After doubling between 1993 and 1994, foreign investment in Mexico then fell dramatically between 1997 and 1998, from $12.7 billion to $9.3 billion (CEPAL 1998, 774). The peso crisis encouraged a significant change in investors' perspectives, with the shortcomings of the PRI's control over the financial system becoming particularly evident (FitzGerald 1999, 113). There was concern that the PRI had begun to slow economic reform so as to keep hold of its political control (Elizondo Mayer-Serra 1999, 146). Even if there was no move to direct external pressure on the PRI, the prospect of political change was, in the words of one European commercial officer, "no longer seen as all risk." The instability caused by the repression of indigenous rights and the alleged links between the PRI and paramilitary groups active in provoking further unrest in Chiapas was seen by some investors as more preoccupying than any prospect that the Zapatista Army of National Liberation's (Ejército Zapatista de Liberación Nacional — EZLN) political representation would radically close off market access. Chase Manhattan's much quoted urging of a harsher suppression of civil unrest did not accord with all investors' views. By the 1997 congressional elections in Mexico, money managers in New York were saying that they would reduce the weight of Mexican assets in their portfolios if the PRI massaged the polls to retain control of the legislature. A similar thing happened in 2000, and after both congressional and presidential elections, Mexican bonds and equities soared (Maxfield 2000, 105).

Many investors acknowledged that the prospect of a PRI defeat appeared less preoccupying as the National Action Party (Partido de Acción Nacional — PAN) overtook the Democratic Revolutionary Party (Partido Revolucionario Democrático — PRD) as the leading opposition party. As one investment organization pointed out, the key for foreign investors was the prospect of a gradual and smoothly managed transition. A crucial factor, it was suggested, was that, as governor of Guanajuato, President Vicente Fox made trips to Europe and the United States to win over the foreign business community (Shirk 2000, 774). In his presidential campaign, he stressed as a top priority his commitment to make the judicial system more impartial. Fox's victory undoubtedly was cause for concern among investors: the president's backing away from the sale of PEMEX, the state oil monopoly; the potentially fractious relationship with PRI-controlled unions; the commitment to meet the population's concerns over *maquiladora* labor standards; Congress's blocking of fiscal reforms during Fox's first eight months in office; and the president's apparent ambivalence toward the Free Trade Area of the Americas (FTAA). However, while more obliged than his autocratic predecessors to take on board the concerns of civil society regarding economic liberalization, Fox was judged to possess the kind of democratic legitimacy that had been lacking in his predecessors. This lack of democratic legitimacy prior to the Fox administration had contributed to the unsatisfactory and unsettled reform process of the late 1990s. Some investors judged that this new legitimacy would reduce the need for profligate pork-barreling of the type that the PRI's credibility had come to depend upon. While domestic businesses, in particular those closely allied to the PRI, expressed unease at the new opening to the Zapatistas, many foreign companies professed to welcome Fox's immediate sending of a new law on indigenous rights to the Congress, this being seen as a likely means of social stabilization and thus helpful to reversing the decline in investment during the late 1990s. By 2001, foreign investment to Mexico had reached a historic high, with a number of notable purchases, such as Citigroup's takeover of Banacci, occurring amidst the turmoil of the Argentine crisis of 2001 — trends that might be interpreted as the rewards of democratization beginning to be reaped by foreign investors, as Mexico's investment climate proved both more robust and more open than in previous crises.

In Peru, there was similar evidence of an investment ceiling having been reached in the mid-1990s. A huge increase in flows, from $136 million to $3.2 billion between 1992 and 1996, was followed by a sharp decline to $1.9 billion in 1998 (CEPAL 1998, 774) and, reportedly, an even sharper fall thereafter through to 2001. The most common sentiment among foreign investors was that Fujimori had "out-stayed his welcome." As the victory over Sendero Luminoso (Shining Path) and early-1990s economic growth faded from memory, Fujimori's legitimacy became increasingly dependent on ad hoc increases in social expenditures, which sat uneasily with those who advocated International Monetary Fund (IMF) reforms (Crabtree 2001). The weakness of broad-ranging institutional structures was felt to be an increasing concern. For example, Tate and Lyle pulled out of a large investment due to the problems of obtaining guarantees over land tenure. By the end of 2000, the international business community was openly calling for Fujimori to step down (*Financial Times*, November 21, 2000). Crucially, business reacted as public support turned against the president, this well before the release of the "Vladivideos" (videotapes of Fujimori's intelligence chief, Vladimiro Montesinos, allegedly participating in bribery and other illegal activities) made transition look increasingly likely (García Calderón 2001). After Fujimori's resignation, political transition occurred relatively smoothly and was favorably viewed by foreign investors. There was some concern about President Alejandro Toledo having to operate with only a minority in Congress and the prospect of additional political space for civil society engendering unrest. In general, however, investors claimed to welcome the move beyond the uncertainties, intrigues, and unpredictability of Fujimori's final years in power.

In Venezuela, the alternate power-sharing arrangement of the Democratic Action Committee for Political Organization and Independent Election Corporatism (AD-COPEI) alliance succeeded only in engendering increasing instability. The bi-party colonization of the Venezuelan state gradually ensured that the liberal reform program became associated with the corrupt and limited nature of the country's democracy. Indeed, many saw the scope of the privatization process as having been limited specifically, so as not to endanger the patronage networks upon which the regime had become so heavily predicated. Growing dissatisfaction contributed to the riots under former President Pérez, the fragility of Caldera's position outside the political party framework, and eventually to President Hugo Chávez's arrival. There was much talk of investors' uncertainty toward Causa R, the center-left opposition excluded by the AD-COPEI "partyocracy," but this party appeared far more moderate than Chávez's populist-nationalism that eventually emerged. After 1998, in some instances — for example in the telecommunications sector — President Chávez cut through local patronage networks in a way that was helpful to foreign investors. However, the idea that his semi-autocratic populism has been an entirely welcome means of injecting life into a sclerotic institutional system and of better serving the interests of foreign capital is categorically not shared by business people. Concerns have grown, as institutional checks and balances have been dismantled and the scope for arbitrary decisionmaking has expanded. Venezuela's GDP fell massively in 1999, and while rising oil prices subsequently assisted recovery, the wider economy has not progressed in a way attractive to foreign investors. A new law increased royalty taxes on foreign oil investors, and a requirement that Petroleos de Venezuela (PDVSA) retain a majority share in foreign investments in the oil sector was pushed through, circumventing parliamentary scrutiny. The nationalism underpinning the legitimacy of Chávez's rule was viewed with some preoccupation. European trade ministries and business organizations recorded a significant decline in interest in Venezuela among investors after 1999. Business worries naturally became even more acute as the country's political instability culminated in the aborted coup of 2002.

In Cuba, the significant opening to foreign investment during the mid-1990s should not detract attention from the serious problems that have faced investors. In some sectors, foreign investors have continued to be subjected to discriminatory treatment. After the first flush of excitement following Cuba's initial *apertura* (opening), disappointment set in among Western companies and trade ministries, as it become clear how few sectors would be liberalized. Even after the liberalizing 1995 foreign investment law, many joint venture requirements remained onerous, as the regime feared a momentum taking root that might eventually threaten its political control (Pérez-López 1999, 283). One trade group highlighted the extent to which investors were uneasy at functioning within an increasingly bifurcated economic system, with the division between dollar-earners and others seen as a potential cause of future instability. Investors frequently pointed to the incongruity of MNCs trying to operate in a society infused with a political ideology that was supposedly quite critical of foreign capital. Cuba was seen as still lacking any deep-seated pro-investment climate, its welcoming in of FDI to a overwhelming degree having reflected an instrumental need for foreign exchange. Investors in Cuba increasingly complained at the lack of institutional capacity to support FDI (Pérez-López 1999, 278). One multinational that had expressly discounted involvement in Cuba suggested, in a confidential interview, that while the nature of the political system was not in itself the crucial factor in this decision, its impact was felt indirectly in the country's pervasive lack of market development and potential. Further south, the Argentine and Chilean economic reform processes have invariably been compared favorably with the constraints imposed by Brazil's fractious party system. Investors' perspectives were, in practice, less clear-cut. After former President Collor de Mello's failure to further economic reform significantly, President Cardoso aimed to build a broader, more positive coalition behind reforms. By 2001, it appeared that this was serving Brazil rather better than was former President Menem's legacy in Argentina (Panizza 2000). Far from benefiting investors, the strong-arm tactics associated with former President Fernando De la Rúa's attempt to push labor market reform through the Senate in 2000 helped unleash the political crisis that, by the end of 2001, had investors withdrawing en masse from Argentina. Reports that Spanish companies, conscious of the increasing backlash against their operations, were offering forward payment of tax liabilities provided a further demonstration of the continuing preference for politically negotiated rather than rules-based solutions. Brazilian and Argentinian FDI receipts were running at similar levels in the mid-1990s; by 1999, flows to Brazil were four times greater. In 1996, Brazil overtook Mexico as the region's largest recipient of FDI, its inflows having increased from $1.3 billion in 1993 to $16.3 billion in 1997, and Brazil was identified as the region's "rising star" in investors' eyes (UNCTAD 1998, 244, 248). Much of this trend was due to Brazil's privatization process having begun later than elsewhere in the region but was arguably also assisted by a more stable and inclusive political process than had prevailed in the early 1990s. In Chile, a proportion of the state copper company, Codelco, was set aside for the military, frustrating attempts to privatize this sector (Barton 2000). Only as President Lagos began to address the remaining constraints to Chile's "controlled democracy," did access to foreign capital begin to expand. At the regional level, while a major positive factor for foreign investors has been the new cooperation between Latin American states that democracy has ushered in, the limits to the same democracy have been relevant to the low level of institutionalization of regional integration projects. Governments have been unwilling to disperse and codify regulatory issues within strongly objective institutional procedures, and the Southern Common Market's (Mercado Común del Sur — MERCOSUR) apparent unraveling has been of particular concern to international investors.

In those Latin American states that have suffered long-running and pervasive violent conflict, contrasting considerations have been in evidence. A standard claim in much investment analysis has been that in the context of civil conflict, firm, rather than open, government is needed to provide the stability so essential to investors' interests. In practice, foreign companies have increasingly acknowledged that heavy-handed efforts to contain conflict have not succeeded in improving investment conditions in a context where the underlying causes of instability have not been addressed in any significant way. Investment flows to Colombia outside the oil sector have remained negligible and have gone down by half from $5.2 billion in 1997 to $2.6 billion in 1998. With the new 1991 Constitution having strengthened democratic procedures — through judicial reforms, restrictions on the executive, the sanctioning of a number of new political parties, and M-19 (a guerrilla group later renamed Democratice Alliance — Alianza Democrática) representation in the Constituent Assembly — Colombia might be cited as a case study in democracy's inability to guarantee stability. Certainly, it was suggested that the most marked decline in investment occurred when parliament did eventually act against then President Ernesto Samper's suspected narcotrafficking links, and political alliances fractured (McBeth 1999, 150).

Alternatively, the continuing *limitations* to democratic processes might be seen as contributing to Colombia's spiraling violence. Former president Andrés Pastrana, rhetorically at least, recognized the need to increase the still limited extent to which social demands were channeled in a more peaceable way through the party system, but his proposals for enhancing the responsiveness of the Congress were blocked by the latter. While Plan Colombia did include references to strengthening democracy, this element was, in practice, subordinate to military strategy. Tough — many would say, repressive — antiterrorist legislation was on occasions used to push through privatizations, only for few foreign companies that registered interest at that time. While there undoubtedly were companies keen primarily to see a firmer clampdown on guerrilla operations, most acknowledged that a sustainable stability could only be achieved if underlying social problems were addressed through the democratic process. A senior representative of one of the largest foreign investors in Colombia insisted that, far from being eager to support paramilitary forces, MNCs had been reviewing their operations in Colombia due to the latter's ascendance. Indeed, the real problem for foreign investors was the destruction of local services and capacities, which had made basic economic operations in the country increasingly difficult (Butler 2000, 159). Concerns intensified as the military displaced local civilian policing, and an exodus of Colombia's middle class deprived foreign investors of partners through which to enter the uncertain Colombian market (Watson 2000, 542). One European manager insisted, in a confidential interview, that his firm's plans to examine the Colombian market seriously had been shelved, as the increasing primacy of the military dimension had rendered even more remote any "stable basis to society." From this perspective, Colombia could hardly be forwarded as a case of low intensity, nepotistic, socially exclusive democracy guaranteeing the interests of transnational capital.

In Central America, much was made of how Presidents Violeta Chamorro and then Arnoldo Alemán bowed to the interests of foreign capital; their failure to develop cleaner and more inclusive democratic procedures helped produce a scenario hardly reassuring to MNCs. In El Salvador, the National Renewal Alliance (Alianza por la Renovación Nacional — ARENA) looked the better bet for investors than the Farabundo Martí National Liberation Front (Frente Farabundo Martí para la Liberación Nacional — FMLN), but the former's hoarding of the benefits of the new democracy and de facto ability to restrict effective citizenship rights perpetuated instability and often appeared to have made former combatants ambiguous in their commitment to democracy. By the end of the 1990s, Guatemala and El Salvador were only just beginning to attract non-negligible amounts of FDI (CEPAL 1998, 774). As often occurs in post-conflict contexts, many extremely cheap assets were on offer to MNCs. However, if the stilted progress in democratic consolidation was beginning to bring Central America onto investors' horizons, the inequalities that first provoked civil conflict had not diminished, and unrest still rumbled on, both within and between the region's different states.

MULTINATIONALS, DEMOCRACY, AND INTERNATIONAL POLITICS

Some multinationals may have increasingly been influenced by concerns integrally related to the poor quality of democratic governance in Latin America, but to what extent have they, as protagonists, conditioned the practical international politics of democracy and human rights promotion? The U.S. and European governments have come ritually to conceptualize their policies focused on the promotion of democracy and good governance as reflecting both strategic and commercial self-interest. However, direct business engagement in and influence over this emphasis on democracy promotion has been conspicuously limited. The emergence of an international agenda focused on human rights and democracy has been pertinent to investors' interests but has not reflected any primary agency on the part of the private sector.

Business engagement has focused overwhelmingly on narrow governance issues: customs procedures, commercial judicial proceedings, and procurement transparency. Despite expressing concerns that broader political conditions have impeded progress on good governance, most investors have still perceived the latter to represent a sufficiently apolitical agenda for them to take an active role in, while being keen to leave the "democracy" agenda to governments. Despite professing worries over the state of democratic governance in Latin America, foreign investors have been highly ambivalent over the politicization of democracy at the international level. Many firms admit to considerable uncertainty over the best way to further their perceived interests in this regard. One U.S. business lobby group acknowledged that a "lot of learning" was still needed. In the words of another trade organization, investors have not wanted "to stick their heads above the parapet" on political issues (confidential interviews). Even if investors' views of democratic procedure have evolved, in their lobbying strategies most have remained extremely cautious. At most, companies have sought an indirect route, encouraging their trade organizations to lobby government officials discreetly. Even then, lobbying priorities have still relegated concerns over political conditions to a position well behind the focus on tariff liberalization or macroeconomic stabilization. Certainly, Latin American elites have not perceived there to be pressure emanating from international business on questions of democratic governance.

Conversely, neither has there been active lobbying to limit Western governments' democracy agendas. Where multinationals have lobbied Western governments, it has often been against the prospect of coercive policies. Even as Spain's Popular Party (Partido Popular) government has in some cases pressed with increasing vigor for judicial reform, the Spanish business community has sought to ensure that coercive pressure did not extend beyond narrow, commercially related procedural issues (Youngs 2001, 116). While British trade officials welcomed the prospect of a trial against Chile's former president, General Augusto Pinochet, presaging democratic reforms that would be highly beneficial to foreign investors, the British private sector — in a rare instance of direct lobbying on political issues — pushed for the general's release from custody. The Spanish government, along with other southern European administrations, resisted proposals for including a good governance clause within the new EU-MERCOSUR agreement. And, most notably, many U.S. firms have lobbied with increasing vigor for engagement with Cuba. Beyond particular instances where coercive approaches to democratic governance have been resisted, however, there has been little active lobbying by the private sector against the international focus on democratic governance. One U.S. business organization insisted that there had been no question of private sector lobbying against the U.S. Agency for International Development's (USAID) increasing budget for democracy assistance projects.

Much of U.S. policy has been driven by a strategic logic. In general, in Latin America, unlike in East Asia, since the 1990s security concerns have not encouraged external actors to support formal limits to democracy (Whitehead 2000, 68). However, the focus on democracy has varied in accordance with security calculations, with experts pointing to the lack of joined-up thinking between economic and strategic objectives.[8] Specifically in relation to South America, one expert laments the "fuzzy" linkage in practice between the political and economic dimensions of U.S. policy (Weintraub 2000, 60). The orientation of U.S. democracy assistance to police and security forces — for example, in the Andean region almost as much has been given by the United States to military assistance as for development assistance (Cerdas Cruz 1999, 130) — might be interpreted as demonstrating a preference for limited, "controlled" democracy. To the extent that such preferences have derived from strategic calculations, the input of the private sector has been relatively mute.

If investors have exerted little influence over the U.S. administration in favor of such approaches to security, neither have they sought to oppose security strategies that appear to have trumped rather than reinforce the focus on democratic governance. U.S. policy on the finer points of Plan Colombia — the balance between eradication assistance, on the one hand, and human rights guarantees and action against paramilitary activity, on the other — was determined primarily by competition between the administration and congressional Democrats. Investors' voices were conspicuously inaudible. In sum, the political-strategic dimension to the democracy promotion project has led to distinct and conceptually autonomous considerations. While critical analysts have usefully warned against unthinkingly seeing the economic and political dimensions as entirely separate, on the evidence of recent policies, it would be just as misguided to conflate the two spheres completely.

The skeptical view would suggest that U.S. policy toward Mexico reflected a business desire for only limited change in the country. Some judged that, having begun to court the PAN under then President Ronald Reagan, the United States reined back from supporting the prospect of precipitate change when the PRD consolidated its position as the leading opposition party in the early 1990s (Coatsworth 1999, 150). Thereafter, it was argued that U.S. policy reflected a business-driven desire for a controlled process of formal democratization without any mitigation of the state's scope for carrying out human rights abuses and the repressive disciplining of labor (Robinson 2000, 317). In fact, elements of U.S. policy suggested exactly the opposite approach, the Clinton administration pressing for limited improvements in basic rights and the rule of law and not formal political transition — NAFTA, after all, included a labor rights clause (at the behest of U.S. unions) but no democracy clause. Overall, even if it was the case that U.S. policy in the 1980s was driven primarily by multinationals' desire for a truncated form of democracy, such a dynamic was not prominent in the evolution and extension of the international agenda on democratic governance during the 1990s. Multinationals' roles as protagonists were both cautious and far from being focused solely or in any detailed fashion on the supposed benefits of low intensity democracy.

European governments' focus on democratic governance in developing markets has been strongly driven by a developmentalist logic. World Bank and Inter-American Development Bank concepts of good governance have increasingly been seen as unduly narrow by European governments and too indulgent of the region's elites. In the broadening of the EU's focus beyond narrow good governance issues, private sector engagement played a relatively limited role. EU policymakers have been much more open to non-governmental organizations (NGOs) in the formulation of external policies, with such civil society representatives being far more heavily engaged in the EU's foreign policy-making machinery than employers' organizations. A frequent complaint among European policymakers was that the private sector has not engaged to any significant extent in the international democracy promotion agenda (Youngs 2002). A number of European trade and foreign ministries solicited views from their respective private sectors on issues of governance structures in Latin America, with limited response. The Union of Industrial and Employers' Confederations of Europe (UNICE), the pan-European employers' organization, expressed concerns that the EU was pushing ahead with a free trade area with Mexico for ostensibly foreign policy reasons prior to securing commitments to good governance reforms but failed to slow this process down. Far from actively seeking a low intensity democracy, EU policy devoted increasing funding to NGOs, many of which were themselves highly critical of European trade policies, and gave limited attention to state institutions within political aid projects.

More notable than private sector agencies' views has been the extent to which external perspectives on democratic governance have been conditioned by international political rivalries, in particular between the United States and the EU. The standard view has been that U.S.-European commercial competition works to undercut democracy and human rights policies in Latin America and other developing parts of the world. However, U.S. and EU policymakers increasingly have seen the governance agendas of these countries in terms of promoting their respective regulatory structures. In this sense, Western governments' emphasis on governance rules was integrally related to EU-United States' rivalry over the evolution of multilateral trading rules. Each has sought to disseminate its own models of regulation with this broader battle in mind. Europeans — especially Spain and the United Kingdom — have reacted with concern at U.S. efforts to influence antitrust regulations as a reaction to big European mergers, especially in the telecommunications sector.

The primacy of political rivalry was seen most clearly in Cuba. The significant increases in European investments in Cuba during the latter half of the 1990s took place despite real difficulties in operating within such a closed political system and were driven primarily by investors' desires to take advantage of U.S. companies' exclusion from the Cuban market. European firms' stated aim was to establish a presence, so as to have a purchase on developments after the inevitable future transition. Conversely, problems deriving from the lack of democratic governance in Cuba were a less serious disincentive to European investors than the prospect of attracting U.S. Helms-Burton sanctions — a prospect that caused several companies, such as Sol Meliá, to review their investment plans for Cuba. The investment "disciplines" agreed upon by the EU and the United States in 1998 failed to resolve differences, Europeans insisting that the United States had committed itself to desist from applying unilateral, extra-territorial sanctions and the United States insisting that the EU had agreed to constraints on investment in nondemocratic regimes. In short, a key factor for issues of democratic governance is that the EU and the United States have developed their links with Latin America in competition with each other and not subsequent to joining up through a Transatlantic Free Trade Area, which would have weakened Latin America's relative position.

These features recall some of the defining work on political process and collective action. Within Mancur Olson's seminal framework, democratic quality might be equated to the very type of collective good in relation to which little joint engagement emerges: the general benefits of this good contrasting with firms' primary concern with relative gains over their competitors. In accordance with this classic logic, we would indeed expect multinational investors as a group to possess little incentive to push for improvements in the democratic quality of host country polities and individually to seek to free ride on any critical pressure brought to bear on developing market governments by other firms (Olson 1965, especially chapter 1). The pertinence of other influential work emphasizing the underlying structural power of the capitalist class can also be seen, thus reducing the urgency of direct engagement on second order issues. From this perspective, features of the productive environment beyond the "accumulation process itself" were, in the face of divisions among individual firms, seen as being shaped with some operational autonomy by the state (Offe 1975, 132-134). The validity of this rule might be seen as being proved by its exception, namely, where the absence of collective action does not preserve the status quo but witnesses a fundamental destabilization of conditions (Przeworski 1999, 64): this consistent with firms' more notable protagonism where a profound undermining of basic political stability renders basic commercial operations increasingly untenable.

If MNCs' proactive engagement with governments has been limited, more notable has been their essentially defensive reaction to Western civil society pressure. Much has been written on the impact of the new Corporate Social Responsibility agenda and the extent to which multinationals have incorporated new codes of conduct. These codes are judged to have been adopted at the behest of NGO pressure, with companies keen to minimize "reputational costs." The prominence of this agenda demonstrates how such defensive perspectives have eclipsed any proactive campaign based on a perception of the positive benefits to be gained from enhanced environmental and labor standards. British Petroleum's hasty elaboration of a new code of conduct after criticism of its alleged links with paramilitary groups in Colombia is often cited as the epitome of such reputation-driven reactions. Moreover, the systemic level features of host countries' political processes have been expressly excluded from the remit of Corporate Social Responsibility. Investors have limited the new commitments within their codes of conduct to respect for labor standards and human rights, where these touch directly upon a company's own operations. The stated concern has been to ensure that the multinational does not contribute through its own operations to abuses of accepted labor, human rights, or environmental standards. Investors have strongly resisted the prospect of the high-profile Corporate Social Responsibility agenda forcing them into broader, more politicized obligations. Significantly, in this they have not been strongly pressed by NGOs, themselves wary of Western governments' democracy agendas shifting the focus away from basic rights. In sum, while highlighting how civil society pressure has made life uncomfortable for investors in relation to certain features common to low intensity democracy, the Corporate Social Responsibility agenda does not, in fact, provide the most helpful lens through which to assess the relationship between democratic quality and investors' interests.

CONCLUSIONS

The foregoing analysis demonstrates that the relationship between FDI trends and the quality of democratic governance in Latin America has been complex. It shows how this issue cuts across both the domestic-international and economic-political divides and is, thus, more pertinent to the study of foreign economic relations than has traditionally been acknowledged.

Significant variations between investors and a self-confessed uncertainty on the part of many multinationals render one-dimensional assertions unsatisfactory.

Statistics themselves are inconclusive, capable of suggesting that Latin America has done less well in attracting international investment than many less democratic nations or, alternatively, that capital inflows have been held back by the limits to democratic quality throughout the region. Some investors have remained focused on the perceived benefits of state autonomy, while others profess concern over the adverse impact of low intensity democracy. Some investors' time horizons remain short-term; others claim longer-term outlooks that have encouraged them to seek a greater sustainability of reform processes. Democratic quality cannot be seen as a panacea for international investors, but neither can limits to pluralistic politics. FDI cannot be seen as entirely indifferent to Latin America's growing inequalities, but neither have investors' concerns uniformly motivated political elites to temper social imbalances. Most investors judge that the broad evolution of the international system means that the realistic option is to seek improvements in democratic quality, rather than an unraveling of the prevailing low quality forms of democracy. In sum, a complex mix of top-down and bottom-up dynamics is needed, capable of expediting specific economic reforms, but also of underpinning these with institutional and ideational contexts most apposite to the particular social, economic, and political patterns of the different host countries targeted by international investors in Latin America.

NOTES

1.   The author wishes to thank William C. Smith for helpful comments on a first draft of this chapter.

2.   The analysis draws from interviews conducted with representatives of multinationals; employers' organizations, including the Center for International Private Enterprise, U.S. Chambers of Commerce, UNICE in Brussels, the CBI and the Latin American Trade Advisory Group in London and the CEOE in Madrid; the president of Transparency International-Latin America; Control Risks Group; diplomats and commercial officers from Germany, Spain, the United Kingdom, the European Commission and the European Council Secretariat; and USAID. The author conducted these interviews between 1999 and 2002.

3.   For one of the most notable expositions of this view, see Gills, Rocamora, and Wilson (1993), and more specifically on particular U.S. policies, Robinson (1996). In a similar vein, Haggard and Kaufman (1995) suggest that limited transitions have best suited business interests. Even where low intensity democracy has not been explicitly forwarded as a conceptual paradigm sought by transnational capital, it was commonplace during the 1990s to point out how "presidential dominance" apparently facilitated neoliberal policymaking — for one example, see Philip (1993).

4.   For such a take on 1990s' developments, see Lievesley (1999). A similar line on civil society is offered by Peeler (1998), especially pages 198-201.

5.   UNCTAD (2000), 43. The incidence of Spanish investment in Latin America has more generally been seen as resulting overwhelmingly from privatization processes, combined with the "push" factors of enhanced competition within the EU single market (Toral 2001).

6.   *El País*, February 2, 2001, reporting on Fundación Euramérica.

7.   Transparency levels have increased in some states, declined in others, but registered no significant overall improvement in Latin America during the late 1990s (Transparency International, press release, June 27, 2001).

8.   See the various contributions to Schoultz, Smith, and Varas (1994), as well as Carothers (1999).

REFERENCES

Armijo, Leslie E. 1999. "Mixed Blessing: Expectations about Foreign Capital Flows and Democracy in Emerging Markets." In *Financial Globalisation and Democracy in Emerging Markets*, ed. Leslie E. Armijo. Basingstoke, UK: Macmillan.

Barton, J. 2000. "'Latin America for Sale': The Privatisation of Power." In *Yearbook on Latin America 2000*, ed. K. Svensen. Oslo: LAG (published in Norwegian).

Bensabat, Kleinberg R. 1999. "Strategic Alliances: States-Business Relations in Mexico under Neo-Liberalism and Crisis." *Bulletin of Latin American Research* 18 (1): 71-87.

Borón, Atilio. 1995. *State, Capitalism, and Democracy in Latin America*. Boulder, Colo.: Lynne Rienner Publishers.

Butler, Nick. 2000. "Companies and International Relations." *Survival* 42 (1): 149-64.

Cammack, Paul. 2000. "The Resurgence of Populism in Latin America." *Bulletin of Latin American Research* 19 (2): 149-63.

Carothers, Thomas. 1999. *Aiding Democracy Abroad*. Washington, D.C.: Carnegie Endowment.

CEPAL. 1998. *Anuario Estadístico*. Santiago, Chile: Comisión Económica para América Latina (CEPAL), Naciones Unidas.

Cerdas Cruz, Rodolfo. 1999. "United States Foreign Relations and the Promotion of Democracy in Latin America." In *The United States and Latin America: The New Agenda*, eds. Victor Bulmer-Thomas and James Dunkerley. London: ILAS.

Coatsworth, John. 1999. "The United States and Democracy in Mexico." In *The United States and Latin America: The New Agenda*, eds. Victor Bulmer-Thomas and James Dunkerley. London: ILAS.

Crabtree, John. 2001. "The Collapse of Fujimorismo: Authoritarianism and Its Limits." *Bulletin of Latin American Research* 20 (3): 287-303.

Dornbusch, Rudiger. 2001. "All Risk and No Reward in Latin America." *Financial Times*, July 11.

Elizondo Mayer-Serra, Carlos. 1999. "Mexico: Foreign Investment and Democracy." In *Financial Globalisation and Democracy in Emerging Markets*, ed. Leslie E. Armijo. Basingstoke, UK: Macmillan.

Figueroa, A. 1998. "Equity, Foreign Investment and International Competitiveness." *CEPAL Review* 65: 45-59.

FitzGerald, E.V.K. 1999. "Trade, Investment and NAFTA: The Economics of Neighbourhood." In *The United States and Latin America: The New Agenda*, eds. Victor Bulmer-Thomas and James Dunkerley. London: ILAS.

García Calderón, Ernesto. 2001. "Peru's Decade of Living Dangerously." *Journal of Democracy* 12 (2): 46-58.

Gills, Barry, Joel Rocamora, and Richard Wilson. 1993. "Low Intensity Democracy." In *Low Intensity Democracy: Political Power in the New World Order*, eds. Barry Gills, Joel Rocamora, and Richard Wilson. London: Pluto Press.

Griffith-Jones, Stephany. 1996. "International Capital Flows to Latin America." In *The New Economic Model in Latin America*, ed. Victor Bulmer-Thomas. Basingstoke, UK: Macmillan.

Haggard, Stephan, and Robert Kaufman. 1995. *The Political Economy of Democratic Transitions*. Princeton, N.J.: Princeton University Press.

Held, G., and R. Szalachman. 1998. "External Capital Flows in Latin America and the Caribbean in the 1990s: Experiences and Policies." *CEPAL Review* 64: 29-47.

Hertz, Noreena. 2000. *The Silent Takeover: Global Capitalism and the Death of Democracy*. London: Random House.

Hirst, Paul Q., and Grahame Thompson. 1999. *Globalization in Question*. 2nd ed. Cambridge, UK: Polity Press.

Inter-American Development Bank (IDB). 1997. *Latin America after a Decade of Reforms: 1997 Report*. Washington, D.C.: IDB.

Karl, Terry Lynn. 2000. "Economic Inequality and Democratic Instability." *Journal of Democracy* 11 (1): 149-156.

Korzeniewicz, Patricio, and William C. Smith. 2001. "Poverty, Inequality, and Growth in Latin America: Searching for the High Road to Globalization." *Latin American Research Review* 35 (3): 7-54.

Landman, Todd. 1999. "Economic Development and Democracy: The View from Latin America." *Political Studies* 47 (4): 607-626.

Leftwich, Adrian. 1996. "Two Cheers for Democracy? Democracy and the Developmental State." In *Democracy and Development*, ed. Adrian Leftwich. Cambridge, UK: Polity Press.

Lievesley, Geraldine. 1999. *Democracy in Latin America: Mobilization, Power and the Search for a New Politics*. Manchester, UK: Manchester University Press.

Lowenthal, Abraham. 2000. "Latin America at the Century's Turn." *Journal of Democracy* 11 (2): 41-55.

Maxfield, Sylvia. 2000. "Capital Mobility and Democratic Stability." *Journal of Democracy* 11 (4): 95-107.

McBeth, Brian S. 1999. "Colombia." In *Case Studies in Latin American Political Economy*, eds. Julia Buxton and Nicola Phillips. Manchester, UK: Manchester University Press.

Nunnenkamp, Peter. 1997. "Foreign Direct Investment in Latin America in the Era of Globalized Production." *Transnational Corporations* 6 (1): 51-81.

Offe, Claus. 1975. "The Theory of the Capitalist State and the Problem of Policy Formation." In *Stress and Contradiction in Modern Capitalism*, eds. Leon N. Lindberg, Robert Alford, Colin Crouch, and Claus Offe. Lexington, Mass.: Lexington Books.

Olson, Mancur. 1965. *The Logic of Collective Action: Public Goods and the Theory of Groups*. Cambridge, Mass.: Harvard University Press.

Olson, Mancur. 2000. *Power and Prosperity: Outgrowing Communist and Capitalist Dictatorships*. New York: Basic Books.

Panizza, Francisco. 2000. "Beyond 'Delegative Democracy': 'Old Politics' and 'New Economics' in Latin America." *Journal of Latin American Studies* 32 (2): 737-764.

Payne, Leigh A., and Ernest Bartell. 1995. "Bringing Business Back in: Business and State Relations and Democratic Stability in Latin America." In *Business and Democracy in Latin America*, eds. Leigh A. Payne and Ernest Bartell. Pittsburgh: Pittsburgh University Press.

Peeler, John. 1998. *Building Democracy in Latin America*. Boulder, Colo.: Lynne Rienner Publishers.

Pérez-López, Jorge. 1999. "The Cuban External Sector in the 1990s." In *The United States and Latin America: The New Agenda*, eds. Victor Bulmer-Thomas and James Dunkerley. London: ILAS.

Philip, George. 1993. "The New Economic Liberalism and Democracy in Latin America: Friends or Enemies?" *Third World Quarterly* 14(3).

Phillips, Nicola. 1999. "Global and Regional Linkages." In *Developments in Latin American Economy: States, Markets, and Actors*, eds. Julia Buxton and Nicola Phillips. Manchester, UK: Manchester University Press.

Przeworski, Adam. 1991. *Democracy and the Market: Political and Economic Reforms in Eastern Europe and Latin America*. Cambridge, UK: Cambridge University Press.

Przeworski, Adam, with Pranah Bardhan et al. (A joint report by 21 authors working together as the Group on East-South Systems Transformations.) 1995. *Sustainable Democracy*. Cambridge, UK: Cambridge University Press.

Robinson, William. 2000. "Promoting Capitalist Polyarchy: The Case of Latin America." In *American Democracy Promotion: Impulses, Strategies, and Impacts*, eds. Michael Cox, G. John Ikenberry, and Takashi Inoguchi. Oxford, UK: Oxford University Press.

Robinson, William I. 1996. *Promoting Polyarchy*. Cambridge, UK: Cambridge University Press.

Rueschemeyer, Dietrich, Evelyne H. Stephens, and John D. Stephens. 1992. *Capitalist Development and Democracy*. Cambridge, UK: Polity Press.

Schoultz, Lars, William C. Smith, and Augusto Varas, eds. 1994. *Security, Democracy, and Development in United States-Latin American Relations*. Coral Gables, Fla.: North-South Center Press at the University of Miami.

Shirk, David A. 2000. "Vicente Fox and the Rise of the PAN." *Journal of Democracy* 11 (4): 25-32.

Tedesco, Laura. 2001. "Between Democracy and Neoliberalism: Conceptualising the State in Argentina." Paper presented at the 2001 meeting of the Latin American Studies Association. Washington, D.C., September.

Toral, Pilar. 2001. "Spanish Investment in Latin America." Paper presented at the 2001 meeting of the Latin American Studies Association, Washington, D.C., September.

United Nations Conference on Trade and Development (UNCTAD). 1998. *World Investment Report 1998: Trends and Determinants*. New York: United Nations.

UNCTAD. 1999. *Trade and Development Report 1999*. New York: United Nations.

UNCTAD. 2000. *Trade and Development Report 2000*. New York: United Nations.

Watson, Cynthia A. 2000. "Civil-Military Relations in Colombia: A Workable Relationship or a Case for Fundamental Reform?" *Third World Quarterly* 21 (3): 529-48.

Weintraub, Sidney. 2000. *Development and Democracy in the Southern Cone: Imperatives for U.S. Policy in South America*. Washington, D.C.: Center for Strategic and International Studies (CSIS).

Whitehead, Laurence. 2000. "Comparing East Asia and Latin America: Stirrings of Mutual Recognition." *Journal of Democracy* 11 (4): 65-78.

Williamson, John. 1993. "Democracy and the 'Washington Consensus.'" *World Development* 21 (8).

Youngs, Richard. 2001. "Spain, Europe and Latin America: The Complex Interaction of Regionalism and Cultural Identification." In *Spain: The European and International Challenges*, eds. Richard Gillespie and Richard Youngs. London: Frank Cass.

Youngs, Richard. 2002. "The European Union and Democracy in Latin America." *Latin American Politics and Society* 44: 3.

Youngs, Richard. 1999-2002. Confidential interviews with diplomats, commercial officers, and individuals representing a variety of companies and governmental and nongovernmental organizations. Please see endnote 2.

Conclusion

THE DEATH OF THE UNIVERSAL DEVELOPMENT MODEL: SUSTAINING GROWTH THROUGH DIFFERENTIATING DOMESTIC NORMS

Brian Potter[1]

For more than a decade, "the Washington consensus" has guided economic policy, both foreign and domestic, of most Latin American countries. The term, coined by John Williamson, describes a standard set of policies that promised a return to growth for the protectionist, state-led, and indebted countries of the region (Williamson 1999). Over time, most elements of the neoliberal growth package have been theoretically and empirically questioned. In a holistic sense, the moderate yet disappointing growth of the post-reform Latin American countries (Stallings and Peres 2000) and the financial collapse of Argentina, one of the most aggressive reformers, have cast doubt on the efficacy of the consensus policies in promoting national economic growth and alleviating poverty. In addition to easily quantifiable measures, the widespread popular discontent of economic prospects and the elections of Presidents Luiz Ignácio Lula da Silva in Brazil and Lucio Gutiérrez in Ecuador signal challenges to the reform policies of the past two decades.

Yet, while "the consensus has been wounded — and potentially fatally so," it is far from dead (Broad and Cavanagh 1999). Defenders seek to legitimate the overall message of the reform package, that markets serve better to allocate resources than do government interventions. Although several reform prescriptions create divisions among economists and policymakers, policies that create a stable macroeconomic environment find widespread support in Washington, D.C., academe, and the Latin American electorate. Moreover, the current U.S. administration, occupied by pressing domestic and foreign policy concerns, seems unlikely to dedicate scarce policy efforts to improve other dimensions of the consensus or to find ways to tailor reforms to individual countries. The consensus, or some subset of it, will most likely continue to influence the domestic and foreign economic policies of Latin American countries.

This chapter builds on recent work in political economy, including the chapters in this volume, to evaluate which standard parts of the consensus Latin American countries should continue to work toward and, by contrast, how countries should modify other prescribed policies to meet national conditions and values more effectively. While the implementation of all reforms has reflected national preferences to some degree, recent financial crises and the changes of leadership in international financial institutions may have opened a "policy window" that can allow substantial deviation from the standard model. This window of opportunity applies to some microeconomic reforms while excluding standard prescriptions for macroeconomic stability. Reconsideration of second generation reforms may serve to create programs that better serve the goal of equitable economic growth and find more legitimacy and, hence, greater compliance in Latin American countries.

This chapter begins with a discussion of the consensus and subsequent challenges to it. A global consensus has emerged to support measures for macroeconomic stability. However, agreement on the correct set of policies to improve the microeconomic environment may not only be out of reach but ill advised. A second section uses some of the works from this volume to illustrate the need for national experimentation with microeconomic reforms. The final section argues that careful attention to national values in designing microeconomic reforms would improve their political acceptability and later compliance, serving to promote stable economic growth. While some elements of the universal development model termed "the Washington consensus" do find widespread support across countries, most consensus policies would best be modified according to differences in the electorates' values in Latin America. In addressing the policy dilemma posed by foreign expectations of economic reform that do not fulfill material expectations in democratic societies, Latin American countries may take advantage of a brief policy window that can allow efficient policy innovation in microeconomic reforms.

PARING DOWN THE CONSENSUS

While adherence to the elements of the consensus might have increased vulnerability to international capital flows and changes in the price of exports, the wave of economic reforms has produced some spectacular successes. Most notably, astronomical inflation has been tamed, typically to less than 20 percent and often to levels similar to those of the developed democracies (Stallings and Peres 2000, 52). Price stability encourages investment, both by firms and households, and prevents the high transaction costs associated with economic actors striving to make the most of their earnings before they wither away. While the reform package has not delivered spectacular growth, it did serve to stabilize economic expectations and improve the general investment climate.

The lengthy process of market-based (or neoliberal) reforms can be divided into the following two stages: stabilization and microeconomic reforms. Although considerable overlap exists among the categories, Moisés Naim (1995) has contributed a clear serialization. Stage one reforms concentrated on stabilizing economies and beginning their opening to more vigorous interaction with the global economy. Stage two or microeconomic reforms have the objective of improving the business and institutional climates that would make more efficient the use of productive factors within each country. The stabilization reforms employed straightforward measures and had a high, immediate, and visible impact on society, while the microeconomic reforms sought less obvious and long-term goals through complex administrative changes.

While the stabilization packages met the loudest opposition, they did enjoy widespread popular support (Weyland 1996). Facing growing economic crises, leaders in several countries initially responded with heterodox adjustment packages (typically a pegged exchange rate combined with price and wage controls) that failed to stabilize the macroeconomy (Edwards 1995, chapter 2). By the end of the 1980s, a standard package of orthodox stabilization measures had gained some acceptance inside countries and considerable enthusiasm from international lenders. Countries were urged to reduce fiscal deficits, expand domestic credit markets, modify exchange rate regimes to reduce inflation, and find means of reducing their foreign debt burdens. The success of stabilization policies in Mexico suggested to other countries in the region that this bitter medicine could yield benefits in a short period of time.

Enjoying their initial taste of the consensus policies, many leaders pushed forward with second generation or microeconomic reforms.[2] These changes included trade liberalization, tax reform (both started under stabilization), eliminating restrictions on portfolio and foreign direct investment (FDI), privatization, deregulation, and securing property rights. As Sidney Weintraub points out in his chapter in this volume, many of the choices made regarding these reforms increased countries' vulnerability to foreign capital flows. The new emphasis on improving the amount of competition within the economy proved less straightforward and more contentious than stabilizing the economy against the whims of the global market. While economists have clear recommendations for reducing inflation and can easily point out the social benefits thereof, the optimal amount of, say, regulation is far more problematic, involving a variety of noneconomic factors. The impact of deregulation in promoting growth is less certain than inflation cutting. Moreover, deregulation involves distributional trade-offs while nearly all citizens gain from controlling inflation. Predictions that such changes would improve economic performance are poorly supported in theory and yet unproved empirically. As they promised uncertain, contentious, and less concentrated results, microeconomic reforms did not always find the widespread support that stabilization measures enjoyed. Inherent delays in the design and implementation of second generation reforms also eroded support from voters and subsequent administrations. Latin American voters rationally responded with less enthusiasm to institutional restructuring, and arguably less has been accomplished in the area of second generation reforms.

The embrace of macroeconomic stability coupled with greater selection of other reforms may reflect a rational choice to implement only those policies that have a major and proven impact in improving economic conditions. Macroeconomic stability has been termed by many a necessary, but not sufficient, condition for growth. Most conceptions of macroeconomic stability are long term instead of lasting just a few years without a major devaluation. Most would agree that stable growth is preferred over volatile gains over a few spectacular years. The Argentine economy performed very well in the early 1990s, yet this success cannot compensate for the current crisis. In fact, spectacular gains may raise expectations of future performance in the belief that the correct model of development has finally been found. East Asian success came not only from high rates of growth, but the ability to avoid major financial crises for several decades.

The East Asian model also suggests that microeconomic reforms are not a necessary condition for growth. State managers in South Korea and Taiwan intervened considerably and illiberally through regulation, creation of state-owned enterprises, capital barriers, and trade protection (Rodrik 1996). Illiberal policies coexisted with years of sustained, high-level growth. Their success was a product of access to export markets, macroeconomic stability, and state intervention. The same could be said of Chile, the most dynamic economy in Latin America. Should the rest of the region follow this interventionist model, the recommendations of the Washington consensus, or their own preferences in reforming the microeconomic environment?

THE PROCESS OF MICROECONOMIC REFORM

In contrast with stabilization packages, the second generation of reforms sought to improve levels of competition within countries. The central role of the state in the import substituting industrialization (ISI) model presented significant opportunities for rent seeking in development programs (Krueger 1990). Tariff-protected infant industries were not weaned and often protested successfully state-led development of intermediate and capital goods industries, which would have increased input costs (Baer 1972). At times, potentially competitive state-owned industries gave in to political pressure to pad payrolls. While state-owned firms providing infrastructure and utilities are not inefficient per se, their monopoly status gave them few incentives to maximize consumer welfare or make long-term investments. Unequal public access to policymaking made regulatory capture a more visible feature than it is in the advanced economies. At the same time, dedication to these programs entailed a significant opportunity cost for other needs, notably education. In contrast with the moving target of a decentralized market, the concentration of power in the state together with its responsiveness allowed the more influential actors the ability to craft public policy and regulation for private interests at the expense of social welfare.

Consensus policies sought to remedy such problems through privatization, deregulation, further trade liberalization, and definition of property rights. The main goal of all the above reforms was to increase the amount of competition in the private and public economies. Contrary to predictions of many political economists, many microeconomic reforms failed to generate widespread opposition; instead, a majority of voters welcomed them in some cases (Geddes 1994; Stokes 2001). The private benefits of ISI were distributed narrowly. As rent seeking was neither hidden nor equitably distributed across society, many voters welcomed the end of privileges for party elites and their clients. A cynic might call this the "easy stage" of microeconomic reform.

Yet, once the obvious fat had been trimmed, further microeconomic reforms suffered from a lack of clear purpose and means. First, in contrast to the clear and single-minded goal of macroeconomic reforms, namely, to restore price stability, the benefits of microlevel reforms were numerous yet opaque. In general, the changes were supposed to create a new competitive environment that would benefit consumers and spur export industries. However, governments had other objectives in mind, notably raising money through privatizations, reducing deficits by cutting subsidies, or enlarging the banking sector through liberalization of capital flows.

While creating a more competitive climate may have been official policy, more pressing demands shaped the nature of reform. Second, it remains unclear if a smaller state and increased competition is the proper means of improving social welfare. Investments in infrastructure and human capital more closely resemble public goods than private ones, implying that markets will undersupply the necessary inputs for development. Banking crises remind us that deregulation can stifle competition as much as encouraging it. Selling state-owned enterprises to a private monopolist hardly encourages competition, yet this was the norm more than the exception. In sum, efforts to advance on the microreform agenda faltered due to a lack of clear purpose and the tricky details of implementation.

While the proper means to achieve greater economic efficiency remains unclear, the larger question is — how much efficiency does a society want? According to Susan Strange, "One obvious lesson is that different societies, in ordering their political economy, will give different values priority over others" (Strange 1999, 5). For Strange, societies measure the value of economic efficiency as opposed to security, justice, and freedom. While electoral campaigns can promise to provide all four, the design and implementation of policy must make difficult trade-offs among competing values. The hidden hand intermittently leads to "creative destruction," posing a trade-off between economic security and efficiency. As Sylvia Maxfield points out in her chapter in this volume, these destructive winds ". . . are likely to remain part of the Latin American landscape for years to come." Given full and asymmetric information, costless transactions, and a great number of buyers and sellers (leading to instantaneous equilibrium), the pursuit of economic freedom leads to efficiency and wealth. However, these conditions have been historically lacking in Latin America. All markets, including ideal markets, are amoral, according to Adam Smith (1776), in that markets themselves do not reward or promote morals, in a narrow sense, and, therefore, offer no guarantee of economic justice, a norm that is in greater demand, as suggested by the growth of social movements in the region. In addition to the uncertainties of how to enact microeconomic reforms that increase efficiency, the question of how much efficiency is socially optimal is debated among and within societies.

Developed countries have resolved the values dilemma by increasing government spending on social programs as their exposure to trade increases (Cameron 1978). Those suffering from changes in the global economy find compensation in insurance, employment, and investment programs that return displaced factors to productive capacity. By providing safety nets, the developed economies have been able to pursue efficient markets, while allowing social programs to provide security, freedom, and justice. John G. Ruggie's (1995) bargain of embedded liberalism describes a social compact where the economic and social roles of governments alleviate risk from a liberal global economy. Social programs and economic growth provide instrumental legitimacy for a liberal global economic order or globalization. The lack of such programs generates a political backlash against liberal policies (Rodrik 1997). Developed countries solve the trade-off of market efficiency versus other values by increasing social spending.

This option is not available for most Latin American countries. As seen in Table 1, government spending per person in Latin America has remained roughly the same since 1980, while the U.S. government has doubled spending per person. Moreover, a greater percentage of the latter is geared toward funding for the social safety net. Chile alone has significantly increased central government expenditure, while current figures for Argentina would be lower than the table suggests. In his chapter in this volume, Gustavo Vega-Cánovas observes that regional disparities in Mexico have "been aggravated by budget constraints, preventing the government from investing in infrastructure and social services." High levels of debt and the worries of international investors constrain the region's financial ability to provide such safety net programs.

Table 1. Central Government Expenditure Per Capita

Expenditure /capita	1980	1990	1995
Argentina	10.7	7.15	13.0
Brazil	7.4	17.5	na
Chile	11.0	14.5	22.7
Mexico	7.4	12.1	12.3
United States	27.9	51.9	62.9

Source: World Bank 1999.
Note: Numbers are in hundreds of dollars at purchasing power parity (PPP).

Table 2 shows that, for three countries, the per capita ratio of external debt to gross domestic product (GDP) has increased since the early 1980s. Announcements of increased social spending raise investors' concerns regarding fiscal imbalances and a leftward shift in Latin American politics. Yet, per David Cameron (1978), the more trade-exposed Latin American countries should feel increased pressures for safety net funding. In Chapter One of this volume, José Salazar-Xirinachs argues that Latin America's "integration into world markets will most likely continue," proving increased pressure for policies to address the uncertainties of globalization. In contrast with the direction of developed countries, Latin American governments will need to find less expensive means of striking their own version of embedded liberalism.

Table 2. External Debt Per Capita

Debt/capita	1980	1990	1995
Argentina	2.8	3.1	3.6
Brazil	2.1	1.0	1.8
Chile	3.8	6.8	9.7
Mexico	2.2	2.6	7.3

Source: World Bank 1999.
Note: Numbers are in hundreds of dollars at purchasing power parity (PPP).

The limited options for encouraging the instrumental legitimacy of a liberal economic order through Ruggie's embedded liberalism turn attention to normative commitments, based on "people's internalized norms of justice and obligation" (Tyler 1990, 4). Instead of calculating the probable costs of noncompliance, people may assess which types of behavior are appropriate for society as a whole. Thus, people are likely to support and comply with policies that reflect the underlying political culture of their society, even when such policies do not benefit them directly. The study of political culture is a psychological approach to politics that is made up of evaluations of current performance of regimes as well as long-standing values transferred across generations through socialization processes (Almond and Verba 1963). While values may differ among groups within a society, distinctions among countries provide a starting point to assess which types of policies would be best received by a democratic majority.

The role of values has been fruitfully applied to explain political and economic liberalization in Latin America. An assessment of democratic prospects in the region at the end of the 1980s found that political culture played some role in every country studied (Diamond, Linz, and Lipset 1989). Matthew Thomas Kenney (2001) found that among countries in the region, individuals' valuations of liberal virtues explain support for and viability of democratic government across countries and time. The enactment of market reforms differed according to underlying democratic values (Welsh and Carrasuero 2000) or when elites could frame policy change as consistent with such values (Armijo and Faucher 2002). Political values play some part in the choice of regime and policy.

Analytically, the study of political values competes with group politics, the structure of institutions, and foreign influence to explain any policy choice. Most scholars view interest groups (based on class or sector) as pursuing material gains that frequently deviate from overall national preferences. However, in presenting their view, group leaders attempt to frame their preferences in terms of national value structures to legitimize their requests. While their creation usually reflects national values, institutions limit political access and policy choices at times in contrast to widely held values. Finally, the imposition of policies by a foreign power (best seen in International Monetary Fund (IMF) conditionality agreements) or the transmission of ideology from one country to another (Drake 2000) may violate or influence national values. From a positive perspective, the role of national values in decisionmaking competes in complex ways with other perspectives in political science.

The focus of this chapter, however, is normative more than positive. Does the reflection of social values in policy formulation and implementation create better social programs to promote equitable economic growth? Programs that sacrifice, to some extent, economic efficiency in favor of value structures may not only serve better to promote sustainable growth, but they may also decrease the governance costs of enacting reform. For many developing countries, maximizing the short-term economic efficiency of growth policies may be less important than ensuring the stability of policies. Economic development requires an environment in which actors can make long-term investments that lead to social gains; stability proves more important than perfecting efficiency. For instance, rapid liberalization of trade and capital movements resulted in macroeconomic imbalances and the loss of productive capacity in Latin America (Agosin and Ffrench-Davis 1995). In terms of trade liberalization, a moderate opening may be more credible, less threatening to the external account, and encourage entrepreneurship in the face of imperfect competition than a dogmatic liberalization (Rodrik 1992). The pursuit of competition in microeconomic reforms to the detriment of other values, namely stability, may be one reason explaining the lackluster growth in the region.

Stability is unlikely when individuals contest economic policies and governments rely on instrumental incentives and coercion instead of legitimacy. Policies crafted to reflect widespread social norms may be easier to design and implement. Agreement on the appropriate values and purposes of policies may deter groups who would seek private gains from particular policies' formulation. Political opposition to their implementation would be hindered by an underlying social consensus. Policies based on prevailing national norms internalize legitimacy and encourage voluntary compliance, lessening the government's cost of monitoring and sanctioning. From an agency perspective, the cost of generating compliance would decrease as programs have normative, instead of instrumental, legitimacy. Tom R. Tyler's (1990) survey evidence on why people comply with the law found instrumental legitimacy an insufficient explanation; instead, individual decisions reflect the degree to which laws reflect values. Value-based policymaking provides the stable economic climate for long-term investments and minimizes the government's cost of crafting and enforcing policy.

VALUES AND MICROECONOMIC POLICIES FOR LATIN AMERICA

To what extent do values in Latin America differ from those of the Washington consensus? Figures 1 and 2 and Table 3 use data from the *World Values Survey* to measure support for economic efficiency, security, freedom, and justice in Argentina, Brazil, Chile, Mexico, and the United States.[3] Figure 1 shows that citizens of the United States and Mexico more than other Americans favor rewarding more efficient job performance with higher pay, with Chileans and Argentines most resistant to performance-based pay. U.S. citizens, more than Latin Americans, disfavor a role for the government in securing welfare (Figure 2) or in promoting economic justice (Table 3). These values maintain high support in Latin America but not in the United States. The percentage of respondents favoring government respect for freedom over order differs little among the five countries. To the extent that the Washington consensus policies reflect U.S. values, they strongly clash with the social norms of Argentina and Brazil and, to a lesser extent, with those of Mexico and Chile.

Works on microeconomic reforms from this volume show the impact of national values in the different types of policies adopted by Latin American governments. Despite hearing similar recommendations for microeconomic reforms, Brazil and Argentina increasingly diverged in this area. Roberto Bouzas explains, "While the Argentine government continued its policy of limited government intervention, based on ideological preferences and institutional constraints, Brazilian central and local authorities gradually moved toward more active sector and horizontal policies. . ." (da Motta Veiga 1999).

Figure 1. Percentage of Respondents in Favor of Pay Efficiency

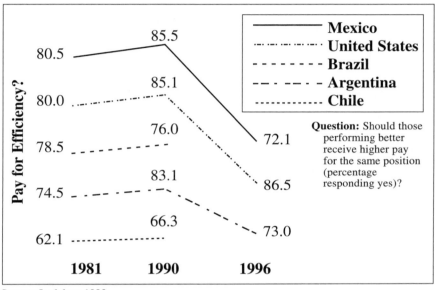

Source: Inglehart 1999.

Figure 2. Individual or Government Provision of Security?

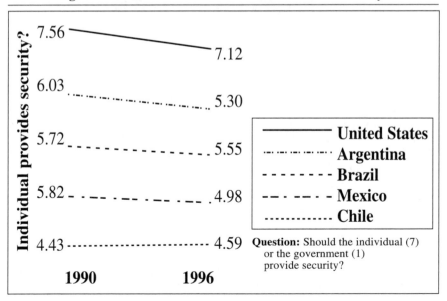

Source: Inglehart 1999.

Table 3. Percentage of Citizens Valuing Justice or Freedom over Wealth

	More justice	More freedom
Argentina	81.8	59.8
Brazil	35.9	49.6
Chile	59.4	48.5
Mexico	71.1	49.5
United States	58.2	51.4

Justice question: Is the government doing enough for the poor?

Freedom question: Should the government maintain order or economic freedom?

Source: Inglehart 1999.

Richard Youngs' analysis of regulations for FDI, in this volume, concludes by recommending that future policy toward FDI needs to reflect the "institutional and ideational contexts most apposite to the particular social, economic, and political patterns of the different host countries." Most directly, the decentralization initiatives described by Eaton demonstrate that policies fruitfully differ not only among countries but also within them.

More important, national values can conflict with the recommendations of international financial institutions. Peter Kingstone's chapter on social security reform describes a conflict between the prescribed model and Brazilian values favoring government provision of security. The Cardoso administration initially proposed the Chilean model of a fully funded, private-risk social security program yet later turned to the more feasible option of "preserving the collective approach to funding the system and to socializing risk." Although interest group pressures played a role in the reform, President Fernando Henrique Cardoso's failure "to connect the reforms to important social and political values" limited the scope of reform. In her discussion of education policy in this volume, Wendy Hunter describes the lack of a consensus blueprint for reform, allowing more of a policy window in this area than others. The impacts of changes in educational programs remain uncertain, complicated by the number of reforms and the lengthy time before they produce results. Moreover, education reform will not lead to productivity gains unless accompanied by the "economic and institutional conditions for production" identified by Suzanne Duryea and Carmen Pagés in Chapter Six. Directly to the point, José Salazar-Xirinachs observes in Chapter One that the core policies for increasing the competitive climate of a country are fundamentally a domestic political matter.

The higher value placed on security and justice in Latin America suggests some tempering of markets to fulfill other societal goals. In general, a decentralized system of exchange tends to work against both values, as markets promote uncertainty and are amoral. Standard substitutes for the market include an active role for the state or monitoring by civil society, although the former remains discredited and the latter awaits more development. To the degree that markets do not supply value needs, they will lose their appeal as legitimate means of allocating resources.

Markets, however, are not pure types, and differences in market design decide whether individual actors bear the full social costs and social benefits of their decisions, the security of ownership, and the cost of transactions. The pure form of neoliberalism pursued over the last two decades has exacerbated externalities, implying a need to correct this through market mechanisms or state monitoring. In Latin America, economic class skews the security of property rights. Land, in particular, may be held by elites for reasons other than production, while those with fewer resources find the process of gaining title lengthy, costly, and uncertain (Alston, Libecap, and Mueller 1999). The cost of measuring marginal value of productive factors and transferring ownership of those factors is higher in Latin America than in the developed world. If an increased role for the state is undesirable, policymakers will have to pay attention to the design of markets in Latin America, where externalities, asymmetrical access to property rights, and transaction costs are greater problems.

CONCLUSION

Fifteen years ago, Albert Hirschman wrote that crises in the region were leading to a more skeptical and pragmatic approach to policymaking in Latin America: "The spectacular miscarriage of ideologically driven economic policies (of the left and the right) has given rise to a new experimental spirit among Latin American economists, intellectuals, and policymakers" (1987, 30). Unfortunately, the financial power of the Washington consensus largely truncated such creativity. Yet, as recent crises may be paring down the consensus to macroeconomic stability, the "policy opportunity" for experimentation may have returned. Through differentiating and following the values present in each electorate, Latin American governments can create microeconomic reforms that are widely supported and complied with but that also allow domestic businesses to compete with foreign firms.

The policy window to tailor microeconomic reforms to local context is opening for several reasons. First, most countries in the region have spent years of effort toward the consensus reforms with mixed success. Instead of rejecting the consensus logic for microeconomic reform, they can credibly claim to have tried the standard recommendations but with limited success. The objective of increasing competition in the domestic economy is not denied; however, the means of doing so will vary according to national context. Second, international investors are more concerned with stable economic growth than maximizing economic efficiency. George Soros, one of the most successful investors of our time, has championed the need to abandon "market fundamentalism" and instead have open societies debate what their particular policy needs are so that they can benefit from and embrace globalization (2002). Third, the IMF has declared the need to "demonstrate to citizens that important public interests such as safety and equity will be safeguarded within dynamic and global markets" by "working on market-led growth supported and tempered by civic values and good governance" (Jacobs 1999). Borrowers and lenders increasingly recognize the need for macroeconomic stability with national adaptation of microeconomic reforms that regulate domestic economic competition.

The adaptation of political and economic institutions to challenges posed by changing technology and population are the hallmark of successful societies throughout economic history (North 1981). Exogenous change affects the workings of markets, including principal-agent relations, transaction costs, and the ability of the state to provide the public goods necessary for continued growth. Ideological rigidity impedes change and encourages economic inefficiency, eventually leading to the secular decline of a society's wealth. Latin American countries, in their yet elusive search for sustainable growth, need to embrace such change in undertaking microeconomic reforms.

NOTES

1.   The author would like to thank Ana Margheritis for helpful comments and Casey Kane Love for research assistance. All errors and omissions are attributable solely to the author.

2.   This view agrees with that of Smith and Acuña (1996) that the stabilization packages led to demands for other reforms. In contrast, Weyland (1996) would argue that, once economic stability set in, the thirst for further reforms diminished.

3.   The data reflect the results from one question per value. Future research might use factor or path analysis to incorporate responses from a variety of questions.

REFERENCES

Agosin, Manuel R., and Ricardo Ffrench-Davis. 1995. "Trade Liberalization and Growth: Recent Experiences in Latin America." *Journal of Interamerican Studies and World Affairs* 37 (3): 9-58.

Almond, Gabriel A., and Sidney Verba. 1963. *The Civic Culture.* Princeton, N.J.: Princeton University Press.

Alston, Lee J., Gary D. Libecap, and Bernardo Mueller. 1999. *Titles, Conflict and Land Use: The Development of Property Rights and Land Reform on the Brazilian Amazon Frontier.* Ann Arbor, Mich.: University of Michigan Press.

Armijo, Leslie Elliot, and Philippe Faucher. 2002. "We Have Consensus: Explaining Political Support for Market Reforms in Latin America." *Latin American Politics and Society* 44 (1): 1-41.

Baer, Werner. 1972. "Import Substitution and Industrialization in Latin America: Experiences and Interpretations." *Latin American Research Review* 7 (1): 95-122.

Broad, Robin, and John Cavanagh. 1999. "The Death of the Washington Consensus?" *World Policy Journal* 16 (3): 79-88.

Cameron, David. 1978. "The Expansion of the Public Economy." *American Political Science Review* 72: 1243-61.

da Motta Veiga, Pedro. 1999. "Brasil en el MERCOSUR: Política y Economía en un Proyecto de Integración." In *MERCOSUR. Entre la Realidad y la Utopía,* ed. Jorge Campbell. Buenos Aires: CEI-Nuevohacer. Cited in Roberto Bouzas, Chapter Two, "Economic Integration in the Southern Cone: Can MERCOSUR Survive?" This volume.

Diamond, Larry, Juan J. Linz, and Seymour Martin Lipset. 1989. *Democracy in Developing Countries: Latin America.* Boulder, Colo.: Lynne Rienner Publishers.

Drake, Paul W. 2000. "The Hegemony of U.S. Economic Doctrines in Latin America." Paper presented at Tulane University, March 18, 2002.

Edwards, Sebastian. 1995. *From Despair to Hope: Crisis and Reform in Latin America.* Washington, D.C.: World Bank.

Geddes, Barbara. 1994. "Challenging the Conventional Wisdom." *Journal of Democracy* 5 (4): 104-18.

Hirschman, Albert. 1987. "The Political Economy of Latin American Development: Seven Exercises in Retrospection." *Latin American Research Review* 22: 7-30.

Inglehart, Ronald. 1999. *World Values Surveys and European Values Surveys, 1981-1984, 1990-1993, and 1995-1997* [Computer file]. ICPSR version. Ann Arbor, Mich.: Institute for Social Research (producer), 1999. Ann Arbor, Mich.: Inter-University Consortium for Political and Social Research (distributor), 2000.

Jacobs, Scott H. 1999. "The Second Generation of Regulatory Reforms." Prepared for delivery at the IMF Conference on Second Generation Reforms, November 8-9. Available at <http://www.imf.org/external/pubs/ft/seminar/1999/reforms/jacobs.htm#III>.

Kenney, Matthew Thomas. 2001. "Liberal Virtues and Democracy." Ph.D. dissertation, Tulane University.

Krueger, Anne O. 1990. "Government Failures in Development." *Journal of Economic Perspectives* 4 (3): 9-23.

Naim, Moisés. 1995. "Latin America: The Second Stage of Reform." In *Economic Reform and Democracy*, eds. Larry Diamond and Marc F. Plattner. Baltimore: The Johns Hopkins University Press.

North, Douglass C. 1981. *Structure and Change in Economic History.* New York: W.W. Norton and Company.

Rodrik, Dani. 1997. *Has Globalization Gone Too Far?* Washington, D.C.: Institute for International Economics.

Rodrik, Dani. 1996. "Understanding Economic Policy Reform." *Journal of Economic Literature* 34 (1): 9-41.

Rodrik, Dani. 1992. "The Limits of Trade Policy Reform in Developing Countries." *Journal of Economic Perspectives* 1: 87-105

Ruggie, John G. 1995. "At Home Abroad, Abroad at Home: International Liberalization and Domestic Stability in the New World Economy." *Millennium: Journal of International Studies* 24 (3): 507-26.

Smith, Adam. [1776] 1994. *The Wealth of Nations: An Inquiry into the Nature and Causes.* Edited with notes and index by Edwin Cannan. Introduction by Robert Reich. New York: Random House Modern Library.

Smith, William C., and Carlos H. Acuña. 1996. "Future Politico-Economic Scenarios for Latin America." In *Democracy, Markets and Structural Reform in Latin America*, eds. William C. Smith, Carlos H. Acuña, and Eduardo A. Gamarra. Coral Gables, Fla.: North-South Center Press at the University of Miami.

Soros, George. 2002. *George Soros on Globalization.* New York: Public Affairs.

Stallings, Barbara, and Wilson Peres. 2000. *Growth, Employment and Equity: The Impact of the Economic Reforms in Latin America and the Caribbean.* Washington, D.C.: The Brookings Institution Press.

Stokes, Susan C. 2001. *Public Support for Market Reforms in New Democracies.* Cambridge, UK: Cambridge University Press.

Strange, Susan. 1999. *States and Markets.* London: Pinter.

Tyler, Tom R. 1990. *Why People Obey the Law.* New Haven, Conn.: Yale University Press.

Welsch, Friedrich J., and José V. Carrasquero. 2000. "Perceptions of State Reform in Latin America." *International Social Science Journal* 52 (1): 31-38.

Weyland, Kurt. 1996. "Risk Taking in Latin American Economic Restructuring: Lessons from Prospect Theory." *International Studies Quarterly* 40 (2):185-208.

Williamson, John. 1999. "What Should the Bank Think About the Washington Consensus?" Paper prepared as background to the *World Bank's World Development Report 2000.* Washington, D.C.: World Bank.

World Bank. 1999. *World Development Indicators 1999.* CD-ROM. Washington, D.C.: World Bank.

CONTRIBUTORS

Roberto Bouzas is a professor at the Universidad de San Andrés and a senior research fellow at the National Council for Scientific and Technical Research. His major fields of study are international economics, economic integration, and international political economy. His latest publications include *Dilemas de la Política Comercial Argentina* (coauthored with Emiliano Pagnotta, Siglo XXI Editores, Buenos Aires, 2003); *Realidades Nacionales Comparadas*, editor (Buenos Aires: Editorial Anagrama, 2002); *Mercosur. Integración y Crecimiento*, coauthored with J.M. Fanelli (Buenos Aires, Editorial Anagrama, 2002); and "Mercosur One Decade After: Learning Process or Déjà Vu?" in *Paths to Regional Integration: The Case of Mercosur*, ed. Joseph Tulchin (Washington, D.C.: The Woodrow Wilson Center for International Scholars, 2002).

Suzanne Duryea is a research economist at the Inter-American Development Bank. She holds a Ph.D. in economics from the University of Michigan. Her areas of expertise include human capital investment and family labor supply. She is the author of articles in journals such as *Journal of Human Resources*, *Emerging Markets Review*, and *World Development*.

Kent Eaton is assistant professor of politics and international affairs at the Woodrow Wilson School, Princeton University. He is the author of *Politicians and Economic Reform in New Democracies: Argentina and the Philippines in the 1990s* (Pennsylvania State University Press, 2002); and *Politics Beyond the Capital: The Design of Subnational Institutions in South America* (Stanford University Press, forthcoming). His articles have appeared in such journals as *Comparative Politics*, *Comparative Political Studies*, *Latin American Research Review*, *The Journal of Asian Studies*, and *The Journal of Latin American Studies*.

Wendy Hunter is associate professor of political science at the University of Texas-Austin. Recent publications include "Democracy and Social Spending in Latin America, 1980-1992" (with David Brown), *American Political Science Review* (December 1999); and "World Bank Directives, Domestic Interests, and the Politics of Human Capital Investment in Latin America" (with David Brown), *Comparative Political Studies* (February 2000). She earned a B.A. from Cornell University and a Ph.D. in political science from the University of California-Berkeley. She is currently writing a book on the growth and transformation of the Workers' Party in Brazil.

Peter Kingstone is associate professor of political science and director of the Center for Latin American and Caribbean Studies at the University of Connecticut. He holds a Ph.D. from the University of California, Berkeley. His interests are in business politics, democratization, and the politics of economic reform. His most recent publications include *Crafting Coalitions for Reform* (Pennsylvania State University Press, 1999); *Democratic Brazil*, coedited with Timothy Power (University of Pittsburgh Press, 2000); and articles in journals such as *Comparative Political Studies*, *Comparative Politics*, and *Latin American Politics and Society*.

Ana Margheritis is assistant professor of political science at the University of Florida. She was Andrew W. Mellon Postdoctoral Fellow at Tulane University during 2002-2003, Neil Allen Visiting Chair of Latin American Studies at The Fletcher School of Law and Diplomacy during 2000-2002, and Fulbright Visiting Fellow at Columbia University and USCD in 2000. A former professor at Universidad Torcuato Di Tella and FLACSO Buenos Aires, researcher at the Argentine National Council for Scientific and Technical Research, and consultant at the Ministry of Foreign Affairs of Argentina, she holds a Ph.D. in political science from the University of Toronto. Her research interests are in international political economy, foreign policy, regional cooperation, and inter-American relations. She is the author of *Ajuste y reforma en Argentina (1989-1995). La economía política de las privatizaciones* (1999); and coauthor of *Historia de las Relaciones Exteriores de la República Argentina* (with Carlos Escudé et al., 1998); and *Malvinas: Los Motivos Económicos de un Conflicto* (with Laura Tedesco, 1991). She has also published several articles in academic journals, as well as chapters in other coauthored books, and is currently working on a coedited volume entitled *Contested Transformation: Processes and Prospects of Structural Reforms in Latin America* (with Anthony Pereira and Brian Potter).

Sylvia Maxfield holds an A.B. from Cornell University and an A.M. and Ph.D. from Harvard University. She is currently professor at the Simmons Graduate School of Management, a Boston-based school whose goal is "training women for positions of power and leadership." She is also an associate of Harvard's David Rockefeller Center for Latin American Studies. Previously, she was professor of political science and public management at Yale University for 10 years. Maxfield has published more than 25 articles on the political economy of developing countries in *International Organization*, *World Politics*, *World Development*, *Journal of Democracy*, and elsewhere. Her most recent books are on central bank independence (Princeton University Press, 1998) and government-business relations in developing countries (Cornell University Press, 1998). From 1995 to 1999, Maxfield worked at the Wall Street firm Lehman Brothers. She has consulted for a variety of public and private organizations, including The World Bank, IBM, Deloite and Touche, and Mitsubishi.

Carmen Pagés holds a Ph.D. in economics from Boston University. She is currently a senior research economist at the Inter-American Development Bank. Her research interests are labor markets, education, and causes and incidence of crime and violence. She is the author of *Law and Employment: Lessons from Latin America and the Caribbean* jointly with Nobel Prize Laureate professor J. Heckman, University of Chicago and NBER editors (forthcoming); and editor of *Good Jobs Wanted: Labor Markets in Latin America* (The Johns Hopkins University Press, forthcoming). She has also published in leading economic journals, such as *European Economic Review* and *Journal of Development Economics*.

Brian Potter is assistant professor of political science at the University of New Orleans. He holds a Ph.D. in political science from the University of California at Los Angeles. With areas of interest in international political economy and environmental policy, he has recently published articles in the *Canadian Journal of Political Science* and *Environmental Politics*. Current work includes a book explaining differences in sustainable resource use for a broad sample of countries.

José M. Salazar-Xirinachs is director of the Trade Unit at the Organization of American States. He was the minister of trade in Costa Rica from 1997 to 1998, a period during which Costa Rica had the Chair of the FTAA process. He has held other positions with the Central Bank of Costa Rica, the Business Network for Hemispheric Integration, the Federation of Private Entities of Central America and Panama, the Costa Rican Development Corporation, and the Ministry of Planning in Costa Rica. He has a Ph.D. in economics from Cambridge University, England. He has written extensively on trade policy and economic integration issues. His most recent publication is a book coedited with Maryse Robert, *Towards Free Trade in the Americas* (The Brookings Institution Press/OAS, 2002).

Gustavo Vega-Cánovas is a professor at the Center for International Studies of El Colegio de México and member of the National System of Researchers at the National Council of Science and Technology of the Education Ministry of Mexico. He was a Fulbright visiting professor at the Watson Institute for International Studies at Brown University for the academic year 2001-2002. He holds a Ph.D. in political science from Yale University and a Licenciatura in Law from the School of Law at the National Autonomous University of Mexico (UNAM). His research interests in the last 15 years have centered on North American integration issues, and he has published extensively on this topic. His most recent publications are (with Gary Hufbauer), "Whither NAFTA: A Common Border?" In *The Rebordering of North America, Integration and Exclusion in a New Security Context*, eds. Peter Andreas and Thomas Biersteker (New York, Routledge, 2003); and a book entitled *La Regulación de las Prácticas Desleales de Comercio Internacional en el Continente Americano: La Experiencia de América del Norte y Chile* (México, UNAM, 2001). He has been a visiting professor at several universities in the United States, such as Brown, Duke, University of North Carolina at Chapel Hill, and Yale. He is also a member of the roster of panelists who adjudicate disputes on matters of antidumping and countervailing duties, according to Chapter 19 of NAFTA, and has participated in five binational panels.

Sidney Weintraub is the director of the Americas Program and holds the William Simon Chair in political economy at the Center for Strategic and International Studies, Washington, D.C. An economist whose specialties are trade and finance, he is also Dean Rusk Professor Emeritus at the University of Texas at Austin. He is a former career diplomat who held positions as assistant administrator of the U.S. Agency for International Development and deputy assistant secretary of state for finance and development. His recent books include *Financial Decision-Making in Mexico: To Bet a Nation* (University of Pittsburgh Press, 2000); *Development and Democracy in the Southern Cone: Imperatives for Policy in South America* (CSIS, 2000); and *NAFTA at Three: A Progress Report* (CSIS, 1997).

Richard Youngs is a research fellow at the Norwegian Institute for International Relations in Oslo, Norway. He has recently coordinated a European Commission project on democracy promotion and has published his research on European and Spanish policies toward Latin America. He is author of *The European Union and the Promotion of Democracy: Europe's Mediterranean and East Asia Policies* (Oxford University Press, 2001).

INDEX